The American Utopian Adventure

THE HARMONISTS

D1548480

THE AMERICAN UTOPIAN ADVENTURE

sources for the study of communitarian socialism in the
United States 1680–1880

Series One

J. S. Duss, Trustee of the Harmony Society, 1890-1903.
Photographed at the age of 33 years in 1893.

The Harmonists

A Personal History

by JOHN S. DUSS

PORCUPINE PRESS INC.
Philadelphia 1972

Library of Congress Cataloging in Publication Data

Duss, John Samuel, 1860–
   The Harmonists; a personal history.

   (The American utopian adventure)
   1. Harmony Society.   I.   Title.
[HX656.H2D82 1972]   335'.9'73   71-187439
ISBN 0-87991-013-5

First edition 1943 (Harrisburg: Pennsylvania Book Service Publishers, 1943)

Copyright © 1943 by John S. Duss. Copyright © renewed 1971 by John S. Duss III. All rights reserved.

Reprinted 1972 by PORCUPINE PRESS, INC., 1317 Filbert St., Philadelphia, Pa. 19107, by arrangement with The Harmonie Associates, Inc.

Manufactured in the United States of America.

TO MY WIFE
WITHOUT WHOSE FAITHFUL DEVOTION
·MINE WOULD BE A
DIFFERENT STORY

Acknowledgment

I wish to express my sincere appreciation for their counsel and assistance in preparing and editing this story to Mrs. Jessica K. Bowman, Mr. E. Gordon Alderfer and my daughter, Vera Duss Houston.

THE AUTHOR.

The Harmonists

J. S. Duss, Trustee of the Harmony Society, 1890-1903.
Photographed at the age of 33 years in 1893.

The Harmonists

A Personal History

by JOHN S. DUSS

Reprinted by
The Harmonie Associates, Inc.
Ambridge, Pa.
1970

Acknowledgment

I wish to express my sincere appreciation for their counsel and assistance in preparing and editing this story to Mrs. Jessica K. Bowman, Mr. E. Gordon Alderfer and my daughter, Vera Duss Houston.

THE AUTHOR.

Preface

IN THIS DAY OF vastly complicated societal mechanics, tremendously powerful governments, and the whole huge web of clashing world economics, we have very nearly lost all concept of the meaning of "community." Human relationships, in the average city, are no longer generated by the spontaneous impulse of mutual cooperation, but rather take a long circuitous route through a complex labyrinth of social organization. When a man is unemployed in the little town down river, an overwhelming confusion of Federal, state and local machinery is set in motion before the helping hand of his fellow man can reach him. The personality of the community, its purpose, and beyond that the natural and spontaneous expression of love in general, are no longer dominant elements in our social life.

Yet, in all the long span of history, no nation or people has risen to a rich maturity either by predatory or violent means, or without that instinctive interweaving of individual efforts for the common welfare of the group which we call mutual aid. The individual instinct of survival is admittedly a great force, but before a social cohesion can be achieved the greater force of love and the instinct of mutual aid must have full play. And without cohesion a people and the permanent cultural products of a people are as nothing.

America herself has been a great testing ground of the principles of community. Out of the stern environmental conditions of a pioneer society, the early isolated settlements developed a sturdy cohesiveness and a sense of communal responsibility. Most of the early settlements were cooperative enterprises. Nature decreed it so. Even after the pressures of hostile natural forces had for the most part been counteracted, numerous communities in nineteenth-century America continued the age-old tradition of cooperative life.

This tradition stems far back through the ages. The gradual emergence of prehistoric man into the dawn of what we know as recorded civilized life was itself an impulse generated primarily by the instinct of mutual aid. The early Greek city-state, the primitive Christian community buffeted by the powerful Roman world, the early monastic communities, the communes of medieval Europe which reared the great cathedrals, the guild towns, the American settlements, the religious communes of the eighteenth and nineteenth centuries, the modern cooperatives of today—all these are the purer evidences of an enduring anti-predatory tradition.

This tradition has received its greatest impetus from the teaching of Jesus of Nazareth, as today it gathers force again in the teaching of Gandhi. The individual example of Jesus and the societal example of the primitive Christian church-community, especially as recorded in the Book of the Acts, like a persistent dream, have haunted the hearts of men and have endowed mankind with an enduring hope.

From the fifteenth to the nineteenth centuries, out of the miseries of a Europe cruelly torn by the wars of petty tyrants and power groups, many simple people reverted to these ancient examples, wandered to new frontiers, seeking an environment where the human destiny might be worked out in the air of freedom, and peace and goodwill might become dynamic realities. This was the extension of the Reformation, not in religion alone, but in the whole web of western civilization.

With the completion of this book we have the great good fortune to read the intimate biography of one of the greatest American communal experiments—one that flourished mightily and for a time became a little empire. For many years the author was an integral part of this community, serving in youth as a worker in various trades of the commune. Later, gaining the perspective of experience in "the outside world," he returned as a teacher, and finally as head of the commune, in the face of stupendous financial difficulties and endless litigation, brought the Experiment to an orderly conclusion. Because his task has been so great, none other could have written so intimately and wisely of this "noble experiment." This is the record of a man, an amazingly versatile man, as well as of a community.

It is particularly appropriate, therefore, that the author should wish this life record to be presented by the simple words of one of the last and most faithful members of the commune. Both the parents and the grandparents of Louisa Rall Schumacher were members of the Harmony Society. Father Rapp himself having joined her grandparents Rall in wedlock. All of her days Mrs. Schumacher was intimately acquainted with the Harmonist way of life. This is what she writes:

> I have read with interest the memories of J. S. Duss and I can safely recommend them as a faithful presentation of the Harmony Society and life at Economy . . . His recollection of facts and circumstances is absolutely perfect . . . All my life I have been either living in the

Society at Economy or have been in close touch with the Society and its traditions, and for these reasons feel myself justified in expressing my authoritative opinion. I have known Mr. Duss ("Johnnie" as we used to call him) from the time he was a baby in 1862, when he arrived at Economy, and I can testify that the community in general regarded him as an unusually gifted and precocious youngster.

Baden, Pennsylvania
December 4, 1923

The story of the Harmony Society and its three settlements in what was the wilderness of western Pennsylvania and southern Indiana is destined, I think, to be one of the truest American illustrations of the meaning of "Community." This people was banded together, not necessarily by any kinship or by any common creed, but by eternal ties of fellowship—the fellowship of men functioning as a common economic and social unit. Such a community is far different from our modern community.

Hence when the author writes of "the community"—be it Harmony or Economy in Pennsylvania or Harmony in Indiana—it must be understood that he means the whole working unit, the entire population, members and non-members dwelling together and functioning as one socio-economic unit. In Butler County the "outsiders" termed all residents "Harmonites," in Indiana "Rappites," in Beaver County "Economites." But these names are confusing colloquialisms; the name of those who actually belonged to the Harmony Society, the organization founded on the principle of community of goods, was the Harmonists. As the years passed, more and more residents of the community were simply hirelings of the Harmony Society, and were not part of the communistic economy. The members of the Society, on the other hand, possessed no worldly goods except as a part of the Society which held the property of all members in common.

Let us not be frightened by the use of the word "communism." I am sure that the author in no way has the slightest interest in or sympathy with modern communism as exemplified by the Communist Party, national or international. Indeed, the philosophy of modern communism is diametrically opposed to the community communism of the Harmonists. In the first place, religion and spiritual experience played a most important role in the life of the Harmony Society, and the social economy of the commune was inspired by the precepts of the New Testament. Moreover, the Harmonists consistently refused to publish abroad their beliefs; they were not evangelists. Their way of life did not permit propaganda. Only by serving as a *working* example did they hope to influence the common life of their fellowmen. Still another contrast to be drawn is the fact that the way of life of the Harmonists had no connection whatsoever with the vast and often cruel machinery of power politics; theirs was a life of peace, fellowship, simplicity, faith, hard work. And everyone worked; stirred on by the sense of communal responsibility, there was no stigma of force or compulsion. Guidance, leadership and direction, yes, but work was accomplished by voluntarily cooperation.

The reader should understand that with the exception of the chronicle of more recent events this history is drawn from the author's work, "My Memoirs," written over twenty years ago when everything was fresh in mind and memory. Due to the severe abridgment of the original story, much of the argumentative and "explanatory" has been omitted—as have been all "references" to documents or other authors. Nevertheless there remains a dramatic and thought-provoking story. It is the record of a great experiment in living, the tremendous accomplishment of a community dedicated to peace and goodwill and joyful endeavor. How great can be the achievements of a simple, unsophisticated people, working and singing together! Perhaps—who knows?—this monument of human endeavor may sometime, after the darkness passes and dawn comes once again, serve as another milestone on the endless road to the more abundant life.

Harrisburg
February 1, 1943.   E. GORDON ALDERFER.

Table of Contents

xiv

List of Illustrations

xvii

xviii

1

Prologue to a New World Experiment

IT IS NOT OFTEN PROCLAIMED, but since the founding of the Jamestown colony in 1607, there have been some hundred experiments in communal life in the United States. The amazing feat of cutting a New World out of a wilderness required the constant coöperation of all group members—in other words, the setting aside of selfish desires for the good of the group. It is no wonder that this requirement of pioneer and frontier conditions penetrated through colonial society and contributed somewhat to a national psychology and to the spread of revolutionary ideas.

But the communal ideal of group coöperation by no means died with the conquering of the American wilderness. Throughout the nineteenth century actual communistic experiments were made in many different regions. Those acquainted with American literature will recall Brook Farm—that strange collection of New England transcendentalists, many of whom were blissfully ignorant of the hard requirements of communal coöperation and manual labor. But how many know of the Shaker settlements scattered through New England, New York, Ohio and Kentucky; or of the Zoar Separatists of Ohio, of the Amana villages of Iowa, the French Icarians, the Oneida Perfectionists, the Aurora and Bethel communes, or of the three towns built by the Harmony Society?

Many of my eighty years were spent as a part of such

a community. As a two-year-old child my mother brought me to Economy, Pennsylvania, the third and greatest settlement of the Harmony Society, where I grew up as one who learned to think in terms of the welfare of all. There being no need for money, I hardly knew the significance of it. Neither was I conscious of social distinctions, for they did not exist. A little later I experienced the shock of meeting the outside world, and even traveled the road to success in the strenuously competitive capitalistic whirl of the last century. When just on the brink of greater success, I returned to the little village on the Ohio River, to find the Harmony Society rapidly declining, the old spirit gone, the great resources of former years dissipated, and the Society verging on bankruptcy. In the tragic last years of this great experiment I became its leader, and although through the ordeal of personal hatreds, newspaper opprobrium, towering financial worries and harrowing court trials, I saw the last members pass away or turn against me, I finally, in the face of disunion and disloyalty, brought this latter-day Noble Experiment to an orderly close.

From the boyhood experiences of Economy in the 1860's to my musical successes in Madison Square Garden, New York, and throughout North America in the early part of this century, mine has been a truly anomalous life. But the story that I have written is not the story of a single life, but one of a community—it is even more than that; from the vantage point of eighty years, it now seems somewhat fantastic, yet it is the true record of an important but neglected segment of American life.

For the beginnings of our story we must roll back several centuries, and scan the fertile lands of central and southwestern Germany. By the early part of the seventeenth century Martin Luther's reformation had accomplished most of its great purposes. But religious thought had by no means become settled, and Luther's ideas were carried to still greater extremes by such preachers as Menno Simon, founder of the Mennonite Church, and by the pious Anabaptists. With the spread of revolutionary religion, the whole Rhine Valley seethed in ferment.

Then came the terror of the Thirty Years' War, waged between political and religious factions. Year after year the pleasant, quiet, industrious towns of southwestern Germany were ravished by lawless marauding soldiers; humble men and women were put to torture and death for their conscientious convictions; barns and crops were destroyed; anarchy reigned in the land. This little corner of Germany, once prosperous and peaceful, was now a bleeding wound in the side of Europe. When in 1648 the Thirty Years' War waned to an end, it left the section naked and desolate.

Where could these poor people turn for succour, where could they find peace for themselves or have in prospect some little hope for their children? William Penn and other English Quakers had visited and preached among these people, and Penn had talked of founding a haven in America both for the oppressed people of England and those of the continent. But even before Penn began his Holy Experiment, a small group of Dutch Mennonites under Pieter Plockhoy came to settle in the Delaware Valley in 1663, intent on finding religious freedom and establishing a communistic community based on the principles of the early Christian Church. Their little settlement was probably destroyed when the English conquered the Dutch possessions along the Delaware, but when Penn formally established his province on the principles of religious freedom, other German and Dutch Anabaptists

3

and Pietists of various beliefs journeyed to the new land. In 1683 Francis Daniel Pastorius led twenty German and Dutch Mennonite families from the Rhine Valley to settle Germantown, now a part of greater Philadelphia. As the early years of the eighteenth century passed, more and more religious radicals fled persecution in war-torn southwestern Germany until they were coming in thousands to Penn's promised land. As time went on they made of this wildnerness a fair and beautiful arable land—truly one of the "garden spots" of America.

Some of these radical protestants established strange ascetic communities based upon their interpretation of Christ's message and the communal life of the early Christian Church. As early as 1694, twelve years after the arrival of William Penn, Johannes Kelpius led forty religious enthusiasts—variously known as Pietists, Rosicrucians and members of the "Society of the Woman in the Wilderness"—to the banks of the beautiful Wissahickon near Philadelphia, where they lived in caves like hermits, studying the stars and discussing their strange mystical beliefs in regard to the spiritual regeneration of mankind. In 1728 a group of Seventh Day Baptists, rebels from various German sects, mostly Dunkards, built the Ephrata Cloisters in Lancaster County and established a self-sufficient, communal and religious society. Mennonites, Baptists, Amish, Dunkards, Moravians, Schwenkfelders came in great numbers to the land of the Quakers.

But what of those who found no escape from Old World tyrannies and persecution? Even if they could have expected rewards or peace for giving up their religious convictions, they would not have done so. For theirs was a religion that gripped the soul—a total philosophy of life and not just a segment of it. During the terrifying devastation of their land and the heartrending persecution of their brethren, their religion was a last refuge, a firm rock in the midst of a wild and stormy sea. As their worldly possessions, their hopes, their security, the very land itself were stripped away, their faith remained. Finding no escape from the hardships of their material world, unable to venture forth to a distant wilderness in a New World, they escaped to a spiritual world—one that no political forces could destroy. Spener and his disciples spread the new Pietistic teachings and distributed their books through southwestern Germany, the Rhine Valley, Holland and Switzerland. Those who craved something more than the uninspiring worldliness of the established Lutheran or Catholic churches, trying to escape the watchful eyes of political and church authorities, met together in humble homes. These "Stunden," or hours of group worship and religious discussion, developed a spirit of community and coöperation, and solidified the spiritual energy of the group.

The established church was, of course, on the alert for such vagaries and disunion, and by appealing to the secular authorities was able more or less to persecute such "heresies". However, as persecution increased, a more radical movement came into being. At first the Pietists did not encourage separation from the established church, but only strove to purify it of its worldliness. Later, seeing the Church and State working hand in hand to suppress the purer religion, and that the Church was becoming unchristian in its intolerance and persecution of those who tried earnestly to find and follow the life principles of the Master, the more radical Pietists began to urge complete separation from the established Church. This movement had begun as early as the latter part of the sixteenth century in certain communities of Holland and the Rhine country. Through the seventeenth and

5

eighteenth centuries the movement gathered momentum, and centering in Wuertemberg, it spread throughout southwestern Germany.

During the eighteenth and early nineteenth centuries Germany was a heterogeneous and disorganized collection of minor principalities, quarreling among themselves and often at the mercy of the greater European powers. By whatever local or international factions these principalities were controlled, the peasant and rising bourgeois classes usually suffered. They were heavily taxed, they were subject to frequent conscriptions for wars—even at times when such wars did not directly concern their own country . . . Then, early in the nineteenth century came the great Napoleon, who in his vast military campaigns forced all the minor principalities under his control to contribute great numbers of men and immense quantities of supplies. No wonder the poor and humble and harassed peoples of Europe turned to other lands, particularly to America, as the New World of their hopes.

On November 1, 1757, in Iptingen, Wuerttemberg, to a peasant vine-grower was born a son who was destined to head one of the most successful experiments in Christian communism in the Western Hemisphere. He was christened Johann Georg Rapp. He received the usual basic education granted to the common people of the land; afterward, like his father, he engaged in vine-growing and learned the trade of weaving. The work in field and workshop strengthened his naturally splendid physique—he had grown nigh to six feet of brawn and muscle; and in spite of his peasant features, he was of striking appearance. A naturally alert and enthusiastic mind soon led him to inquire into the religious controversies of his time. Early in life he became acquainted with the mystical writings of Spener, Boehme, Swedenborg, Jung-Stilling, Arndt and other Pietists and mystics. He was convinced of the individual's power of personal communication with God, and of the layman's inalienable right to interpret the teachings of Jesus. By the time he was thirty he had become a preacher of radical separatist ideas. Full of religious fervor, endowed with a magnetic personality and a rich and powerful voice, George Rapp gathered about him a small coterie of farmers and mechanics.

Wuertemberg for at least two centuries had been a hotbed for the germination of new ideas in religion. Protestantism had been carried to extremes. Indeed even before the death of Luther in 1546, a preacher of Waibligen complained that there were as many sects in Wuerttemberg as there were houses. However, the established Lutheran Church, as the official religious representative of political authority, affected a surface solidarity and never permitted the radical protestant groups to crystallize into a really formidable opposition. On the alert for religious movements independent of their authority, they succeeded in making extremely uncomfortable those who wavered from the official religion.

Happily for our story, the original written records of George Rapp and his associates are still extant. The protocols or minutes of the Church Convocation in Iptingen in April, 1785 disclose that George Rapp had refused to submit to Church discipline, and his privilege of partaking of Holy Communion was taken away until he should mend his ways. This seems to have greatly affected the twenty-eight year old peasant-preacher, for when asked if he intended to withdraw permanently from the Church, his answer was unhesitating and decisive: "Yes, for all time."

"Why have you persisted in your offense?" continued the representative of the established faith.

"Because I have found the fountain-head myself, and the substance itself is in Jesus Christ."

"Do you promulgate your principia to others?" they inquired.

"No," said Rapp, "so long as no one asks me, I say nothing." But he did admit that he had talked with Christian Hoernle and Michael Conzelmann, both present at the hearing, and that they had held midweek meetings together for prayer and religious discussion. Rapp's wife joined with her husband in holding firmly to their convictions.

In 1787 the minutes of the Ducal Consistory record an admonition to the "Separatistic married couple and consorts to change their views, to hold to the Church and not to hold separate meetings." Whereupon Rapp declared that he could not assent to the present way of the Church and would adhere to his former declarations. In the questioning that followed, the utterances of Rapp strike us with their simple intensity: "Whatsoever stands in the Bible is only a testimony of the independent Word, which no one but I and my brethren understand" . . . "The Lord's Supper is idolatry and abhorrent blasphemy" . . . "I will not acknowledge the minister as called of God" . . . Christian and Susanne Hoernle, Johannes Hoernle, Michael Conzelmann and Katherine Walz express themselves in full concurrence with Rapp's testimony. Remonstrances were in vain, and Rapp even refused to apologize for his disparagement of the minister. There was nothing to do but refer the matter to the political authorities.

In the old Rathaus or town hall of Iptingen the records of the time show much concern over the separatist movement led by Rapp. The political authorities believe that Rapp's "despotism" is dangerous to Church, school and police and is "therefore to be apprehended." These records also point out that, while other Separatists worship in silence and "leave the public institutions unassailed," Rapp and his adherents "have the impudence" to refuse to recognize the clergy, to oppose sovereign ordinances of district authorities, to judge lightly of the Bible, to blaspheme Holy Communion, to pronounce church-goers as hypocrites, and—worst of all—"to constitute a Church of their own instead of the public Church, and a State of their own within the State."

These were dangerous activities, certainly. One can hardly blame the authorities for taking measures against them, especially when we realize that for the most part the accusations were true. Thus in return for their outright flouting of the Church and political authorities, their separatistic literature was confiscated—indeed, all books except the Bible and the school and common devotional books. Secondly, "the civil beneficences, particularly the donation of wood, were to be withheld until Rapp and his followers learned to submit to regulations of Church and State." Rapp himself was to apologize to the local parson before a tribunal, or suffer imprisonment. The authorities even threatened the lunatic asylum for Susanna Hoernle if she persisted in her declarations. And those who continued to refuse to obey the Sabbath injunctions of the established Church and gad about freely on Sunday were henceforth liable to be driven from their homes.

This was in 1787. During the next several years the unrest continued. Sometime during this period Rapp was imprisoned in the tower of Maulbronn. But the protocols continued to record the "calumnious" utterances of the

9

fiery preacher, such as, "The Church is a Babel" . . .
"The Church is not of God, it is of the Devil" . . . "The
parsons eat and drink and fatten their bellies, and do not
provide for the poor." Burdensome fines were levied on
some of the dissenters, and in 1798 Rapp himself paid a
heavy fine. Again in the next year he was fined—this time
for splitting wood and distilling whiskey on Sunday! Also
four others were fined because "on Good Friday, during
the morning Church services, they bought a herd of swine
from a dealer and drove them through the streets"! (Past
the church, probably).

By this unvarnished spirit of contumacy the halo of
martyrdom is somewhat tarnished. By no stretch of the
imagination can these acts be tortured into conformity
with their ideals of worshipping God according to the
dictates of their conscience. We cannot blame either
church or civil authorities for taking measures against
such unseemly conduct. As a matter of fact, the civil
government of Germany was very lenient toward them.
Surely our own civil authority in America today would
not condone similar actions.

Let it also be known that the religious tenets preached
by Rapp by no means constituted a well-defined creed
for the Iptingen Separatists. Furthermore, that basically
in the theology of these rebels, was the principle of the
conscience—that each individual had the potential power
of communicating directly with God, and therefore the
purified individual was divinely ordained to judge most
things for himself. Like the Quakers, these humble folk
saw a spark of the Divine—an Inner Light, to use the
Quaker phrase—in all men.

But in order to present a petition to the Diet at Lomersheim in 1798 in an attempt to protect the brethren from
further recriminations, the Iptingen Separatists had to

formulate certain general principles of faith. From this we learn that their chief objection to attending church was that it did not permit the individual to express himself as the spirit of God moved him. And for this reason they wished to be allowed to worship in their own homes in small groups where all could talk freely. This was their major objective. However, they did record their belief in the Christian Church, but one founded according to the principles of the Apostles and the "primitive" Christians.

In regard to religious ceremonies and forms of worship, they acknowledged that baptism was good and just, but they argued one becomes a true Christian, only through the free exercise of will and faith in God to overcome sin, not because of any ceremony. The placing of emphasis on the *ceremony* of baptism, especially in the baptism of infants and children, did not allow the true significance of this dedication to God and Christian brotherhood to shine forth. That was also true in the matter of confirmation where the children were more interested in the new clothes that they were to receive than they were in the rite itself. They did not oppose the celebration of the Lord's Supper, but they called it the Lovefeast, and they insisted upon observing it as a reestablishment of spiritual and social harmony.

Within the ranks of the Separatist Group there were undoubtedly wide divergences of religious ideas, and in all likelihood we need not imply that George Rapp's preachments represented the concentrated opinions of the Group as a whole, or even that Rapp's own mystical ideology was crystallized and constant. As early as 1794, or even earlier, Rapp announced his belief in the bi-une nature of the perfected man. Did not God create Adam in perfection, balancing within his being the fire of the male and

11

the light of the female attributes of human nature? Historians sometimes assume that these mystic concepts of Rapp's early days were the direct evidences of a tendency toward celibacy, but I do not regard these beliefs as anything but vague tendencies of an evolving theology, for the precept of celibacy was not preached by Rapp until after its introduction as a custom in 1807 at Harmony, Pennsylvania.

In temporal matters the Separatist petition recorded an objection to the worldliness of public schools under the dominance of the established clergy. Not that they did not believe in education and guidance for their children, but that they preferred to establish their own methods of instruction. Then, after their children were sufficiently matured, they were to be left free to join "any religion, be it Lutheran, Catholic or Reformed."

The petition also grants that political authority and government is necessary, and consequently "we perform our duties so long as we are tolerated in the country." Nevertheless, they object to the corporeal oath required on official occasions, and wish instead to substitute the Scriptural "yea" and "nay". Equally obnoxious to them is military service—indeed, all war—which manifestly is inconsistent with the great love of all mankind required of the true follower of Jesus. However, in lieu of such service they declare themselves willing to submit to extra taxes.

But neither Rapp nor his followers ever claimed that the higher civil authorities of Wuertemberg treated them unfairly. The King himself showed his tolerance in their behalf. Many an aged member have I heard recount how the local clergy incited the civil authorities to address a petition to the King, asking for a decree of banishment against Rapp and his growing congregation.

After scanning the petition, the King asked, "Who are these people? Are they good citizens? Do they pay their taxes?"

The courtiers and petitioners had to admit that the Separatists were quiet, industrious and peaceful; and that they paid their taxes faithfully.

Whereupon, the King slowly tore the petition to shreds. "Then let them believe what they please," he said.

Harassment of the Iptingen Separatists, however, at the hands of local church authorities, continued. There seemed to be little enough peace for these fervent people. And it was but natural that they began secretly to talk of finding a haven in some distant country. The romantic appeal of the New World, and especially that thriving new republic called the United States, caught their imagination. Perhaps when news came that President Jefferson had made the Louisiana Purchase, opening up immense new territories, the impulse to move to the new nation became irresistible.

America was young and free, its vast fertile lands were cheap, it was thousands of miles away from the tyrannies of old Europe . . . One day in July 1803, the magnetic preacher of Iptingen, with his son John and a certain learned Doctor Friedrich Conrad Haller, boarded a boat on the river Rhine—the first step toward a new life in a New World.

2

Harmonie in Pennsylvania
(1804-1815)

AFTER A DIFFICULT, TEDIOUS VOYAGE of more than a month the three travelers early in September disembarked at Baltimore. Perhaps they had known or corresponded with some of the German sectarians of Lancaster County in Pennsylvania. At any rate, within a week or two Rapp was in Lancaster, largest of the inland villages, scouting for land. He soon explored large sections in Pennsylvania and Maryland, and considered tracts on the Susquehanna, the Conestoga, the Potomac and even on Lake Erie.

Almost from the time he had laid eyes on the New World, he felt invigorated by the new environment. "Here is a very rich land," he wrote Friedrich Reichert in September. He was surprised to find that everyone had employment, that there was practically no real poverty, that everyone could go wherever he desired. He notes the characteristic friendliness of the people and their open-hearted, frank demeanor. Even the taxes amounted to practically nothing. "All the people are good toward each other; one must admire their friendliness." Best of all was the absolute freedom of religious worship. America was still a blossoming wilderness, especially Lancaster County and westward. People were a bit crude perhaps—"women ride just like men," "one may go shooting for his dinner . . . the wilderness belongs to everyone."

"I shall never return to Germany," he wrote; "if my citizenship still continues, I will give it up. I am already a citizen here."

After his various explorations George Rapp contracted for the purchase of some three thousand acres in Butler County, Pennsylvania. The tract was situated about twenty-five miles north of Pittsburgh, on the Conoquenessing Creek and about twelve miles from the Ohio River at Beaver. There were as yet few settlers in the neighborhood, and the price of the land was only $3.00 an acre. Doubtless, Rapp as a down payment used a portion of his two thousand Gulden, about $800, which he had saved and brought from the old country.

Meanwhile, preparations were being made in Wuertemberg for the migration of Rapp's associates. Among these, Friedrich Reichert, an intelligent, stalwart, handsome man somewhat younger than Rapp took charge of the Herculean preparations for the migration. As an organizer and executive, this Friedrich or Frederick was a born genius. While George Rapp was still searching for a permanent location for his flock across the waters, Frederick took matters into his own hands. Not hearing from Rapp, Frederick wrote, "I notified the brethren and declared that I had decided on the journey, and though this caused a great commotion, nearly all of them were in agreement." He very fortunately realized the economic requirements of a self-sustaining community in the sparsely settled wilderness regions of the New World, for he took great care that enough mechanics, such as smiths, shoemakers, tailors, carpenters and even wheelwrights joined with the emigrants. Even in these early days Frederick showed his foresight and keen financial ability by borrowing funds from the more wealthy for those he wanted but who could not pay their way.

However, after anxious waiting, came word from George Rapp. Evidently he hoped that only the hardiest would emigrate, for he added, "You must not urge anyone to come—it is a long and perilous journey." Despite this admonition on July 4, 1804, about three hundred arrived at Baltimore on the ship *Aurora*. About a month later under the leadership of Frederick, two hundred and sixty more arrived at Philadelphia where the elder Rapp met them. Still later another similar group arrived on a third ship, though most of these separated from the main body and the following year under the leadership of Dr. Haller, settled in Lycoming County, Pennsylvania.

The season being too far advanced for emigrants to risk a harsh winter in the forests of western Pennsylvania, most of these people through the assistance of the friendly Quakers of Philadelphia and southeastern Pennsylvania obtained employment; thus the families became divided and scattered. Haller and others, for example, settled among the Dunkards and Mennonites of Germantown, where Haller was converted to Dunkard beliefs.

Unlike the learned Haller, who stayed in cosy civilized quarters during the winter months, Rapp with eighty hand-picked men proceeded at once to Butler County, and began the erection of log cabins and the clearing of land. In several months, apparently in the dead of winter, others who cast their lot with George Rapp journeyed over the long hills three hundred miles westward to Harmonie—the name which they had given their new home.

Not all of those who had arrived in the autumn went with this group. Some quibbled on points of religious faith, others thought that George Rapp was not sufficiently educated to serve as leader. As to Haller, he was not only judge and lawgiver for the Lycoming County settlement, but also a physician who distinguished himself some years later in the epidemic of 1813-15. He was a scholar and linguist familiar with six different languages. A widely learned man of his calibre, some thought, was beyond compare with the simple vine-grower. Moreover, this group had been somewhat separated from the Butler County migration even in Germany. At any rate, in the spring of 1804, while the Rapp contingent was being established in its Butler County home, the followers of Dr. Haller reached Lycoming County, and on May 20 they first beheld their haven of rest. Seven miles north of Williamsport a little gem of a valley, two miles long and half a mile wide, drained by a little brook that was fed by many springs in the adjacent hillside, lay in the warm May sunlight. The woods were full of rhododendron and dogwood in full bloom, so they called the valley Blooming Grove.

The segregation of the Blooming Grove group from the main body fortunately helped to clear the latter of some discordant elements, so that the Rapp group in Butler County, Pennsylvania, went to work with a will.

Though many of the original members sold their property in Germany, before their departure, many others were unable to do so; not only because of economic conditions and the hostility of the civil authorities, but because these properties were thrown on the market at the same time. At any rate, not long after the arrival of the immigrants at Harmony, necessity drove them into an "each-for-all-and-all-for-each" organization. On the fifteenth day of February, 1805, Articles of Agreement were entered into, establishing the Harmony Society as a communistic unit with a common fund. In no way is it to be understood that any of the Harmonists had previously looked for an actual economic organization based upon community of interests, though the admiration of the primitive Christian church, with its communal organization, undoubtedly stimulated the ideal in their minds.

The 1805 Articles of Agreement—a model of simplicity —were in the form of a contract between the signers and "George Rapp and his Associates." In substance the subscribers pledged, first, to give absolutely all their property to George Rapp and Associates for the common benefit of the Society; second, to obey all rules and regulations of the community and to labor obediently and unselfishly for its well-being; and third, not to demand any reward for their labor or services in case they should desire to withdraw. In return George Rapp and his Associates pledged, first, to adopt subscribers as members of the Association and provide the privileges of Church and school to all; secondly, to supply the subscribers with all the necessaries of life, both in sickness and in health, and after their death to provide for their families; and finally, to return to those desiring to withdraw, the value of property contributed, and to provide those who had contributed nothing with a sum of money upon their withdrawal. It is noteworthy that not a single tenet of religion is mentioned in the Articles. Wisely so. Had they attempted such a move, there likely would not have come into being a Harmony Society. (See Appendix).

At the time of this simple, sweeping dedication of labor and property to the common welfare of the community, the Society also held an election. Though there were a number of members with better education and higher intellectual attainments, the simple weaver and vine-dresser, George Rapp, was elected head of the Society by a nearly unanimous vote. During the first hard months he had proven himself endowed with unerring common sense and remarkable judgment of human nature. In the old country he had filled the hearts of these people with a common inspiration. Now he became a kind of spiritual elder to the flock, at times stern and commanding but eminently fair, so that in the course of time the community began to refer to him as "Father Rapp"—a name that toward the close of his earthly career, deservedly became a major tradition.

Another position of equal importance was filled at this time by the brilliant young Frederick Reichert. This budding genius, who had already proven his metal in conducting the migration, was elected industrial superintendent and manager of the Society's external affairs. At the same time he changed the name of Reichert to Rapp and became George Rapp's adopted son. What George Rapp lacked in the dispatch of the Society's practical business and in executive ability, Frederick made up in the organization and maintenance of a perfectly coördinated economy. To Frederick were entrusted all external and financial affairs of the Society, and in course of time he held title to the total estate of the Society in his own name as Trustee.

They were a splendid pair, these two. Without them the Harmony Society could never have succeeded so brilliantly. Each complemented the other. Father Rapp, now in the high noon of life, unified and inspired the spiritual and internal life of the community; Frederick, still a virile young man, with worlds to conquer, managed its material, external life. The elder Rapp was intensely mystical, a fervent believer, an inspirer of men's souls; Frederick, on the other hand, was more realistic and practical in his dreams of a new life—a splendid artist in such realities as community planning and architecture, and a natural captain of industry. Yet the differences of the two Rapps are not to be exaggerated—the hymns written by both are distinguished by spiritual qualities fused into splendid phrases, and both were capable in the everyday management of work and of men. It is a tribute to the good sense of these people that without much doubt or hesitation they elected the two men best qualified to be their leaders.

Seven other men were elected as a Board of Elders, who were to aid in the control of internal affairs and to see that the Society's laws and regulations were enforced. However, it seems that during the lifetime of George and Frederick Rapp this board did not exercise much authority—the exercise of its powers was not deemed necessary or advisable under the banner of Harmony's two geniuses. Now and then, however, the Board assisted Father Rapp in judging complaints.

As to its internal organization, Frederick Rapp divided the Society into departments, each with an appointed superintendent. Each department—such as the store, the tavern, the orchards, the brewery, and the several factories—kept its own accounts. The superintendent was charged with money and materials entrusted to him, and credited for his products. In this way Frederick Rapp could immediately judge, from the periodic reports, precisely where the Society was making money or losing it.

By 1806 there were some seven hundred persons in the community, and about a third of them were operative male members engaged in community labor. Division of labor shows that nearly a hundred were engaged in farming, while masons, carpenters, smiths and weavers functioned in proportionate number. The women, too, contributed to the economy of the commune and engaged regularly in the activities of farm and workshop, as well as of those in the homes,

In spite of a smoothly working communal organization, days of severest trial followed. Nevertheless the gigantic task of clearing the land and erecting more permanent dwellings in late wintertime and combining these major tasks with agriculture in the summer, was accomplished by these hardy people. But some of the necessaries of life had to be brought from Pittsburgh, twenty-four miles away, over the crudest frontier roads. What's more, the Society had to depend upon its unestablished credit to purchase even these basic necessities. When credit failed— and this was not seldom in the early days—a good many people went hungry. For a time the daily ration had been cut to one spoonful of flour per capita. In August 1805 George Rapp writes to Frederick, "For eight days we have had no bread and very little flour, but are not suffering because of various cookables from the garden." Hungry enough to eat roots, some of them were poisoned and would have died had it not been for their capable community doctor.

Even as late as July 1806, George Rapp wrote to his friend and benefactor, Jacob Neff of Lancaster: "We are hard pressed. For about three months there has not been a cent in the treasury—and from the money of the store and the inn subsist seven hundred souls." But down deep in his heart there was always the germ of faith. "We have an unusual blessing . . . There is complete peace, and we have become much closer to each other."

On account of the extreme hardships, the pangs of hunger, and the endless hours of strenuous labor, some soon withdrew from the Society. The disaffected, who in our modern jargon "could not take it," found fault with the Rapp leadership, the communal economy and the rigid equality of reward extended to all alike. Some of these flocked to Dr. Haller's Lycoming County settle-

21

ment where no community of goods was enforced. Those withdrawing, who had contributed considerable sums of money to the settlement, now demanded its return. But this was obviously an impossibility, and when such cases were brought to court, the latter, with Solomonic wisdom, decreed that since the Society was practically penniless, the claimants must content themselves to wait until the Society was able to reimburse them. Some of the seceders became even more troublesome, circulating fantastic reports detrimental to the Society. The result was that credit was refused everywhere.

From the time when new German immigrants began to arrive, "the brotherhood spirit separated the pure and the ignoble," as George Rapp wrote. The late arrivals from Germany, who came after the hardest work was done and were not schooled in the religious enthusiasm and brotherhood of the original group, tended to disrupt the spirit of equality, self-sacrifice and unity of the original members. "It is most trying," wrote George to Frederick, "to send me such leprous people . . . We cannot permit ourselves to be corrected by new arrivals . . . The community will purify itself." Several even conspired to wrest control away from the Rapps and reorganize the whole community, "but suddenly the community, old and young, separated from them and they were thrown out as dirt."

Still, credit was not forthcoming. But now and then at crucial moments, real angels would appear on the scene. One time a stranger and his family visited Harmony and before he left he loaned George Rapp and Associates seven hundred dollars. Several times Jacob Neff, Father Rapp's dear friend of Lancaster County, came or offered to come to the rescue.

One evening Frederick Rapp, after vainly trying all

day to get supplies in Pittsburgh on credit, was sitting on a stone beside the Monongahela River, brooding, wondering how he could bear to return empty-handed on the morrow to his hungry brethren. He had reached the depths of despair; perhaps he was wondering if the Great Venture was a lost cause. A man had just walked past him and now was retracing his steps. Noticing Frederick's downcast expression, he gradually extracted the facts from Frederick. The stranger was George Sutton, a liberal minded merchant of the growing town of Pittsburgh. When he had heard the tale of woe and the sorry condition of the Society, he immediately offered to extend credit to Frederick until the Society would be able to pay him . . . Tradition has it that some years later this same merchant faced financial ruin, and when the Society heard of it they quickly came to the rescue of their former benefactor.

For several years the community worked frantically to gain security. The Society's affairs at home and abroad must have been a tremendous ordeal for both Rapps. As early as September 30, 1805, George wrote, to Frederick: "I am often inclined to tire of living, yet my feet shall stand in the portals of Jerusalem." In his letters one often notices that added spiritual enthusiasm, which helped him and his people to conquer the harsh circumstances of frontier settlement. Five years later he still wrote in a similar vein to Frederick, "I am tired of every-. thing. It is time you should come back, though I have nothing to complain as to the community . . ."

Time and again he depends upon Frederick. He signed his letters, "thy loyal father and brother." A true spirit of kinship and brotherhood shines through their letters to each other. "I withdraw myself," wrote the elder in 1810, "as much as I can so that your affairs may be com-

23

pleted, so that we may longer enjoy each others' company. I can hardly recollect when you journeyed away—it seems such a long time. I will be very glad to have you again." But if Frederick evinced the least sign of despair, the elder Rapp's spiritual faith and enthusiasm would again shine forth: "Many absurd things, no doubt, come your way, but you can bear much in the hope for the Kingdom of God. Believe it, we are destined to no other end than to serve the community all our lifetime . . . Every day I become more and more convinced of the great destination of the plan of the Kingdom of God in our point of time . . . God is with us . . . I am in high spirits and hope the same for you."

To endure the insecurity and hardships of the early years—indeed to risk such a New World venture at all—required a dominant faith and a religious enthusiasm and belief in the community's high destiny. This was George Rapp's major contribution, for he sought to infuse in the minds of his associates a mystical belief that the Harmony Society was destined to play a very important part in the establishment of the Kingdom of God *on earth*.

The people gathered around George Rapp as their teacher, "My small room," he wrote to Frederick in 1805, "is filled every night with people, as is the yard, who do not go to sleep until they have been with me and prayed," and five years later he wrote: "Some men and women wept as I spoke of the great destination of Harmonie."

But even his closest followers sometimes questioned the elder Rapp's practical vision. In less than a year after the settlement was established, many complained of the site chosen by Rapp. So strong was this dissatisfaction that, in December 1805, two hundred male members of the Society signed a petition to President Thomas Jefferson, requesting permission to purchase on terms,

30,000 acres of land in the Western Country for the chief purpose of cultivating the vine and making wine, the present location in Butler County not being suitable for this purpose. Both George and Frederick Rapp, unselfishly signed the petition, and the elder Rapp even went to Washington to confer and report on the bill which had been drawn and presented in Congress.

On January 29, 1806, this bill passed the Senate and was referred to the House. It had slipped smoothly along until it was vigorously debated on the floor of the House, February 13. Some days later it was amended, and when brought to a vote the result was a tie, forty-six to forty-six. The same day, February 18, the Speaker of the House cast the deciding vote against the bill.

While the bill was still being debated in the Senate, George Rapp wrote home, and after reporting its progress, he added, as a kind of afterthought, "Enclosed are some verses from the desert of wisdom." The hymn, *Kinder seid nun alle munter* (Children All Rejoice Anew), is the most clever expression of Rapp's expansive mysticism and the great destiny and purpose of the Society in the entire hymn literature of the Harmonists . . . Some of its twenty-four verses are as strangely beautiful as any mystical poetry ever written in America, and a translation cannot possibly do full justice to the poem:

> *Kinder, seid nun alle munter,*
> *Weil der inn're Liebes-Zunder,*
> *Freunde Jesu wieder paart,*
> *Sonnen-Blicke, Lichtes-Strahlen,*
> *Lassen Geistes-Funken fahren,*
> *Auf die Paradieses-Saat.*

A translation of this beautiful opening stanza may run something like this:

> *Children, all rejoice anew,*
> *For love's inner amadou*
> > *Jesus' friends re-pairs thuswise:*
> *Sunlight flashes, rays agleaming,*
> *Sending spirit-sparks forth streaming*
> > *On seed fields of Paradise . . . .*

(The "re-pairs" in the foregoing stanza refers to the re-pairing of the two sexes into one bi-une, or whole being.)

This came to the Society in the midst of its dissensions and controversies. The members sang it at morning worship the next Sunday to the tune "O wie seelig sind die Seelen," as Rapp requested. The result was magical, electrifying. Tears came to the eyes of the fervent, and some of the old members told me it was like a great dawning of light. The factional leaders felt like whipped curs. For all their superior education, they, as poets and inspirers of the souls of men, were not fit to touch the hem of George Rapp's garment.

In 1807 the memorable custom of celibacy was introduced—a subject of peculiar fascination for the more sensational historians. None of the original members with whom I have talked ever claimed that celibacy was mentioned in the old country, and all emphatically stated that George Rapp did *not* set the custom in motion—this in flat contradiction to most commentators on the Harmonists. According to Jonathan Lenz, a Trustee of the Society in later years, the movement began with the young people. Economic and social necessity naturally contributed to the establishment of the custom. From the purely economic point of view, the pregnancies and deliveries of the mothers and the suckling of the young, considerably hindered the progress of work—and labor was a precious thing in those early days. Moreover, the more children born into the Society, the more severe the rationing. Then, too, from the viewpoint of social organization, the division of the membership into family units, consisting of blood-relations, each family with its own desires and rank, did not so well contribute to the brotherhood and stern equality of the community as a whole. Hence in course of time the members abjured not only the use of tobacco but every other unnecessary thing.

There are several important things to be remembered in regard to the custom of celibacy. And it was a custom, voluntarily applied and accepted, and not a rule. After its adoption, George Rapp in his sermons no doubt elevated the celibate state above that of wedlock, but he had neither the wish nor the power to enforce celibacy. Indeed, both at Harmony, Pennsylvania and at Harmony, Indiana, he married a number of couples. In a letter to Frederick Rapp, he put it thus: "This narrow way is not for every one, I have already united several couples and expect to unite several more." The sanest words ever written on this moot point of celibacy are those of Ross F. Lockridge, Director of the New Harmony Indiana Memorial, "It is possible that these remarkable people realized the benefits of sublimation to a degree seldom if ever attained in community living. Perhaps they transferred the psychic energy of sex impulses into higher nonsexual channels of creative endeavor. Their natural emotional cravings may have found happy expression in their marvellous material productivity, their almost unequalled thrift, and especially in their rare cultivation of fine flowers and wonderful music." However, let us also note that a number of married couples flagrantly disregarded the custom—for example, Martin and Philli-pina Rall had four children between 1814 and 1829, Christoph Schwartz's wife bore six youngsters between 1813 and 1826, Daniel Vogt's wife Magdalena gave birth to six children between 1805 and 1819, and the Christoph Killingers had eight children between 1808 and 1830. Some of these children perhaps were born prior to the parents' admission to the Society, but unquestionably, quite a number were born within the Society and *while the parents were in full membership.*

The story was often told how in the early Economy days there came to George Rapp, Brother Martin Rall, requesting that an addition be built to his house—the appeal evoking from Father George at once the trenchant reply, "If you would stop adding to your family there would not be need for additions to the house." However Rapp gave Rall permission to go to the lumber yard and select the necessary material—"but you will have to build the addition yourself and not during working-hours," added Rapp.

Celibacy may have been adopted as a temporary meas-ure, but once adopted, Rapp searched out all passages of Scripture in support of the custom. The superior purity of the brother-sister relationship of the members was constantly eulogized, and as time went on, marital rela-tions were more and more derided. Result—the birthrate steadily diminished, until in the 1830's it came to an end.

The original family organization, however, continued, though after the adoption of celibacy there were subtle and gradual changes. The family became more of a house unit and an intrinsic part of the larger Society, rather than a separate and basically selfish organization of par-ents and children. Family names were unimportant any-way, for "brothers and sisters" were called by the first name—the merest child addressing hoary elders as "Jacob," or "Frederick," or "Romeli." And when parents died, the children became part of entirely different "families"; adults were moved around in like manner. Thus over a period of years the real family merged with, or was scattered throughout, the community. The creation of these "artificial families" proved a pronounced success. Each such family unit had its house and a quarter-acre lot, a milk cow and as many chickens as could be kept on the feed rations, which, like all of their provisions, were furnished by the Society.

Children were kept at the community school until fourteen years of age. But the older of these attended school at this time only in the forenoon, while the afternoon was devoted to such labor as they could easily perform. Children learned to work happily together, and were taught to think in terms of the whole community and its welfare. In school were taught all common branches as writing, arithmetic, geography, reading, history, in both German and English—though the former was used in conducting classes. Upon reaching the age of fourteen the youth was granted his choice of a profession and the opportunity to learn it where it was practiced in the Society.

Throughout the years the moral tone of the Society was more than praiseworthy. John Melish, Philadelphia traveler who visited the Society in 1810, reported, "There is no vicious habit among them. There is not an instance of swearing, or lying, or debauchery of any kind; and, as to cheating, so commonly practised in civilized society, they have no temptation to it whatever. As individuals, they have no use for money—and they have no fear of want."

I suppose in these idyllic days and nights there was

29

little need for the night watch. But every night one of the members took his turn, and on each hour he would chant a different All's Well—at twelve o'clock for instance:

> Hört ihr Leute last euch sagen
> Uns're Glock hat zwölf geschlagen.
> Zwölf Thor hat die güld'ne Stadt,
> Wohl dem der den Eingnug hat.

> List unto me all ye people
> Twelve strokes sound from out the steeple
> Twelve gates has the city of gold
> Blest is he who enters the fold.

Though, during the Harmonie settlement, these sober industrious people spent tremendous energy in developing their "garden in the wilderness," the community was never without a social program. Much of this revolved around the church which they built in 1808. Prior to this, for religious instruction and divine worship, they met in houses, which was in consonance with their petition to the Diet, at Lomersheim. George Rapp divided the community into five groups—old men, old women, young men, young women, and youngsters of both sexes—for social intercourse and mutual improvement during the week days. Then, too, there was always music to soothe the souls of the Harmonists. In the best German traditions all learned how to sing. They sang not only at worship and at their annual festivals, but at their work in field and shop. Five years after their settlement had been established, they had a little chamber orchestra—three violins, a bass, a clarinet, a flute and two French horns—which played secular as well as sacred music. This was the modest beginning of one of the most famous institutions of the Harmony settlements, and a tradition in which at a later day I had the happiness to play a major rôle.

Despite dissensions, withdrawals, privations and suffering, the community achieved a high degree of prosperity —indeed, in view of the difficulties which they faced and conquered, their achievements in this first New World settlement are amazing. During the very first year of their settlement they cleared a hundred and fifty acres, erected nearly fifty log houses, and a very respectable grist mill. The second year they cleared nearly four hundred more acres, and planted four acres of vineyard. In addition to a number of dwellings they erected a two-story hotel mostly of stone, a hundred foot barn, a sawmill, an oil mill, a dye-house, a tannery, a distillery and a brick storehouse. The same year they raised enough grain to supply their own needs and to sell a surplus of six hundred bushels, not to mention the manufacturing of 3000 gallons of whiskey! (Though it became famous throughout hard-drinking western Pennsylvania, the Harmonists used it very sparingly—in course of time only as a medicine.) Year after year new additions were made, and production greatly increased. By 1809 they were becoming an important economic factor in western Pennsylvania— this only five years after the erection of the first log hut!

By the time they were to embark on still another great adventure far to the west, they had paid for nearly 7000 acres of land, more than 2000 of which were cleared and cultivated. Besides the town of Harmonie, this included three tiny outlying hamlets,—Ramsthal, Edenau and Oelbrunn, settled by some members who wanted the advantages of Harmonie but did not wish to submit to its strict customs. The town of Harmonie itself included 150 dwellings, largely brick structures which had soon

31

replaced the early log and frame buildings, six larger and more superior brick houses, a large comfortable inn, a brick store with vaulted wine cellars, a brick weavery, two brick buildings for textile manufacturing, another for dyeing, a woolen factory, a spacious brick meetinghouse, a four-story granary, two distilleries, two flour mills, two fulling mills, an oil mill, hempmill, brewery, blacksmith shop, nail factory, brickyard, potash boilery, and a number of other buildings for various tradesmen. Below the town were four large barns and a number of scattered stables. Also a large brick warehouse erected at the confluence of the Ohio and Beaver Rivers.

In less than ten years the community outgrew its original self-sustaining economy, and throughout southwestern Pennsylvania was selling its growing surpluses. The community mechanics also served the surrounding countryside. Moreover, a reputation had been established for the excellence of Harmonie craftsmanship; people were willing to pay more than the average market price for Harmonie products.

Harmonie, with its neat streets and prim architectural quaintness, its broad fields of waving grain, its green lush meadows, its well kept woodlands, and its peaceful industrious atmosphere, was truly like a garden in the wilderness. Frederick, always with a discerning eye for beauty, had adapted colonial architectural style with Old World town planning. The elegant simplicity of late eighteenth century motifs adapted by Frederick to Harmonie's needs remind us not a little of the old buildings of Philadelphia, Lancaster and southeastern Pennsylvania. As the traveler approached from Pittsburgh over the southern hills, Harmonie must have looked like some remote Utopia.

John Melish, the cultured traveler from Philadelphia came upon it one day in August, 1810, and wrote:

32

The whole country, from Pittsburgh to this place (a country tavern not far from Harmonie), is rather rough and uncultivated, and land sells from two to three dollars an acre. Beyond this, as we continued our journey, we found the country to improve, and approaching the precincts of the Harmonist Society, we passed some of their well cultivated farms. Here the road passes over a considerable hill, and on reaching the top, we saw at a little distance the town of Harmonie, elegantly situated amid flourishing and well cultivated fields."

By 1810 Harmonie could even enjoy certain luxuries. Indeed, even before that time a splendid community garden had been established under the direction of the artistic Frederick and the mystical Father Rapp. The greater part of this garden was a kind of luxuriant labyrinth, with circular paths lined with tall hedgerows and leading circuitously to a simple structure in the center within which were benches for seats.

Near the labyrinth was the botanic garden, well stocked with valuable plants and herbs, many of which were used by the community physician. The doctor had a remarkable collection of native plants all carefully catalogued according to the Linnaean system.

On the north side of the Creek were the sheep pens, and on the hills round about one might see more than a thousand sheep. The Society had been among the first to introduce the Merino breed into this country. They paid $1000 for a ram and proportionate prices for a flock of ewes, and had unusual success in breeding them and in the manufacture of woolen cloth from such superior wool. The flocks were under the watchful eyes of

33

three shepherds, who during the nights slept in tents which were moved from hill to hill.

To the northward, facing the community and outlying fields, was a very steep hill which one might ascend by a regular flight of 137 steps. George Rapp often ascended to this point of vantage and, like the patriarchs of old, surveyed his domain. According to legend, he sometimes directed via megaphone, the daily routine of the community from this little peak. I was told that it was the intention of the Society, at one time, to build a little temple at the hilltop to be called Harmonie Hall, where practising musicians could assemble and send forth their melodies over the quiet town and fields below. The hill was terraced with stone to permit cultivation of the splendid vineyards, the source of the wine of Harmonie which became justly famous throughout western Pennsylvania.

As year by year the surplus products of the community increased, and greater trade facilities were required, the location proved more and more inadequate. In an effort to overcome this handicap, Frederick built a warehouse at the junction of the Ohio and Beaver Rivers, near the present site of Bridgewater. Raw cotton from the South, and wrought iron and other bulk materials from Pittsburgh, were poled on the Ohio to this point, from whence transportation to and from Harmonie took place. But this transportation system proved unsatisfactory to Frederick. Under his direction the community had grown from a predominately agricultural unit with a simple economy to one of diversified industries. This had always been his dream. But now that the dream was realized, the community and its expanding economic system had outgrown its location.

There were other reasons for seeking a new locale.

For example, the soil of Butler County, though sufficient for ordinary purposes, was not suitable for grape culture— an occupation which many of the members had followed in the old country. Moreover, a new method of transportation, namely steam navigation, had begun to appear on western waters and the ever-progressive Frederick wanted to take advantage of it.

Accordingly in the spring of 1814, a party of exploration—George Rapp, John L. Baker and Louis Schreiber— in search of another haven in the American wilderness, boarded a river boat headed for Louisville.

3

Harmonie on the Wabash
(1815-1825)

MAKING PART OF THEIR WAY by horseback so that they could more intently examine every possible site, our three explorers finally came to Louisville late in April. They had letters of introduction to leading citizens of this thriving outpost of civilization and were well received. But gradually it became obvious that the best sites along the Ohio and in the Louisville region were already taken. The recently Indian-infested areas of what is now Ohio, Indiana, Michigan and Illinois had just begun to open up to extensive settlement, and the more adventuresome land speculators and settlers had pretty well honey-combed the whole area along the major waterways. However, the search for a new haven was continued.

Early in May the explorers were at Vincennes on the Wabash, a small frontier settlement and fort, where the redoutable Clark had but recently rallied his men against the redskins. When George Rapp saw the great clusters of black locust trees along the prairie streams below Vincennes, he knew there was good land there. At the land office they scrutinized all the available tracts in the territory of Indiana, but their hearts were really taken by a large section, some miles below Vincennes, which sloped from the gentle hills to a fertile plain along the Wabash. "You will not believe what a rich and beautiful land is found there," George Rapp wrote to the flock at home. Opposite the tract lay an island of some three thousand acres, frequently inundated by spring floods.

The explorers did not long hesitate. A few days after viewing the land they made the first purchase of 7000 acres. Well pleased with their accomplishments, they returned to their Pennsylvania home.

They had every right to be proud of the purchase. Located about seventy miles above the junction of the Wabash with the Ohio, the peace of the new community was not so liable to be disturbed by rough, hard-drinking rivermen, raftsmen and keelboatmen, yet the location permitted ready access to river trade. People in Pittsburgh and the river towns were beginning to talk of steamboats to replace the slow-moving, one-way flatboats, and the Wabash had a deep enough channel for a middle class steamboat. Adventuresome souls from the sleepy East were moving down the Ohio River, which was the great highway to the immense lands of middle and western America and to the deep South. With these massive movements of men, river trade was at the point of its first great expansion. No wonder that in the midst of such expansion, with the richest land in the country, and with the agricultural and industrial skills of the members, this community, welded into one intrepid organization, accomplished the seemingly impossible!

About a month after the first purchase, John L. Baker and a hundred members of the Society floated down the Ohio in flatboats, and two weeks later poled up the placid Wabash to the new location. There, adjoining a spreading meadow separating it from the river, the Society's second Harmonie, was laid out according to the cardinal points of the compass. Allowance was made for a garden adjacent to each house; this to enable each family to raise its own vegetables and as a prevention against the spread of fire.

37

Untold hardships lay in wait for these first settlers. The summer was especially hot. Temporary sod huts were built, but such living conditions, combined with the heat, aided the spread of fever and ague. Soon an epidemic so debilitated their ranks that progress was cut in half. Some of the children died. Even John Baker, a veritable Hercules in charge of the advance guard, succumbed for a time and could not attend to the strenuous business at hand.

With the coming of cooler weather, the hardier workers were able to erect better quarters. The fever subsided and finally disappeared. Nevertheless, it was an heroic struggle. Only ten years before, many of these same men and women had emerged from similar hardships, so now, as they had done before, they put their trust in God and worked away. After a time George Rapp, with additional families, arrived and stimulated the work anew.

Meanwhile Frederick Rapp, at old Harmonie, in making preparations for departure, was having difficulties. In the first place, fines were levied on those who had left because they had missed serving in the state militia. The collectors, thinking they could capitalize on a simple unworldly people, tried to collect twice as much as was due. Frederick paid $640, the amount legally due. But the young upstarts in charge of collection were unsatisfied and proceeded to make trouble. They stopped two wagons loaded with trading goods and wanted to unload them. Frederick having no faith in the collectors' authority, indignantly rode to Butler, the county seat, where he entered suit against them as thieves. Even this action failed to stop the rascals, but when they attempted to make way with several horses, the women and girls of the Society armed with brooms marched down upon the marauders and fought them off. Even when Frederick arrived and gave security for the amount demanded, the officers wanted to force the sale of the property within ten days, and some of Harmony's neighbors sided with them. Thereupon, Frederick with his attorney visited the Brigade Inspector in Beaver. Finding that he could prosecute the collectors as thieves, he held them dangling for awhile between freedom and a possible jail sentence, then proudly dismissed the whole affair.

This was by no means the end of trouble. The community's neighbors, many of whom had prospered via the Society's regime, but who were envious of the peaceful unity and great economic successes, trespassed at large over the Society's lands and rambled through their houses and gardens. The matter was getting out of control, and the noisy neighbors demanded the right to elect a commandant over the village—a direct insult to Frederick. In May 1815, in the midst of these difficult affairs, a group of six Mennonites came from Bethlehem, Pennsylvania, to view the grounds and buildings of the quaint village on the Conoquenessing. One of these, a man by the name of Abraham Ziegler, purchased the village and adjacent lands for $100,000, which according to Frederick left the community a profit of about $8000. Having received the powers of agent for the new purchaser, Frederick threatened to take all trespassers to the county courthouse as thieves. Harmonie had evidently prospered after the early hardships, since, concerning the purchase of Harmonie Frederick writes to his adopted father, "I did not ask payment in hand because I did not see that we need it . . . I still have twelve thousand dollars in the bank besides the stock therein." As to the foregoing I am compelled to state that Mr. Ziegler was unable to meet his obligation. A part of his indebtedness seemingly was cancelled and in 1826 and succeeding years he paid $50,000 in cash and produce. Even without immediate payment the Society was able to bear not only the expenses incidental to the new migration westward, but also to pay for 24,734 acres of land the sum of $61,050.

Late in June, via flatboats, the migration down the majestic Ohio began, and after a pleasant voyage of fifteen days the people disembarked at the new village on the Wabash. Frederick was well pleased with their new home —"They have done immense work, already 125 acres are in corn eight to ten feet high." Nothing meagre about this land! The wheat and rye harvest had already proved splendid, and the new vineyards and orchards were thriving better than those in Pennsylvania. Frederick was filled with optimism about the future of the new settlement: "It appears that this country in a few years, in regard to the cultivation of small grain and commerce, will become one of the most important parts of the Union."

According to the plan of Frederick Rapp, surveyors from Vincennes, by way of two wide intersecting streets, had laid out the town into four sections. The east-west road led to Vincennes; while the other led south to Mt. Vernon and Shawneetown. To the eastward lay the cultivated fields and along other edges of the town extended the sheep pastures, vineyards and orchards.

After the first sod houses with thatched roofs had served their purpose, they were replaced by log houses, which in turn were gradually replaced by neat brick and frame structures—rarities for a frontier village.

Besides the family houses there were four large three-story brick dormitories, harboring sixty to eighty individuals. The dormitories served as dwellings for the unmarried.

Due to Frederick Rapp's inborn artistic sense, the new

Harmonie became a garden in the wilderness. Here was a scene of Arcadian beauty—this well planned village nestling in the fertile valley by the Wabash; surrounded by low vine-covered hills, gently rolling pastures and fruited orchards. There, too, was the famous horticultural design, the labyrinth, a replica of the one at old Harmonie, and, since the Harmonists were extraordinarily fond of flowers, the family gardens and the public garden must have been models of perfection. On the workbenches of the factories and in the shops were flowers to brighten the lives of those blessed people.

Among the public buildings were two churches. The smaller, older one was a frame building with a clock steeple; the other, newer one was a large, cross-shaped structure of brick. Imagine a church with a transept 120 feet long and a nave of the same length. Surrounding the middle a circle of twenty-eight huge, polished pillars of walnut, cherry and sassafras, which supported the gallery and the lofty dome. Other conspicuous features were its graceful lines and its four immense doorways—over one of which, designed by Frederick, is carved a gilt rose under date of 1822, followed by the inscription from Micah 4—8, which in the German Lutheran version reads:

And thou tower Eder, the stronghold of the daughter of Zion, thy golden rose shall come, the former dominion, the kingdom of the daughter of Jerusalem.

William Herbert, a London traveler, wrote of this church: "I can scarcely imagine myself in the wilds of Indiana, on the borders of the Wabash, while passing through the long and resounding aisles and surveying the stately colonnades of this church."

Southwardly on the opposite side of the street was the brick mansion of George and Frederick Rapp, larger than the other homes and further distinguished by more spacious and elegant gardens. An early English traveler Thomas Hulme, declared in amazement that "the dwelling house they have built for their pastor more resembles a Bishop's palace" than the humble dwelling place of a mystical teacher of the principles of the primitive Christian Church. Nearby was a massive brick and stone granary with loop holes so constructed that, if river pirates invaded the peaceful scene, the building could quickly be turned into a fortress. Not far off was the community tavern and inn, haven of western travelers and famous for its good food and clean service. Southward on the main street was the well-stocked community store where neighboring settlers from miles around purchased the Society's own manufactures and the imported wares sold by the community. The store of course supplied the community as well, according to the flexible rationing system used. Small manufacturing establishments and shops were scattered appropriately at points throughout the village.

Less than a year after the Harmonists moved to the territory of Indiana, Congress enabled the territory to form a constitution and a new state. On June 10 the convention convened at Corydon, where the most eminent of the territory, including Frederick Rapp, were present. Harmonie, later called New Harmony, it is well to remember, was at that time the largest community in Posey County and one of the largest in the state. Its political importance was therefore obvious. However, most of its inhabitants (George Rapp among them) neither spoke nor understood the English language, so that Frederick, by virtue of his office and his fluency in the adopted tongue, naturally became the political key to the entire community. Influential men throughout the state and nation came to recognize Frederick Rapp as a cultured gentleman, honest and magnetic; and a vastly capable business genius.

Although he received many letters from political candidates requesting the vote of Harmonie, he always remained detached, objective and unbiased in the discussion of political recommendations with the other leaders of the community. He never abused his power, in fact never made the most of it. But when called upon by the state, he gave wholehearted coöperation to whatever project was assigned. As one of the eight commissioners selected by the legislature, he helped choose Indianapolis as the permanent site of the state capital. Frequently, through the district representative, he made proposals to the legislature for the stabilization of currency, the encouragement of industry, the improvement of roads, of river traffic, and the protection of domestic manufactures. Frederick ardently championed a substantial tariff which he believed was necessary for the sound development of domestic industry, and from henceforth the Society as a unit became identified with Frederick's intelligent protective tariff philosophy which had not a little influence on the political ideas of his contemporaries.

In those early days of a simple state economy, taxes were comparatively light, and Harmonie with its vastly growing financial resources bore them easily. But other state laws caused difficulties and were frowned upon by the Harmonists. Such was the militia service required of every male adult. After all, had not this people abandoned Old World tyrannies and military conscriptions to come to free America to live a life of peace and productiveness? And now the new state had passed a law requiring all men from eighteen to fifty to be on call for a period of militia duty each year or pay a fine of seventy-five cents a day. Five days of work on public roads was also required—a burden gladly assumed by the hard working Harmonists. The refusal of most of the members to serve in the militia, on grounds of conscientious objection to war and the bearing of arms against one's fellow man, brought a series of fines which Frederick protested. His efforts to ameliorate this burden resulted in a reduction of fines to an extent satisfactory to the Society.

But there was nothing evangelistic about the religion and philosophy of the Harmony Society. Not the least inclined to proselyte, their interest in the "world outside" was quite limited. *They believed it was their destiny to set an illustrious example of the harmony of human relations, the natural coöperative economy of the community of goods, and the peaceful reign of Christian fellowship under such conditions; so that other communities observing this marvel of communal life, would gradually be led to adopt a similar policy.* In short, they believed that a Heaven on Earth was not only possible but, under conditions of so-called Christian communism, inevitable. Enough work, the Lord knows, was required to keep their own environs trim and neat; why should they meddle in the muddy affairs of the world?

Prosperity had been achieved in Pennsylvania and under most trying circumstances. But the progress of the new settlement was even more remarkable. For sheer fertility the land outrivaled that of the highly extolled acres of Lancaster County, Pennsylvania. Due to better climatic conditions, richer soil, easier marketing conditions and more extensive land holdings, agricultural production increased by leaps and bounds. From the beginning Frederick kept adding to the Society's holdings so that within three years they came to be nearly 30,000 acres.

The vineyards on the surrounding hills took up fifteen acres of southern exposure where the large variety of grapes that Frederick imported from Germany were especially successful. Wines from these grapes were not equaled in the western country.

Interspersing the vineyards, were orchards containing about fifteen hundred bearing apple and pear trees from which were gathered immense quantities of fruit; and also a peach orchard from which one year, so it is recorded, the peaches yielded so abundantly that the surpluses, which the community could neither market nor consume, were fed to the *hogs* for an entire month! Nor were the expert orchardists satisfied merely with perfect fruit and tremendous yields, but constantly experimented in producing new varieties. Behind the Rapp mansion there was a large greenhouse, so constructed, that it could be rolled away in summer leaving the plants in the open air. In it one might find even orange and lemon trees which produced excellent fruit. Vast quantities of the orchard crops were annually preserved by the industrious matrons of the Society, whose preserves, jellies and fruit butters were seldom short of perfection.

Even without its vineyards and orchards, Harmonie's agricultural production was astonishing. Two thousand acres of wheat, rye, barley, oats and flax had to be harvested each year. In harvest time it must have been a magnificent sight to watch from one of the vineyard hills a line of brawny men with sickles cutting away across a hundred acre field of waving grain—the women, too, doing their part. Now and then someone would strike up a song, or the community band would gather on the hillside to cheer the workers and escort them home from labor at the end of day. Looking over the fruitful fields and the bursting barns at dusk, hearing the soft slow faraway

45

sounds of the village below, one might easily fancy himself dreaming of a beautiful and perfect Nowhere . . .

One will remember that in Pennsylvania, the Society although predominantly an agricultural community, under Frederick's management developed sufficient diversified crafts and industries to make the community not only self-sustaining but productive to the extent of a considerable trade throughout the neighborhood. Recognizing the potential values of the mechanical and industrial skills of these German craftsmen and mechanics, Frederick saw to it that in their new home, these crafts and industries took a proportionately greater place in the Society's economy. Though agriculture naturally remained basic, industrial expansion took place, and the sphere of commercial activity widened.

Many of their industries were built up on the principle of the production of the raw material through various phases of manufacturing to the distribution of the finished product. This was in large measure true of the textile manufactures of the community. Wool, cotton and flax were produced abundantly and prepared for processing by the community itself; while the Society also ginned the cotton of neighboring farmers and planters at a toll of one-eighth of the cleaned cotton. Machinery for spinning and weaving of cotton fibres was operated by young women. The spinning machinery was driven by the use of two oxen walking on an inclined plane; and four power looms were run by a steam engine.

Complicated machinery was also used in wool manufacture—one of Harmonie's pet industries. A dyeing and bleaching-house completed the manufacturing process. Harmonie textiles, because of the superior craftsmanship and the excellence of materials used, commanded highest

46

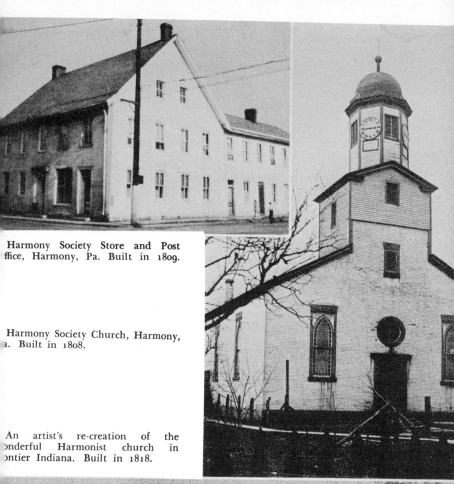

Harmony Society Store and Post Office, Harmony, Pa. Built in 1809.

Harmony Society Church, Harmony, a. Built in 1808.

An artist's re-creation of the onderful Harmonist church in ontier Indiana. Built in 1818.

prices throughout the western country. The steam engines used in these factories were among the very first in the western country. The Harmonists apparently, and Frederick especially, were always in the vanguard as to new industrial methods. It has also been claimed that the first threshing machine in this part of the world was used and owned by the Society.

On the wild Indiana-Illinois frontier there was, as might be expected of a hardy, crude and rugged people, a great demand for all kinds of spirits. The log distillery at Harmonie, a unique but simple device, performed the whole process of converting rye into whisky ready for use. Two dogs working hourly turns on a treadmill pumped the necessary water. Twelve gallons of whisky could be prepared in about six hours. A small still added about twenty gallons to the daily production. And in the nearby brewery about 500 gallons of beer were brewed every other day. These beverages were in great demand in neighboring and river towns. But the wines and cider were something special, and were kept in mammoth hundred-gallon casks in the wine cellar under the Rapp mansion for distribution throughout the western country. The Harmonists, of course, drank only wine and cider—and these in moderation. It seems that there was never any inebriety among the sober Harmonists.

Nearly all of the products required by the community were made by members of the Society. The coopers made barrels and other containers; a self-taught tinsmith manufactured the tinware; blacksmiths tended six forges which turned out all the iron work; chandlers made a thousand candles a day; rope-makers made six thousand pounds of flax and hempen rope in a season; and the stocking weaver had four looms, upon each of which four

47

pairs of stockings could be woven in a day. Brick kilns turned out thousands of excellent bricks; an oil-mill made oils from linseed, hemp, walnuts, and peach-stones; the large grist-mill (four miles from the village on a "cut-off" of the Wabash), could grind fifty-six barrels of grain in twenty-four hours—enough to supply both the community and the foreign trade. There was also the flour-mill proper, to which the farmers of the neighborhood brought their grain to have it ground.

Besides the surpluses of agriculture and industrial crafts already mentioned, the little community sold seed, hops, hemp, tobacco, sugar, cheese, butter, wax, linen, shingles, cattle, sheep, horses, hogs, furs and hides. There was good hunting and trapping in these early days by the Wabash, for many hundreds of skins of deer, bears, wolves, raccoons, otters, beavers, minks, muskrats and rabbits were sold. Still other products added to the community's exchequer: venison, pork, lard, tallow, eggs, bacon, honey, apples, cider, wine, spirits, beer, feathers, quills, bristles, tar, powder and all sorts of textile products. It was a rich, rich land, especially in the hands of sober, industrious, men and women, welded into an effective working unit, striving coöperatively toward an ideal life. Though hundreds of miles away from large markets, the surpluses in 1818 brought $13,141.83 in hard cash. And in 1819, when the young nation was suffering from its first national economic crisis and hard money was almost non-existent in the western country, the community's surpluses sold for $12,441.85.

Always on the alert for new industrial and commercial methods Frederick studied complicated machinery with the eyes of an expert and he kept pace with the latest improvements in management and industrial or commercial techniques. He never applied new methods without testing their practicability; but once proved, they were adapted to the community's requirements. . . . These were the years when, largely through his efforts, the Harmony Society rose from a limited, self-sustaining economy to a small agricultural and industrial empire.

The production of large surpluses naturally demanded an extension of trade and commerce. In Pennsylvania the Society had bartered and sold goods within a restricted area, and one of the chief motivations for moving to Indiana was the greater facility of trading and shipping by inland waterways. Although Frederick had dreamed of building a river steamboat (such were introduced on inland waterways in 1811) for the Society at the time of their leaving Harmony, the project was postponed because steamboating was still generally regarded as too venturesome or dangerous. Thus even in Indiana the community continued to ship much of its produce via the old fashioned flatboats and keelboats. In this way their trading area extended downriver to St. Louis and New Orleans.

The sixteen-year-old Jonathan Lenz, later the kindly junior Trustee of the Society, directed a flatboat shipment of the community's products in 1823 to New Orleans—typical of many similar shipments to this and other river ports on the Ohio and Mississippi Rivers. The cargo, valued at $1369, consisted of 39 kegs of lard, 100 kegs of butter, 680 bushels of corn and oats, 40 barrels of whiskey, 88 barrels of flour, 130 barrels of pork, 32 oxen and 16 hogs. Some members of the community must have been splendid river navigators to guide such an unwieldy cargo down the swift-flowing, broad-breasted rivers.

Frederick established agencies in a number of river towns—Abishai Way and Company at Pittsburgh, Frederick Dent at St. Louis, James Olde and Company at New

Orleans, still another at Louisville. For trade closer home he opened branch stores at Vincennes and Shawneetown, Illinois.

Almost from the beginning of the Indiana settlement, the Society had been confronted with the problems of paper money, its fluctuations in different areas and its general instability. In 1815 Frederick had accepted Kentucky state paper at only 37½ cents on the dollar; later he refused it altogether. State paper depreciated rapidly, until in 1819 the whole nation found itself in a financial crisis. Frederick did what he could; he submitted proposals to the state legislature and indirectly to Congress. But because specie went to England for purchases—the chief reason for Federick's advocacy of protective tariff,— and because of wild-cat banking, especially in the western states where speculation was rife, the bottom seemed to be dropping out of everything. Banks and business houses failed, and the more conservative financiers refused to purchase or to draw bills other than those deemed absolutely necessary. Sales nearly disappeared, particularly those of the more staple articles.

However by careful planning and business management, Frederick managed to keep the Society on an even economic keel, even while business everywhere around sank to a new low. Naturally, the Society suffered insofar as its trade and commerce became more limited, but the community was still a self-sufficient economic unit and its standards of living were not at all affected.

The major effect of the crisis of 1819 was the embarrassment of the community's wool industry. Demand for woolen goods was so unsatisfactory and competition with foreign goods so keen because a protective tariff was lacking, that the leaders debated whether to close down this industry altogether. It is well to remember that this industry was the pride and joy of Harmonie: its woolen goods were sold from Pittsburgh to New Orleans, commanding higher prices than similar goods from other establishments. Some of this was due probably to the splendid merino sheep which had been purchased in Pennsylvania at great expense . . . Next year, 1820, the market was worse than ever.

When by force of national economic circumstances the manufacture of textiles bogged down, and commerce continued on a restricted scale, the Society devoted itself with added zest to agriculture. Notwithstanding the general depression, this band of frugal people did not at all feel the pressure of hard times. Their internal economic structure, so admirably flexible and adaptable, became soundly balanced between industry, agriculture and commerce, and all of it proportioned according to the community requirements. When depression came, it simply meant a partial reduction of cash profits without decline in living standards. The accumulation of wealth also continued so that by 1819, the Society's economic valuation rose to $368,690.92. This sum in the main is to be credited to the rise in value of their land. In 1823, they offered to lend money to the state of Indiana at six percent. And in 1824 they were able to pay in full for an entirely new tract of land as well as the expense of moving the entire community, not to mention the building of a steamboat—this before they received any money for the sale of Harmonie!

Thus, in spite of the vagaries of a national economic breakdown they continued their industrious, calm, contented life. To the casual visitor it may have seemed dull and monotonous. On the other hand, to the neighboring backwoodsmen, Harmony seemed a paradise, thus engendering feelings of jealousy. But to those within, life was filled with humble pleasure—the joy of working to-gether, the luxury of social integrity, the security from the turmoil of the strange, wild world outside.

In the mornings between five and six the community arose; breakfast was served between six and seven, where-upon the men and some of the women departed to their various tasks, sometimes noted on individual schedules on the milk-wagon bulletin. The Harmonists worked steadily and intently, but were relieved at intervals by refresh-ments—besides the regular three meals they had a lunch at nine in the morning and a Vesperbrod in mid-after-noon. Curfew rang at 9:00 P. M., and all but the shepherds and watchmen were to be in their homes by that hour, although during festal or social activities of the evenings, the hour was not regarded. (Herdsmen, by the way, slept in a wagon on wheels—a so-called "Noah's Ark.")

The Harmonists were interested in music, in the true German fashion, and it was probably their chief form of pleasure. Instead of the alarm clock, mellow French horns awakened the people and on every possible occa-sion the community band was put to use. This estimable organization was under the direction of Doctor J. Christoph Müller, who served as school teacher as well as printer. Every festal occasion was a signal for the band to function and it was with regularity that it played on summer Sunday evenings in the public garden.

In the shops when work was slack or slow, the workers sang in harmony. The younger people were trained to sing the favorite songs of the old world, and some of the American tunes. In church, if we may believe the journals of travelers, their singing had a wonderfully uplifting effect. Many of their hymns were indeed compositions of the members themselves. George Rapp being especially capable in the assembling of words; while Frederick composed both words and music. Frederick's hymns and secular songs were generally built about the theme of Friendship. Gertrude Rapp, granddaughter of George, was given a special musical education and performed brilliantly on the piano and organ. . . . They all had music and harmony in their hearts, in conformity to the peace and community friendship that ruled their little world.

Frederick's influence seems to have dominated the cultural as well as the industrial life of Harmonie. Aside from his commercial and architectural talents, he had a flair for the literary, the artistic and the scientific interests. He was often in the market for books, and through his efforts, the Society accumulated a considerable community library. Soon after settling on the Wabash, he ordered many copies of Klopstock's *Messias,* one of the great epics of German literature, and some paintings such as "Christ Healing the Sick" and "Peter Preaching at Pentecost." When J. Reichert and J. L. Baker were on Society business in Germany, collecting money still due to individual members, Frederick ordered them to bring back choice varieties of grapes from the Rhineland, many books, a small telescope, a new kind of musical instrument called the Jubel horn, a camera obscura, and astronomical charts. He himself was an enthusiastic amateur painter, and a splendid judge of works of art. Although he traveled much in the world of men, in the metropolitan centers of the still young nation; although he enjoyed attendance at concerts, the opera and theaters of the cities, he was always happiest among his own people. In 1817 he wrote to George Sutton:

> "On my journey I became so weary of the world, and particularly of city life, that I am glad to live again among my friends, who have up-

rightness for their rule, and where, instead of fashionable luxury, simple frugality governs the rudder."

Among the intellectual and cultural pursuits was one that prevailed among the "classes" mentioned in the previous chapter—the members vying in the jotting down of "rays of purest thought serene," inspirational gems generally devoted to praise and exaltation of HARMONIE. The choicest of these were brought to Father Rapp who in turn made a selection and had it printed under the title *Stück-Buch* (Piece Book). The essays or encomiums were short as a rule, and some were set to music— one of these, "Fair art thou Harmonie," became quite a favorite.

Another little volume from the 1824 printing press is the "Thoughts on the destiny of man," containing matter which Father Rapp adopted in slightly different language from the great German philosopher Herder. The latter called his chief work, "Ideas on the destiny of man."

The booklet was not printed for dissemination—indeed the numerous repetitions in the subject matter lend color to the story "that the printer, for practice on the new 1824 printing press, compiled the Rapp philosophical jottings". In any event, George Rapp during many years, in terms less erudite, had preached a similar philosophy.

Soon after its founding, the Society began to receive requests for a statement of its principles, but the answer was invariably to the effect that it did not publish anything of the kind. However, all over the United States people wanted to know what was in the hearts and minds of this band of religiously inclined communists. Samuel Worcester of Boston, apparently writing for a group of Swedenborgians, who were contemplating a similar community, asked Frederick about the underlying philosophy and basic Economy of the Society. Mr. Worcester had heard of the Society's successes through that enthusiastic traveler, John Melish. Quoting at random from Frederick's reply of Oct. 1822:

"We can not refer you to any book nor send you a pamphlet informing you of our principles and management . . . There is nothing written or printed . . . except a sort of agreement. We . . . see how everything is shaken in its base by the present period; how all kingdoms and states tremble and totter; also all religious societies, sects and parties have no solid hold upon their old systems and forms . . . how moral corruption has universally crept into all ranks, so that most of the people are lawless and unconscionable and regard neither civil order nor care to exercise true Christian religion. . . . Of all these evils and calamities Harmonie knows nothing; eighteen years ago she laid the foundation to a new period—indeed, after the original pattern of the primitive church described in Acts of Apostles, chapters 2 and 4 . . . and now our Community stands proof firm and immovable upon its rock of truth . . . although unknown and disdained, we have lived in happiness and peace, hence our unity, temporal as well as spiritual, has increased from year to year . . . Since the moral worth of right and wrong is already implanted into the heart of each man at his creation, there remains nothing to do but to open the inward feeling and keep it open. Then it follows of course, that those susceptible of Light exert themselves to lead a virtuous and godly course of life, and when they inadvertently act against the truth and commit sins or errors they are ashamed of it, come and reveal it themselves to the superintendent . . . No hypocrite can exist here, therefore they withdraw from the Community, sooner or later, and flee to the world at large, . . . and in this manner our Community remains pure without using constraint or rigor. . . . We also believe for certain that the nigh approaching Kingdom of Jesus Christ will be governed and conducted in the same manner as well here upon earth as in the Realm of Spirits. . . . For in the Kingdom of God no person possesses aught of any thing as his own, but all things in common, and therefore we all have only one Social Interest here, and Brotherly love gives sufficient impulse . . . freely without compulsion."

Frederick writes in accordance with his own sentiments and those of George Rapp and of a majority (perhaps) of the members but this does not mean that the Society as a whole constituted a legal religious organization, church or sect. Frederick's letter indicates that, at the time, the various religious sentiments of the members had coalesced to a degree sufficient to enable him to liken the situation to that of the early Christians.

Yet for all the blessings of the village by the Wabash, Frederick and others failed to be satisfied. Frederick realized that here the workers had attained a highly valuable technical and industrial proficiency. Yet, through the influx of foreign goods, the efforts of the community to expand its industrial activities were largely frustrated. Moreover, the western country was not developing fast enough to provide the markets necessary for the absorbtion of the industrial output of the Society. Eastern markets were far away, and the currency question was still a vexatious problem. Other things also influenced the community's decision to move eastward. The neighbors were envious, jealous and sometimes troublesome. In actions at law the tribunals naturally favored the Society's opponents. Some complained, too, that the climate was too warm and none too healthful.

On April 11, 1824, Frederick Rapp instructed Richard Flower (of Albion—the English colony, west of the Wabash in Illinois) who was about to journey to England, to advertize for a purchaser of Harmonie. While traveling in England, Flower succeeded in interesting the famous socialist and manufacturer, Robert Owen of New Lanark, Scotland.

Meanwhile, Frederick had been roaming the country, ostensibly on business but keeping a sharp eye for desirable tracts for a new home. He inspected lands along the Ohio River, considered tracts in Virginia, but finally selected a lovely tract of about 3000 acres on the Ohio River, eighteen miles north of Pittsburgh.

Robert Owen visited Harmonie in January 1825, and after going over the property with Frederick Rapp, agreed to pay $150,000 for the land and $40,000 for certain manufactured products and livestock. The bargain for the sale was concluded at the home of George Flower, in Albion, Illinois, at Christmas time.

Frederick Rapp had purchased the new Pennsylvania site in April of 1824, and a month later the advance guard under George Rapp started via steamboat up river to begin work on the new location.

But before we go to Pennsylvania let us pause . . .

The much publicised transcendentalist experiment at

Brook Farm seemed to have had its incipiency in the philosophical trend pervading Germany at the time. The experiment lasted six years.

The Social System inaugurated by Robert Owen at Harmonie, Indiana, seems to owe its origin to Owen's observation regarding the havoc resulting from the displacement of manual labor through the introduction of machinery. The experiment lasted only three years.

The Harmony Society, organized by George Rapp and his associates, came about through the oppression of these people while still in the old country, on the part of the clergy and the established church, and because of conscription into the armies of Napoleon. They all wanted freedom as to religion and no one wanted to bear arms. The Harmony Society lasted one hundred years.

The collapse of the Owen experiment is easily accounted for. Far from being the (practically) handpicked group as was that which Frederick Rapp brought to America, the group which flocked to Owen was a motley assemblage of savants, reformers, well-meaning ordinary decent folk—not to mention a heterogeneous mediocrity which came solely for the purpose of finding an easy living.

Secondly, as Karl Knortz noted author and educator, pertinently put it: "He (Owen) committed the unpardonable sin of at once going back to England and leaving the project in the hands of his inexperienced sons."

The Knortz criticism brings to mind that the Owen sons also became critics. Failing in their endeavor to persuade leading mechanics to transfer their allegiance from the Harmony Society to that of the Owen Commune, they mistook loyalty for ignorance. The Owen Movement not proving a success, comparison with the Harmony Society engendered jealousy and the casting of aspersions on the Harmonists. It was now explained that the success of the latter was due to the "despotic rule of George Rapp" and the "slavish asquiescence of his ignorant and superstitious underlings".

In line with this sort of reasoning certain stories became current. Among these are two outstanding falsehoods that (incredible as it seems) have maintained a firm hold not only on the people of Southwestern Indiana but on historians of recent days.

Story number one is that of a stone slab which Frederick Rapp brought from the bank of the Mississippi River. The stone contained the imprint of what seemed to be that of two human feet. The stone was placed in front of the home of the two Rapps. After the departure of the Harmonists some wag or evil-minded person invented the tale that father Rapp told his people that the "foot prints" were those of the Angel Gabriel, who had appeared to him and delivered certain revelations. The Harmonists are supposed to have swallowed the announcement "hook, line and sinker". This tale was bandied about and written about, in spite of the fact that William Owen in his Diary plainly sets forth the facts as told him by Frederick Rapp.

Silly as is the foregoing, the height of absurdity is reached in the myth that George Rapp, in order to lead his people to believe that he could appear or disappear at will, for this purpose utilized an underground passage.

Credence in such utterly impossible things can be accounted for only on the ground of "wishful thinking". And he who proclaims these myths as facts, even if only for the purpose of tickling an unthinking or romantically inclined public, nevertheless unmistakably places himself among malefactors and slanderers.

Frederick Rapp used to accommodate some of the neighbors by cashing drafts on foreign exchange. One such transaction was according to the wishes of Morris Birkbeck—two drafts amounting to $2150. When the drafts came back with protests, Frederick Rapp called Birkbeck's attention to the law which "entitles me to 20 per cent damages on the principal of the protested bills beside the interest from the date the bills were made until paid." I can understand how this "fine" of more than $400 may have had something to do with Birkbeck's feeling toward the two Rapps and their "brethren"—as he puts it "abhorrence of the hypocracy, if it be such, which governs the ignorant by nursing them in superstition." George B. Lockwood in his "New Harmony Movement" states: "The failure of George Rapp's success stands out in vivid contrast to the success of Robert Owen's failure."

A beautiful play on words is the foregoing—as clever as it is illogical and unjust. However, a man's success is to be measured by the degree to which he attains his goal—not by what some wiseacre thinks the goal ought to be.

There was a great difference between the movement started by Owen and other similar reformers and the movement started by George Rapp. Whereas the former contemplated a speedy reform of the world at large, the Harmonists under the guidance of George Rapp, concerned themselves with the perfecting of the individual—*i.e.* by way of self denial, humility and an attitude of "each in honor preferring the other"—separate from the world, to become welded into such a perfect commune that it would serve as an example to the rest of the world. That the members of the Harmony Society, in this self discipline, succeeded beyond any one's expectations, proves that talk of the Society's failure is sheer nonsense.

The Owen Community adopted a motto—"If we cannot reconcile all opinions, let us endeavor to unite all hearts." Get it? The *"endeavor"* plainly shows that the motto was to remain a dream—something to talk about and write about. In a similar motto adopted by the Harmony Society there would not have been *endeavor* but *doing*. The Harmony Society never adopted any particular motto but it did have some sayings that were a wonderful help toward welding different opinions—whether of religion or any other thing—into one harmonious whole. Take simply the saying, "The wisest gives in". If a dispute began, it got exactly nowhere, due to the fact that each disputant instantly recalled that the one who first entered into silence would stand the higher in the estimation of the Commune. The first to subside, he would be regarded as having more of the "Harmonische Geist" (Harmonist Spirit)—a thing that was more tangible than the Holy Ghost, and therefore became not only what might be termed the religion of the Society but is very life.

Much has been written on the subject of the rise and fall of various communistic experiments—some of it by savants or men in high places. As should be expected—to any one like the author who has *lived the life*—much of such analysis is but idle speculation. The sum and substance of it all is that success in communistic life, as in any other endeavor, depends:

On wise leadership, able management and sensible, capable, loyal followers.

Imagine, for instance, what it would have meant to the well-meaning transcendentalists of Brook Farm had they been blest with a "Frederick Rapp".

4

The Golden Age of Economy
(1825-1868)

IT WAS NO EASY TASK to move seven hundred people and a large amount of freight six hundred miles up river to the new Eden. The manager *par excellence*, Frederick Rapp, was as usual superintendent of this gigantic task. He tried to get a steamboat large enough to do the moving—offered a thousand dollars in hard money for the hire of one. But finally, discovering that ordinary boats could hardly be trusted, he put into effect his old dream— the building of a steamboat. In November 1824 Father Rapp at Pittsburgh christened it the *William Penn*. (Some Wabash wine was used on the occasion). With this and several other steamboats, the moving was soon accomplished.

When the last unit arrived on June 6, 1825, at the new home, they found that the advance guard had already built thirty-three "roomy and convenient frame buildings, besides twenty comfortable log houses," not to mention a large brick L-shaped four-story manufacturing building with wings eighty feet long—the woolen-mill. Building went on with astonishing rapidity. Soon a steam grist-mill was added, a steam driven saw mill, and a large hotel for visitors, the large handsome brick music hall, a school house, a store with apothecary shop and post office, some eighty two story brick and frame dwellings, and in 1831

Village of Economy and environs on the Ohio River.

Frame, steam-driven flour and grist mill, built in 1825.
Brick, steam-heated cotton factory, built in 1829.

the beautifully simple brick church with its lofty, graceful, well-balanced steeple.

About 3000 acres of good land had been purchased from nine different owners. Part of this tract was called Legionville—in memory of General Anthony Wayne's "legions" consisting of fifteen to eighteen hundred men, quartered here in the winter of 1792-93, before he started on his campaign against the Ohio Indians which resulted in the Battle of Fallen Timbers and opened the entire Northwest Territory to white settlement. About twenty stone chimneys were still standing when the Harmonists took possession. (Gen. Wayne's log-cabin, in my day, still stood staunch).

The selection of this pleasant site furnishes strongest proof of Frederick's managerial wisdom. Old Harmony in Butler County and New Harmony on the Wabash were chosen by the elder Rapp with a view toward a self-sufficing agricultural economy. If the industry of the people produced marketable surpluses or industrial products well and good, but that was not his major objective. Frederick, however, preached "the diversification of industries,"—believing that every possible industrial talent should be given full opportunity for development.

The site of the new settlement compared in no way either in size or fertility with the New Harmony location. But, these new 3000 acres were more than adequate to supply the Society's agricultural needs; and other advantages more than compensated for the smaller acreage. Pittsburgh, only sixteen miles up river, was now a booming city, "the Gateway to the West," as everybody called it. People were flocking westward from the eastern seaboard cities, looking for new land, new opportunities and greater freedom. And the new Harmonist settlement was located on the main highway to the new western country.

63

River traffic on the Ohio passed along five miles of the Economy tract. To the weary traveler the new settlement seemed like an oasis, and the westward moving peoples remembered what they heard in Pittsburgh about the industry and the honest dealings of the Harmony Society. Its wines and whiskeys, its textiles and cloths, its grains and food products—all of them the best that money could buy. This the travelers did not forget. Wherever they settled, Harmony Society products followed.

The Society named its third settlement, Economy. This is significant. They did not use the term in the ordinary sense of saving, but as embracing the science of economics. The new name also indicates a slight but fundamental shifting in the subconscious ideals of the Society, from the intangible mystic unity of old to the tangible practical life of the new "heaven on earth". The name also establishes in concrete evidence the shift from a predominantly agricultural community to a predominantly industrial one.

As a whole, the new town was quite similar to the previous settlements, but most of the shops, and the homes, were on a larger, better, more comfortable scale. The huge woolen mill, the equally large cotton factory, and the five-story grist and flour mill, were all equipped with the best steam driven machinery. All this activity and progress augured the dawn of a Golden Day.

Yet, these people were never merely dull utilitarians, as represented to the world by careless scribblers. Look you, the Harmonists not only took a deep interest in the cultivation of flowers but they were passionately fond of music; it was a necessary part of their life and much more than a social indulgence. Their choral singing with its modulated beauties surprised the most cultured visitors. And, though the orchestra lacked the symphonic proportions of those of the present day, many came to hear its regular concerts. There were about thirty instrumentalists—eighteen violins, five flutes, two clarinets, a bassoon, two horns, a trombone, a trumpet and a bugle. One of the young men even *made* a piano, which was later sold, but Frederick soon saw to it that several handsome pianos and organs were purchased.

Frederick spent thousands of dollars in collecting works of art and museum curiosities. Among the fine paintings that decorated the walls of the home of the Rapps was the splendid copy of Benjamin West's "Christ Healing the Sick". The natural history museum located in several apartments of the music hall was Frederick's special pride and joy. It contained rare minerals, specimens of meteoric iron, collections of mounted birds, insects, shells and numerous Indian antiques. William Harrison of Brighton, in writing to Jacob Henrici for a loan of a meteoric iron specimen, declared, "You are, I know, a friend to science and the progress and the development of the Valley." The same might be applied to all the leaders of the Society. Later, many valuable specimens were stolen from the museum, and the remainder, I believe, was sold to the University of Pittsburgh.

Of course, the new town was as beautifully planned as the former ones. Frederick, in a general way, not only designed the leading houses, the graceful church and the music hall, but laid out the town and part of the Great Garden. The latter, with its winding walks, its beautiful flowers and shrubs, its cool and cozy arbors, and its tempting fruit trees blossoming beautifully in springtime, came to a focal point at the large round fish-pond. In the center of this rose the graceful, stately arches and columns of a sexagonal structure, a masterpiece of design supposedly by Frederick. From here the narrow, tangled paths led to a distant corner where a small, round, rude, structure, built of roughest stone and with a door of rough bark, was overgrown with wild vines. The Grotto, so rough and crude on the outside, was decorated within, and the leading events of the Society were recorded on its walls. It was symbolic of man—no matter how crude he be without, so long as he be beautiful within. The Deer Park and the Labyrinth at the eastern outskirt of the village also added to the quaint interests of the community.

It was not long before romantic tourists and travelers began to speak and write of Economy as a place of Arcadian charm and beauty. Its fame spread throughout America and Europe. Travelers made special journeys to visit it, and generally went away believing that Economy was as near a Utopia as one might ever find on earth. In 1826, within two years after Economy's birth, came two of the most distinguished travelers from Europe. Both left glowing written records of Economy's simple Utopian life.

First came Friedrich List, famous German economist, who later led the movement for the construction of railroads in Germany. In Wuerttemberg he was expelled from the Chamber of Deputies in 1821 for the expression of ideas too liberal for his time. For this he suffered ten months' imprisonment at hard labor. Fleeing to France, he became a close friend of Lafayette, who in 1824 invited List to join him in his visit to America. Circumstances arising which prevented List from going at that time, he followed a year later and joined the great French hero of the American Revolution in Philadelphia.

Tired of old world tyrannies, List decided to look for a permanent abode in America. Thus seeking, he came to Pittsburgh, and from there visited Economy.

"It was evening when I arrived," he wrote, "and evening

bells were tolling as in the Swabian homeland." The next day he inspected the factories, the workshops, the barns and the fields of the Society, amazed that in fourteen months these people had been able to transform a forested frontier into a beautiful village. He was quite pleased with Father Rapp and the other leaders, and was especially impressed by the wonderful spirit of harmony among the people. With all these evidences of coöperative community life before him, List here conceived his plan for youth education in practical living, built upon the idea of combining theoretical learning with productive group labor. Many years later this idea found its way into the educational systems of the world.

In the same year came Duke Bernhard of Saxe-Weimar, second son of Karl August who befriended Goethe and Schiller and made Weimar the cultural center of Germany. Duke Bernhard's career began in the Napoleonic wars, and he served under Napoleon with such distinction that the Little Corporal decorated him with the Legion of Honor. After Waterloo he traveled in the British Isles, and early in 1825 started on a fourteen months' visit of the United States. He was so well received, so frequently honored, and so impressed with the rising dignity of the young nation, that he even thought of settling here. But later, international affairs abroad called him back to the Old World. Twice, *i.e.* in 1825 and again in 1829, he rejected Russia's imperial plan to place him on the throne of Greece.

While in America the Duke visited both New Harmony on the Wabash and Economy on the Ohio. When in May 1826 he appeared at Pittsburgh, intending to visit Economy the next day, he was pleasantly surprised by a visit from Frederick Rapp who invited the Duke to go home with him.

In a lengthy, enthusiastic description of his visit, the Duke wrote, "As we neared the settlement, three hornists played a melody of welcome. At the large frame hotel, we were received by prominent men of the Society led by George Rapp—a dignified band of gray-heads." Then came a sumptuous dinner of German dishes. "All was good fellowship." After dinner the Duke and the Patriarch wandered about the village. Like List, the economist, the nobleman was amazed at the progress made in less than two years' time—"It is astonishing," he wrote, "what united and properly directed powers can accomplish in so short a time." Then he writes of the neat dwelling houses, the large and active factories with their steam power and steam-heating pipes (an innovation which Frederick introduced), and he notices especially how "the bloom of health is on all the faces of the workers, especially on those of the women."

We get a charming glimpse of Economy entertainment from the Duke's travel journal. "After supper Rapp called together the musicians of the Society to entertain with music. Miss Gertrude [Rapp's granddaughter] also played the piano, and three girls sang."

From the sound of horns echoing over the fields on the Duke's arrival to his last farewell, music played a great part in his visit, and he no doubt realized the vast and integrating importance of this art to the Society. He writes further, "The following day we were shown the warehouse, where all their manufactured articles are stored, ready for shipment. I was simply astonished at the quality of all these things. Again, Rapp took me to the factory to hear the girls, some sixty or seventy, sing songs, first of a religious then of a gay character. Rapp takes great interest in music. . . . Later, we again ate a hearty dinner, while the orchestra played really excellently; and it was with peculiar emotions that we departed at 3:00 o'clock, from the friendly and industrious town of Economy."

"Through what I had read of Mr. Rapp and his Society, and *what I recently heard in New Harmony,* I was really prejudiced against him and his adherents. It pleases me all the more therefore that I came here and through my eyes learned something different and became convinced of something better."

Somewhat later Nikolaus Lenau, one of the great romantic poets of Germany, made his abode at Economy. What the circumstances were that led him to Economy, I know not. Perhaps it was the Society's universal fame and its romantic and utopian quaintness. Perhaps the words of Duke Bernhard led him hither. At any rate, it appears that during his sojourn at Economy, Lenau became seriously ill, and the good sisters of the Commune nursed him back to health from the very gates of Death. . . . It is strange that only a tradition remains of his long stay. Could it have been from the Great Garden that he penned that lovely lyric?

> *Diese Rose pflück' ich hier*
> *In der fremden Ferne;*
> *Liebes Mädchen, dir, ach dir*
> *Brächt' ich sie so gerne!*

Other notables, from both Europe and the United States, stopped from time to time or made special visits to Economy. They always received the kind and generous attentions of Father Rapp, Frederick, or Romelius Baker, and of the succeeding heads of the Society.

In 1839 Chief Justice Gibson and Judge Rogers of the Pennsylvania Supreme Court came for a visit. Two years later General William Henry Harrison, after emerging victorious from his hot campaign against Van Buren, stopped at Economy on his way to his inauguration as President of the United States. Still later we read in the Society correspondence that President Zachary Taylor and his friend, William F. Johnston, Governor of Pennsylvania, were given a reception and entertainment at Economy.

The fame of Economy gradually spread to all the western world. Before his death in 1824 Lord Byron, wandering over Europe as the romantic scorner, and as champion of freedom, heard of the Harmony experiment in communal life, and in the fifteenth canto of his greatest work, *Don Juan,* flung mockery at marriage by describing the celibacy of the Harmonists:

> When Rapp the Harmonist embargoed marriage,
> In his harmonious settlement, which flourishes
> Strangely enough as yet without miscarriage,
> Why called he "Harmony" a state *sans* wedlock?
> Now here I've got the preacher at a deadlock.
> Because he either means to sneer at harmony
> Or marriage, by divorcing them thus oddly:
> But whether the Reverend Rapp learned this in
>   Germany
> Or not, 'tis said his sect is rich and godly,
> Pious and pure, beyond what I can term any
> Of ours. . . .

Notice that Byron tacitly assumes that the reader has some knowledge of the Harmony Society; also that the common, world-wide impression of Harmony and Economy is that of a communal society "rich and godly, pious and pure."

From Indiana the Society brought $35,000 worth of manufactured goods, with which they supplied their trade until their factories were again in operation. The splendid $30,000 wool factory was soon under way, and in 1826 the cotton factory was built at an estimated value of $25,000. The value of manufactured woolen goods rose from $35,000 in 1827 to $84,000 in 1831. But due to cutthroat competition, cotton manufacture did not prosper so well, decreasing in value of product from $22,000 in 1827 and 1828 to $18,000 in 1831. Wool, moreover, seems to have been under a protective tariff.

This was the heyday of the Society's prosperity—the day of triumph for Frederick and his wise policies. In a short time the Society had agents or "factors" stationed throughout the country, watching and reporting on local market conditions, making sales, and handling the extensive business of the Society. Agents were stationed at Baltimore; Philadelphia, Pittsburgh and Washington, Pennsylvania; Steubenville and Cincinnati, Ohio; Vincennes and Coridon, Indiana; Shawneetown, Illinois; Louisville, Kentucky; St. Louis, Missouri; and at New Orleans. Good David Shields, dear friend to Frederick and to R. L. Baker, kept the post at Washington, Pennsylvania, until its removal to Sewickleyville. At Pittsburgh the firm of Abishai Way represented the Society, and for a short time Ephraim L. Blaine, father of James G. Blaine (statesman and one time candidate for the Presidency) joined Way in partnership. And in Cincinnati Nicholas Longworth, great-grandfather of our former great Speaker of the House of Representatives, served as the Society's agent. These men were well chosen, and by their attentive watchfulness of the Society's interests, contributed to the trade successes of these years.

The Harmony Society had become a little inland empire. Its industrial and trade success, beyond the wildest dreams of many of its own members, was so great that in certain instances the Society controlled the Pittsburgh market—and that probably meant a similar influence throughout the whole Ohio-Mississippi Valley market to New Orleans. Then too, Frederick Rapp, a true industrial and business genius, was a shrewd observer of market potentialities—knew the demand and knew how to meet it. Finally, these people were such excellent farmers and craftsmen that their workmanship, all directed toward one splendid harmonious effort, could hardly be equaled in the western country.

Competitors, knowing that they could not possibly outdo the efforts of the Society, resorted to propaganda against Economy. The newspapers of Pittsburgh began to raise the cry of MONOPOLY—"a great monopoly with which the individual manufacturer could not compete because he was forced to buy wool at Economy prices as well as to sell his wares at Economy prices." Moreover, the farmers who raised the fine Spanish wool had to sell it to Frederick because the small factories could not work up such a fine quality of wool. Nor could the Society be outdone in cotton manufacture. When the commodious cotton factory burned to the ground in 1829, Frederick at once built a still larger and better one.

Press criticisms became still louder. The *Allegheny Democrat* in 1829 declared: "Economy has the power—and uses the same— to regulate the trade in our market. This is a fact too palpable to be permitted to pass unnoticed." And in conclusion the same paper advocated the total dissolution of the Society by Act of Legislature . . . To warrant such strenuous demands, Economy must indeed have been a powerful economic force.

Besides cotton and woolen yarn and cloth, the most important articles of Economy's trade were hats, raw wool, blankets, flannels, and whiskey. The bills of lading also show large shipments of leather, cider, plants, apples, flax-seed oil, flour, fruit trees, hides and wine. Shipments of these products went to New Orleans, St. Louis, numerous points in the Ohio Valley, Pittsburgh and western Pennsylvania communities, and to cities as far east as Boston. During the first fourteen years of Economy's trade, 1826 to 1843, sales totaled well over a million and a half dollars.

At the same time agriculture was continued, but on a more modest scale than in the flush days of New Harmony. At Economy most of the agricultural products were consumed by the community itself. However, the men of Economy were specialists in the making of beer, wines, liquors and whiskey. Vast quantities of these stimulants were kept in the Society's spacious wine cellars and the Economy label became a synonym for the best to be had in wine and whiskey.

One can but pause and speculate as to what might have been the outcome of such amazing industrial progress and prosperity, had it not been for certain misfortunes that beset the Commune. With a throttle hold on the trade of much of the western country, this stirring example of coöperative effort might materially have altered the course of the economy of most of the trans-Allegheny region. Without interference, Economy might have developed into a financial octopus of gigantic proportions. The name of Frederick Rapp was not only a talisman in the Pittsburgh region, but a name to be reckoned with throughout the land. He was a personal friend of Henry Clay and other prominent statesmen. Some styled him "Frederick the Great," and certainly his star was in the ascendent.

Although Frederick made no pretense, the folks at Economy realized what he had accomplished for them. They loved him dearly and recognized him as their genius.

Father Rapp may not have been losing out, but he was only the symbol of the spiritual intent of the Commune. And now that material, tangible prosperity flushed the Society, spiritual direction was not regarded with such adulation as before. Indeed, from what I have gathered in conversations with the last of those early Communists, the common adoration of Frederick began to arouse feelings akin to jealousy in George Rapp. And this circumstance subtly prepared the way for Economy's greatest crisis.

Although in the Old Country, George Rapp was the leading Spirit in the movement which culminated in the organization of the Harmony Society in America, he was not a founder in the sense of "one who founds, establishes, erects or endows". In matters religious, he was the Society's leader or teacher, but as founder he was one of a group of men and women, numbering some 180, who by signing the ARTICLES of ASSOCIATION on February 15, 1805, became partners in the founding of the Society.

The Society was looked upon as religious—and rightfully so, especially from the standpoint of the exemplary life of the members. But the Articles of Association do not contain a single tenet of belief and the signatories were of various beliefs and unbelief; hence eminent Theologians and Jurists declared the Society neither Sect, Church nor Religious Society. (See Escheat Case, Ch. 14 and Articles of Association in Appendix).

The fact that George Rapp preached the nearness of "the Second Advent" and that it now and then was stated that the Society was founded on Acts 2 -44, "and all that believed were together, and had all things in common," constitutes no proof of sectarianism or denominationalism. In quoting the Apostolic communism, none of the

74

spiritual heads ever had the hardihood to quote the full story. Had they attempted to do so, they would have quickly found themselves entangled in a web of confusion. The *communism of the Harmony Society consisted in the purchase of large tracts of land—the cultivation of the same; the erection of dwellings, shops and factories, later by the investment in stocks and bonds: Also at all times in commercial activities with Industry as the watchword of the hour.* What about the Apostolic communism?

Verse 45 of ch. 2, continues "and *sold their possessions and goods and parted them to all men as every man had need. And they, continuing daily with one accord in the temple, and breaking bread from house to house, did eat their meat with gladness and singleness of heart.*" How long the consumption of their substance in this wonderful festivity lasted, we know not. But one comparative glance at the matter sufficeth to show the unbridgeable chasm that separates the communism of the Apostles and that of the Harmony Society.

Regarding the Second Advent—George Rapp's theology must have been in flux (as it was on some other points). Whatever his theory was in early days as to this Advent, it changed to the expectation of its taking place not in America, but in Jerusalem after the Society, together with the Lost Ten Tribes of Israel, had put the place in order. For this purpose, selfevidently, there was needed a large sum of money—which sum was not in evidence until Economy's Golden Day.

Be it known that while still on the Wabash, the Society had met with its first important law suit. One Eugene Müller, having withdrawn from membership, in 1821 brought suit in the U. S. Circuit Court in Pittsburgh to recover wages for services rendered by him while a

75

member of the Society. But inasmuch as all such claims were emphatically renounced in the Articles of Association, Müller's demand met with no success at all. Representing the Society was the best legal talent west of the Alleghenies—the brilliant James Ross, nearing the end of his turbulent career as United States Senator, "Whiskey Rebellion" commissioner appointed by Washington, twice Federalist candidate for governor, and Pittsburgh's greatest lawyer; and John H. Hopkins, who later became senior bishop of the Episcopal Church in the United States.

In comparison with other law suits that later confronted the Society, this case was rather petty. Viewed more closely, however, its importance is epochal in the Society's history, for it was the first test of the validity of this voluntary Society's Articles. Informed of the victory in the case Frederick at once wrote to Abishai Way to remunerate the counsel properly, and to see *that no one lost any money through the litigation.* Although Frederick and his associates achieved total victory in the case, it put the Society on guard for further court attacks. Perhaps this started the elder Rapp thinking about further safeguarding the Society's property and his own position by a revised constitution. At any rate, soon after the new settlement was fully underway, Lawyer Hopkins was engaged to draw up new Articles of Association—the way Rapp himself wanted them.

Not having heard or seen anything to the contrary, I doubt whether Father Rapp even consulted Frederick as to this fatal step. The two were no longer the close friends of old; feelings of variance in the older Rapp led almost to an open breach. Frederick's scathing letter to Father Rapp, criticizing him for having as laboratory assistant the young and unreliable, Hildegard Mutschler, indicates that the two, at that time, were not on speaking terms. (See Chapter 11.)

The new Articles of Association were nevertheless put into execution March 9, 1827. This time the Articles were prefaced with a Preamble, stating that the community was formed on the principles of Christian fellowship—including the community of goods and *patriarchial government*. Though the new Articles were drawn so that the agreement between the members and George Rapp and Associates were more clearly and legally defined, especially in regard to those expelled or leaving of their own volition, the introduction of the new and daring phrase, "patriarchal government," caused considerable commotion. Quite a number refused to sign the Articles, and others signed them only under duress.

Previously, George Rapp was considered the first and foremost brother among equals united in one common cause. Now his status had become that of a monarch. The accusations of Rapp's "tyranny" began to assume dangerous proportions. And what effect did Rapp's new government have upon his "Associates"? Looking at the Society's *Seelen Register* I discover that in the three years from 1823 to and including 1825, only six members withdrew from the Society. In 1826, the year in which George Rapp began to preach and propagandize in favor of the Articles he had in mind, no less than twenty-six members withdrew. Twenty more withdrew in 1827, the year the new Articles were put into effect; eight left in 1828; and twenty-four members followed suit in 1829. An average of twenty departures a year in contrast with an average of two in previous years certainly is proof positive of the disturbance that rocked the community pursuant to the revamping of the Society's Articles. Dissatisfaction with George Rapp's attitude spread throughout the community during these years, and created fertile ground for the Count Leon imbroglio which follows anon. Many of those seceding during these years chose a section just beyond the Ohio-Pennsylvania border in Columbiana County, where they and their descendants were to cause the Society not a little trouble.

Whether these disaffected people had anything to do with other serious troubles that arose in February, 1827, I am not able definitely to say, but the likelihood is obvious. At any rate we read in the correspondence of George to Frederick, that "the Bull-Creekers"—an Ohio group of recently withdrawn former members and others opposed to the Economy regime—collected together as an armed company at the house of Martin Stahl on an expedition to rescue Stahl's children from Economy. The sheriff was with them. Four of the Bull-Creekers came to Economy as spies. But faithful Romeli Baker came to the rescue, got the law after the group, and settled the matter in favor of the Society. "The enemy," wrote Rapp, "raves terribly."

But the old Patriarch was as steadfast as ever. Neither his own basically generous heart, nor the love of his granddaughter, Gertrude, and of Frederick would permit a shift in his course. The disaffection between the two Rapps could not have lasted long. Without the splendid guidance of Frederick, George Rapp knew he was lost. Thus affiliation of the two always gained the upper hand. When Frederick takes Gertrude for a visit to Philadelphia on a business trip, the elder Rapp in March 1828 writes to Gertrude and Frederick: "Since your departure our house seems vacant as a church on week-days . . . Experience teaches what a true friendship is in the loyal circle of the family and the communal spirit."

It will be recalled that a major tenet of George Rapp was the imminence of the "Second Advent." Inherent in this was the pilgrimage to the Holy Land by the Society, together with the Lost Ten Tribes; the rebuilding of the temple at Jerusalem, the welcoming of the Savior and the ushering in of the thousand year reign on earth. There was also the tenet of the Elect—among whom the Harmonists were to have a conspicuous place. All these were not only to symbolize the majestic destiny of the Commune, but also to serve as a literal ideal plan. "Jesus will be the Morningstar, and his good people with Him will also be stars, and will illuminate all the worlds" . . . Such beautifully mystic sentences flowed regularly from Rapp's prophetic pulpit. However they laid the groundwork whereon conspiracy might be built.

Now after the rising discontent over the Articles of 1827, the old Patriarch to stir his people into a consciousness of their destiny, dwelt more and more upon the pilgrimage to Jerusalem. Thus matters might have moved placidly along had it not been for a letter that came, announcing in the most glowing and dramatic terms, the coming of a man who regarded himself as "the anointed of the Lord" or as "the organ of God." Frequently stirred by Rapp's discourse regarding the Second Advent, many of the faithful in the community—and many of those dissatisfied with the rule of Rapp—waited either hopefully or skeptically for the appearance of the "Anointed."

The letter aforementioned, dated July 14, 1829, to George Rapp, was written at far-away Frankfort-on-the-Main in Germany, under the pompous signature of "Sàmuel, a fellow servant and consecrated servant of God, in the profane world now really subsisting, chief librarian of the city of Frankford, doctor of Philosophy and Theology." The letter was from Johann Georg Goentgen, chief lieutenant and secretary of Count Leon, whom Goentgen announced as Minister of Christ and Anointed of the

79

Lord, who has descended upon this earth to act as the herald and "organ" of God. Dr. Goentgen announced the coming of Count Leon and his followers to America for the purpose either of affiliating with the Harmony Society or of forming a separate Commune.

The letter reached Economy at the proper psychological moment. George Rapp replied courteously but propounded certain specific questions.

Days, months, two years passed. Suddenly, in September 1831, came a second letter from Goentgen announcing the Count's arrival in New York. The letter is well worth quoting in part:

"In the name and in commission of his Royal Highness, the Archduke Maximilian von Este, as the anointed of God, from the tribe of Judah and the root of David, who announced to you in the year 1829, through the undersigned, the return of Christ in Spirit, for Judgment and for preparation of the Kingdom of God, by laying the foundation of the Philadelphia Church in North America. I herewith inform you that he has now personally and in the first place incognito, by the name of Count Leon, touched the free ground of the United States, in a holy design, in conformity to the external decree and particular commandment of God, to gather and unite all those who intend to live in conformity to the law of God and the Gospel of Jesus Christ to be preserved in time and Eternity.

With the most intimate joy of heart we received in due time, your faithful and loving reply in that brotherly letter which furnished confirmation of all that which we had heard from your Christian society in regard to your pure evangelical Spirit, your pleasing endeavors, your confidential hopes for the near fulfillment of the Divine promises and for the deliverance and sanctification of all the true children of God; this we heard from natural and higher sources.

We regret, however, that we are unable to make the communication you wish and to give you more explanation; had even your enquiries been stated with less precision, for to reply to you then we could not have, at all events, given you so early an information, for the written declaration of the Divine Judgment had already been sent to all the higher authorities of the European states and churches, and we could not foresee at the time we received your letter how those authorities would accept that revelation of the Divine decree, intended for their own preservation as well as for that of their believing subjects. Many thousands will follow our example and escape the chaos of Europe over which is designed the slow progressing judgments of God, which have already commenced in pestilence and revolution . . .

The name of the Messianic pretender who challenged the powers of the world was in reality plain Bernhard Mueller. However, Dr. Goentgen, in an article dated April 13, 1833, writes.

"Maximillian Bernhard Lewis (Leon) a descendant of one of the oldest houses of European Regents, was born March 21, 1788, previous to a twin sister—the twin sister is mentioned in genealogical records not so the brother. The latter, against his mother's will, was brought to the cottage of a peasant from whence in some manner he was stolen. The immediate inducement for this diplomatic violence was . . . a traditional family belief of which the mother was animated before her delivery; namely, that she should bear a son who had the destination of God to raise mankind to an improved spiritual and physical state, especially by a universal reformation of the church."

Other sources disclose that the boy was brought up in strictly monastic fashion. Apprenticed to a tailor, he stole away to join a group of trick riders. Soon tiring of this life, he entered the cloister of Aschaffenburg to study theology. Next he journeyed to Rome for further light. Disappointed, he went to Regensburg and joined hands with an English missionary Wm. Sykson. Sykson stimulated Mueller's belief in his divine mission and the development of the gift of prophecy which in 1810 led to the menacing note sent to Napoleon I, predicting his early downfall. This so enraged the great Frenchman that he set a price on Mueller's head.

Finding his prediction verified in 1815, Mueller became thoroughly convinced of his mission as Savior of the world. After entering the evangelistic church, armed with letters of introduction, he joined the Pietist Society of London. After he acquired a sufficient knowledge of the English language, this society sent him as a missionary to Ireland. Here he made the acquaintance of a wealthy maiden lady, among whose swarm of parasites was a pseudo-Jesuit by name of Martin. The latter, for his own purposes, convinced the lady that it was Mueller's mission to usher in "the thousand year's reign". To this end the lady contributed a large sum—the greater part of which was appropriated by Martin who absconded. Mueller thereupon proceeded to Offenbach, Germany; bought a large estate, built a magnificent villa, furnished it in princely fashion and proceeded to gather members for his community. He applied to the Grand Duke of Hesse for permission, lawfully, to change his name to Proli—a favor the Duke readily granted. Proli yearly subscribed 1000 thalers to the support of the poor of Offenbach and was given the freedom of the city.

At Offenbach he early made the acquaintance of the learned Dr. Goentgen, who, becoming an ardent disciple, soon resigned his office of librarian of Frankfurt and became Proli's private secretary.

In 1829 Proli issued 72 notes to crowned heads and church dignitaries of Europe, commanding them to free their peoples so that he could prepare them for "the 1000 year's reign". Not receiving any reply, he sent a second, more highly powered epistle. When this was likewise treated with silent contempt, Goentgen bethought himself of America and the Harmony Society—hence his letters to George Rapp.

The quaint Bavarian costumes of his followers and the aura of nobility around the ostentatious Count Leon made quite a stir in New York City, Albany, Buffalo and Pittsburgh on their journey to Economy. From Pittsburgh Leon dispatched two heralds, as if his visit were indeed a royal one. The Harmonists waited expectantly for "The Messenger of God" to shed his glory upon them. As Leon's coach and four rolled into the village, the band, stationed on the church tower balcony, burst into music. Father Rapp welcomed Count Leon at the hotel. Leon emerged in full military dress, even to epaulets and gem bestudded sword . . . Jonathan Lenz, who played the French Horn in the band, in later years recounted from the pulpit how inconsistent the count's conduct appeared to him. "He did not come like the Saviour humbly riding on an ass, but in a coach-and-four with epaulets and sword and uniformed courtiers." Jonathan sensed at once, as did others, that no good would come of the Count's advent.

It should not be difficult to guess what went on in the mind of Father Rapp, as he attended the Count to the church and the pulpit within. Then instead of a stirring, poetic prophecy, the Count said little else than: "This meeting is the most important since the Creation, and henceforth all sorrows and troubles of the Lord's people will cease." Rapp's reply was cool and, to the effect that he "doubted whether the happy period anticipated by the count had yet arrived." Then without further ado he dismissed the assembly. There never was mention of any meeting of Rapp and Leon but meetings between the leading men on both sides led nowhere. It soon became obvious to Rapp and his faithful followers that Leon's extravagant view of communal union could in no way be adjusted to the Economy way of life. Leon favored high living, luxury and fancy dress; Rapp preached the goodness of the simple, agrarian life. Leon favored the restoration of matrimony, while Rapp believed in the subjugation of the flesh. Leon favored a shorter working day and less strenuous labor and toil, but Rapp's experience had taught him that steady collective labor not only brought material prosperity but was conducive to a harmonious spirit.

However, since it was late in the frosty autumn, Leon and his disciples were permitted to remain. Five houses were assigned to them, while the Count and his closest followers dwelt at the hotel. Thus during the whole winter of 1831-32 Leon and his forty followers mingled freely with the whole community, making converts particularly of members who were disgruntled or disaffected by Rapp's rule. Leon held meetings in the evening, calculated to win the affections of the younger Harmonists, while his followers talked of Leon's supernatural capacities, among them the claim that he could make gold out of rocks.

The situation resolved itself into a disagreeable paradox. Those of the Society who had been looking hopefully for the dawn of the Millenium and had anxiously awaited the coming of Count Leon were cruelly disappointed, while those who had no such expectations and at first had regarded the whole affair with contempt were now attracted to the Count's banner of money, luxury, and matrimony. The latter in great part were malcontents even before the coming of the Count: Leon, moreover, tacitly assumed, from the very beginning, that the Harmonists should come under his guidance; it would be perfectly natural for him to look upon Father Rapp as merely a forceful commoner without any of the majesty and noble pretension that befitted the leader of God's chosen.

Rapp did little to counteract the activities of Leon and his band. Soon the followers of Leon drew up a paper—signed by 250 men, women and children—to be published in the daily press of Pittsburgh, proclaiming Leon the rightful director of the Harmony Society. To counteract this audacious and ridiculous move, the faithful Harmonists, greatly outnumbering the opposing camp, likewise drew up a paper for public consumption, proclaiming that George and Frederick Rapp still maintained the leadership of the Society. Thus was the Society rent and threatened with disruption.

Meanwhile, Frederick, appalled by the impending loss of his galaxy of youthful and efficient factory operatives and the destruction of his business and his commerce, counseled Father Rapp to compromise, suggesting that the elder Rapp again encourage matrimony or at least not frown upon it. George Rapp's reply to Frederick was a Caesar's, "And thou too Brutus!"

In addition to the Hildegard entanglement, there was something radically amiss between George and Frederick in that period. Probably the disagreement had to do with the sequestration of specie by George toward the pilgrimage to the Holy Land. In my day the story still persisted that Frederick, in the course of taking invoices at the factories, wanted these in a way to hoodwink Father Rapp. In other words the account to show a loss instead of a gain. There seems to be conclusive evidence of this matter by way of the following:

Statement of Imports and Exports of the Economy Establishment during the year of 1831.

Amount of Merchandise, Lumber and Cattle	....	
Rolled and Cast Iron, Dyestuffs, Grain, etc. ..	41,251.55	
151 Bales Cotton and Freight	5,653.16	
194,212 lbs. Wool of every description	106,311.44	
Amount of Goods, etc. sold by wholesale		121,228.50
Amount of Goods, etc. sold by retail, etc.		7,025.00
Amount of Cash taken in by Tavern and Mechanics		9,327.80
Amount of Balance of trade against us		15,634.85
Dollars	153,216.15	153,216.15
To balance of Trade against us	15,634.85	

Economy January 20, 1832

Without the invoice of stock on hand at the beginning and end of the year, this statement can have only one object—namely, to mislead some one who is not versed in the science of accounting. For instance, if one-third of the wool was still on hand, the account, instead of a loss, would show a profit of $19,802.29.

As the Leon imbroglio developed and gained the support of one-third of the total membership of the Society, George Rapp was driven to accept at least certain suggested compromises. These suggestions were incorporated in supplementary Articles of Agreement, and signed by a large majority of the members on February 20, 1832— in the midst of the prevailing insurgency, and exactly one month after the preparation of the statement as to the business of the year 1831.

Obviously this new Agreement was designed to curb the patriarchal severity of George Rapp. Cleverly enough, however, he was retained in full authority as Spiritual Head. But the management of nearly everything else fell upon the shoulders of Frederick, who was henceforth to conduct all business of the Society, to appoint and supervise foremen in workshops and factories, and to assign members to their duties and their dwellings. Moreover, Frederick was made responsible for submitting a complete financial statement whenever called upon.

Furthermore, a Board of twelve elders was created to assist both George and Frederick in adjusting and adjudicating any disputes or matters of disobedience within the Society.

Among the 425 signatories to this Agreement it is significant to note the names of George Rapp's own family—his wife, his unmarried daughter Rosina, his granddaughter Gertrude and her mother Jacobina. Although these new Articles did not heal the breach between the two parties, they did bring back into the fold about seventy-five of those who had signed the Leon document.

In spite of this partial reconciliation, Geo. Rapp and his faithful adherents were forced to extend a compromise to Count Leon and the insurgents. An agreement was signed on March 6 between the two parties. (Appeals to the law would only result in long-drawn-out litigation; better to be rid of the malcontents at once). The terms of agreement stipulated that Leon and his followers were to leave Economy within six weeks, that the seceding members of the Society were to depart in three months and were to receive the sum of $105,000 in three installments within the year. In return, those withdrawing were to relinquish all claims of any kind on the property, money or real estate of the Society. An additional payment of 60,000 francs went to seceding Huber heirs—Mrs. Wagner and Mrs. Bentel.

The seceders now joined with Leon in purchasing a site of present-day Monaca. Here by the beautiful Ohio, opposite the mouth of the Beaver River, Count Leon and his followers built the village of Phillipsburg. The community was established as a theocratic government fashioned after the Old Testament, with communistic principles, similar to those of Economy, but allowing matrimony and greater individual freedom. The laws of this "New Philadelphia" aggregation were signed by nearly 400 people. How their numbers were so greatly augmented in so short a time is astonishing indeed, and something for which history does not give us an answer. Inasmuch as only 176 of those who went with him had been members of the Society, the Count and his men apparently had been recruiting throughout the whole region.

The fate of Phillipsburg strongly testifies to its weaknesses. The Count himself as a leader of pioneers, was in no way to be compared with George Rapp.

But the greatest contrast in the makeup of the two colonies existed in the differences between Frederick Rapp, the practical genius of Economy, and Doctor Goentgen, Leon's chief lieutenant of daily affairs. Goentgen was solely a German scholar and theologian but lacking in the organization and dispatch of practical life. Unlike Frederick, whose feet, in regard to George Rapp, were planted firmly on the ground, Goentgen failed to act as a healthy check on the Count's aberrant mysticism, and dreams of world dominion.

Under such leadership, there could be little directive guidance of daily work. Filled as they had been with promises of ease and wealth, Leon's followers failed to apply themselves to the gigantic task ahead of them, and soon the community began to disintegrate. Most of their money gone within the first year and their creditors pressing them, the Phillipsburgers became impatient, and began to make threats against Economy.

When certain conditions of the agreement of separation were not fulfilled by the Phillipsburg group, Frederick Rapp withheld payment of the last installment. But rather than fulfill the written agreement's conditions, eighty able-bodied Phillipsburgers marched to Economy in a vicious endeavor to obtain the last payment. A friend of the Society having sent word of the proposed invasion, Rapp at once ordered the men to go in hiding and the women to take charge of affairs.

It was on the second day of April, 1833, that the Phillipsburgers came. They attempted to gain entrance to the Great House. Finding the doors barricaded, they proceeded to batter them down. But being dragged by the legs down the steps and subjected to a baptism of hot water from the windows above, not to mention brick bats, coal and other weapons on which the women could lay hands, the entry to the house proved a fiasco. After some of the women began to stick the invaders "head-first" into the watering troughs (placed here and there) the mob lost heart and hied to the hotel where refreshment was in order.

At this juncture there arrived a quondam military company from the back woods. The big captain strode into the midst of the revelers, grasped the ringleader and threw him out—the others quickly found an exit.

The captain thereupon marshaled the invaders, read them the riot act, bound them over to court and (to the tune of the "Rogues March," played by fife and drum), escorted them to the river on their homeward way.

(It was my privilege to become well acquainted with

89

the man who as a youth played the fife in the parade to the river.)

Litigation facing the Phillipsburgers caused the Count and a number of his faithful followers to board a keelboat for a long, hazardous journey, namely to the Red River in Louisiana. At his little village in this wilderness the turbulent career of "the Anointed of God, of the Stem of Judah and the Root of David" came to a sudden close the following year. He died in August 1834.

Whether or not George Rapp ever realized it, the Count Leon Insurrection proved a blessing in disguise. Since the disaffected malcontents were thus separated from the faithful, many of those who remained were henceforth heart and soul wrapped up in Father Rapp—to them he seemed to be prophet, priest and king. A whispering campaign proclaimed that he would not see death. Now it came to Rapp's ears that the 16-year-old Jacob Stahl had expressed his doubt in reference to this subject. Rapp coming upon the youth in the harvest field, accosted him with: "And are you too, one of those who do not believe that I will not die?" "O well," said Jacob, "you'd be the first one that ever remained." Whack! came a box on Jacob's ear from the palm of Father Rapp.

But look upon the Patriarch now, as on a Sunday morn he marches into the church. Although along in years, his upright carriage still proclaims the vigor of his frame. His calves and thighs arrayed in velvet breeches, his barrel chest in flowered brocade as silken frock-coat hangs from massive shoulders, he, the observed of all observers, to outsiders seems a Viking donned in ornate garb; but to his own he is simply Father . . . And then he speaks. What flow of mystic, transcendental eloquence is this that sweeps beyond all bounds of the imagination? . . . We must forgive these people if they almost worship him,

Meanwhile, Frederick, heartbroken by the defection of so many of his friends, fell upon evil days. He for whom Friendship was a constant theme in song and conversation, had watched the flower of Economy's young manhood and womanhood depart—an experience that broke his spirit. A broken spirit soon ushered in a broken body. For two years after the Leon defection he lingered with his beloved brethren, until June 24, 1834, when his generous beautiful spirit passed from earth. . . .

Romelius L. Baker, his close friend and protege pronounced the last words over his unmarked grave. Romelius' heart must have been flooded with grief, and he must have sensed that the death of Frederick symbolized the waning of the Golden Day of Economy. Nevertheless, there is still an importunate hope in his words. . . . "Although our chain of brotherhood has suffered a violent break, we will not become either weak or lax in the battle; but the more firmly and intimately united, that the bond of brotherly love and friendship be still more closely drawn. . . ."

With the passing of this gentle, forceful soul, the Society, viewed from the standpoint of practical working communism with vision and purpose, began its long decline— almost imperceptible for some years—into a final state of desuetude, the members more and more contenting themselves to live in memories of a glorious, golden past.

True, the factories and workshops fitfully continued, for a time, but after some years the great woolen and cotton factories closed permanently—an event that presaged the desultory abandonment of a *positive* economy and the ushering in of an era of external investments to take the place of internal production.

In 1836 the Society again deemed it wise to amend the Articles of Agreement, the purpose being to forestall litigation that might be brought by former members or their heirs. In the first place, the new amendments entirely repealed that section of the Articles of 1827 which provided that to those expelled or voluntarily withdrawing from the Society, there was to be refunded the value of all property contributed on joining the Society. This article had proved itself a sore spot and a source of much contention, and the Society was well rid of it.

In the second place, the new amendments provided that all property of the Society should be regarded as common, indivisible stock, each member having given up all property to the Society absolutely and irrevocably. As a final safeguard, the third amendment provided that if any member should withdraw, or depart this life, neither he nor any of his heirs should have any claim to remuneration for services or to property donated to the Society. The superintendent of the Society was henceforth to have sole jurisdiction as to how much money should be given in cases of withdrawal.

Frederick Rapp in 1825 had executed an instrument providing that all property in his name was to be considered as the property of the Society. Pursuant to his death the Society executed a power of attorney to George Rapp, making him the general agent of the Society. Father Rapp realizing that he had neither the ability nor the youthful strength to carry this burden, at once appointed agents to attend to all temporal affairs. Two worthies, Romelius L. Baker and Jacob Henrici, thus became the managers of the industrial, financial and material affairs of the Society.

After the exodus of members, law suits against the Society became more and more common. The first of these was that of Jacob Schreiber. Jacob was the fourth son of Peter Schreiber who had become acquainted with

92

George Rapp in 1803. In 1806 Peter sold all of his worldly belongings including a well-stocked farm in frontier Ohio, and with his wife and nine children and $8000 came to the Society. Jacob becoming dissatisfied, left the Society in 1826.

Two years later this same Jacob sent a petition to the Governor and the Assembly of Pennsylvania. The document contained absurdly untrue accusations as to George Rapp's tyranny and represented the common members as mere slaves. The petitioner asked that Rapp be publicly declared an infidel, and that he and his son Frederick be charged as transgressors of both Divine laws and those of the State. In conclusion Schreiber asked that the Harmony Society be dissolved and the whole estate divided equally among the present and former members. This vicious memorial was signed by a number of other seceders.

The Assembly's Committee on Judiciary rejected the request of Schreiber and his fellows because sufficient evidence and testimony were lacking; also because it was not a proper subject for Assembly investigation.

After the death of his father in 1833, Jacob, as one of the heirs of his father's estate, took out letters of administration. But the Court of Common Pleas at Beaver quickly handed down an unfavorable decision. Thereupon Jacob appealed to the Supreme Court of Pennsylvania where the case came to trial in 1836. Justice Gibson, (who at a later day became one of the most famous legal figures in the country and who also paid a kindly visit to Economy) handed down a significant opinion, emphasizing that a mutual benefit association based on community of property is not prohibited by law, that an heir cannot claim property thus put into common stock, and finally that no one joining a religious society of such principles can avoid

93

his contract with it on the basis of the extravagance of its doctrines. . . . Although this was the last of Jacob Schreiber, the Trustees were to be harassed for many years by litigation.

In 1847 a new circumstance arose to alter the organization of the Society. On the seventh day of August, Father Rapp, almost ninety years of age, closed his eyes in death. It was hard to believe that he had gone at last, this patriarchal prophet—this stalwart peasant who had led his people out of hopelessness in Europe to faith and aspiration in a New World, this courageous pioneer who had helped to build three settlements in the wilderness, and who had guided the souls of hundreds of people to faith and brotherly love. The presence of the man had given confidence to all . . . Now, like many of his associates, he lay beneath the apple trees in God's green acre.

Many communal organizations, after the death of their chief leaders, have crumbled and passed away. But the Harmonists were made of sterner stuff. The conversion of three virgin forests into comfortable habitations, the trials, vexations and sacrifices of pioneer life, the self-denials necessary for the welfare of the communal group had tested these men and women as by fire. Sturdy, valiant, hard-working, godfearing, and ever ready to sacrifice for the common welfare, they could lift up their heads even after the death of their foremost brother.

And so, five days after the death of Father Rapp, the members entered into new Articles of Association. In this document more specific duties were shifted to a Council of Elders, composed of nine members—Romelius Baker, Jacob Henrici, Jonathan Lenz, John Stahl, John Schnabel, Matthew Scholle, Joseph Hoernle, John Eberle, and Adam Nachtrieb. And these were men to reckon with. The Council's business included the management of all internal affairs, deciding disputes, giving advice or reproof, receiving and expelling members, directing community morals and education, filling of vacancies in the council, and keeping of the records of its important proceedings, appointing two of its members as trustees for the transaction of the Society's external and financial affairs.

The two trustees chosen were Romelius L. Baker and Jacob Henrici, both experienced in the business management of the Society, the first as understudy of Frederick Rapp, the latter as a protege of Father Rapp. Both had served as business agents of George Rapp since 1834. With the exception of fifteen months Brother Romeli, (as his fellows were fond of calling him) from henceforth served as the spiritual head of the Society. Although the combined powers of these two men who worked so harmoniously together were as great as those of George Rapp, those powers were never abused, and matters of extreme importance were generally submitted to the vote of the Society as a whole.

But even with this careful reorganization of the commune, other troubles came apace. Joshua Nachtrieb withdrew from the Society in 1846, signing a paper that he had voluntarily withdrawn and acknowledging the receipt of $200 as a donation from the Society. In spite of these precautions, suit was brought by Nachtrieb, in the U. S. Circuit Court of Western Pennsylvania as of November term 1849, claiming that he was unjustly excluded from the Society and deprived of any participation in the property and benefits of the association. He requested an accurate account of all the Society's property in which he hoped to share as an equal.

It was a long court duel. Eminent attorneys of Western Pennsylvania participated, among them on the side of the opposition the fiery Edwin M. Stanton, later Lincoln's Secretary of War and still later a member of the Supreme Court appointed by President Grant. During the years 1850-51 a mass of testimony was collected, and in the November term of 1851 the case was argued in court. In the following April, after taking the case under advisement, Judges Grier and Irwin delivered an opinion sustaining the complainant—the first and only major legal set-back ever to be received by the Society.

Trustees Baker and Henrici were ordered to render a full account of the Society's estate during the twenty-seven years of Nachtrieb's membership. A protracted and tedious investigation followed, in which all the pecuniary affairs of the Society were inquisitorially examined. Finally in 1855 Nachtrieb was awarded 1/321 part of the Society's total estate. Said part, as of the date of his withdrawal amounted to $3890.

The Society promptly appealed to the United States Supreme Court. This eminent body, in the December term of 1856, reversed the decree of the lower court and barred Nachtrieb from all claims. The decree of the court was due to Nachtrieb's signature on the paper averring that he withdrew voluntarily from the Society . . . Thus the "seven years' war" was ended.

In spite of the heavy expenses of this protracted litigation, the whole affair redounded to the credit and benefit of the Society. In the first place, the Harmony Society became better known and understood. As a result of the public inquisition into its financial and industrial interests—the account proving that the Society's property was worth less than $902,000—the wild talk of "Economy's Millions," heralded far and wide by press and public, for the time being, at least, was stilled. Also public sympathy, at first strongly in favor of Nachtrieb, waned to the advantage of the Society. And not least of the beneficial effects of the case was the renewed confidence, public and local, in the leadership of Trustee Romeli Baker. On the witness stand Brother Romeli showed such a remarkable exhibition of honesty, clarity, and knowledge of the minute details not only of the Society's business, but also such profound understanding of national economics and the principles of finance, that he confounded his opponents.

At the time when victory seemed assured to Nachtrieb, an additional lawsuit faced the Society. Immediately after the lower court's decision in favor of Nachtrieb, Elijah Lemmix, a friend and associate of Nachtrieb, brought suit before the same U. S. Circuit Court of Western Pennsylvania in 1852. Lemmix had left the Society under substantially the same circumstances as Nachtrieb, but his withdrawal was still more manifestly a voluntary one. A similar investigation took place under the same attorneys, but in the February term of 1855, the court pronounced a brief but decidedly adverse opinion against Lemmix.

In all these difficult affairs the new leaders, Baker and Henrici, showed foresight and wisdom. The continued success of the Society, in spite of the death of the Rapps and the partial retrenchment of industrial activities, is to be credited in large measure to these two trustees. In those days the Society, though no longer increasing in momentum, still maintained a somewhat positive course. Its true direction we cannot understand, however, without a closer, more intimate knowledge of the men at the helm.

Nearly the entire life-story of Senior Trustee Baker is intimately connected with the Society. Early in life he foreshortened his original name, Gottlieb Romelius Langenbacher, to Romelius L. Baker. Romelius was born inWuerttemberg in 1793. Both his parents, his brother John and he, early became interested in the teachings of George Rapp, and decided to cast their lot with the emigrants to the New World. Once in the New World, all signed the original Articles of Association, and remained forever faithful to the cause of brotherly love and community of goods. John, the elder brother, soon came to be regarded as Frederick Rapp's chief assistant, so that in the frequent absences of Frederick from the home base, John served as business director. Alas, John's brilliant and promising career came to an untimely end—he died in 1825.

Romeli, who heretofore had occupied a secondary position, now "stepped into his brother's shoes." Through the years of association and friendship with Frederick, until the latter's death in 1834, Romeli absorbed his mentor's caution, foresight, and general business acumen and genius. Like Frederick, he was exact in his accounts and regarded every branch of Society business with love and care. At any time he knew the exact status of the Society's industries and investments.

As the agent of George Rapp, after Frederick's death, Romeli had the opportunity to broaden still more his experience. Extensive travel widened his cultural background. In his service he was so faithful and efficient that he enjoyed the fullest confidence of Father Rapp. Even though the old Patriarch knew that their opinions at certain points were widely at variance, there is in his letters to Baker a kindly benevolence, at times even tenderness toward the younger man, also an expressed desire for his early return.

In the Baker correspondence I have found only one

letter hinting of a romance. Perhaps it originated at New Harmony, or more likely when Baker paid business visits to Vincennes in later years. At any rate, it is interesting to note a letter from Mrs. Nancy Ann Hay Maddox of Vincennes, dated 1851, and recounting sad yet pleasant memories of Baker's visit to her father's home.

"I have often felt ashamed in thinking of the time I bid you farewell on the Steam Boat, I wept so bitterly, and with all my heart, it was because I felt that I was saying good bye forever. I never thought I would see your face again on earth."

Baker's reply is full of recollections and sentiments of the past; tactfully he writes:

"The songs, an important one of which I have as a keepsake from you . . . and the wolf and the lamb you have from me, I can still remember, the youthful sweet voices of you all, the apples we used to cut . . . the sweet-cake you brought from Mother, and the stock glass of wine which George served up, are all fresh in my memory . . . I felt for you at our departure on the Steam Boat which you mention. I saw your tears and emotions and I understand them, they were all pure friendship, emanating from a tender heart. You have become the partner of a worthy husband now, entitled to all your affection. I felt strange and perhaps I did not externally show what my inward feelings were, and may have left a vacuum, but we will forgive and forget."

There are no other evidences of romantic affections

entering into Romeli's calm, sweet life. The kindness and beauty of his own affectionate nature were lifted up, in true Harmonie idealism, to a love of all men.

Often sent to distant parts of the country on business, he invariably longs for home and the brotherhood of his people. On a trip to New Orleans by steam boat in 1844, he writes to Father Rapp:

> Never before in all my travels did I feel and see the difference between our innocence and simplicity and the complexity and luxury of the world so forcibly as at this time. As the world hastens toward her periphery, so it becomes our duty in whatsoever location we may be to move forward so that we may attain the opposite unity right soon, and in the communal spirit become for the world and her complex chaos a leaven . . .

We note the echo of Father Rapp's own mysticism, but whereas Rapp's spirit was often fevered and sometimes harsh, the spirit of Romeli is always serene and loving. And there is purpose and direction in his thoughts and actions. In far away New Orleans, worldly and luxurious, he writes again—

> . . . In the stillness of the night on my couch I exercise my thoughts; there is and still remains in the bonds of love the communal spirit which is what the pole is to the magnetic needle. Everything except my business affairs are strange and side issues . . .

In many respects Romeli seems to have combined the spiritual idealism of George Rapp with the practical and material idealism of Fredrick. His sermons, replete as they certainly were with nuggets of profound philosophy, through his own ingenuity and the use of the Swabian patois, resolved themselves into simple homilies facile to the understanding and delightful to the ear. But he was equally capable in the daily dispatch of affairs.

Although a man of great simplicity, Romeli was one of the most cultured men in the country. Like Frederick and his brother John, he cultivated the English language assiduously, keeping most of his accounts and some of his other papers in that language. But he studied the German language almost as diligently—though he usually spoke in the Swabian dialect. He even left a manuscript of a hundred pages, a commentary on the history of Joseph, bearing witness to his interest in composition, his searching biblical interpretations, as well as his attractive handwriting. In 1855 he became a charter member of the Historical Society of Pennsylvania, and for some years continued to maintain his interest in its activities as well as in the activities of the Pennsylvania Society of Agriculture. He was an unusually well-read man, and much of his leisure time was spent in the well-stocked Society library, where he became especially well acquainted with the great works of German literature and philosophy.

He must have been a wonderful man. I vividly recall, how kindly and lovingly the men and women of Economy used to speak of Romeli. He was particularly tender toward children, and though I was but a child of eight when the sad news of Romeli's death went abroad I well remember his kindnesses to me. He had all the qualities that make a great and beloved leader of men—tactful yet firm, kind and generous yet business-like and practical, pious yet wholesomely human. In his many business trips throughout the United States and Europe, he learned to know the world, and to acquire an exceedingly rare ability in judging men. He had associated with Yankees and Southerners, Negroes and Indians, cultivated Europeans and crude frontiersmen. Wonderful were the tales that fell from his lips.

But on the thirteenth of January, 1868, beloved Romeli passed away. This sad event somewhat lowered the sun of Economy's Golden Day.

In his place Jacob Henrici, who as junior trustee during 34 years had worked harmoniously with Romeli, succeeded to the senior trusteeship, and my guardian, Jonathan Lenz, became junior trustee. Henrici's business methods, however, were different from those of Romeli. Whereas Baker followed the footsteps of Frederick Rapp, Henrici followed the shining mystic light of George Rapp, who had paid little attention to the keeping of accounts. Let us take a closer look at this remarkable man.

Jacob Henrici was born in the little village of Grosskarlbach, in the Palatinate, Germany, on January 15, 1804. As the Palatinate was at that time under the government of the French Republic, Henrici enjoyed disconcerting the American "Know-Nothings" in the middle of the last century in a typical sharp thrust of satirical humor: "You are citizens of this republic by accident of birth; I am a citizen by choice." Then proudly, "But I too was born a Republican—a citizen of the Republic of France." Both father and grandfather were linen weavers, but young Jacob studied to be a teacher at the government school at Kaiserslautern. During this educational process the reaction against the radical and atheistic principles of the French Revolution set in, and Henrici became ardently interested in the deeply religious movements which from time to time stirred that corner of southwestern Germany.

Glancing through an encyclopedia he read of George

Rapp and the Harmony Society in America. The fervent mysticism of George Rapp and the primitive Christianity practiced by the Harmonists in America instilled in young Henrici an ardent desire to visit and perhaps to join the Society. Difficulties were, however, almost insurmountable —his family was loath to move, and since he had been educated in a government school his father would have to pay a large sum to the government to gain permission for young Henrici's departure. For some time Jacob prayed fervently for divine guidance, and through the psychical experience that followed, he felt reborn and determined to find his way to Rapp and America in search of a newer and a better life. He thereupon succeeded in inducing his father to pay what was due to the government, whereupon the whole family emigrated to the land beyond the seas.

They landed at Baltimore in June 1825. The family temporarily established, young Jacob started afoot on his nine hundred-mile journey, over mountain and forest to far off Harmonie, Indiana. (Henrici, by the way, nigh unto his dying day, was an inveterate pedestrian). Arriving in Pittsburgh, after three hundred miles of travel, he learned that the Society had just moved to nearby Economy. It being midafternoon, he at once set out for Economy. Midway, he stopped for the night.

Emerging from the woods near the edge of the Economy settlement the following forenoon he came upon a party of men and women at their labor in the field. "They looked happy, well disciplined, and glowing with health and good spirits." When he entered the village, just then in the process of construction, Father Rapp met him. The patriarch must have been wonderfully impressed by the ardor of this young man in the light of what he went through to reach his goal. Equally certain is it that the young man was well pleased with the Patriarch, even though on his journey he had heard many evil stories of the mystical communist and the commune. Heaven seemed to be about him here in this quiet village. He used to tell of a dream he had in the Old Country as to Economy and that on his arrival here everything came true exactly as he had dreamed it. Pledged to return the following year, he returned to Baltimore.

Here, however, difficulties again surrounded him. In the first place, try as he might, he could not convert his parents and his brothers to the Economy way of life, and under no circumstances would they consent to join the Society; his mother especially was opposed to the plan. But the family later did move to Pittsburgh, and there successfully made their way in the world. As a clan, the Henricis are all endowed with real sincerity and superior mentality. Max Henrici, for example, a grand-nephew of Jacob, even now is one of Pittsburgh's leading journalists as editor of the Pittsburgh *Sun Telegraph*, while his father J. F. Henrici attained considerable note as a scholar. I have known a number of the family personally, and it has been a joy to see the Henricis follow in the footsteps of their "Uncle Jacob" in their devotion to the nobler things of life. The Henricis are scattered over the civilized world, and I feel safe in claiming that wherever occurs the name it is a synonym for integrity and ability.

But there was still another and perhaps more potent difficulty—love. Few people know that while Jacob was sojourning in Baltimore, he met a young woman, beautiful, accomplished, lovable. The acquaintanceship ripened into love, and for some time he was undecided about returning to Economy. But a man who has given his pledge as Jacob gave it; a man who felt in the vast depths of his conscience that even many thousands of miles away in the ravaged land of Europe, God had shown him the way to follow; a man who had borne mental anguish and had striven for years to attain peace in a new way of life—such a man could take but one course. He sacrificed love for communal brotherhood—and never afterward did he regret it . . . When one of his nephews told him long afterwards that the Henricis should have a "Jubelfeier" on the fiftieth anniversary of Uncle Jacob's coming to Economy, Jacob only replied that if he thought about it he would go out among his vines and praise God and have a little Jubelfeier all by himself . . . This is the story that I have from his own lips, when once I asked him if there were any truth in the romantic tattle of journalists about his affection for Gertrude Rapp.

So back to Economy he came in 1826 to be the village schoolmaster, and after the usual probationary period to become one of the most trusted and faithful members of the Harmony Society . . .

He put his whole soul into the Harmonist way of life. Religion was his daily food, and he was perhaps the only one who adopted the theology and the fervent mysticism of Father Rapp in all its facets. I can remember his long and devout prayers, and that when he sang with all the earnestness of his great heart, he seemed like a saint.

From the very beginning of his career at Economy, he was a special favorite of Father Rapp's, and unquestionably the old Patriarch saw in him a worthy successor. They were alike in many respects. In the first place, the protege was as fiery a religious zealot as Father Rapp himself. Oftentimes Henrici was intolerant of other opinions, and to counteract them he gloried in hurling his shafts of irony or scorn at these having the temerity to question his beliefs. There is no doubt about it, Henrici, otherwise kind, lovable and sweet-natured, in matters pertaining to morality and religion was as hard as flint. Like Father Rapp, he was a champion of simplicity, and severely chided all unnecessary adornment as well as the foibles of fashion. Once at a Love Feast, when he was administering the Sacrament, he noticed Elizabeth Ott, his cousin, wearing ear-rings. When he came to her, he extended with one hand the bread, quietly intoned the words—"Take, eat; this is my body" . . . as with the other hand, he vigorously tweaked her ear! He even refused to attend his mother's funeral in Pittsburgh, probably because of her former opposition to joining the Society. "Let the dead bury their dead," he said.

However as a leaven to this rigorous sternness, Henrici possessed a real sense of humor. But even this was not always kind and gentle. His shafts of wit were like arrows that seldom missed their mark. Even some of his puns had barbed edges. Nevertheless, there was something very lovable about Brother Jacob—perhaps it was the essential dignity and grandeur of the man. His soul was clear as purest crystal; his heart embraced all mankind; his boundless generosity even made a significant dent in the huge treasury of the Society. For all his blunt severity, no one justly could accuse Brother Jacob of being a bigot.

One thing Henrici lacked, but perhaps this made him the greatest of us all. He had not the slightest patience with any equivocations or half-truths, nor even with St. Paul's remark—"All things are lawful unto me, but all things are not expedient." Henrici's honesty and integrity was so far beyond question, that the Society's attorneys rarely called him to the witness stand for fear that he would "lean backward" in his endeavor to be absolutely truthful. So, like the Rock of Gibraltar stood Henrici in his rugged integrity and defiance of the opinion of men.

Even before Henrici came to Economy a young man

by the name of Jonathan Lenz had risen to considerable importance in the Society. He was destined to be the only leader to have the distinction of being born in the Society. Jonathan first saw the light of day on June 10th in 1807 at Harmony in Butler County, and as he grew in stature he showed all the evidences of that stalwart original stock which within a quarter of a century cleared away three virgin forests, built three towns each of which were flanked by orchards, vineyards and gardens.

I well remember that in the days of my childhood, I used to liken him in physical aspects to Saul the son of Kish—that "choice young man and goodly" who "from his shoulders and upward was higher than any of the people." For Jonathan's body seemed almost monumental —his handsome head resting easily on his great shoulders, his entire body in proportion—all in all he was one of the finest specimens of masculinity that I have ever seen.

The fact that Jonathan, as a lad of only sixteen summers, was sent from New Harmony on the Wabash to far away New Orleans in charge of an immense cargo transported on flatboats, is proof positive that Jonathan was regarded as one of the most trustworthy and capable men of the Commune.

His chief interests, however, were not in commerce and the amassing of wealth for the Society. This he regarded simply as a means of exchange. His natural bent seems to have been toward mechanics and the making of real things. And indeed he was one of the Society's most careful and capable craftsmen. When new buildings or machinery were to be built, Jonathan delighted in drawing the plans, making the designs, and perhaps supervising construction. He was a fine draftsman, and some of his sketches of new buildings, machinery or mechanical devices are still extant and treasured.

Prior to the death of Trustee Baker, Jonathan was placed in charge of the Society's lumber operations in its great tract of forest land in Warren County, far up on the Allegheny River, and was often commissioned to look after other less important business. But modest Jonathan regarded his position as the Society's chief wagonwright as his real job. Even when he arose to junior trusteeship, instead of sharing in the responsibility of managing the Society's complicated external affairs, Jonathan spent most of his time managing the shops and farms at Economy.

During the early years of Jonathan's visits to the timber tracts of Warren County, he became acquainted with a young and lovely woman with whom he fell deeply in love. The attachment between the two was so strong and tender, and the conflicting emotions in Jonathan's heart between the love of his brethren of the Society and the love of this woman that for a time it somewhat affected his sanity. Baker and Henrici, and also my mother, extended all their kindness and prayerful advice to win him back to Economy.

But the power that had most to do with winning him back to happiness and his duty was the calm, sweet counsel and consolation of Simira Hoehr, one of Economy's outstanding women.

Jonathan was not only the largest man in the village, but his heart was in proportion. When as a child I was orphaned by the Civil War, Jonathan was appointed my guardian. In this I could not have been more fortunate, for generosity and kindliness characterized all his actions. His heart was a mansion where all could find a place.

I used to watch the Society's expert cradlers go to the fields of yellow grain simply for the joy of seeing Jonathan lead the assault with his mammoth cradle, an extra large one which he himself had made. Down the field he led all the cradlers—cutting almost a double swath. One might see his rippling muscles flex in the sunlight, and his face beam with the sheer joy of physical strength and activity. At the 3:00 o'clock "Vesperbrot" the workers—men and women—gathered under one of the mighty oaks, where Jonathan *as raconteur* would regale them with anecdotes of the settlement on the Wabash, or of his experiences throughout the Ohio and Mississippi River Valleys. He had a pleasant sense of humor—not sharp and brilliant like Henrici's, but amiable and wise, and a little mischievous, as his eyes would light up with an impish twinkle.

Like Romeli, he was generally beloved, and all of us, members and hirelings, felt more at ease with him than with any of the other leaders, a fact which implies more than words can tell.

Yet another character stands out as a representative of Economy's Golden Day, namely Gertrude Rapp, the much loved granddaughter of Father Rapp. Gertrude was born at Harmony in Butler County in 1808, one year after the adoption of celibacy. She was the daughter of George Rapp's son John, and his wife Jacobina, *nee* Diehm. The sad and early death of John, due to an accident, not only shook the community but gave rise among outsiders to the fantastic tale that, because of the birth of Gertrude some time after the adoption of celibacy, the elder Rapp had emasculated the son. Like Jonathan, Gertrude belonged to the Society from the cradle to the grave.

As the years passed by, the beautiful child became a beautiful woman, and a favorite of all. George Rapp saw to it that she was carefully educated; even at the age of fifteen she assisted her grandfather in his correspondence.

She studied German, French and English; mathematics, music and painting; the old gentleman was especially careful of her musical education, and her talent at the pianoforte and organ in this whole community of musicians was equaled by none, except the assiduous Henrici. Eminent visitors, like the Duke of Saxe-Weimar, always made mention of Gertrude and paid her their respects.

One would imagine that the special attentions lavished upon Gertrude by everyone would spoil her or at least give rise to jealousy in others. But neither seems to have been the case. Everyone—men and women, humble and important—looked upon Gertrude with love, respect and admiration. When she was still but a child or a lass, the leading men—Frederick Rapp, John Baker, Romeli Baker —when absent on business trips to Philadelphia, New York and other points, always wrote her letters. By them she sometimes sent presents to her numerous friends in these cities, from whence she generally received gifts in return.

Her letters will always stand as a refutation to those historians who stupidly imply that the Society was composed of common peasants who thought only of their daily bread and their fantastic religion. She writes to her friends about Economy's natural history museum, about favorite musical classics, the new books, her accomplishments in embroidery and the making of wax flowers, the Great Garden, her new sketches, the cultural activities of Frederick and other leaders, the Society's band and orchestra, or perhaps her attendance at the grand ball in honor of Lafayette in Pittsburgh. If she visits Philadelphia she writes home about the opera and concerts or the new music and books she has received.

She played one of the two harmoniums in the church, while Henrici played the other (the musical Economites would not be satisfied with just one). Perhaps this musical affinity was responsible for the remarkable rumors of

Great House. Executive mansion of the Trustees and the Music Hall at Economy.

Pumping drinking-water at the Kotrba corner "Hotel Pump."

the Henrici and Gertrude life-long love affair. Newspapers often carried the story; thus it spread throughout the country. It never seemed to embarrass either of them. When Henrici, in a private conversation with me some time after Gertrude's death, flatly denied such affections, he told me a story which few have ever heard.

There was a time when Gertrude and one of her tutors fell deeply in love with each other. At the height of their infatuation, the two actually eloped. But her bosom friend and constant companion, Pauline Speidel, hearing of the elopement, swiftly followed, and succeeded in enticing Gertrude safely back to the fold. Henceforth Gertrude never wavered in her duty and love to the community. Her whole life was one of service. However, the bonds that existed between Pauline and Gertrude were peculiar; I never could divine whether or not the feelings of Gertrude toward Pauline were those of genuine gratitude.

As to the alleged affection between Gertrude and Henrici, he certainly showed no favoritism toward her. In their youthful days at a weekly singing class, which Henrici and Gertrude led with two pianos, Gertrude made a slight mistake. Henrici stopped the singing and vigorously criticized Gertrude. Behold, when the passage was repeated, Gertrude made the same mistake. Quick as a flash, Henrici rose from his piano, walked to Gertrude—and boxed her ears!

But all in all, to Henrici, as well as to Romeli and Jonathan and others, Gertrude was both a mother and a sister. She became mistress of the Great House, dignified and gracious, and at this post served the Society more than half a century. To have produced even one such character is enough honor for any Community.

But Gertrude was not merely a beautiful flower, nor

simply the lovely and dignified mistress of the Great House. Shortly before 1826 she became interested in the culture of silk-worms and the manufacture of silk. Urged on by Frederick, she took the lead in establishing a silk factory at Economy, and this was at a time when it was universally believed that silk culture could not possibly be carried on in this country. Gertrude's effort, therefore, became the earliest attempt in this country to raise silk on a large and profitable scale.

At first the factory produced only enough cloth to supply the community's own needs—in itself a large task in those days of abundance and a populous membership. But so successful had these trials become, that by 1838 the Society was encouraged to enter the business on a larger scale. Thereupon they produced, yearly, from five to six thousand pounds of cocoons which were manufactured into silk, satin, velvet, florentine, brocade, and by-products such as satinets and velveteens.

Governor Joseph Ritner became interested in the venture, for he was well impressed with the textiles of Economy. After he bought coat cloth, he wrote to Rapp in his own hand: "I had a coat made of it and take great pleasure in saying that I never wore a better one." As to the waistcoat silk sent him: "The silk vest has been made up and amply sustains the high grade of your amiable and intelligent granddaughter, Gertrude, to whom you will please present my kind regards. She will be glad to hear that the Legislature which has just closed its session has done something to encourage the culture of silk, for which her industry has accomplished so much."

The fame of Economy's silk spread far and wide. Letters were sent from all over the country, inquiring about the methods and techniques used and the history of the industry at Economy. A special letter book was kept for this purpose. At various exhibits and fairs Economy silk received gold medals and honorable diplomas—at the Boston Fair of 1844, at a special exhibit of the Franklin Institute of Philadelphia in 1838, at the American Institute in New York in 1844, and at the great Columbian Exposition in Chicago.

As Economy's silk trade expanded beyond the bounds of its own community, the leaders of the Society, always champions of a tariff, felt that without such protection the industry could not long prosper in this country. Thus in 1846 a silk exhibit was sent to Congress, and owing to the extremely fine quality of the material it attained no little notice. But Congress refused to take any action on the protective tariff question in regard to silk; hence from that time on the industry gradually declined and shortly after 1852 it was abandoned.

In 1837, owing to the too rapid extension of credit, the unwise multiplication of banks that flooded the country with depreciated currency, and the wild spending of public funds for internal improvements, a long period of hard times had set in throughout the country. It was a real panic and banks failed by the dozens. President Jackson and the Democrats had failed to stabilize the tottering financial structure of the country, and depression and chaos froze the trade of the nation. In the Society's correspondence one finds that debtors and agents of the Society complain that "the times are sadly out of joint," "nobody knows what to do," "our manufactories are all idle, or doing worse," "no one today knows what money is good."

Yet in spite of all this chaos, Economy did not feel the extreme pressure of hard times—a real tribute to the community and its economic system. About a dozen years before the outbreak of the panic, Mayor John M. Snowden of Pittsburgh wrote Frederick Rapp requesting a loan of no less than $20,000 to the City of Pittsburgh for a new water system. It seemed to be a crucial time in the development of that city, and the Society responded with a prompt loan of the amount requested. Even at the time when, after the Society's treasury had been depleted by the Leon insurrectionists and the financial condition of the country was just beginning to totter, the Society extended the time of payment on the Pittsburgh loan. Baker wrote: "Should the city want the amount for two or three years [longer] we shall be at her service."

For some years after the panic, trade was almost at a standstill, but one must remember that the economy of the Commune did not depend wholly upon trade with the outside world. Its industries and agriculture continued to produce the necessities for home consumption, and all its needs were easily met by its own farms and workshops—a vast advantage over other individualistic communities. Whatever was produced over and above home-consumed goods was profit. Though the external trade of the Society greatly declined during these years, the people of Economy lived as comfortable and secure a life as ever.

However, by the end of the 1840's trade again spurted ahead, rising from a money income of $13,000 in 1849 to $19,000 in 1853, and in the next year suddenly shooting up to $40,000; though this latter accretion was probably due to the first gradual absorption into the common fund of the $510,000 which Rapp had formerly sequestered for the pilgrimage to Jerusalem.

Then came the days of Economy's greatest wealth. The assets of the Society in 1855, according to the Harmony Township tax report, totaled $1,053,699, not including numerous land holdings in other areas—and these were still days when evaluations could hardly correspond to the actual worth in more normal times. It is to be noted, moreover, that the chief assets of the Society no longer consisted in the land, industries, workshops, homes and equipment of Economy itself, but in external investments —bonds, stocks, mortgages, notes. And thus the economy of the Commune was no longer a positive and dynamic one; foreign investments outgrew domestic production; it had become principally a money economy.

According to the same tax report, the Society had interests in the Little Sawmill Run Railroad, the Cleveland and Pittsburgh Railroad, the Darlington Railroad, the Perryville and Zelienople Plank Road, the Bank of Kentucky, Brighton Bridge, and holdings in the Ohio and Pennsylvania Railroad. By 1866 the Society reached its high water mark of material prosperity with the development of oil production in the Warren County tract. From henceforth Economy, as a producing community and a little vested empire, began its long and troublesome decline.

There were obvious reasons for this deterioration. In the first place, the Society, from an early membership of some 700 souls, by 1862 had decreased to less than 200 members. The custom of celibacy long ago had cut the birth-rate to nothing, while the members grew aged and less useful. Moreover, the Society had never put forth any evangelistic endeavors toward gaining converts. From time to time a few members were added to the membership rolls, but at no time did the number of these equal the number that died or abandoned the Society.

To keep the farms and workshops active, the Trustees began to hire outside help of both sexes. The increase of hirelings, many of whom had little respect for, or knowledge of, the community's high principles, tended further

115

to destroy the integrity of the home economy. Wishing to avoid this as much as possible, the trustees entered upon a long period of external investments, which in the end proved disastrous. Much of my own life as trustee of the Society was spent in disentangling what had come to be a stupendously complex and unfortunate financial economy. But that is another story.

During the expansive 1850's and 1860's the Society was faced with other difficult problems. In spite of the depletion of membership and the influx of hirelings, the Society itself did not forthwith lose its great influence in the affairs of Western Pennsylvania. In evidence of this are the political squabbles in which the Society became entangled. Radical Locofoco movements in Western Pennsylvania combined with the democracy of Jacksonism. The combined movement, once attaining power, became more and more arrogant and undisciplined. Knowing that the Society favored a restoration of conservative Whiggery, because that party endeavored to stimulate domestic industry, the Democrats began threatening the Society.

The Society, generally voting as a unit, cast its 200 and more votes regularly against the Democratic ticket. Undoubtedly Frederick Rapp advised the members and influenced them, but never exercised any coercion. The same may be said to a lesser degree of Baker and Henrici. In 1839 a large political meeting at Bridgewater assembled and passed resolutions protesting against the Economy vote. Baker coolly and soberly replied that everyone at Economy was granted both legal and constitutional rights in regard to voting. By 1844 the ridiculous arrogance of the radical Democrats of Western Pennsylvania led to an attempt to blackmail the Society and prohibit the members from voting because their vote might be helpful to Henry Clay as candidate for President. The vote of Economy seemingly was so strategic that it might easily swing Western Pennsylvania to the Clay banner. In former years Henry Clay was a close friend to Frederick Rapp; and thus also a friend to the Society; the situation therefore was all the more trying. Father Rapp continued to insist that every individual freedom be exercised at Economy. Letters were sent to him threatening physical force. Three letters finally arrived threatening the Society with death, fire and total destruction, the authors of course remaining anonymous. In 1846 a mob even gathered at the mouth of Beaver Creek in a conspiracy against Economy. The threats grew more ominous, and one of the Harmonists, a township school director, was violently attacked and beaten; also one of the Society's frame houses at Legionville was burned. At the time it was thought best to withdraw the whole Economy vote, though individual freedom remained for the members to exercise at their own risk. However the Society soon got even with their enemy neighbors. Trustee Baker, succeeded in having the Legislature take away from Economy Township the Harmony Society real estate and establish it as a separate Township called Harmony. One can imagine how this loss must have struck the denizens of the Economy "hinterland."

Another event of importance before the close of this period was the effort of other communal societies, which like the Harmony Society were on an obvious decline, to unite their groups. Both the Shakers of New Lebanon, New York, and the Zoarites of Zoar, Ohio, made overtures. The Shakers entered into a long correspondence with Henrici and the Society, sent Shaker hymns and music, and explained Shaker beliefs. Hiram Rude, a

117

leader of the Shakers, paid Economy a visit in 1856, but his overtures for a union of the two bodies were declined.

About the same time the Zoar community, much more closely allied both in nationality and in basic principles to Economy, entered into correspondence with the Harmony Society leaders. Though a trustee and an elder of Zoarites came to visit Economy, perhaps to make overtures for union, the two representatives of the Separatist Society left in a huff, because Henrici deliberately hurt their feelings by offering them pork at the dinner table knowing as he did that the eating of the flesh of swine was against their religious principles!

At the outbreak of the Civil War, although beyond the age of conscription, the members of the Society heartily championed the Union Cause, and Abraham Lincoln even before his election was regarded as a hero. With the formation of the Republican party, and its stand as to a protective tariff, the community naturally became for the rest of its days politically identified with said party.

Shipments of farm produce, clothing, food, money and whiskey were sent to the Union lines from Economy's warehouses, and letters from army officers and statesmen testify to the patriotism of the Society.

Economy's Golden Day now obviously at an end, the little village by the Ohio sank into a sort of Sleepy Hollow lethargy. The old men and women, once valiant pioneers in a noble cause, passed into the last long sleep or lingered in recollections of days when the Harmony spirit was a dynamic ideal and Economy a bustling little empire of the west.

5

A Lonely Boy in a Strange Little World (1860-1868)

M Y LIFE BEGAN IN THAT DARK, fateful year of 1860; in the very month in which from Illinois to Cooper Union, New York City, came the towering Abraham Lincoln to deliver his memorable speech in favor of the restriction of slavery. Slavery, indeed, and sometimes secession, were words of the hour, and the nation was confronted with the threat of being rent asunder.

Yet I doubt if any such thoughts entered the mind of my mother. It was on the twenty-second of February that I first saw the light of day. My parents lived in Cincinnati at that time, but my father was in New Orleans in the interests of a Cincinnati brewing company. Both my parents had emigrated from Württemberg—my father from Effringen in the Black Forest, my mother from Hoheneck on the River Neckar. In the chain of events that rapidly followed I was destined never to know my father intimately. But I imagine he contrasted somewhat with my mother who was intensely religious, stern, and ardent in her beliefs.

At any rate, during the outbreak of hostilities my father, still in New Orleans, was summarily conscripted into the Confederate Army. Unwilling to fight at variance with his own convictions, he feigned illness until the Battle of Bull Run. Then he found an opportunity to escape, and to join the Army of the North. Being a deserter from Confederate ranks, upon advice of certain Federal officers he changed his name to John Rutz, and thereupon became a private in Company H, 75th Pennsylvania Volunteers, 11th Corps. (See his name on Gettysburg Monument).

Meanwhile, my mother, sadly aware of the exigencies of war, decided to return with me to the communistic community of Zoar, where by the way, my parents had been married. The Zoar Separatists had settled and organized in Tuscarawas County, Ohio, in 1817. They had emigrated from southern Germany, and, like the Harmonists had adopted the principle of Christian Communism, established a celibate society, in general had striven to emulate the primitive Christianity of the early church, and under the leadership of one Joseph Bäumler in the New World had thrived as an agricultural and industrial unit. But in their religious separatism they seemed even more uncompromising than the Harmonists though they abandoned the rule of celibacy after a cholera epidemic had depleted their numbers.

There might have been a place among them for my mother, but the baby was too much of a handicap. Friends came to the rescue, however. Not far from Zoar lived Samuel Siber with his wife and son. Though nearly eighty years have passed I readily recall the small unpainted cottage nestling against the hillside, the narrow lane leading to the road to Zoar. There comes to me also the picture of dear old generous Samuel Siber, willing to share with us—indeed voluntarily proffering his very humble home. Pious as he was, even the Zoarites were too worldly for him. Rather than join them and acquire an easy livelihood, he preferred to cultivate his scant acreage and ply his trade of basket weaving.

It was difficult enough for the elder Siber to eke out a

livelihood for his own little family, and well nigh impossible to feed extra mouths. Hence in behalf of my mother and her auburn-haired child, he wrote a letter to the trustees of the Harmony Society at Economy, recommending us to their care. Soon there came a favorable reply.

Most of the members of the Harmony Society were well advanced in years—hence there was need of housekeepers, nurses and of help in general. My mother was to be employed as housekeeper, and as nurse.

I was only two years and one month old when we arrived at the scene of our new life, but I well recall a certain episode. Brother Weber, the community potter, had committed suicide. From the religious or ethical viewpoint such action was of course unspeakable; from the standpoint of practical economics—what now was to be done? . . . Brother Weber had been the Society's last and only potter. Why should I, a babe of two years, become so impressed by this episode? The answer—because Brother Weber had been a member of the household into which my mother and I now entered.

He had been an inmate of the very house to which Trustees Romelius L. Baker and Jacob Henrici assigned us, namely, the household of aged Brother Peter Rosdan, composed of himself and Sister Marie Vester. Marie was well advanced in years and no longer able to attend properly to household duties. These duties my mother was now to assume.

The whole community lived according to this "family" system—it was basic to the Economy way of life. At this time there were about fifty families in the community, each composed of from two to eight members, five or six generally, the sexes being about equal in number. There is more to be said for this way of communal life than may at first appear. When individuals of different traits are thus grouped, selfishness and jealousy tend to disappear, yet the economic convenience and efficiency of the small "family" unit is preserved or even increased. Rearrangements within the Society were constantly being made especially whenever death occurred—sometimes involving many changes. It was natural therefore that individuals came to think in terms of the entire community rather than of their own small immediate "family" unit.

In those days every home had an outbuilding containing a hay loft, cow stable, a chicken coop, a root cellar, a fuel section, and a carpentry shop equipped for the making of ordinary repairs. The home itself was as fully equipped. I well remember the old fashioned pewter platter in addition to the china ware. Once, when my family was on an all-day harvesting or haymaking jaunt, in order to warm my dinner I set it in the hearth of the monstrous chimney, shortly to find my victuals surrounded by a lake of molten pewter. Before the days of the community bakery—established in 1866—each family did its own baking in one of the large, arched, brick ovens located on each street at convenient points. Each family also had a cow. Every morning and evening the milkman made his rounds, collecting the milk from the family cows. And though our cow contributed almost a tubful of milk per day, which was poured into the cedar, brass-bound vat—we, from the spigot below, received only about a gallon in return. When I became indignant at this procedure, my mother retorted, "Silly boy, what would the other families do which now have little or no milk?" In this same year of 1866 the Society collected the family cows into one dairy, from which the milkman delivered the milk. However each family made its own butter and cheese.

The houses were heated with woodstoves of the type invented by Benjamin Franklin, still the most efficient and economical of their kind. Furthermore, a pipe extended from the stove in the large downstairs sitting room to a big drum on the second floor, allowing but few heat units to escape. We always cut the fuel a year in advance; matters like these were perfectly planned and efficiently executed.

Concerted effort was the adage of the hour, all contributed to the community, even the youngest. It was a strange little world, stern and uncompromising in some respects perhaps, but generally snug and wholesome. Soon after our arrival Brother Peter took to his bed and on July 19, fell into his last long sleep. Thereupon Marie, my mother and I were moved to the Woehrle family.

Always an intensely spiritual person, my mother's mind was filled with the dreams of the prophets and a striving for "something better." Even after my father was reported seriously wounded in the Battle of Gettysburg, July 3, 1863, his recovery was of negligible importance in comparison with the saving of his soul. To this end she designed her letters which I heard her discussing with the old folks.

Some days after my father, with a bullet wound in his shoulder, had been removed to a Baltimore hospital, my mother and I experienced a strange psychologic phenomenon. . . . It was late in the night; deep silence had settled on the village. Suddenly my mother and I, asleep in the same room, awoke. The quaint old room appeared strangely illuminated from without the east window. My mother arose and approaching the window, whispered "Come here quickly." In the sky there seemed to be a great light, much larger than the moon. Only a few seconds it lasted, then faded away . . .

123

Inquiry the next day developed the fact that no one else had any knowledge of the phenomenon, whereupon my mother construed it as an omen in reference to my wounded father. Perhaps she was correct—who knows? At any rate word soon came from the hospital in Baltimore that my father had breathed his last—at about the time we had perceived the light in the sky. . . .

The peaceful village of Economy was alert to the great civil conflict. Although most of the Society members were too old for service in the field and some objected to armed force as a matter of conscience or of religious scruples, they were intensely patriotic. Heavy contributions of money, manufactured drygoods, fruits and fruit juices, medicine and other necessaries had been given to the Northern army. Aid also was rendered to widows, orphans and injured soldiers. But the fighting being many miles away, harsh realities of the war did not affect us very intimately.

But suddenly came news that Confederate General John Hunt Morgan with his troops was raiding into Ohio. The news electrified the community. If the raids were successful, Economy might well tremble, for like as not the raiders would be after the "hidden wealth." One Saturday we heard that Morgan was only a hundred miles away, whereupon next day was proclaimed by the Society leaders as "Buss und Bettag"—day of fasting and prayer. When on Sunday evening, after a day of fasting, long church services and prayerful meditation word came that Morgan and his company were captured, great was the rejoicing.

The Woehrle household consisted of the brothers Jacob and Christoph and their sister Marie. Domestic supervision of this household was more than a job for my mother—Marie Vester now spent most of the time in sick-

bed and Marie Woehrle was also an invalid. My mother
served as nurse, housekeeper and cook, as well as caretaker of the garden and the cow. I remember, too, that
Brother Christoph, violinist in the community orchestra,
lost some left hand fingers at his post in the sawmill. And
I shall never forget the flogging Brother Jacob gave me
for what to me seemed an innocent throwing of stones
through the shed window—a beating that moved even my
mother, stern disciplinarian that she was, to interfere on
my behalf. However we were destined soon again to move.

Serious illness in the Weingartner family in 1865, occasioned another readjustment. I well recall that at the
Weingartners my mother's lot was more than burdensome.
Besides nursing Marie Vester who came with us, my
mother had to take care of old Clemens Weingartner who
was utterly helpless with dropsy. Finally an assistant,
whom I recall only by the nickname "der Capuziner,"
was hired by the trustees. Formerly a Catholic—now an
infidel—he likened our potpourri of vegetables to a mixture served by the Capuchin monks, hence his nickname.
Yet he apparently enjoyed equality with other Economy
folk who, for the most part, were then intensely religious
—a significant comment on Economy tolerance. Being a
disbeliever, he and my mother naturally entered into
long arguments about religion. Brother Clemens died in
January 1867, and exit the Capuziner.

My mother having presented me with an accordion, I
soon was looked upon as the "boy wonder accordionist"
and the musicians of the community made frequent visits
to hear me perform.

Contrary to opinion outside, Economy was always alert
to contemporary events. Newspapers and the modern reports were read and discussed; political opinions were
aired; foreign and domestic problems were debated. Often

there was considerable unanimity of opinion, since the affairs of the world were generally and naturally subjected to a criticism based on the belief in the Economy way of life. Then, too, the forceful influence of the opinions of the leaders—like Trustees Baker, Henrici and Lenz—was very noticeable. For example, Henrici, speaking in Sunday school, deprecated Lincoln's attending a theatre on the fateful Good Friday when he met his death. Of course, all Economy felt the profoundest gloom at the news of the great President's assassination, but with the possible exception of Christmas, Good Friday was in Economy the day of days most sacred. For Christmas meant joy and happiness and festivity, while Good Friday had to do with death by crucifixion. The Society, by the way, observed four religious holidays, celebrated appropriately according to their meaning and significance—Christmas, Good Friday, Easter, and Pentecost. But days of festivity also were observed. Each February 15th was the day of the "Harmonie Fest," commemorating the founding of the Harmony Society. In August, frequently the seventh, the community celebrated its "Erntefest"—Harvest Home. The selection of such an early date for the Harvest festival, was due to the fact that George Rapp's death had occurred on the said date, so it was an opportunity to honor his memory. Of course, the Society opposed individual ostentation of any sort, and a celebration in honor of any individual was not a part of the Society's ideals. Hence, to avoid misconceptions and the honoring of one man too highly, the Harvest festival was just as often held on other dates. The "Liebesmahl" or Love Feast, celebrated near the close of October, corresponded to the Lord's Supper observances of Christian churches in general.

At all of these celebrations, feasting and music were

Economy's stately church.

Scene in Great House Garden. On left is Frederick Rapp's symbolic, architural (but unfinished) "Harmonie" founta

Marie Diehm. Cousin of Gertrude Rapp, in typical work-a-day garb.

a part. Indeed, Economy was famous for its music, its wholesome food and its unadulterated wines. The Harmonie Fest, weather permitting, always meant an early morning concert of band music from the church tower balcony. I can still remember my first attendance at an Erntefest—entering the spacious Music Hall with its vaulted dome of blue, watching the glassware sparkle in the midday sun, smelling the appetizing viands heaped on the tables, listening to sweet strains of the orchestra . . . It seemed indeed as if these good people, with a fore-knowledge of heaven, were giving a foretaste of the life to come.

Haymaking, harvesting, and fruit picking resolved themselves into festivities less formal. Inasmuch as the Economy tract was extensive we were often in the fields and orchards for a full day. At such times we carried along our "vesper-saekle" or lunch bag for the midday meal as well as our "niner" and "vesper" snacks of food for refreshment. At events like the currant pickings, for example, nearly the whole community put forth its efforts —talked and laughed and sang. Perhaps the grape harvest was the time of most rejoicing, for the grape was looked upon as the final product of the good earth-year. Special delicacies were distributed, such as a piece of the choicest cheese and a glass of extra fine wine. Economy, in spite of its lofty, serious atmosphere, was not without good fellowship and merriment.

In the winter came the annual fox-hunt, regarded as the king of sports. On that day the men and boys resident in the village who were still sufficiently spry and nimble would join together in hunting down all foxes within range of the drive. A line of men and boys, extending a mile or more eastwardly from the Ohio River along Sewickley Creek on the south or Legionville Creek on the north, would drive toward the center of the property where sharpshooters were stationed and where poor Reynard came to grief. But individual hunting, though not exactly forbidden, was taboo. Brother Michael Killinger it was who could not overcome temptation, and time and again he wandered off to take potshots at squirrels, coons and other wild life still abundant. But Brother Michael, a "queer" fellow, all ways considered, every now and then for having "conducted himself unseemly" was deprived of some such pleasure as his drink allowance.

The subject of punishment recalls the one meted out to me by my mother in the babyhood days of 1862. School boys, one day, were splashing each other at the hydrant water-trough adjacent to our house. Though I was an innocent onlooker, my mother, mistaking my presence for participation, took me by the legs and thrust my head into the water. Scolding the boys, who were scuttling away, and heedless of the time, she almost drowned me.

An incident of that same summer, trivial in itself but of moment in connection with the last dark days of the Harmony Society, is here pertinent.

Being the only baby in the village, the women folk naturally wanted to fondle me and kiss me. Against this latter expression of sentiment I had an utter abhorrence. My mother evidently had discovered this, for she never kissed me. Two young women of Economy, having made the discovery that I was fond of strawberries, came to bribe me—offering strawberries in exchange for kisses. I am still somewhat puzzled at the precocity of the mind which at the age of 2 years and 4 months, drove the hard and fast bargain that they give me all the strawberries I could eat but kiss me only once.

The first proviso was forthwith carried out—as to the second, the reader's guess is as good as mine.

A difficult position was that of my mother. The rearing of a child in a community such as Economy presented problems which at times must have been exasperating, and which partly explains why I was the recipient of many whippings. Also, besides the duties of nursing and the work in general, she often had a sick child to care for. Colds innumerable, scarlet fever, measles—a whole gamut of illnesses—left me pale and delicate. Small wonder this, for sleeping in rooms with the aged and the sick, in days when windows and doors were kept tightly closed, the vivifying power of fresh air was denied me; and the food, though good enough for the workers, was not the proper diet for a child. Imagine a breakfast of fried potatoes and meats. It was certainly not to my taste, so I had to be content with a slice of bread and a cup of weak coffee. The noon meal was an improvement and I managed to partake somewhat of the soups and meats. Supper was on the order of breakfast. Thus, the only delightful meal was the midafternoon snack called "Vesper." Ladwerk (a butter made of pumpkins and apple juice) with wholesome bread and butter. Sometimes smoked summer sausages and other delicacies added zest to this snack. Albeit, the old folks would comment on my frailness, and it seemed the general opinion that tuberculosis or some other malady would claim me at an early age.

These remarks sometimes made me sad; at other times I did not care, for time dragged heavily. My many sicknesses, the painful punishments at times for "innocent" misdeeds, the lack of companions with whom to play, led me to reflect that my childhood days were one slow adventureless procession, dull and full of woe. Sometimes, in my vague childish way, I almost hoped that the prophecy of my early departure from this life might prove correct.

Due to the depletion in numbers and the advanced age of the living members, in addition to the hiring of help, the Society began to adopt orphans. By this agreement boys under twenty-one and girls under eighteen were clothed and boarded and sent to school until fourteen years of age, at which time the boys learned trades toward which they seemed inclined, while the girls were instructed in the care and management of the household. On reaching the age of twenty-one, for their "start in life," the boys were granted a compensation of two hundred dollars, whereas the girls at the age of eighteen received one hundred dollars.

Thus it came that when I passed the six-year mark, I was happy in the companionship of children, and in the thought that, after all, this was a pretty good old world. Of my new playmates Chris Schlaegel proved the most congenial, yet he was neither bound to the Society nor an orphan. His father, employed in the community shoemaker's shop, had brought his family there to live. Two additional chums were Chris Loeffler and Chris Schmidt. There were five of the Loefflers scattered in four different "families." Two, Joseph and Rosina, had the honor of living in the Great House which gave them what one might call political prestige. One of the peculiar angles of life at Economy was that not only "outsiders", but lay members also, hardly dared to incur the ill will of these favored youngsters at the Great House. Indeed the influx of the young people often gave rise to some of the few major disputes in the community—the various families "sticking up" for their "children." But the Loefflers were all above average in intelligence and ability, all good-looking. Joseph, the eldest, especially took my eye. He was the most ambitious and superior of the "big boys," and an indefatigable worker. Arriving at majority, after he left the quiet village on the Ohio, he made a notable success in business and, in course of time, became the proud father of the famous operatic star, Emma Loeffler.

From the beginning of my years at Economy I attended school. My mother finding me a plaguing interference in her duties, came to an agreement with Mrs. Elizabeth Ott, the teacher at the schoolhouse across the street, permitting little Johnnie to come to school, and a place was fitted for him in the chimney corner. In the first years, before I had attained school age, I amused myself by learning to write and to draw pictures on my slate. As the years advanced I made commensurate progress, and by my sixth or seventh year had become extraordinarily nimble in mathematics. It was in the year 1866 that I began the study of the English language. All branches of studies, by the way, in that day were conducted in German.

Outside of school hours—did we enjoy our play and games! The sheep folds near the school and a street of deserted houses were ideal for "hide and seek." Back of the school we played "blackman" or "What will you do" (abbreviated to "warlyloo") or "townball," the interesting forerunner of the much more scientific baseball of today. Discovering that smoking was taboo, we ventured on the partaking of stolen sweets. Purloining a large sugar hogshead, we rolled it into a nearby shed and placed the open end toward the wall. We crawled into this unique hideout by turns to smoke cigars—made of grapevines! In this shed at other times, we stretched a large curtain back of which we operated all sorts of outlandish pasteboard figures on the end of long sticks. Lights placed in the rear of the operator threw the shadow of these figures on the curtain, and thus we instituted what was probably the first "motion picture theatre" in Western Pennsylvania!

Of course we were not like children of "the outside world"—we did not have holidays such as Saturdays or half days for play time. We contributed our share to the community work and took it as a matter of course. Perhaps the potatoes in the great community cellars under the old log church or the Blaine schoolhouse needed sorting and culling, or the grain on the floors of the large granaries was to be "turned," or the last remnant of the apple crop was to be gathered—whatever the work, we went through it like a prairie fire. When we finished our work ahead of schedule we were declared "free."

On such occasions we roamed the broad Economy acres in boyish glee. The whole countryside was ours, for the Economy tract enclosed nearly 3000 acres. Sometimes we devoted ourselves to a game of hide-and-seek of magnificent proportions. Out through the barns, out through the orchards, behind fences, over the hills and through woods and hollows we scuttled away.

One of our favorite jaunts was down to the site of the former Indian village of Logstown nearly two miles away. A century and more had passed since Celeron de Bienville had camped here with his French soldiers and Indian allies. Washington on his expeditions into the French territory had tarried here in 1752 and 1770. We might even continue to the plateau beyond Legionville Creek, where "Mad" Anthony Wayne had quartered his troops in the winter of 1792-93, and prowl around the log cabin that had been his headquarters. And so the chase would go. By supper time we ambled homeward, agreeably tired, to "Lovers' Lane," and vociferously related our experiences. This lane, formed by mulberry trees in the days of silk culture, later replaced by appletrees, had become a favorite trysting place for the young people.

In the autumn we often went nutting, combining

work with play. In the "old-fashioned winters" we had our share of coasting—on sleds made by ourselves, of course. And sleighriding was a community custom in which both old and young took part. Farm bobsleds were transformed into sleighs by the addition of wagonbeds filled with straw. One of these was reserved for the community band. All of the community's magnificent teams were requisitioned and to the jingle of the sleighbells and the music of the band, away we'd ride . . . to Rochester, or to Sewickley. If the latter was our destination, the sleighing party would hie to an auditorium where the band and choir proceeded to give an impromptu concert. It seems to me that in spite of its multifarious amusements and sophistication, the present generation can have but faint conception of the inherent joys of those collective festivities.

In the winter, too, our skating pond, formed by the overflow of the brook adjacent to the village and in which at the age of five years I nearly met a watery grave, became a scene of activity. Since the Society did not indulge in such luxuries we were forced to make our skates. The runners we made of hard wood and the straps of cast-away scrap leather—we spent more time, probably, in repairing than in skating. At that, this enforced self reliance undoubtedly proved beneficial, both mentally and mechanically.

During the long winter evenings we gathered around the large table in the living-room. After finishing my lessons assigned by the teacher; Walrath Weingartner, having presented me with a water color outfit, instructed me in the rudiments of drawing and painting. On other evenings plaiting of braids for strawhats was a favorite pastime. I still recall the calm enjoyment of those evenings Brother David Bauer—a tailor—and I plaiting, my mother and the hired girl sewing or knitting, while Brother Walrath played the guitar (made by himself), read aloud some interesting story or regaled us with noteworthy experiences "on the Wabash."

To the quota of straw hats made by the hatter, who in scientific manner went through the rye fields and picked the best of straws, some of us added hats as follows: During the noon hour, in the straw shed we chose the best straws there, brought them home and for the purpose of sizing, shoved them through a block containing knife sections which divided the straws into three, four or five segments. These were thereupon immersed in water. After supper, the straws having become pliable, were ready for the plaiting. The sewing of the braids into hats was generally left to the hatter. One woman's hat containing 120 yards of braid or two men's hats each of 60 to 70 yards was considered a winter's work.

At the age of seven years one of my chores was to help in the ringing of the church bells. There were three (two of which are still doing their duty). The big bell called the people to worship and to fires; the "middle" bell was rung for breakfast and for dinner, while the little bell announced the time for return to afternoon work. Peg-legged Brother Ulmer was greatly pleased at my being able to relieve him of the ringing of both the middle and little bells.

In this same year I was given the job of herding the hogs to and from the pasture. Returning them to the piggery at the end of day was an heroic job. Having to count them singly as they came through the gate, it was all that I could do to hold the gate against the onrush of fifty big porkers. One evening after they had slushed down the swill from the troughs, the hogs were in a tumultuous commotion. Brother John Bessan and I rushed from the distillery where the mill feed was steamed for the hogs. We found the animals in violent uproar, fighting and carrying on. The fracas on the increase, John got a black-snake whip and began to lay to, but quickly he was forced to escape and leave the wild, crazed hogs to their completely insane circus. Directly we found that the old man had emptied the wrong barrel into the troughs—the hogs were hopelessly drunk on whiskey. It was the greatest circus I ever beheld . . . Later I took part in driving the sheep to pasture and returning them to the fold. This was one chore to my liking, especially in lambing season with its interesting daily increase of the flock.

In summer months there was much to be done in field and orchard. There were two large apple orchards of thirty and forty-two acres respectively, a crab-apple orchard of six acres and a nursery of seven acres. There were small vineyards at the north and south edges of the village, and here and there were berry patches, particularly currants (they made the choicest of wines), and the streets were lined with cherry trees. The whole community joined in harvesting the currants, the apples and the cherries—every gathering becoming a sort of festal celebration.

In the spring we youngsters were kept busy planting corn and potatoes, gathering the twigs and brush left by the trimmers of the fruit trees and grapevines and currant bushes, gathering stones in the fields and heaping them in orderly piles, hoeing out thistles and the mullein which came up in field and pasture. During the summer we took part in haymaking and harvesting. In the fall we were busy at gathering apples, husking corn etc. We took no little pride in doing the work of older folks.

In this same seventh year I was also installed as a sort of man Friday in the slaughterhouse or butchershop, a

job that was extremely distasteful. To see animals, especially those that I had helped to raise, ruthlessly killed,
was something I could hardly bear. Jacob Stump, the
butcher (*and* blacksmith) killed twice a week. He weighed
the beef or mutton, divided the weight by the total
number of community members to find the individual
quota, and thereupon with rare sagacity cut the family
portions and arranged them on long tables. He knew the
favorite cuts of most members and he did his best to make
distribution in accordance. When the portions were so
arranged for half of the families, I trotted from house
to house issuing the call "fleisch holen." Thereupon the
streets became lively with women and children, armed
with pails to get their rations. In winter-time all of the
hogs, together with some beeves, were slaughtered—this,
for the year's supply of bacon, ham and sausages. The
sausages, by the way, were made by the families—thus were
they enabled to flavor them according to different tastes.
The men of the families took the meats to the smoke-
house, where, tagged with the family name, they were
suspended until properly smoked.

The division of the products by the butcher was of
"share and share alike," but the housewives after receiving
their portions had a way of subdividing the same. Certain
families might have men employed at heavy labor, whereas
the men in other families might be engaged in sedentary
work—as tailoring or shoemaking. Appetites thus differed
and so did tastes, hence there developed the clever custom
of readjustment according to the real needs of the different families.

I discover a defect in the Society's management in those
days, to wit: Twice a week, during the twilight hours
of summer months, we boys were permitted to bathe in
the Ohio River—under the supervision of a bathingmaster

who taught us how to swim. At other times we sneaked away to the "ole swimmin' hole" up Sewickley Creek. For the girls there was no such opportunity.

The death of our beloved Romeli, (Trustee Romelius L. Baker), in January 1868, marked the extinction of the Lenz and Weingartner families, and in the general reorganization we found ourselves moved to the Duerwächter family in the north wing of the Great House. The families were generally named after the head of the house, but now and then a man stood so high in the community that his name was continued through a remaining sister or daughter. This was indeed the case with the Duerwächter household. Elizabeth Duerwächter, one of the most highly respected women of the Society and daughter of Elder Duerwächter, was confined to bed and needed a nurse, so once again my mother's hands were more than full. Eusebius Boehm, (who alone with Henrici shared the secret of the Society's hidden wealth) Michael Ulmer, Elder Johannes Eberle and I were the males of our new household, while the female entourage consisted of Sibilla Hurlebaus, Elizabeth Duerwächter and my mother.

During our stay in the Duerwächter family, Eusebius Boehm, the Society's expert arboriculturist, initiated me into the mysteries of planting, grafting, budding, shifting and general care of shrubs and trees. Brother Eusebius had charge of the wine cellars, the apiary and the "Great Garden." But in that day the floral part of it was of little moment. The northern third was partly vineyard and partly vegetable garden. In the 1890's, during my trusteeship, Mrs. Duss and I transformed the garden—I doing the landscaping, she attending to the flowers—in a manner that soon enabled connoisseurs to pronounce it one of the most beautiful spots in America.

Living in the Great House—a title which in later years

137

I bestowed on the lovely old Rapp mansion—carried with it a certain prestige. In the main section of the Great House lived the Trustees, Baker and Henrici; Christoph Keppler, the coachman; Gertrude Rapp, First Lady of the Society; her mother, Johanna; her bosom friend, Pauline Speidel; Gertrude's aunt, Rosina Rapp; Katherine Langenbacher, sister of R. L. Baker; and, after Baker's death, Jonathan Lenz.

In a communistic society it would be difficult to judge salaries in relation to modern capitalistic standards; for instance many things were rendered free to my mother and to me, that in different surroundings would have had their price—such as the intensive music training I received. My mother received one dollar and fifty cents per week and her board; but she paid back twenty dollars a year for my board. With the remaining fifty-eight dollars she not only managed to clothe herself and her child, but to lay by a goodly portion of her yearly wage. It may be difficult for the casual reader to understand or to appreciate the cooperative spirit and the nobility of these simple folk of Economy.

Laboring together, as they did, for the good of "the greater family," they arrived at a stage of contentment, peace and plenty beyond the ken of the ordinary community. The fact that many who seceded, soon or late, in person or by letter, applied for readmission, speaks volumes. That indefinable hidden "manna," or food for the soul, the "Harmonische Geist" was not to be found in the world outside.

There were sacrifices, of course—some even voluntarily imposed. There is on file among the relics a resolution written by David Aegerter, who having four times strayed from the Society, directs that he be punished "with cane or whip" each time that he might transgress the unwritten code of the Society . . . "for I have found that in the world outside I can find neither peace nor enjoyment."

A communal life which can so reclaim the wayward, must have worth indeed. As to myself, I have never regretted my bringing up in Economy. And, looking at the subject in its widest sense, the loneliness, discipline and sacrifice to which I was subject in the days of my childhood, constituted a wholesome and indispensable preparation for epochal Economy days that lay in wait a quarter of a century later.

6

The Years of Growth *(1868-1874)*

SOMETIME IN THE YEAR 1868 my mother's pension was granted by the government, though she had the greatest difficulties in laying proper claim to it. Chief of these obstacles was my father's change in name from Duss to Rutz. After an enormous amount of testimony was submitted and the claim was allowed to a point where the proper documents and $200 bounty were sent to her attorney, this crafty rascal, pocketing both the money and the papers, forthwith absconded. After years of endeavor, Dr. Benjamin Feucht, formerly Economy's bandmaster, but now successfully practicing medicine in Pittsburgh, brought mother in contact with Noah Schaefer, one of Pittsburgh's bright young lawyers, who soon brought Uncle Sam to acknowledge her pension claim.

My mother's salary has already been mentioned; one would hardly believe that she saved $200 from it. This sum plus a back pension of $700, minus $100 for lawyer's fee, brought her total savings to $800. So, tired and worn from continuous nursing of the sick and the burden of household duties of the past six years, now feeling secure with her savings and her assured pension of eight dollars per month and mine of two dollars, she decided to seek life in some other corner of the world.

After some correspondence with David Haufler—formerly of the Society who with his wife Elizabeth had set up a tailor shop in the Ohio village—we moved to Strassburg,

Ohio. David had rented a little cottage of two rooms for our use, which mother with her savings proceeded to furnish. This was all a vastly new experience for me, and I greatly enjoyed the new companions, who played games new to me and vied to show the newcomer a good time. As to my mother it was entirely different—soon she complained that everything was "so different from Economy," that there were none of the Economy conveniences like the steam laundry and the community bakery. She found that the effortless procession of Economy days, the freedom from worry and the steady assurance of friends were feelings that were lacking in the outside world. It just wasn't Economy. Besides, my mother was very lonely, and did not succeed in getting employment to give us greater security.

After two months a solution came through one of her friends of former days at Zoar, who had married a Mr. Groetzinger. The Groetzingers were farmers at "the old furnace," about a mile and a half from Zoar, and they invited mother to make her home with them. Mother was to work for her board and mine. I well remember the pleasurable days of the summer, for close at hand were the Tuscarawas River and a canal for towboats with lock and switch or a dead end, where I spent many hours at fishing.

Alas, my mother had evidently become "an Economite" (inhabitant of Economy). Everything in the outside world was well enough in itself, "but it was not like Economy." Soon she wrote to Trustees Henrici and Lenz, asking whether they again could place her in the little old village on the banks of the Ohio. At once a reply came, welcoming us back—and mother "would not again be obliged to nurse the aged and the sick."

Arriving in Economy we were added to the Breichle

household. The Breichle family was composed of Mr. and Mrs. Breichle and their teen-age son Rudolph. The elder Breichle was employed in the Society's tannery, and his son was apprenticed in the blacksmith-shop. Little do I remember of this household because we soon moved into another house, and not long after that we became a part of the Geier household. There were only two people in this "family"—Brother Sylvestus Geier, the Society's tinsmith, book-binder and painter, and Magdalena Bamesberger. Sylvestus was very kind and patient in teaching me the rudiments of his trades. Sister Magdalena had long been regarded as difficult to live with; Brother Sylvestus seems to have been the only one to tolerate her peculiarities. Of course my mother, too, had her peculiarities, and both women were sharp-tongued. Though for a time life moved placidly along, there soon developed that exasperating condition described by the German proverb—"no house is big enough for two women." Dear Brother Sylvestus was happy as could be during the first days of household peace and unity—a happiness destined soon to be replaced with sadness as the squabbling from day to day increased in violence.

Soon the Trustees, ever wary to avoid disharmony, told my mother to move up the street into part of a big frame double dwelling. By this time the Society had a number of hired-hands of both sexes, scattered among the various families. They were referred to as "Kostgaenger" or boarders. Our Kostgaenger was Bill Kocher, the sawyer at the Society's sawmill. Because his job required expert care and judgment, he received twenty or twenty-five dollars a month in addition to his board rather than the customary wage of twelve or fifteen dollars.

Here we lived in peace and quiet until I was about ten years old—when Brother Andreas Kotrba, the boss blacksmith, began his pilgrimages to our house to induce my mother to become his housekeeper. The present head of domestic affairs in his family, Christiana Aschinger, was sickly and other help was unsatisfactory. So finally, in accordance with the pleadings of Andreas, we moved once more. The Kotrba family consisted of Andreas Kotrba, August Grueninger ("der kleine August" because he was the most diminutive adult of the Society), Sister Christiana, Benjamin Loeffler a lad aged thirteen, and a hired-girl. Of all my "family" experiences at Economy, this was perhaps the most memorable. Sister Christiana, a kind, good-natured, easy-going affable soul, soon took to her bed and departed this life.

"The little August," the Society's dwarf and one of the shoemakers, had an immense forehead, a full heavy black beard, and carried one shoulder much higher than the other. This caricature of a man, like so many Harmonists, had musical aspirations, also he professed to play the violin and the trumpet. The poor fellow used no system in his violin efforts, and his clawing and sliding of fingers, plus the fervent sawing of his bow, invoked from Brother Andreas the terse understatement, "The Little August is again searching for tones." To the accompaniment of this searching his whole physiognomy became a living contortion. Finally practice on this instrument was vetoed by everybody. Happily he discovered that blowing the trumpet terrified the rats, so whenever rodents made their appearance "Gabriel's understudy" from cellar to attic brought into play the trumpet.

Brother Andreas was an outstanding Harmonist. Muscular and heavily constructed, he held two offices, namely that of boss of the blacksmith-shop and that of village constable. Of course not a single member of the Society ever did anything to call for the presence of a constable; he was elected solely to look after offending "outsiders." Andreas' prowess was proverbial in the community, and it was confidently believed he could break a man in two should occasion call for such action. Besides, he had an indescribably heavy tread that seemed to set the earth atremble. This tread I set about to imitate. Soon I discovered that shoes several sizes too large would do the trick. Thus equipped I achieved with diligent effort something of an echo of Andreas' thudding walk—a style that other small boys quickly affected. You may be sure the shoemakers could not understand why suddenly the little boys' feet had grown so big.

Deaths in the Society were taken as a matter of course —even the death of beloved Trustee Romeli Baker created a sorrow that was of but short duration.

Came October 28, 1871—a day when hearts were stirred to inmost depths by the news of Bennie Loeffler's death, after an illness of only a few days. He was the first youth in years to be claimed by the "Grim Reaper"— and he was a "Loeffler"; thus through his sister and his three brothers, four families were affected directly. Indeed it was a time of sorrow that struck a deeper note than any we had ever experienced. To Bennie's funeral flocked old and young; and eyes that had been dry for years, were bathed anew in tears. Even Andreas Kotrba, man of iron, gave way.

But whatever the parting meant to others, it was I who was most concerned. Between Bennie and me there existed bonds of more than brotherhood—our relationship was that of a Jonathan and a David (1 Sam. 18) "I am distressed for thee my brother Jonathan, very pleasant hast thou been to me." Indeed, the perusal at that time, of the history of Jonathan and David, proved strongly comforting.

Yet, wounds however deep, soon heal. The healing balm at this time, was the arrival of Albert Linnenbrink, a boy of my age. Albert was the youngest of nine children of Doctor Linnenbrink—former physician of the Society. The widow Linnenbrink wanted Albert to have the advantage of learning the German language and the benefit of the Economy discipline. She appealed to Henrici, who in turn appealed to my mother—soon Albert came and was installed in Bennie's place. My mother took him fully to heart and at times, to my chagrin, discriminated in his favor.

I recall a winter evening in the Kotrba family circle, when, after Albert and I had "finished our lessons," my mother directed me to study the Bible. Soon Albert and I became so deeply absorbed in the Good Book that we failed to notice my mother's furtive movements. Slipping up behind me to scrutinize what we were reading, she suddenly boxed my ears . . . "'Tis a pity you can't find something better than that", said she. We were reading the "detective" story of Susanna and Daniel as narrated in the Apocrypha—a case of stolen sweets to us. Methinks I saw a merry twinkle in Andreas' eye. Life in the Kotrba family was seldom without interest. At the corner of our house stood one of the two "community pumps," where one half of the community got its drinking water as well as its share of "small talk." For these same things the other half patronized the "Rapp pump" at the Great House. In those days menageries and circuses traveled by wagon—the elephants and camels afoot. The animals insisted on being watered here; which forced the keepers to long exertions at pumping, which in turn resulted in expletives from the keepers of such lurid and variegated profanity as never smote upon my ear—before or since.

145

The story was often told how Father Rapp, instead of dogs for companions, chose a wolf and a bear. He trained these animals to follow him about, and—well, this is where his showmanship asserted itself—to frighten the wits out of strangers and in general to prove his power over beasts as well as over men. This wolf-and-bear affair lasted until one day when the beasts proceeded to attack some women who were pumping water at the Rapp pump. Luckily some men, on the way home from the hayfield, armed with forks, forced the animals away. But, much as he disliked it, Rapp had to do away with his strange pets.

Pursuant to the Weingaertner instruction in water colors, I executed an amateur attempt at still life. It attracted considerable attention. Henrici heard of it and came to see it. Finding that Albert Linnenbrink also had artistic inclination Henrici proceeded to furnish us with progressive drawing-lessons and the necessary materials to develop whatever talent we possessed in this direction.

Along about this time the boys took to making and flying kites. Always ambitious to outshine or outdo others, I proceeded to make a mammoth sixteen-foot kite. In the ripping in two of a long scantling, I inadvertently got my left thumb under the ripsaw—off came a half-inch of nail and flesh. Hurt as it might, there was the mitigating fact that my mother was ill in bed, else would there come to me a hurt on a bigger end than that of thumb.

At the Kotrba public corner we got glimpses of all the life from the outer world that came to Economy. The seedy looking organgrinder and his monkey garbed in red flannel, and importuning our contribution with a tiny tambourine, at intervals made their rounds . . . though generally disappointed in the lack of real money. Or there might come a Pole with his dancing bear, singing with raucous voice and melancholy intonation—

146

Grze zelony majem
Lank otkryte tlo . . .
"In the merry May-time, when the flowers bloom." . . .

The bear would do a sidewise lumbering dance, then go through tricks dictated by his master. When the hat was passed the answer was generally, "Wir haben kein Geld." And it was true—the community's economic system consisting of production and exchange of commodities, there was no need for money.

In my early youth the great Van Amburg with his circus and menagerie exhibited at Sewickley. In Economy's earlier years such shows came there direct, this being the first important stop west of Pittsburgh, but later the circus center had moved five miles southward—to Sewickley. Immense posters and glowing handbills announced the coming of the show. So, now many of us traveled forth to our rival community to behold "the greatest animal trainer ever known" and all his wonders of wonders.

Sewickley at that time had become Pittsburgh's aristocratic suburb. Sewickleyans naturally took just pride in their community. To such an extent was this the case, that some seemed to adopt a patronizing air toward the rest of the world. The story was told of one of the town's respected ministers who, in conducting a funeral service, so far forgot himself that he said "the departed has gone to a better place." Well, after such concession there was only one course left for him—resign his charge and embark for other parts! Joking aside—Sewickley was the home of many outstanding western Pennsylvanians.

But we of Economy looked patronizingly not only on the world at large, but also on Sewickley. My mother's experience in the outside world was not unique. We all felt as she did, that "Everything in the world outside was

147

perhaps all right enough in itself, but it was not like Economy." We had all the advantages, and besides, a highly integrated collective fellowship and an unequalled spiritual life. The old folks with one accord always referred to Sewickley as Sewickleyville, which by some was understood as a deliberate minimization of the town since as far back as 1855 the borough had discarded its swaddling raiment, "ville."

Often one or more of Sewickley's superior beings, in splendid equipage, would drive through our streets, perhaps descend to visit the Great Garden or to linger at the old inn for supper or a glass of lager or wine. But when we went to the circus at Sewickley, we went *tout ensemble*, and in holiday spirit,

> *The show was therefore double-bill*
> *Two birds with one stone we would kill,*
> *Van Amburg and Sewickleyville!*

The relative isolation in which we lived, and the fact that money did not circulate in Economy, made my mother's yearly shopping expedition to Pittsburgh an important event. On such occasions I got my first knowledge of capitalistic methods of living. The stores were not operated like ours; at Economy things were picked out and handed over, while in Pittsburgh one looked and looked, and ended by haggling over prices; then my mother would hand over a greenback and receive perhaps a number of bills in return. Having no conception what this was all about, I was greatly puzzled at the storekeepers- returning several pieces of money in exchange for one. Those were the paper-money days of five, ten, twenty-five and fifty cent "shinplasters."

Yet for all our natural isolation from the world outside, we were always fairly well informed of the significant current events. I well remember how the Franco-Prussian War of 1870-71 roused the community to a high pitch. These people still clung to the traditions of their "Vater-land." When France, regarded generally as a dissipated and immoral nation, declared war on Germany, the good people of Economy, though far from the scene of battle, were full of resentment; and great was the rejoicing when news came of German superiority and victory. One must remember that Napoleon I was still deeply resented by the old folks, for his campaigns had devastated their home-land, and his conscription of their forebears in Germany had often driven them to prison, exile or other fates. The very name of Bonaparte roused their ire, and when Napoleon I regained the throne, Frederick Rapp had written, "Would that Heaven had decreed the old snake's destruction." (Though the quiet peaceful Harmonists sincerely loved America, supported the Union, and held high the principles of American freedom, no amount of propaganda could have persuaded them that by the time of World War I, Germany had so deteriorated and atheistic France had so improved as the American daily press of that time made it appear. One source of satis-faction to me, during those hysterical days of 1914-1918, was that these peaceful, harmless people, who had contrib-uted much to the building of our nation, were all at rest in the quiet little cemetery, for all of them would have been under the ban, perhaps doomed to imprison-ment).

Economy people kept in close contact with neighbors on farms adjoining Economy lands and in nearby towns. Several of their neighbors were surprisingly alert and cosmopolitan in spite of their backcountry existence. There were the Stoners, McPhersons, Macrums, Leisys, Bergmans, Ehmans, Thirets, and Hayses. These and others

149

came to Economy on festal days to listen to the splendid music and to join the festivities. They always had a pleasant word for us. Some, of course, were not quite so agreeable. On a nearby farm, for example, lived Mary Kelly—old Katzen-Marie we used to call her, for she accumulated all the cats she could find—dozens of them. It was disagreeable, to say the least, to visit the old spinster surrounded as she was with the vicious, spitting cats. But with the other neighbors we visited freely and whenever the spirit moved us.

Though some intercourse with the outside world was always maintained, the expression "draussen in der Welt" (out in the world) was a by-word familiar to all, calculated to stress the beauties of our prosperous, secure, communal way of life. We did not exactly disparage the outside world; we only viewed it comparatively, namely the security and happiness that was ours, with the insecurity and misery that prevailed beyond our borders. Truthfully, we had every reason to appreciate the superior conditions under which we lived and worked. Was not the Press, then as now, filled with the woes of mankind—unemployment and starvation, epidemics, city slums, robbery and murder, wars and rumors of wars, wickedness and immorality? Economy, indeed, was it not like an oasis in a burning desert, standing aloof from all this journalistic din of suffering and of crime . . . a home of plenty and of peace, a tabernacle of the elect?

We of the Kotrba household were especially well located to watch the "come-and-go" of outsiders. Across the street was the hotel barn, and diagonally across the inn itself. At almost any time we could witness something worthy of note. Economy was always famous for its hospitality, and the hotel was the centerpoint of this virtue. It was, in fact, a rule of the Society that no one should come to Economy and be left destitute of food and shelter. Of course, word of this got abroad among the perennial knights of the road, and every evening a procession of tramps, often numbering thirty or more, appeared in squads of twos or threes to ring the innkeeper's bell and to await the appearance of Brother Daniel Schreiber, master of the establishment.

Directly Daniel would appear, stand a moment in the doorway, and with judicial mien look down on the motley lot of pilgrims. Thereupon ensued the usual colloquy:

"You been here before? And you? And you?" said he, pointing to the different ones.

"No, O no, never," they chorussed.

"Why don't you stay at home," Brother Daniel counters.

"We haven't got any home."

"Why haven't you got any home?" Daniel perseveres.

Sundry reasons of a stock character were advanced; the tramps, knowing beforehand what would be the catechism, had the answers ready. Finally Daniel followed through with a lecture on man's duty, to labor, to save, to found a home, to live peaceably with one's fellowman, and so on. No matter how many groups appeared, these questions had to be propounded and answered before the good man led the way to the corner and sent the vagrants to the "tramp-auberge" across the way. Here they received supper, lodging and breakfast.

It was thus, that far and wide, Economy became known as "Tramp's Paradise." Better entertain a hundred unworthy ones than to turn away one who is worthy, was the Harmonist sentiment.

The personnel of the hotel was in itself remarkable. Since only they came in constant contact with the outside world, they were chosen with considerable circumspection. Joseph Goetz, rolypoly with a jovial round face topped with white curls, a jolly disposition and the spryness of a cricket, was a prince among landlords. When visitors familiar to him appeared, he flooded them with greetings and questions, almost taking them in his arms. The land-lady was Simira Hoehr—"stately enough for an empress," beautifully statuesque, as well poised and dignified a woman as I have ever seen. Her name was often linked with that of Jonathan Lenz, splendid specimen of man-hood and big of heart, and many would whisper that they were affinities. Certainly her striking figure and splendid mental poise corresponded well with Jonathan's hand-some, muscular body and his clear, wholesome, sparkling intellect. (They sleep now side by side in the silent cemetery beneath the apple trees.) Andy Oestreicher, the peglegged hostler, for whom I climbed into the hay mow to gather eggs; David, the friendly waiter; rosy, wrinkled, blind, but cheerful Melena; Rosina, the cham-ber-maid and other helpers—all contributed their share to the quaint, unique atmosphere of the old village inn.

In those days a Mr. Shiras was the star boarder at the hotel. He was neither a member of the Society nor a hireling, he dressed more expensively than anyone else in the community, and wonder of wonders he never worked. In this respect, Mr. Shiras was something of a phenomenon. In previous years he had been a successful brewer, and when age crept upon him he came to Econ-omy to retire. Well mannered, well read, kindly, George Shiras the elder, personified the dignified, affable "gentle-man of the old school." In his long daily walks, dressed in Prince Albert coat and high silk hat, he contrasted greatly with the humble folk who labored in the shops and fields. Yet all admired his simple way of life. We little fellows were at his beck and call, for he was a true disciple of Isaac Walton, and we vied in supplying him with bait. His name has been preserved in Pittsburgh and the Nation through his son George II, in his day an Associate Justice of the United States Supreme Court; and the two grandsons—staunch attorney Winfield H., and the famous student photographer of wild life, George III.

In the 1860's and 1870's there were still a number of interesting characters among the Harmonists. Some there were who, though not actual leaders of the community, nevertheless helped to give it a characteristic tone or social atmosphere. There were those of philosophical trend for instance—hardy workers, humble, devoted to the principles of the community. Such was Brother John Bessahn, one of the carpenters (and our carpenters were real craftsmen). I well remember the sound advice he gave me in my earliest years; "Whatever you do, do it as well as possible." Brother John Georg Bauer, responsible for the steam-engine which ran the laundry, the machine-shop, and in the fall the cider-press, was still another of this type of genius. He was well read, intelligent, calm and dignified; one of the best mechanics; also a capable musician, playing the bass viol in the orchestra and being one of the "Vorsaenger" in the church. In the repetition of a tale some of the members might make mistakes. Not so Bauer—anything he said was taken as absolutely correct.

Chief among Economy philosophers was Friedrich Eckensperger, school-teacher of the early years. He was a man of considerable learning. Scripture, of course, was plentyfully quoted at Economy, especially that of Solomon the Wise; but I honestly believe that even Solomon had to play second-fiddle to Eckensperger. Besides, Brother Friedrich was what people call "a character." The Trustees, seeing he was advancing rapidly in age, relieved him of the onerous duty of teaching, and appointed him to take charge of the hotel-bar and stable. At that time, members of the Society did not receive whiskey as a beverage, but only as a medicine upon doctor's prescription, though it was on sale to strangers. The story was told of Eckensperger that, just after he had taken over these duties, Brother Jacob Wohlgemuth decided to try out the new bartender. One morning Jacob appeared before Eckensperger, bemoaning his aching stomach and calling for a "bitters." Though he got his portion he returned again on the two following days. On the third day Eckensperger drawing his imposing figure to its full height, blurted, "Listen to me, Wohlgemuth, no bitters is also bitter! Good morning!" Eckensperger, accustomed to give orders to Johnnie or to Gretchen and no longer able to receive orders at the bar or at the stable, one morning stalks into the store and throwing down a bunch of keys, tells Trustee Baker "this means that I have quit, I am accustomed to command—not to obey."

Another of our schoolmasters was a small man of good education and fine address, Paul Wagner, who had wandered into Economy. He had risen from store clerk to teacher, and meantime was preparing himself to become the Society's doctor. Though he may have been a capable teacher, his school methods are not a pleasant memory for me—with Wagner it seemed to be a case of

> *Count that day lost whose setting sun*
> *Marks not considerable whipping done—*

and I seemed to be his special target. Now I never missed my lessons, so he used all sorts of methods to place me in the wrong. Later I learned that the man was an adventurer pure and simple. His ambition was to become head of the Society, and to this end with the aid of Brother Louis Pfeil, was quietly working among the members. Trustee

Baker was growing old and feeble; Henrici as Junior Trustee was next in line, so if Henrici could be ousted, Wagner would have clear sailing. Somehow my mother got next to the plot and carried the news to Henrici . . . Wagner was to have joined the Society at the next Harmonie Fest; instead, he went to the railway ticket-office and purchased a fare for parts unknown.

That there was a wholesome respect for Henrici is not to be denied. Henrici never minced matters, always called a spade a spade, or worse. After the death of George Rapp in 1847, Henrici preached for fifteen months; then at a Wednesday evening church-meeting, Brother Louis Pfeil took unto himself the role of chief spokesman, and in his Swabian brogue, assailed Henrici: "This is now no longer to be endured the way you blatter; we feel as though we sat here in our shirt tails!" Henrici, driven into a corner, lost his head and finally proclaimed that the whole method of dual leadership of the Society was wrong—a statement that caused a major sensation, and led Henrici to resign. A day or two later Henrici was missing; he could not be found anywhere. Jonathan Lenz, one of the Elders and boss of the wagon shop, followed an intuition and found Brother Jacob at Father Rapp's grave, busy with lamentations. Jonathan soon persuaded Henrici to come and live with him. This done, Henrici devoted himself to assisting at the silk mill and studying the French language. In course of time finding the Society's business proceeding as if nothing had happened, he submitted an apology and request for reinstatement to the Board of Elders. The Elders readily granted forgiveness, adding that since they had never accepted his resignation, there was no need for any action.

But to return to the schoolmasters, I must not fail to mention Brother Jacob Bitzer—"der Bitzer" to the community and simply "Yawcob" to his pupils—for he was portly, dignified and impressive; yet his education above the "common branches" was self-acquired. Not a great teacher, perhaps, but under his surveillance what we learned we learned thoroughly; and his gentle but firm direction in regard to morals, manners, and character must have made a lasting impression.

After "der Bitzer" came Caspar Henning. Whereas Bitzer had been satisfied with his knowledge and attainments, young Caspar was ever seeking to expand his fund of learning. Their formal education had been about the same, but Caspar keenly felt his shortcomings. His very superior intellect and ambition led him to gravitate toward the more highly educated people of the outside world, and he would have left the Society had it not been for his ailing father. Being by far the youngest of the members, he did not feel at ease among the older men; and, because of the dignity of his office, he could not freely fraternize with his students—a situation this, that left him practically without companionship. Though in his earlier years virile, good-natured, jovial and full of hope and aspiration, this isolation in later years made him both cynical and misanthropic.

Caspar's love and search for learning was not a new thing in the Society. In the early days the Society could boast of experts in mathematics, chemistry, physics, men who were conversant with the Latin, Greek, French, German and English languages. Some had been trained in the best German university traditions. Learning among the Harmonists was thus at its apex in the early days. But the clearing of three forest areas and the building of three beautiful communities, left little time for academic education. The younger generations therefore received instruction only in the common branches.

With the passing of the old patriarchs and sisters much of the "old" passed likewise. Since my arrival in 1862 up to 1871 there had been sixty-seven funerals. Each year some eight or nine of the "old stock" passed on to their peaceful, unmarked resting places in God's acre. And, as less and less remained to carry on the labor, more and more hirelings filled their shoes. With the introduction of this competitive element into the communism of Economy, the prosperity of the Commune henceforth gradually declined.

Though death was regarded as a distinct community and family loss, it was taken philosophically. Most of the members, because of their simple and well-balanced life, had achieved a ripe old age before death visited them. Life's end was a natural and expected event.

Now and then a procession of plainly dressed men might be seen following a narrow hearse bearing a curious hexagonal casket down the grassy street out to the "Friedhof," there to gather around the open grave, to sing a hymn and listen gravely to the sermon and the prayer and to drop a flower. Thus there was added one more mound, unmarked except perhaps by a shrub or floral plant placed there by some particular friend. . . .

Equality was to be practiced even in death; hence the elders attempted to equalize the attendance at funerals. The first experiment consisted in having the sexton count off twenty-four men from the cortege—these alone to perform the last sad rites. This method, though at first successful, soon proved a fiasco—some good folks being escorted to the grave by a mere half dozen men. A plan of issuing invitations also proved a failure. Having learned their lesson, the Elders henceforth left the attendance to an all-wise Providence.

Economy also had its Memorial Day—the annual procession to the Friedhof in the springtime when all was brilliantly green or evolving into color, and apple blossom perfume filled the air. The whole Society clad in the festive silken garb of their own manufacture, to the dirge intoned by the band, marched solemnly to God's Acre—there to listen to the measured words, for instance, of kindly Romeli Baker. Having been with the Society from its inception, he could speak authoritatively and from the heart. An appropriate number by the band, the singing of a hymn by the gathered throng, a short address and prayer by Romeli, constituted the service. Thereupon the band again fell into line; and, followed by the community, marched on through the orchard to another burial ground. This consisted of a large mound where Indian Chiefs or members of a prehistoric race were buried—so tradition had it.

Here followed more music by the band, speaking by the leaders, singing of appropriate vocal selections by young and old. At last the homeward march led by the band, playing not funeral music but the liveliest of airs.

Music, as a matter of course, was always of importance in the social life of the community. The Society's orchestra founded in early days made excellent headway for many years. But in the 1860's, as the players grew old, a brass band was organized by young Dr. Benjamin Feicht. But when he and his brother Henry in 1865 left the Society to take unto themselves wives, the cornet chairs were left vacant. Rivalry arose as to who should be the leader—a rivalry that boded ill for the embryonic organization. Mostly composed of lusty young fellows, the band at all times had its rivalries. I recall the incident of a concert at which Gustaf Schumacher's tuba failed to respond and he made the discovery that a jealous predecessor had crammed a towel well down into the tuba's bell.

When for one reason and another it became apparent that the band would not be able to play at the ensuing Harvest Home, the old men of the erstwhile orchestra were coaxed or bullied into action by the women. It seems that the old men, playing the old familiar numbers, had not forgotten the fine art. In any case, the orchestra performed so nobly that many said that they preferred the orchestra to the band. But lusty young bucks of the band decided to nip this sentiment in the bud. One night a little later, some of them entered the music room and smashed to pieces the double bases, 'cellos, and bassoons. (To this day some of the fragments are preserved). Although the chief instigators were given their walking papers, the occurrence marked the end of the orchestra.

However, the band continued to function but it was something of a disappointment. Hence the Trustees, always careful to encourage music in every conceivable way, hired as teacher Professor Jacob Rohr of Pittsburgh. Rohr was an expert teacher and cornetist and, being an Alsatian, a happy combination of German thoroughness and French finesse. When the band was thus revived, the trustees purchased new instruments. Soon even a second band, composed of younger boys, was developed. In this "cheese band," as it was opprobriously called, I was started as second alto horn; in a short time I rose to first cornetist and boy leader of the "kleine Musikanten." We even progressed to a point where we performed at some of the Sunday evening garden concerts. Alas, it was soon after this triumphant innovation that my mother forbade me to play the cornet. Some misguided soul had convinced her that blowing a wind instrument was injurious to a child of nine years. No amount of pleading, even on the part of Henrici, Lenz, and Professor Rohr, could alter her conviction. This separation from my cornet left me disconsolate for weeks . . . Soon after I left my post, the junior band disbanded and most of its members merged with the "grosse Musikanten."

Throughout the years the instrumental music of Economy was justly famous. At our concerts and festivals, neighboring communities, Pittsburgh and other areas were represented in the audience.

The programs contained the standard works of the classic composers such as Haydn, Mozart, Beethoven, Weber, Rossini, Wagner, and Gounod. In the early days —1820 to 1832—a concert record was kept by the leader, J. Christoph Mueller, and he jotted down criticisms for future reference. Other critics from Pittsburgh and its environs often attended, and lauded the performances. Since music always filled such an important niche in the life of the community, we youngsters had a long and important tradition to uphold.

Regarding my part in the musical efforts in Economy, it will be recalled that at the age of seven years I attracted attention as an accordionist, at the age of eight years with the "kleine Musikanten" had played the alto horn and the cornet. At the age of twelve I was studying the violin, and Henrici saw to it that I was given lessons by our "Herr Feldwebel," a former sergeant in the army of one of the German states. I do not recall his name but he was a man of unusual refinement and artistic talents. Later I studied the clarinet, organ and piano. This, as will be seen, in after years to me, proved of inestimable worth.

In speaking at length of the instrumental organizations, it goes without saying that music played a dominant role in our community church, and vocal music surpassed the instrumental in importance. Sometimes the chorus joined the band or orchestra in concerts, especially in the rendition of cantatas. Two pianos with organ or reed attachments stabilized the congregational singing; in my day Henrici played the one and Gertrude Rapp the other.

Some of the hymns used by the congregation were compositions of members of the Society. George and Frederick Rapp composed a number, others added to the stock, until a whole hymnal of several hundred pages was collected and published by the Society. In the early days, however, when Dr. Mueller assumed musical leadership, he had some of the members hum the tunes which he in turn transcribed to paper. The results at times were astonishing. Later, Henrici corrected some of the glaring vagaries. One Sunday Baker chose one of the revised hymns. Henrici and Gertrude played it the new way, while the congregation, having no written music before them, sang it the old way. Confusion—then Baker turned to the organ loft, shouted in his Swabian dialect:

"Hei, Jakob, was machts den du?"

Jacob arose and in purest High German politely explained, "You see, Romeli, these hymns are not properly arranged; this one, for instance, I even had to put into correct time. (He used the German word "Takt," which also stands for "step.")

"Ei was," retorted Romeli, "What do we know about takt—play it the way we are accustomed."

The title of the hymn was "And entire nations still are marching, in night and darkness round about." Henrici, who had a fine sense of humor, at once took his pencil and added, "aber nicht im Takt" (but not in step).

Henrici and Gertrude at the organs were backed by a number of important personages—we called them "Vorsaenger" or leading singers, three women and five men at that time, but they were growing old and their voices no longer possessed their former resonance and strength. It so happened that at a time when young and old were gathered together in practicing an oratorio, Brother Louis Pfeil interrupted the proceedings by pointing at me, proclaiming that I had a wonderful voice "just what we need to help lead the singing in Sunday church." Willie Wagner was also chosen for this bulwarking of the Vor-saenger. Henrici added his approval of the plan. Thus we became "the nightingales," (as someone dubbed us) and proud as peacocks you may well believe.

Economy church services were, to outsiders, always an interesting spectacle. For instance, the bells were not rung until *after* the lay members had assembled and taken their proper pews. The women occupied the westerly half of the church, and the men the other half. Seven elders occupied the front bench on the speaker's right, and the prominent "foreladies," like Simira Hoehr, the Frank sisters and others, the opposite front bench. Newcomers, of course, at first were seated in the rear. At the age of six years however, I had managed to wriggle halfway toward the front. No, it was not the pulpit, which I was destined to occupy a quarter of a century later, that attracted me, but one George Kirschbaum, a young man, stalwart and handsome, who was always especially kind to me.

But let us attend a typical church service. While the bells are ringing—in sweeps Gertrude, closely followed by Baker and Henrici. The Senior Trustee files to the right and ascends to the pulpit as Gertrude and Henrici to the left, ascend to the organ loft. The service opens with the singing of some stanzas from one of the Society's hymns. After a short prayer comes the sermon, preached in sitting posture—a desk being used instead of a pulpit. On said desk, particularly in winter-time, is a bouquet of flowers. After the sermon the remaining stanzas of the hymn are sung, whereupon comes the benediction—which means that we are dismissed. Are we—and how! The woman nearest the exist rushes forth; wide open flings the double doors, through which the throng of women simply pours. A casual visitor, aghast, exclaims "is there a fire"—"Oh, no," he is informed, "the rush is in deference to the Trustees, who follow immediately and whose egress must not be impeded."

One day in the summer of 1873, Henrici came to my mother. He had been talking with the Reverend Mr. W. G. Taylor, principal of the Phillipsburg Soldiers Orphans School at Water Cure Postoffice, now Monaca. When the Reverend Mr. Taylor had heard that Johnnie Duss was the orphan of a soldier in the Union Army, he pointed out that my place was properly in his school. Henrici told my mother he disliked to see me go, but he knew the value of superior educational advantages and would leave the matter to our decision.

One can fancy how my young imagination ran riot with such an opportunity. It sounded like a proposed journey to the moon, this going into "the world outside." After much argument pro and con, in which practically the whole community joined, it was decided that I should go. My own decision was in large part due to Caspar Henning's arguments—dear fellow, he himself had always wanted just such an opportunity.

So Little David Haufler took my measure for a new suit of clothes, Adam Geier made me a felt hat, and the "magnificent John Goetz" had his best shoemaker make me a beautiful pair of boots with red leather tops and copper toes. It was in July 1873 that, among much shedding of tears, I said goodbye to the good people of Economy.

7

Wandering in the Outside World (1874-1882)

WE YOUNGER FOLKS, isolated as we were within the boundaries of our own little world, often looked beyond Economy with longings to investigate the larger world outside. When distinguished visitors stopped, as they often did, at the community's hotel, or even when way worn hobos wandered in at eventide to ask for food and quarters, they brought a sense of adventure from beyond the boundaries of our 3000-acre plot which often kindled the fires of boyish imagination.

After Henrici proposed that I attend the Phillipsburg Soldiers Orphans School, a natural feeling of superiority helped me to assuage the pangs of breaking home ties. Was I not going into a new world, a big world of which I had dreamed but had never really known? . . .

Alas for human hopes and expectations! The big new world or part of it that I had hoped to see at Phillipsburg was very much smaller than that of Economy, and the happy visions I had conjured up proved but a snare and a delusion. At Economy, of acres to romp in and explore, we had three thousand; at Phillipsburg, we had but three. Inasmuch as the boys and girls attending the school were not permitted to leave the premises, my proposed investigation of the outside world resolved itself into an acquaintance with the narrow quarters of a dormitory, dining room, schoolhouse, bathhouse, woodshed, carpenter shop and a two-acre playground. For this tiny world had I left the wide open spaces of a beautiful 3000-acre tract, a charming community with its wonderful economic system, and people and playmates I understood and loved.

The property of my new domain was owned by the principal, the Reverend Mr. W. G. Taylor. It was on a low level, completely encircled by the village of Phillips-burg and the hills paralleling the Ohio River. It was shaped like a rightangled triangle. Few outsiders entered its boundaries, few students left them during the term.

Yet for all its narrow limits, the school was in a sense a state institution, and a gathering place for different kinds of young people. The fact that I was "an Econo-mite"—made of me an object that elicited both wonder and curiosity. Moreover, an interesting corps of teachers added to the circumstances which combined to make my three years at the school a valuable and interesting experience.

It was during vacation time that I first arrived at my new destination. Reverend Taylor had suggested to Henrici that it would be well for me to enter the institution while the 160 pupils were absent on the six-weeks' summer vacation, thus enabling me better to accustom myself to the surroundings and to become acquainted with him and his family.

The chief of our little fortress of learning was, of course, the estimable Reverend Taylor, a Presbyterian D. D., pious, upright, just and keen minded. Like Henrici, he believed fervently in the maxims of Solomon. As a strict discipli-narian he did not believe in many punishments, but wherever necessity forced him, he sought to make a lasting impression. The boys in the dormitories preferred their chastisements from anyone but him. Apparently Old

Taylor, as they dubbed him, had a powerful right arm, though I cannot speak from personal experience. At times, to win the coöperation of the boys, Taylor employed the shrewdest psychology. He won me heart and soul by his oft repeated and enthusiastic references to Economy and the Harmonists during his after-table lectures and other talks, describing their sterling virtues and amazing accomplishments. He had been particularly pleased with Trustee Romelius Baker, and invariably pointed out that he should have been president of the United States. In some respects Taylor's administration of the school was probably influenced by the Economy example. Our table fare was very simple, but prepared with scrupulous care. Then too, as at Economy, the boys and girls had to take part in productive work—engendering at least a semblance of Economy coöperation.

The family consisted of Rev. Taylor, his wife, their three sons and three daughters. My arrival during vacation time enabled me to become acquainted with the family and to learn more intimately the ways of the institution from them than would have otherwise been possible.

But when the students flocked back from vacation, I had a very trying time. Unluckily for me, among the industries sponsored by the Harmony Society at Beaver Falls was a cutlery factory which had resulted in considerable loss to the Society. After trying various remedies to no avail, the management decided to import Chinese workmen. Naturally the townspeople were up in arms. The Chinese, importing most of what they consumed, spent but little money in the town. I recall the delegation of 100 men from Beaver Falls that early in the 1870's came to Economy and protested against this employing of Chinese workers. Whereupon Henrici soon got rid of the Orientals. The subject is worthy of a chapter for which, alas, I have not space. But the resulting antagonism against both the Chinese and the Harmony Society had entered the hearts of the large contingent of soldiers' orphans who hailed from this vicinity. And, to add to my difficulties, Adam Geyer, Economy's hatter, had fitted me with what he termed a very stylish hat—an unusually low crowned one, which very much resembled the hats in vogue among the Chinese.

When the Beaver Falls boys spied my hat and found that I was from Economy, an avalanche of vitriolic nicknames descended upon me. On the instant I became John Chuck, John Chinaman, John Chicken Thief, John Rat, etc. Since in Economy nicknames had always been pet names applied in a friendly or affectionate spirit, this vengeful application was something radically different and hard to bear.

This, however, was not my only grievance. In resolving to deport myself according to the rules laid down by the school, I laid myself open to persecution by some who noted that I would neither fight nor tell on anyone who committed a transgression. A few mean and cowardly spirits thus were able to make my life miserable.

Another circumstance that prompted my fellow students to make me feel uncomfortable was my noticeable German accent. A hasty examination had placed me in the third grade, though at Economy I had read the fifth reader with ease. Having listened to the efforts of the others with disgust, when my turn came, I promptly rose and reeled off—

"*A zuberzilious Nabop uv de Easd . . .*"

when came a roar of laughter. Even the teacher could not suppress her amusement. "Never mind," she said, "he may soon surprise you all." Her prophecy came true, for in a short time I was placed in the fifth grade.

The efficient daily program of the school left little open time. Each day was divided into five parts: One part, school, one part work, one part study, two parts playtime —fifteen minutes in the morning and fifteen minutes in the afternoon. The four two-hour school periods lasted from 7:45 A.M. to noon, and from 1:00 P.M. to 5:15. But only the teachers attended the whole eight hours. For the students the program was so arranged that during every two-hour period one-fourth of the students were engaged in various forms of manual labor—on Doctor Taylor's farm, at the woodyard, in the laundry or at the bakery; while the girls attended to the chamber work, sewing and cooking. In the evening there were two study hours before bedtime, and the scholars gathered in the study hall where Miss Mary Chambers sedately and effectually presided.

Miss Mary was about ten years my senior, and a fair and blooming specimen of young womanhood. Of splendid dignity and poise, she took me captive, heart and soul. It seems that my diligent application to my studies was not so much for the noble sake of acquiring knowledge as it was to please my teacher. And, since the students were seated in the old-fashioned way, according to their behaviour, it was no wonder that I earned the farthermost seat. Miss Mary was just kind enough and stern enough to maintain almost perfect decorum; hardly ever was it necessary to admonish any of her pupils. I have seen other women teachers who maintained this same superior control over their charges.

I always had my work well prepared at the end of the study hour—it was a principle with me. But one night, I recall, I went to bed with a sinking heart. A problem in

Dean's Intellectual Arithmetic, used in the class taught by Miss Mary, had me completely confused. My rival classmate, David C. Reed, was also up the same tree, and though we compared notes, nothing resulted. He and the other members of the class somehow suspected that I had found the solution but selfishly refrained from passing it around. Assuring them this was not the case, we all took our places in class next day. Just as Miss Mary tapped the bell for class changes, the solution flashed through my mind. When the problem came before the class, I was the only one to raise my hand. The class looked thunderclouds at me. Even Miss Mary was startled, since none of her former pupils had ever solved this problem. Alas, having formed the habit of demonstrating it herself, to my disappointment she proceeded on her usual course, though I was quick enough to take part in the analysis.

Although Professor S. H. Piersol was known as principal of the school under the supervision of Doctor Taylor, he had wisely placed the major burdens of this office on Miss Mary. While she presided in the main school room, he was in other rooms hearing recitation classes. Like Miss Mary he was both kind and stern, and understood the students sympathetically. And I remember him as the embodiment of strength—moral, mental, physical—moreover, deeply humble and profoundly spiritual. I am afraid the likes of him and Miss Mary have become all too rare in the field of secondary education. They made an admirable couple, and, sometime after I had left the school, were united in wedlock; also they founded the Piersol Academy at Bridgewater, Pennsylvania.

Occasionally after study hours several of the teachers would corral me in their sitting room. Being an Economite my views about life sounded strange but to them the teachers loved to give ear. Apparently I was a side

169

show, offering them amusement, though at times they were seriously impressed. For in that day everyone knew about Economy in a general way and wanted to know more. Also there were the rumors of its tremendous wealth, of which not a dollar was in circulation at Economy. The Society's far-flung industrial holdings, its strange unworldly doctrines, its communistic regime and the periodical law suits, had made the people of Western Pennsylvania aware of something strange in their midst. Interested in me thuswise, the teachers were generally kind and generous toward me.

At one time I became aware of sly smiles and knowing looks among them, an undercurrent of whispers—all somehow concerning me. After a long while the cat got out of the bag at one of our night-sessions. Fate had played me a merry prank, for a love-note had been discovered in my handwriting. Now, though Doctor Taylor believed in the refining influence of co-education, love-letters were utterly taboo, and if discovered, were destined to be read before the entire school. Not wishing to humiliate me, however, the teachers had kept the matter to themselves. . . . The facts were that I had written a note to Ira Graham, a companion whom I instructed on the violin, asking him why he had suddenly refused to speak to me and telling him that I felt deeply hurt. We had been speedily reconciled, but someone had picked up the note and handed it to the teachers. Ira, however, had a sister named Ida, and some scamp had transformed the "r" into a "d!" The story is here told as a warning against partiality—which is always an error or an evil.

Life within the narrow confines of the school was not so very different from life at Economy. Sometimes, however, I got that hemmed-in feeling, as though I might be a favored prisoner. Though the most stringent rules laid down by Doctor Taylor forbade students to venture beyond the grounds and buildings, some of the boys took delight in slipping out to a village store for candy, to raid neighborhood orchards or to go nutting in nearby woods, ventures in which I had no part. To do so meant running the risk of losing my perfect record as to behavior. Also having to remain within the bounds of the grounds was no hardship—my previous life having been somewhat similarly confined and regimented. Here, as at Economy, each one had specific jobs to perform. Soon after I came to the school I had been given charge of the schoolrooms—sweeping and dusting the rooms, and cleaning, filling and trimming the kerosene lamps. Though heretofore such assignments were made by the month, I was continued on this job month after month. These chores were not only distasteful, but required too much time. Since the two-hour work period was consumed in taking care of the lamps, I had to spend the dinner-hour sweeping and dusting. Besides, I thought the swallowing of quantities of dust was injurying my health. One day, mustering up sufficient courage, I took my grievances to Doctor Taylor. Alas, my arguments did not impress him; at any rate he wished me for the time being to continue. . . . Sometime after the interview he was showing visitors through the institution. As the party came toward the schoolrooms, I could hear him descant on how clean everything was kept. Out of sight but within hearing distance, I heard him say, "You know, insurance companies are very particular about the handling of lamps, therefore I must guarantee that they are tended only by trustworthy persons. But I have a boy who is thoroughly reliable." My task henceforth seemed easier, and the dust no longer mattered.

But the Doctor's averment was not mere subtle flattery.

171

From the very beginning he had confidence in me; Henrici must have recommended me most highly. For instance, there were three divisions of the dormitory, and, as in the classes, quarters were assigned according to behaviour. At once I was placed at the head of "the holy of holies," the south wing occupied only by boys of best behaviour. Such division and regimentation in an educational institution will seem very old-fashioned to those believing in the theories of so-called individual expression of youngsters. But in that day it was taken for granted, and all my life had been lived not according to individual desires but according to communal needs.

Even so, we all were happy as vacation time drew nigh. When the sap in the trees began to rise and force the buds, as perfume of spring was in the air, the young blood in our veins coursed more freely and we longed for the close of another season of imprisonment. By Decoration Day one might notice the unexpressed feeling of expectation. On that day the soldiers' orphans made their annual pilgrimage to the cemetery at Beaver to decorate the graves of the soldiers. We marched from the school to the wharf, then away to Beaver. The Harmonists on these occasions always sent a wagon load of cut flowers for our purposes. All this was a kind of prelude to our six-weeks' summer vacation.

It was good to return to Economy, even though throughout the year I had kept in touch with the community—as when the Phillipsburg school would now and then receive a barrel of "schnitz" (quartered dried apples) or other good things to eat from Economy—donations in a sense accredited to me. When the great day arrived we all marched to the wharf, embarked first for Rochester on the ferryboat "Mary Campbell." At Rochester we entrained for our respective goals. I was soon whisked home on the train. Once there, proud of my uniform and soldierly appearance, I was roundly welcomed. Alas, my mother immediately discovered a scar on my forehead—the result of a stone-throwing duel across a high board fence at the school. She at once embarked upon a campaign of upbraiding that lasted throughout the vacation, though methinks that there was a certain degree of gladness in her to have me back alive. Vacation time was harvest time, so naturally I was busy from day to day in the hayfields, wheatfields, or at picking berries and gathering of fruit. The change from the schoolroom to outdoor life and coöperative manual labor was not only good for my health, but thoroughly enjoyable.

Attending the Phillipsburg school for only three years, this vacation came but twice.

On the twenty-second of February 1876 I became 16 years of age. The date meant departure from the school. As a rule the orphans looked forward expectantly to the day when they would be "of age"—to go their own sweet way into the larger world. But in my case something happened that was new. On good terms with the teaching staff and well satisfied with life at the institution, February 22 passed without my calling Doctor Taylor's attention to it. Some days later discovering the fact, he put forth extra efforts to have me fitted with a new suit of clothes and to dispatch me to Economy. To be thus ruthlessly hurried off somewhat hurt my feelings—a hurt that was not assuaged by the discovery that the State no longer paid my board.

Still, I left in high feather. At my last breakfast Doctor Taylor spoke to the whole school of my departure, and accorded me the most extravagant praise . . .

My return to Economy was opportune. William Goll

and Jacob Zimmerman, last of the brethren who had charge of the orchards and nurseries, had passed from this life, and the work was now in the hands of hired help. Because at the age of eight I had been apprenticed to Eusebius Boehm, the Society's expert in this field of endeavor, I was again placed in this employment. Much work was to be done. In the spring of my return, some four thousand one-year-old apple sprouts were to be grafted. Then too, the crab-apple orchard on the hilltop a mile east of the village was in disreputable condition, and I decided it needed a severe pruning. Adolf, the hired man who had been in charge and was now my assistant, agreed; but the farm and garden bosses held contrary opinions. Finally I decided to proceed regardless of them.

The orchard had never received so rigorous a trimming. Nearly two months it took us. At its completion the combined teams of the Society worked a week dragging the trimmings to the adjacent old stone quarry to be burned. John Scheid, the farm boss, and others loudly condemned the outrage we had perpetrated.

"And who was the Society's tree expert?" I parried.

"Eusebius Boehm, of course," was the usual answer.

"Very well," I said, "my method is the Boehm method; wait and see." Things finally quieted down, and the next year I had the satisfaction to see that orchard produce a crop that dumbfounded the community—all admitted that here was a yield beyond any that they had ever seen.

The four months after my return constituted one round of happy days. The old folks manifested their pleasure at having me back in the community circle, and I soon became an integral part of the village. My occupation as tree expert was wholly to my liking. In the band I was assigned to the position of solo alto horn, doubling now and then on the small snare drum, the playing of which

The Economy Hotel. Famous haven of hospitality.

Typical Economy dwelling. Here Nikolaus Lenau, famous German poet, was nursed back to health by the good sisters.

I had learned at Phillipsburg. I even had the most beautiful suit of clothes in Economy—my mother had it made for my confirmation—an event that had taken place in the German Lutheran Church at Phillipsburg after I had left the Soldiers Orphan School.

Alas, these happy days came to a sudden termination. My mother, whose health had somewhat failed, unexpectedly determined again to leave Economy. Convinced by former experiences that she could not be happy elsewhere in America, she decided to return to the Fatherland,—not to the place of her birth, but to the exclusive, renownedly religious village of Kornthal.

And so it came to pass that I really was to see the great, wide world. The train trip eastwardly at once impressed me—the majestic sweep of Horseshoe Curve on the Pennsylvania Railroad near Altoona, the beauty and luxuriance of Lancaster County, and finally the overpowering magnitude of New York, (though in 1876 Central Park was still in the suburbs).

We crossed on the "Donau," one of the North German Lloyd steamships, and after eleven uneventful days docked at Bremerhaven. From there we went by train to Bremen where we entrained for Kornthal.

Though not a communistic colony, Kornthal was a religious community. Everyone living there had to be above reproach. The community authorities permitted no one to settle there unless he bore the necessary credentials as to character and general worth, and was willing to live subject to the rules of church and community. Church services were held every night, and thrice on Sunday. To my mother this seemed to be an earthly paradise. She presented the credentials, with which Henrici had provided us, and we received permission to dwell within the sacred precincts of this exclusive and

175

pious village. We soon found living quarters with the family of Jacob Seher.

Before settling down to the quiet life of this community, we made excursions into the heart of Germany and even into western France. We journeyed to Effringen in the Black Forest to visit my father's brother and other relatives, and we visited my mother's brother, Gottlieb Kroll, on his farm near Marbach (where had lived the famous poet Schiller). On our several trips to Stuttgart we spent some time with a relative, Oswald Ottendorfer, a renowned architect. Finally we journeyed to Hoheneck, my mother's birthplace, to visit a granduncle. It was he who threatened to lock the door if his son did not return from the inn by ten o'clock. When the father proceeded to carry out his threat he found that the bibulous son had carried away the door.

These little journeys were indeed enlightening, but I had not a minute's peace. At the beginning of our ocean voyage fleas attacked me, causing infection followed by numerous boils, which caused me untold suffering and misery. I very much disliked the European railway compartment coaches—one could not change one's seat in spite of disagreeable company. On our little journeys there was much to be heard and seen—the superb military bands as at Stuttgart, the splendid German public parks and museums—though I was horrified by the brazen nudity of statues scattered everywhere.

At Economy my mother had often spoken of the Fatherland and of Wuerttemberg in particular—"there the meat is sweeter and more nutritious, and the fruit has a better flavor." Now she found that she had been mistaken. Even the Neckar River flowing past her birthplace disappointed her memory; instead of being broader than the Ohio, as she had described it, it was less than one-fourth such width. Disappointed in one thing after another, both of us soon grew tired of it all and we decided to return to America. Indeed, the itinerary of our European journey seemed to have been arranged for the sole purpose of speedily returning to America. Altogether we had been gone less than three months. My mother's dream of the Fatherland's superiority was quite banished from her mind by the time we embarked for New York. It was all very well in itself, "but it was not like Economy." . . .

En route from New York to Economy we met at Philadelphia my guardian, Jonathan Lenz, and a number of the Society's prominent men on their way to the U. S. Centennial. But we were so anxious to return to Economy that we continued our journey. After our arrival, Henrici came to greet us warmly, and the whole community manifested its pleasure at our return. Before we had left, many prophecies had been made to my mother: "You won't be gone long," "you will find no better place than Economy" . . . So now all joined the chorus: "I told you so!"

The Trustees had arranged a place for us with the Frank family. In my childhood days this family consisted of good Brother Eberhard Frank, a shoemaker, and his two charming sisters, Persida and Veronika, experts with the needle in the women's clothing shop. Now only Veronika remained as head of the Frank household. Karl Ulrich, Frederick Marquart, my mother and I, Hannah Mayer the servant girl, and a little girl called Hannah Seitz, constituted the rest of the household. Ulrich, a recent emigre from Wuerttemberg, was a curly-headed, handsome young man, a superior cabinet maker who soon became foreman of the cabinet shop. Because of his fine cultural background, heroic tenor voice, and splendid craftsmanship, he was soon prominent in community affairs. Though he was not a member of the Society, Henrici turned over to him the office of Sunday School teacher. He was one of the very few in Economy who achieved the honor of being called "Herr". Frederick Marquart, a lad of nineteen, who ten years earlier had saved me from a premature and watery grave, since then had acquired the tailor's trade but was now in charge of the community bakery. He too was competent and versatile, and with his baritone horn held an important position in the community band. Hannah Mayer was above the average in education and culture, and her sober, inscrutable countenance masked a spirit of humor and mischief which contributed not a little to our household joy. Our "school girl," twelve year old Hannah Seitz, helped with the women's work in house and garden while she attended school. I remember her as a sprightly little bud and a good pal . . . Upon the whole we were rather proud of our family, thus living and working in harmony.

It was always good to return to Economy. So now, in the late summer and autumn of 1876,—in the company of other men and women of the Commune, busy at gathering apples and potatoes, stripping sugar cane and shucking corn—I was again a happy harvester.

The garnering of the corn, like the grape or currant harvest, was something akin to a festival or community reunion. Farm hands went to the far fields, tore the ears from the stalk, and heaped them into little piles. Then came the gondola wagons, each with a driver and a "little boy." The driver scooped the corn into a basket and tossed it into the wagon bed, and the little boy emptied and returned it. When the wagonbed was full, the boy set up a row of ears around the top; this space was filled in, and then a second row set up, until a complete arch was made. Back came the great loads to the "Kornhof" each wagon stopping between two rows of cribs, where the corn was unloaded and husked by the women and the older men. Little was wasted: the best husks were selected for platting into doormats, and the rest were used for livestock bedding.

Late in the autumn our "sugar-cane bee" took place in front of the silk factory, where the necessary machinery and an evaporator finished the work. Here was made a molasses of such excellence that to this day I have not tasted the like anywhere else.

About this time Henrici inaugurated the brewing of boneset tea on a large scale. The Harmonists had always held the boneset herb in high esteem, using it for medicine. But Henrici now planned to secure a large amount of boneset extract to mix with crab-apple cider, whiskey and sugar into a "bitters". The whole process took place at Economy; the young people went in parties through all the fields in the vicinity to gather the blossoms; these were spread in the Music Hall until dry, after which the extract, made in the laundry's evaporating annex, was stored in the wine cellar.

Then came the time for apple jelly—another of Economy's choice delicacies. The extract of the pomace from the cider mill, like the boneset, was boiled down in the large evaporating trough after seemingly endless stirring. Reduced to the level of the steam coils, the juice was drawn off into a smaller trough. Further boiling, the addition of sugar and more stirring produced as perfect a jelly as ever was made. This process, too, was a favorite occupation with Henrici, but since he had many other duties he left much of the job to me. The stirring process continued all day and much of the night so that at times only the counting of strokes kept me awake and saved me from falling into the cauldron.

When the work of the harvest season was completed, I was appointed to the tailor shop. Though I had little inclination toward this field of endeavor I felt that the acquiring of the trade of tailor would not harm me and in any event, in Economy one did whatever was required for the common welfare. With the approach of spring I was again given charge of my favorite occupation—the planting, pruning, grafting and general care of trees. During the summer months, when much building and roof shingling and repair work was to be done, most of us were also drawn into the ranks of the carpenters. In fact throughout the year we gained wide experience both in mechanics and at common labor. Any of us who had spent some years at Economy were bound to be well equipped, resourceful and self-reliant. (Here I must beg pardon for a chuckle at the wiseacres who claim that a community life such as that of the Harmonists is destructive of ambition, initiative and ability.)

It would be difficult to judge the Economy wage system according to modern standards, or even according to the standards of private enterprise in those days. There were a few who received higher wages than the ordinary hired help. Karl Ulrich, for example, received twelve dollars a month plus board and lodging—a princely stipend, according to our standards,—because he was a very skillful craftsman. Frederick Marquart and I belonged to those "on age"—we received our clothing, board and lodging with the expectancy of only $200 and an extra suit of clothes and pair of boots upon attaining our majority. At that I believe that the average 21-year-old Economy youth had more wealth than many a youth of the same age now earning five or more dollars a day.

Working hours were long but rarely arduous. We worked carefully and thoroughly, and in a common effort. As an apprentice in the tailor shop it was my duty in the winter to rise at 4:30 and kindle the fire so that the shop was warm and comfortable when the others arrived one hour later to work an hour before breakfast. Even after a full day's work, during the winter tailors and shoemakers worked two additional hours after supper.

Circumstances in our family, late in the year 1876, decreed that I was to learn somewhat about nursing. When Hannah Mayer left Economy, her place in our family was filled by a young widow whom I only remember as Sallie. In December Veronika was taken seriously ill, and soon became utterly helpless. At the same time my mother, the young widow and Hannah Seitz were also confined to their sickbeds. Then Frederick Marquart injured his hand and was disabled, while even Herr Ulrich was somewhat *hors de combat*. So while Emma Heinsberg, one of the Society's hired girls, came thrice daily to cook our meals, I became the household nurse. Poor Veronika, in the first floor addition, was very restless and required constant attention. With my mother upstairs it was the same. Hannah and the widow of course also needed my care. The days and nights crept on, and I became weary and worn; for sleep is one thing that my body cannot well forbear. After several harrowing weeks, I too became ill and took to bed . . . Whereupon, lo and behold, my mother at once was able to rise, and Hannah and the widow also recovered. But on February 15, Feast Day of the Society's founding, dear Veronika, sweet and charming to the end, breathed her last. Sometime after Veronika was laid to rest, the trustees installed Fredericka Dingler as head of the house, "Rika," as we called her, was an important personage, both because of her own great worth and her late father's prominence.

For the most part these years held real happiness for me. Here at Economy I had opportunity to satisfy my great love for music. As soon as I returned from Phillipsburg I was again drawn into the choir, and in the tenor section stood elbow to elbow with Herr Ulrich. Ulrich, a cultivated German, during one of our first rehearsals noticed my Swabian patois. His offhand criticism of my pronunciation of the German language led me diligently to improve my German by the very best standards. It was at this time that the Moody and Sankey revival excitement was at its height. Henrici was much interested in this movement, and took great delight in translating Sankey's hymns into German. He aimed to present a new hymn every Sunday—"Hold the Fort," "What Shall the Harvest Be," "Pull for the Shore," etc. Though Henrici had rare gifts in translating hymns he chose at this time Herr Ulrich to assist him.

In the band, after my return from Phillipsburg, I first occupied the chair of second B-flat cornet, to which I gave serious study, but was soon promoted to that of E-flat cornet which in that day was the ranking instrument. At the same time I acquired proficiency on the clarinet. By the time of the Harvest Festival concert in 1878 I not only played a difficult solo on the E-flat cornet but had progressed far enough to play the leading part of a clarinet duet with Chris Loeffler. This varied training on different instruments and in different types of music, encouraged by our musical organizations and the community in general, played an important part in the preparation for my short but brilliant professional musical career of later years in New York and throughout the country.

One day Caspar Henning, the teacher, came to me. "Henrici and Gertrude are getting well along in years," he said, "and one of these days it will be necessary for someone to preside in church at one instrument or the other. I do not want anyone else but you to occupy the seat." The seed was well planted, and I took his advice, though not for his reasons, but rather to broaden my musical knowledge and ability. To this end, I spent long hours at practice at the Harmonium in the old Blaine schoolhouse. Soon I wrote down my first musical composition, a jolly waltz. After playing it on the organ I arranged it for the band, and it was soon played at a Sunday evening concert in the Big Garden. Dr. Benjamin Feucht, a very competent musician and former bandmaster, heard it and immediately urged me to take up seriously the study of composition and harmony.

Came the year 1877. Dark clouds settled on America, and tempests were brewing . . .

The spiritual life of the Society had always been linked with the Second Coming of Christ, "Judgment Day," in common parlance "The End of the World." It is described as a time of sorrow and distress; a time of fears, and plagues, and dire calamities. It is spoken of as sudden, like the flood in the days of Noah, or like the fire which overwhelmed Gomorrah.

George Rapp had taught that the Second Coming was to be preceded by the gathering of the Lost Ten Tribes at Economy, who with the vast savings of the Society were to be transported to the Holy Land to rebuild the Temple at Jerusalem. Two thousand barrels of flour had been roasted and stored away for this purpose, and $510,000 in gold and silver had been collected in secret hiding places. But after Father Rapp's death in 1847 the rank and file of the Society had confiscated the flour which he had roasted and stored away and transformed it into whiskey, and a court decision had vitiated the purpose of the Hidden Wealth . . . However, each of Father Rapp's spiritual successors—Baker, Henrici, Lenz— had somewhat to say concerning the Second Coming, particularly so, Henrici.

Late in 1876 Henrici became engrossed with the Great Pyramid of Ghizeh. Certain engineers and theologians, by adopting a unit of measurement, had discovered that a given number of Pyramid inches corresponded to a given number of years, epochal in human events, which thus prophetically recorded the history of the world. The time from Creation to Abraham, that from the Exodus to the Birth of Jesus, the length of his time on earth are all apparent in the measurements. A magnificent chamber opens forth to symbolize the Christian era . . . And beyond is the granite King's chamber, in which all consummates. Certain measurements seemed indicative of the year 1877 as marking "the End of the World." As time went on, Henrici expounded the prophecy more and more ardently, but the attitude of the community as a whole was about the same as that adopted by the Society at a meeting held shortly after Rapp's death— "No man knoweth the hour: forty years or forty thousand years might intervene."

The morning of July 17, 1877, was ushered in with unusual quiet. Was there something in the air, some missing undertone of our daily life, that made us apprehensive? Nothing much was said, yet people looked at each other with a vague wondering. Soon someone discovered that it was the unusual quiet that prevailed—in other words the absence of thundering roll of freight trains in the valley. Reports soon reached us of the railroad strike at Pittsburgh, and of the strikers taking possession of the railroad's property. This was before the day of telephonic communication and Economy did not boast of a telegraph office, but from eye witnesses and the "grapevine telegraph" along the Ohio Valley, we were kept in touch with these happenings only seventeen miles away. We learned of the increasing disorders, the looting of stores and warehouses and traincars for food and drink, the wholesale drunkenness and the street fighting, the influx of lawless people and the reign of terror. We learned that the Allegheny County Sheriff had appealed to the Governor for militia to quell the mob and that one home regiment, sympathizing with the strikers, had refused to clash with them. Word came of the arrival of a thousand vicious adventurers from Philadelphia who ushered in a period of tumult and riot and violence and plundering of the freightyards; of the clash of militia and rioters; of the burning of the huge freight sheds and many other buildings; of the retreat of the Philadelphia militia, of the killing of a hundred people . . .

We who dwelt "in the shadow of the cloud by day and in the glare of the pillar of fire by night," we had some cause to wonder whether this reign of terror marked the beginning of the harvest-time spoken of in Scripture and expounded by Brother Jacob Henrici—namely the time when "the Heavens and the earth, which are now by that same word of God kept in store, reserved unto fire against the Day of Judgment and perdition of ungodly men."

After ten fearsome days our doubts were set at rest with the arrival of General W. S. Hancock who ordered the trains to move and placed authority in the hands of General Joseph Brown, who in turn promised the strikers that their grievances would be considered and differences compromised. Editorials in the *Pittsburgh Press* warned those who sympathized with the rioters that under ex-isting statute Allegheny County would be compelled to pay vast sums in damages. And this came true in course of time—the people of the county paid five million dollars to the Pennsylvania Railroad.

What at first disturbed and excited the good people of Economy was not so much the strike in Pittsburgh but the different sides taken by the two leaders, Henrici and Lenz. Never before had these two leaders publicly taken opposite stands. But here Henrici favored the rail-roads, while Lenz championed the cause of the strikers. However, the reports of the holocaust and reign of terror quickly caused Brother Jonathan to change his point of view.

Brother Johannes Wolfangel, since the passing of Eusebius Boehm, had been in charge of the community wine vault and cellars. Gentle and kind, he was beloved by all, and though there were of Johns a goodly number, he was immortalized as "*der* Johannes" (*the* John) of the community. But now, on the day of the Harmoniefest, February 15, 1878, he too passed away. Though the Society ordinarily did not permit even death to interfere with the even tenor of its ways, the passing of Johannes cast a gloom over the day of rejoicing. Everyone knew his place would be hard to fill. But after due considera-tion the elders chose my good friend, teacher Caspar Henning, to fill Johannes' important post. And in Cas-par's place at the school, Miss Kate Creese was to conduct the classes in English while I was to hold forth in Ger-man.

As a teacher Miss Kate had considerable experience, and like Miss Mary of the Phillipsburg school, possessed that indefinable ability of women teachers, who without seeming effort achieve a perfect mastery over their pupils. Friend Caspar often came to see us and to express his pleasure at our progress.

Directly across the street from the schoolhouse lived the Creese family. Inasmuch as there was often need of consultation with Miss Kate, I became well acquainted with a charming trio of ladies—Miss Kate, her mother, and Miss Susanna, Kate's younger sister. Susanna Creese was particularly attractive and lovely, and gradually my visits increased . . .

But "the course of true love ne'er runs smoothly." At a Sunday concert in the Garden, Professor Rohr invited me to play with the Great Western Band on a jaunt down the river. At the close of the concert I asked Henrici's permission to thus absent myself.

"Absolutely no!" shouted Henrici. "You cannot go." He proceeded to work himself into a ferment, and after some sharp words, continued: "Also you are too sentimental toward a young lady."

I defied him to point out any misconduct whatsoever. Having nothing specific, he took recourse in further bluster. My own part in the colloquy had not been exactly in a whisper. And there we were, blocking the exit from the Garden, while the whole community listened to our altercation.

After putting away my instrument, I went home and reviewed the incident with my mother. In the discussion my mother's cousin, Gottlieb Ruthmueller, lately arrived from Wuerttemberg and now a member of our family, also took part.

"John," said he, "there's no use in remaining here. No matter what you do or leave undone, you'll find no peace. Take my advice and go to college; more education will not hurt you."

I talked the matter over with friend Casper, who all his days had yearned for an opportunity to broaden his knowledge. He was greatly enthused about my going to college. And his stimulus helped me to decide. I had often dreamed of further study so now I made a quick decision. Instead of playing for a day with Pittsburgh's splendid band, I sallied forth on new adventure—this time to Mount Union, Ohio.

In September 1879 I matriculated at Mount Union College, and except for vacation periods, remained there for two years. My student days, though of real importance to my later life, were comparatively uneventful.

I entered upon the Scientific Course with real purpose, and during one term added pedagogy, preparatory to teaching. Though I was always well prepared, there was, alas, no Casper of Economy to pat me on the back and urge me on, nor any lady like Miss Mary to appeal to youthful and romantic fancy. But several of my instructors made a lasting impression on my mind: particularly President Hartshorn and Professors Shunk, Brush and Clarke.

Our course in pedagogy was under the tutelage of Professor Clarke. Somehow I had become unusually proficient in the science of grammar, a subject dear to the heart of our instructor. Nearly every day points were raised in class discussion that led to so much argument that there was left but scant time for recitation. Generally I was the one who argued with the good professor. One day near the close of the term he turned upon me.

"Now," he said, "I'm just beginning to see what this is all about. You and I have spent the greater part of the term in argument; the others simply fold their arms and enjoy the show." "Also," he continued, pointing to a shelf of books, "there is a row of different authorities on grammar, many of which you have made me purchase. Now I am not going to buy any more grammars, nor indulge in any more hair-splitting arguments." "And," turning to the rest of the class, "a full share of work will be expected from the rest of you." But one would have to know this jolly good fellow, Professor Clarke, to appreciate the world of merriment and good fellowship which such incidents as these enfolded.

At first I found board and lodging at the Madden House, but soon accepted an invitation to join "The Club," the purpose of which organization was to obtain first class food and cooking at lowest cost. And here my classmate, Elmore Davisson, and I luckily secured confortable quarters.

Davisson hailed from Clarksburg, Virginia, was hot-headed and full of antebellum spirit. Since he was Mount Union's only Southerner, his views encouraged opposition; and since lustily he sang the praises of the Sunny South, we dubbed him "Sunny."

But there were bonds that made us close friends. We had come to Mount Union at the same time; we pursued the same studies; belonged to the same literary society; and both of us were oddities of a sort—He our only Southerner, I from that quaint village in Pennsylvania called Economy. Though we had our arguments, especially concerning States Rights, in opposing which my father had laid down his life, our battles never went beyond a war of words and always ended in a friendly truce.

Those were the days of spectacular student pranks, and we had our full allotment. Mount Union was especially proud of its splendid little museum, but suddenly the magnificent full-grown male gorilla in the corner glass-case disappeared. "The King" had been abducted! After a time, when the culprits were promised immunity, a group advanced on "Castle Thunder," where the "King" was secretly entombed, and, accompanied by the entire student body, returned him to his throne. At another time a precious Egyptian mummy disappeared, and was actually buried. And one Commencement Day, the janitor, early in the morning, discovered all the beasts from the museum lurking here and there on the campus; he had to rout out the members of the faculty to help him restore them to their rightful places. Nor will I ever forget the morning when we marched into chapel only to find a cow in the balcony.

Not having been reared on such droll pranks, I had little time for them. However, one day three of us were sitting rather forlornly in my room, when the conversation turned to a student named, let us say, Smith, who by spouting extemporaneously at the weekly meetings of our literary society, proved himself a nuisance. He was a bundle of conceit, and needed a good stiff jolt to make him human. I got the inspiration of writing him a letter, informing him that he was to represent Mount Union College at the intercollegiate oratorical contest at Oberlin that year, and suggesting that he prepare an oration on "The Miracles of Our Lord" but that he keep the matter in strictest confidence. The letter was signed "Geo. W. Clarke, Secretary of the Faculty." After his return Smith for a week or two was very important, and obviously hard at work on his oration. Two weeks later he came to have a quiet confidential word with Professor Clarke. The Professor at first was mystified, but when he saw through the joke he nearly went into hysterics . . . The hoax may have been a bitter dose but it certainly proved a cure for egotism. Young Mr. Smith henceforth was a different man.

rched wine cellar. Form-
filled with huge casks
the storage of famous
nomy wine.

e of three large gran-
in which the Society
in reserve a year's
y of grain. Under this
ry is the cider cellar
e the members came
heir daily portion.

During my second year I lived with the Lane family to tutor their youngest son Albert or "Bert." It was a splendid family—Mr. and Mrs. Lane and their four sons, James, Charles, Samuel and Bert. Another son, William was married and living in Alliance. The Lane brothers were exceptionally talented in music; James played the violin, Charles played the piano, and all of them sang well. When I brought out my cornet I was hailed with joy. At the music store in Alliance, Charles and James presided. Whenever an instrument was placed in the home of a prospective customer, we gathered together and offered them a free entertainment in their own home —solos, duets, trios, quartets, both vocal and instrumental. It was splendid sales technique.

Those were the days when I gave much time to a mastery of the cornet. Every day I shut myself in a large closet to study tone production, sometimes for hours. The result was such that it led critics to proclaim that the beauty of my cornet tone was equalled by only one artist, Matthew Arbuckle, the famous church cornetist of New York.

As usual I kept in constant touch with Economy, and when vacation time came, I returned there for the summer. No longer undersized or feeble, I now was of full stature and athletic. I had developed very quickly, and found myself to be one of the strongest men in the county. During vacation I joined the crew that swung the cradle in the harvest field . . . And then came the great fire.

There had been fires before at Economy, but none of such consequence. The Society never invested in insurance, partly because fire prevention was conscientiously followed by all. Everything in the community was kept clean and safe; absolutely no rubbish was to be seen; everything inflammable was cautiously guarded; smoking was forbidden; matches were kept in iron wall brackets with two compartments, one for used matches and one for the unused; and both old and young passed through a daily discipline of caution.

On June 7, 1881, in the evening during a storm, a heavy bolt of lightning struck the largest barn. Partly filled with straw, it immediately burst into a mass of flame. The strong wind very quickly carried the flames to a large shed nearby, and thence to nearly every building in that block. With a crew of helpers I took charge of the fire-engine, and we worked desperately to keep the large stables as well as other nearby buildings intact. The whole community had joined the fire-fighting in various capacities, and of course our bucket-brigades were well organized. We worked feverishly for an hour or more, when, with the aid of a heavy shower, the fire passed its zenith. The total loss to the Society was estimated at a hundred thousand dollars, but, because the entire village had narrowly escaped complete destruction, and because the fire had occurred before the harvest, there was a general spirit of thanksgiving.

After the harvest I again returned to Mount Union. It was a long but satisfactory year. During said year I became acquainted with Mr. J. F. Buck, head of the Fairmount Children's Home, located two miles south of Mt. Union. When my school term ended it was he who asked me to accompany him on an entirely new adventure, a thousand miles to westward . . .

8

Westward Ho! (1882-1888)

J. F. BUCK AND HIS WIFE had most ably conducted The Fairmount Children's Home; severity and kindness were blended to a nicety in the man, and a love of justice and all around motherliness characterized the woman. So superior had been their administration that their fame penetrated to far-off Kansas. The Kansas State Reform School at Topeka needed new and able management, and Mr. Buck was asked to direct the new regime as Superintendent. He accepted, but only with the wise proviso that he be permitted to bring along a nucleus of dependable assistants. In the spring of 1882, therefore, a group of six people headed westward—Mr. and Mrs. Buck, their nineteen year old daughter Lillie, Mr. and Mrs. Kale, and myself.

Mr. and Mrs. Buck were to serve as Superintendent and Matron of the institution, while Miss Lillie was to be Mrs. Buck's assistant. Mr. Kale, a farmer tried and true, and Mrs. Kale, as seamstress, were to preside over departments for which their abilities fitted them. To me there fell the post of master and teacher of one of the two "families" into which the inmates were divided.

The inmates were a motley lot indeed, ranging from the ordinary "bad boy" to young experienced criminals—horse and cattle thieves, train wreckers and robbers, and so on. Some of them were of the nondescript jetsam, floating back and forth between Texas and the Dakota

Bad Lands, but apprehended in Kansas. Some also were men posing as boys, having been saved from the penitentiary by their parents attesting that they were only sixteen years of age.

As we arrived and entered the hallway of the main building, we found a boy scrubbing the floor while an officer with a cudgel stood threateningly over him. We discovered that the boy was in disgrace for some misconduct, and was therefore forced to do this work. Until Mr. Buck took charge, the inmates ordinarily did no work whatsoever, except when assigned as punishment. I can still see Mr. Buck's frown.

"A fine state of affairs," he said, "to make work a subject of disgrace!"

At mealtime the complete lack of thorough discipline was obvious—the boys ran helter-skelter to the dining room where an officer with the inevitable cudgel managed to bring about some semblance of order. The same state of affairs prevailed at bedtime when the boys ascended to the third story dormitory. The officer and his cudgel were busy for an hour controlling the pillow fights and other riotous proceedings.

But within forty-eight hours Mr. Buck and his corps of workers had eliminated the prevailing disorder. First of all, the officer was instructed to discard his cudgel. And within three weeks the conduct of the boys had so improved that the officer followed in its wake. Instead of the wholesale scramble for the dining room at mealtimes, the boys were ordered to assemble outside and form a procession according to their heighth, when at a given signal they marched orderly to their victuals. To top it all, ladies supplanted the men at waiting upon tables. The same kind of decorum was inaugurated at bedtime. The dormitory was divided into two parts—one for the older boys and the other for the younger. The boys were also put more and more upon their honor, and the two groups vied for the attainment of the best record. Labor was put upon a pedestal of honor, and all were led to work together. On the school farm only several acres had been cleared and cultivated when we arrived, but soon the boys were working heartily on the hundred acres of woodland to increase the area for the plow. Conditions of study were also vastly improved.

This, of course, was my first real job in the outside world, and I was determined to make a success of it. Real difficulties had to be overcome, and I gave my whole position much serious thought. The first question was, what are the prime requisites of governing such young ruffians successfully? To gain their admiration, confidence and respect seemed the real problem, and the first step to be taken was to demonstrate my physical prowess. I was in splendid condition at that time, and watched for a chance to display my natural strength. One day, while the boys were playing football—I nonchalantly whittling by the boiler house—the pigskin got out of control and rolled in my direction. Though keenly awake to the situation, with apparent unconcern, I picked up the ball, doubled up my fist, and drove the ball with all my might. Up it sailed, up over the tall boiler house chimney. "Whoo-oo-ee-ee! Who kicked that ball?" someone asked. A whole chorus of boys replied, "No one kicked it; that man there hit it with his fist!" There were mutterings of unbelief, and I overheard someone say, "Wow! I don't want to get within range of his fist." Other feats of strength naturally followed. Little Jimmie Williams once contended that Mr. Duss could pull up a certain tree with his bare hands. It was about two inches in diameter, and there was good reason for several bigger boys calling little Jimmie an idiot for such an idea. Foolishly I examined it—then knew there was nothing to do but justify Jimmie's claim. I tugged and tugged, and finally, up it came. The tree had a five-foot tap-root,— but Jimmie's triumphant, "There, I told you so!" justified all the pain of bruised and bleeding hands. Presumably, I had lifted a weight of 1500 pounds.

Having thus begun to gain their confidence, I still remained ever watchful and wary. Gradually I made them feel that they were too manly to do wrong or to sneak away, and often I wandered off to put them to the test. If some of them planned escape, I generally got wind of it, and by subtle means would let them know that I was aware of their plans. A new addition to my "family" arrived. Having stepped aside into dense underbrush, I heard someone call the boy's attention to my leaving them unguarded so frequently, and vowed that if I didn't carry a revolver he would certainly skip out immediately. Big Bill, one of our negroes, laughed heartily.

"Mist' Duss do'ant carry no volvuh—don' need one. You all try run away an' you fine out what happen gwine be wuss'n shootin'—dat man sho in cahoots wid de debbil or sumpin. He done eben know what us tinks!"

Every night I scanned the happenings of the day and made of them a study in psychology. I also planned my course of action to follow, and gave careful attention to each individual under my care. Eventually this special and individual attention wove bonds of fellowship, and the boys came to look upon me as "a regular guy."

In spite of the fact that I was proud and happy at my success, there were definite reasons for feeling dissatisfied. My "family," in the first place, seemed to be composed of all the worst elements in the Reform School, while the other family under a Mr. Shumway was almost entirely free of such like. When Mr. Buck had asked Shumway (who previous to our coming had been at the school for sometime) to segregate the boys into two families, Shumway allotted me all of the negroes, the one and only idiot, the biggest boys and the smallest. Naturally such an incongruous group proved a constant source of harrassment. Even against such odds, I lost not a single boy of my group, while seven of Shumway's boys ran away. Then too, I found it difficult to adjust myself to the caste or social status of the staff members seemingly imposed by Mr. Buck. At Economy such a thing as social discrimination was quite unknown, and one and all were considered as absolutely equal. But after our staff became settled at the Reform School, I was politely asked to dine with the servants and lesser officers downstairs. Moreover, Mr. Buck hardly ever conferred with me, seeemingly preferring the confidence of Shumway.

In the course of some months I was seriously stricken with a fever. Though delirious at that time, there linger in my memory the doctor's ominous words, "Well, it's kill or cure." Oblivion set in. A day or so later, when I returned to consciousness, the doctor's medicine had knocked the fever, but also left me feeling as if some heaven-high giant had picked me up and hurled me down to hard earth. No strength was left me—and it was the only time in my life when I wanted to die. After some days I gradually recuperated, but I had lost twenty-seven pounds. I was so greatly weakened both in mind and body that I felt unable to cope with the difficulties confronting me.

One day Mr. Buck was walking about with me and chatting. It was easily perceived that something more than common engrossed him.

"Mr. Duss, you may not know it," he said, "but from

our very beginning here I have had a special eye on you and your work. Of course, we all know about the division of the families. So you may know that it was an added gratification that in spite of your great handicap you have succeeded far beyond my expectations." Commensurate reward for my good work was to follow, things of importance, such as organizing a band, and so on.

I waited until he had finished the alluring picture. Then I replied, "but this is all too late, for I am going to leave."

"But—what—why this sudden . . ."

"It's not so sudden as you think," I interrupted. "You very well know what obstacles I have had to face, and never until now have you given me the slightest encouragement." He hastily promised things would be far different henceforth. "No use," I continued. "The die is cast, for I have written Miss Susanna Creese to set our wedding day. After we are married I shall return to Ohio to sell organs and pianos."

Two weeks later I departed.

During my college vacation at Economy I had called regularly at the Creese home, and spent many unforgetable hours with Susanna. And when I left for my last year at Mount Union and the Kansas adventure, we pledged our life and love to each other. Letters flew back and forth, resulting finally in a meeting at Keokuk, Iowa, at the home of her brother David where on July 17, 1882, we were married.

During the month of August we settled happily in one wing of the Lane mansion near Mount Union. At first my salesmanship, measured by actual sales of organs (the parlor variety then technically known as reed-harmoniums) and pianos, was not exactly dazzling. I greatly missed the assistance of the Lane brothers—Charles and James. Both now traveling for manufacturers of pianos, it was impossible to present the very unusual entertainment of the former days. Obviously, too, the slow, sweet life of Economy had done anything but sharpen my commercial instincts and my sales thinking. Thus my sales conversation was more concerned with art than with the dollar. Though I made some sales, I soon discovered that in this line the future held but little in store for me.

At some time my mother had received word that her brother on his "Birkenhof" or beech farm in Germany was financially headed in the wrong direction. I counseled that he sell his farm and with his family come to America. Out West vast homestead lands had opened up. If he and his eldest three husky sons and I would follow the beaten trail, we would be entitled to file claims for a ranch of 800 acres, each adult male being entitled to 160 acres. My mother's ready cash would start us on the way; thus out on the western prairie, with the efforts of five industrious men, we were bound to carve at least a state of comfort if not of affluence.

Agreeably to this plan, my uncle sold his property, discharged his debts, and with his wife and eleven children came to Economy. They arrived in the autumn, a time of year not propitious for a western expedition. Besides, the chiefs and elders of Economy extended a most cordial welcome to our relatives. Uncle Kroll, the three eldest sons, and the oldest daughter were placed on the Economy payroll, while the seven younger children attended the public school. Now when this large family became thus comfortably situated, no one felt inclined to change a sure thing for an uncertainty. Thus my initial homesteading plans went glimmering.

But the fascination of the West had quite engulfed me. The words of Horace Greeley still lingered and, like a national call they rang: "Go West, young man, go West!" . . . After consultation with my wife, and in spite of flattering offers from the musical stage, I decided to cast our future with the West.

Our first move was to Burr Oak, Kansas, where Mrs. Duss' brother Mitchell had built first a cottage, then a large home, and finally sold the former to his sister Susanna. The cottage being too small for us, I immediately added a lean-to kitchen and a storm-cave. In the frontier towns of the rolling prairie lands in those days the buildings were all frame, lightly and cheaply constructed. When the great winds blew, as they often did in Kansas, the light structures were dangerous for the occupants. Cyclones were frequent, and whenever one appeared on the horizon, people scurried to their caves of refuge. These caves were simply outside cellars liberally covered with earth.

From Burr Oak in Jewell County, as a point of vantage, I now explored the country round about. My investigations soon revealed that in this part of the country all worthwhile homestead lands had already been taken, and the prices for whatever remained for sale were unduly high. However, in the adjoining state of Nebraska, nine miles southwest of Red Cloud and three miles north of the Kansas line, I found a quarter section that had the right appeal. A small brook, Buffalo Creek, traversed the land from south to north, cutting the land in two. The larger eastern part of the land sloped gently from the boundary to the creek, and the major portion of the western tract was also suitable for cultivation. The creek was fringed on either bank by heavy virgin timber—cottonwood, elm, ash, hackberry and the like—which in this almost treeless country would not only add beauty but also profit to the land. The layout was ideal for a stock farm. Thus when the owner, C. W. Kaley, a reputable lawyer of Red Cloud, quoted me its price at eight dollars an acre, I purchased it at once. Not having the necessary capital for active operation of the stock farm, I was forced to bide my time.

Meanwhile, my brother-in-law, "Creese, the Photographer," was operating two photo galleries, one at Burr Oak and the other at Mankato, and was badly in need of an assistant. I entered into this work with zest, for it promised not only a further development of my artistic sense but also a rare opportunity to study the people of this region. Soon I learned the technique of photography, and operated one gallery while Creese was at the other.

Burr Oak, like many another town at that time, had an organization,—alas, now almost extinct—the Village Band. The enterprising merchants of the little town, realizing the value and the splendid form of amusement provided by such a musical organization, had provided funds for the band and hired me as teacher. Some of the members were talented beyond the average, and we progressed by leaps and bounds. At the ensuing Fourth of July celebration the band rendered an ambitious program, thus delighting hundreds of people who had come from near and far. As a result of this activity, two representatives of the Kansas Organ Company—manufacturers of parlor organs—came and asked me to take the agency of their product in our county.

Brother Mitch and I jointly accepted their offer, using the studio waiting-room for display purposes. With this venture we gradually made a success. Oftentimes sales could only be made by barter—Would we take a cow, a calf, a colt, as part pay for the organ? It became a splendid method of stocking my Nebraska ranch.

Came the thirtieth of August, 1883—a ne'er-to-be-forgotten day—for on that day there came to our cozy cottage a charming bit of humanity, a baby daughter. At the suggestion of Aunt Kate, Mrs. Duss's sister, we called her Vera, and in honor of friend Casper of Economy, attached the name Caspera. Happy days indeed! Although my various lines of endeavor at Burr Oak held much in promise my dream of a livestock ranch was uppermost in mind. Planning and scheming, my wife and I in full accord, finally decided in the coming spring to migrate to the gentle slopes of Buffalo Creek in the Republican River Valley of South Central Nebraska.

Nebraska, youthful and picturesque in the brotherhood of states, at that time made a strong appeal to me. Its snappy, variable climate, where windy springs faded into hot and sometimes dry summers; the autumns beautiful, extending sometimes to the holidays; then followed by short and severe winters—all gave urge to young and virile manhood. The extended view of prairie land, rolling like a vast sea, and the infinite blue sky brought a sense of lofty aspiration.

Romance of the past and present mixed as one on its soil. Forty years before our adventure in ranching the state had been almost completely unsettled. John C. Fremont and his companions trailed across the state in 1842. Several years later the vanguard of the Mormons, some 15,000, camped north of what is now Omaha. In 1847 the entire sect joined them and began their mass migration to Great Salt Lake. In 1849 and the early 1850's thousands raised the dust of the buffalo trails on their trek to the California gold fields. Then came the first Overland Mail across the state from Independence, Missouri, to Great Salt Lake—1200 miles. When silver was discovered at Cherry Creek, Colorado, food and merchandise began to be transported through Nebraska, on to the mining camps and Salt Lake City. By 1869 (when as a nine year old Economy boy I listened to Henrici's glowing account in Sunday school) the Union Pacific Railroad was completed, and the gold spike driven that united East and West. The same year the Burlington Railroad entered the state at Platsmouth and started construction westward toward Denver.

With the railroads came the homeseeking people, many of them from overseas. When we arrived in Nebraska, the eastern part of the state was fairly well settled, but the central portion, where we lived, and the land to the westward was largely raw prairie. The roving herd and its picturesque guardian, the cowboy, were still somewhat in evidence, though gradually pushed west-ward by the great fenced fields. Dugouts and sodhouses were still to be seen. The latter were constructed of our buffalo-grass sod, cut and laid like stone. These houses were warm in winter and cool in summer, and they proved to be comfortable and practical dwellings.

"Colonies of European people, Slavonic, Germanic, Scandinavian, Latin, spread across our bronze prairies like daubs of color on a painter's palette," wrote Willa Cather for *The Nation*. "They brought with them some-thing that this neutral new world needed even more than the immigrants needed land." As late as 1910 the census showed 228,648 foreign and native born Germans living in Nebraska; 105-503 Scandinavians; 50,600 Czechs—making a foreign population total of 900,571 compared with about 300,000 native stock.

We lived on the line where cultivated area trod the heels of cattle ranges and forced them ever westward. Except for a single small frame house of my immediate neighbor, John Robinson, there was no house to the west and south of us for many miles.

Our pilgrimage from Burr Oak to the new home in Nebraska took place in the month of May 1884. With my team and that of a neighboring farmer, we transported our possessions over crude wagon trails which inadequately served for roads. Part of the time it rained, and once we were caught in a severe hailstorm. Two days it took us to travel the forty miles. Several trips back and forth had to be made, and finally the cattle were driven northward. Temporarily we found quarters in a dugout dwelling, a spacious cave dug in the side of a large bank on a neighboring farm. We would have been fairly comfortable during our residence in this primitive dugout, had it not been for fleas that beset us and nearly broke our patience. This mode of living is hardly to be recommended for a young couple with a tiny child.

Some time before I had ordered from Chicago a shipment of lumber for a house, twelve feet by twenty-four with two equal rooms below and two upstairs. When the lumber arrived at Red Cloud, I hired my neighbor, Mahlon Points, to help me haul it to my ranch with his team. The lumber had indeed arrived with a bill amounting to $187, but an expected letter with a promised draft had not come to the Post Office; without money we could not carry away the shipment of lumber. Then I did what in the East would have been unprecendented. I, as a total stranger went to the State Bank, poured out my tale of woe to the cashier, and asked him simply to lend me enough money to pay the freight. Fixing me with a sort of serio-comic scrutiny, he pondered the matter for a half minute, then said: "I've never done a thing like this before, but I am going to help you." He counted out the money. The following day came the expected letter with the draft, so all was well. In due course of time, with the aid of a carpenter, I built the house.

Soon another project engrossed my mind. Just to the east of my quarter section, another good quarter of Government upland lay unused. Several had filed claim for it, but one after another deserted it because they failed to locate any water. Since my farm was well watered, the logical thing to do was to annex this 160 acres. The Federal government required a six months residence on the property to establish a preemption claim. The present incumbent, a Mr. Gardner, agreed to relinquish his claim if I would reimburse him for his costs in prospecting for water—some two hundred dollars. This done, I filed claim and six months later proved continuous residence, paid Uncle Sam $200, and received my patent signed by President Grover Cleveland.

On the new land I had reared a twelve by twelve shack of plain boards, furnished with a cookstove, table, cupboard and bed. Nearby I excavated a dugout to serve as a storm cave and a cellar. I also tried my hand at prospecting for water. Somewhere I had picked up the theory that ants always establish a nest not far from water. Near our shack was a large ant heap; I bored a hole with a test augur right through this nest; and only twenty feet from the spot where a previous homesteader had drilled to 140 feet without success, at the depth of ten feet, I struck a plentiful supply of water. The "find" naturally increased the land's value, and, neighbors spreading the word that I had almost magically found water there, the whole project brought me considerable publicity. True, some derisively referred to me as a "book farmer." However, in spite of the implied derogation of the term, my neighbors began calling on me for advice, particularly when it concerned farm animals.

I had always been unusually fond of animals. At Economy, when only five years old, I began feeding the family cow and soon assumed general care of that mild creature. When I was seven I drove the swine to pasture in summer time, and in winter did the same with the sheep. When I was nine, and at the Groetzingers near Zoar, I learned to ride and drive horses and helped with the harrowing. On through the years I had to do with farm animals, studied them closely, loved them and acquired a knowledge of them.

My intention was to specialize in the breeding of horses and of registered shorthorn (Durham) cattle, and of the latter I acquired a number of fancy specimens. At the county fair these animals captured some blue ribbons and led me into the company of the leading stockmen in that section, such as old Peter Marsden, and the brothers McCall.

But in the breeding of fancy shorthorns I was anything but wise. Of course the animals were beautiful, and because of "balanced rations," careful grooming and perfect all around care bestowed upon them, the creatures at fairs and other exhibitions earned their blue ribbons. Although I bought the best that money could buy, I failed to consider the question of marketing the progeny. As to my beautiful brood mares, although they received most scrupulous attention, untoward happenings outside of my control undid all my efforts.

In those days stock farmers had been in the habit of buying, in the fall of the year, steers from the range at about three and one-half cents per pound on foot. These with a herd of swine were turned into corrals and corn-fattened during the winter. The following spring the beeves brought seven cents a pound or more. When in the fall, the time came to buy range steers, the stock farmers went to the banks to borrow freely the necessary funds on promissory notes endorsed by each other. I joined the procession and both Alf and Ol. McCall endorsed my note. But when we came to sell our steers the following spring, the price of former years had quite been cut in half,—just enough to lift our promissory notes.

We soon discovered that the beef combine in Chicago —the "big fellows" who owned the slaughter houses—had banded together and were thus enabled to buy western cattle at prices they alone dictated. After serious deliberations my friends and most of the other stockmen agreed to try it again next season. What could they do? They were in the habit of cultivating immense areas of corn, which in those years was such a drug on the market that it was freely used as fuel. Indeed, what sense was there in loading forty bushels of corn and hauling it say fifteen miles to an elevator in order to get only $3.20 with which to buy a little jag of coal to be hauled fifteen miles back home? Although these stockmen made scarcely any profit by feeding the corn to cattle, the process at least afforded an easy way to transport corn to market.

But for myself, I refused absolutely to have anything more to do with a business in which a coterie of capitalists pulled the strings according to their own sweet will, and from city offices hindered the initiative of thousands of farmers throughout the land. Too much of an American rebel to submit to capitalist tyranny, my dream of breeding shorthorns and horses having vanished, and there being no profit in raising grain, it was time to try a different course. Indeed I was on the verge of forsaking ranch life and entering the world of music, when I happened to read of hog fanciers in Missouri selling large English Berkshires at fancy prices. Why could not I do the same in our fast growing section farther west? With the monetary assistance of mother Creese, I purchased some fine large registered Berkshires. By good luck and good management, the herd grew miraculously. At weaning time the pigs were sold at extravagant prices, and for us literally "brought home the bacon."

During those long, monotonous pioneer days on the Gardner preemption claim, my mother came to stay with us. Once again she had grown weary of Economy; she needed rest and an abiding place in a more healthful climate. Along with her came young Jacob Seher, a lad of eighteen lately arrived from Kornthal, Germany. At the time of their arrival our house on Buffalo Creek was not yet ready for occupancy, hence we had to bunk in the shack erected on the "claim"—a trying experience for my mother. I shall never forget that first night. I was nearly asleep when she called to me in a stage whisper more penetrating than her normal voice.

"John, get up and chase them away," I didn't realize what she was talking about. "The rats, of course," she said. "I hear them." "Mother," I said, "there are no rats in this country, these are only harmless field mice."

"Nonsense," she replied in her stage whisper, "rats are everywhere. I know what rats are—get up and chase them away." I refused to budge from my bed, and soon she was scampering about the room essaying to drive the imaginery rats away. No use, the mice were soon at work again—and so was my mother throughout the night.

Later: "John," she commanded, "get up—there are people coming."

208

"Nothing of the sort," I mumbled. But she insisted. I was now thoroughly aroused, and explained that what she heard were only prairie wolves or coyotes.

"What!" she shrieked, the stage whisper now forgotten. "Do you mean to tell me you have wolves out here? Had I known that, I would not have come at all." It was useless to tell her that the coyotes or prairie wolves were quite harmless and more afraid of her than she could be of them. Later still, she heard Old Pap, our biggest horse, rubbing against the shack, and when she discovered that the animals were not fenced away, she was utterly disgusted.

Even when we moved into our new house the day after her arrival, her satisfaction was of short duration. And no wonder. On the one hand, mother sorely missed the steam laundry and the thousand other conveniences of Economy, while on the other, pioneering entailed many irregularities quite beyond her power of adaptation. Within a fortnight she moved to Red Cloud where I had secured rooms for her. Though town life was more acceptable, we had hardly comfortably installed her when, bag and baggage, back she went to Economy. It had been just another unavailing journey which my mother had made to where "Everything was all right in itself, but not like it was at Economy!"

While my mother was still in Nebraska, there came another from Economy to strike his fortune in the West. Gottfried Lauppe had come from Wuerttemberg to Economy a year or so previously. He was an extreme mystic and pietist, a real "Stundenganger," (a term applied to those who regularly attended the meetings for prayer, worship and meditation peculiar to these pietists). In the old country they had been left unmolested by civil authorities and clergy, but when Lauppe tried to inaugurate a Stundengang at the old hat-shop in Economy, Henrici wasted no time in hinting that if Lauppe were not satisfied with the worship services at Economy he need no longer eat the bread of the Society.

Nothing daunted, Lauppe followed my mother to Nebraska, planning to use her as a beginning of another "Stundengang." Both he and my mother criticized the lack of true religion (as they conceived true religion) at Economy and the worldliness that had come in vogue. But Lauppe's main concern was to find a livelihood. Though it was autumn and not·much work was available when he came, I found a place for him on a well ordered farm five miles from our ranch, owned by a German family named Kuehn.

In those sod-breaking days Westerners had of necessity learned to work furiously, morning, noon and into the night if possible. To this gait, Lauppe, used to the easy going system at Economy, could not adjust himself. Soon he was complaining—the three daily meals were not enough without Economy's "Neuner" and "Vesper," and worst of all there was no wine or cider as at Economy. "And look how they rush about," he would say. "This is surely no way to work."

"You will have to learn," I explained to him. "Our produce is so much lower in price than it is in the East, that we have to make up the difference by raising it in large quantities—which means not only long hours but faster work."

Mr. Kuehn, meeting me in Red Cloud, complained that Lauppe had proved to be a great trial. Because he worked so slowly, Kuehn could not use him in conjunction with other workers, but had to shunt him off into odd jobs. At corn-husking time Westerners worked so fast that one farm hand, driving his own team, was expected to husk fifty bushels of corn a day and shovel it into the crib. Some even hit well above a hundred bushels. Lauppe, awestruck and demolished, shortly hit the trail back to Economy.

Mildly eventful though our ranch life had been up to now, on March 25, 1885, there transpired the most important event since our arrival in Nebraska—the birth of John S. Duss, Jr.—a little son to gladden well our hearts, auguring the perpetuation of the family name and giving new impetus to our labor.

Sometime after we were established on Buffalo Creek, two more former Economites came to us—Mrs. Creese, my wife's mother, and her daughter Miss Kate, with whom I had shared duties at Economy's school. More adaptable than my own mother and poor Lauppe, they soon fitted into the varying scheme of things. The McCalls, our closest friends and members of the district school board, soon discovered in Miss Kate, a rarely gifted teacher. It was not long until they engaged her as teacher in our district school. As the schoolhouse was two miles away from our home it was agreed that whensoever the weather proved inclement, I was to take her place. Miss Kate inaugurated modern teaching methods, and our work elated the school board, so that we were re-engaged term after term until Miss Kate was married. Averse to any change in policy, the board sent me a special request to continue as full time teacher. Though I continued the management of our ranch, the winter months that followed found me regularly at the little district school.

The provision regarding winter weather was a perfectly natural one. In those days we were now and then subject to a phenomenon of nature for which somebody had invented the name "Blizzard." My newest dictionary defines blizzard as "a blinding snowstorm." No wonder that the phenomenon is regarded by the public in general as a snowstorm.

Now a Western blizzard in the 1880's had little in common with a snowstorm. A snowstorm was something that could be seen—at fairly moderate wind and temperature, it brought us downy flakes of snow. But a blizzard brought below-zero cold, with a gale raging at sixty or more miles per hour, driving minutest particles of ice, which pricked the face as would a thousand needles and filled the air to such a density that you could not see your hand before your face. And that is why here and there men lost their way in going from house to barn to be found as frozen corpses after the abatement of the storm.

Came now a day when it was imperative for me to be in our county seat, the town of Red Cloud. A blizzard having started, driving was out of the question—horses will not permit themselves to be led in this kind of weather. To walk nine miles in a blizzard may seem foolhardy to the utmost degree but to me it held no whit of terror. Possessing absolute certainty as to direction; unsurpassed judgment of distances; knowing that the wind blowing from the north would so continue and serve me as a compass; familiar with the trail as well as with the topography of the surrounding terrain; I had no misgivings regarding the adventure on which I was about to embark. Courageously I sallied forth. First—with eyes tightly closed—straight south a distance of two miles over upland prairie, to the corner of a fence. There I oriented myself in a certain diagonal south-easterly direction, which at the end of a mile and a half brought me downhill to bottom land where the trail led through forest southwardly about four miles to a very large tree opposite the Republican River bridge. Up to this point I had gotten along swimmingly. (I use the word advisedly, for through the forest my hands and arms were just as busy as were my feet). Fortunately, I soon found the tree in question. Thereupon on hands and knees I proceeded to explore my way toward the bridge. Having found the same, I arose and forged northwardly straight into the blast a distance of a mile to where my feet struck the tracks of the B. & M. Railroad; thence up the street where sidewalks, posts and houses served as guides, to the Post Office. My eyelashes, long since frozen tight, soon thawed and I beheld the postmaster gaping at me in open-mouth astonishment. "Where in the world did you come from?" he asked. "From Buffalo Creek, nine miles," said I. "Through all this storm?" he questioned, "I can't believe it—why there are merchants in this block who have not ventured out to get their mail." However, when I had taken off my outer garments and he saw that down to the waistline I was encased in a solid crust of ice, he understood and sympathetically helped me to remove the icy armor. Gradually drawing near the fire I dried my clothes, and as a healthy glow pervaded my being, I felt that I would be none the worse from having passed through the hazardous experience.

Strange as it may seem, the return home, after the three-day storm, was an even more trying experience. The icy particles lay at a depth of anywhere between six inches and six feet. A crust on the surface at certain points was strong enough to bear my weight; at other points it let me down. The "let-down" was more liable to happen when the drift was deep than when it was but shallow. The let-downs in the snow banks meant the breaking down of the crust ahead by flailing arms and fists until I found it sufficiently strong to bear my weight. If the reader has imagination, let him pursue the journey thus. At one point (in order to save distance around a ravine) I lay face downward and "swam" across. At this point the drift was twenty feet in depth. The last part of the journey was to me a blank. Instinctively I must have trudged along, and at the point of utter exhaustion reached my home and fireside. Here, I must greatly compliment Mrs. Duss, who without the least worry about her spouse in whom she had absolute faith, busied herself with our chore-boy Jacob Seher in feeding and watering the stock and not getting lost twixt house and barn. I had experience in two other blizzards, but let us to a different sort of adventure.

One bitter cold evening in Red Cloud, when with a pair of lively colts and buggy, I was about to start driving home, I learned that it was safe to drive across the frozen river. Accordingly I proceeded to take this shorter route. Crossing the river at dusk, my eyes drawn to the far bank, beheld black sentinels, here and there in the rushes—charred tree-stumps, remains of campfires of the Indian, the hunter or the pioneer. The spectral aspect engaged the attention of the colts. Ears pricked, wary and on edge, the moment we struck the river bank ahead, where buffalo trails reached the river, they bolted into two of these ruts and galloped wildly on. My clumsy mits prevented me from controlling the lines and suddenly each colt jumped one rut to the right. The sudden elevation of the right side of the buggy threw me out on the left side but, luckily, the handhold on the left side of the seat caught me under the right knee. Held thus suspended twixt the wheels and body of the vehicle, which being yanked along at frightful speed, had me wondering, was I to be mangled for life or to be killed outright . . . when suddenly the colts jumped to the left. The buggy careening in the opposite direction, I was thrown back into the seat.

Thankful for my miraculous escape, I discarded my

mits, gradually led the colts out of the ruts, and driving them 'round and 'round the prairie, wore them down. Tranquility restored, I retraced our route imprinted in the snow—gathered in the groceries and other effects that we had sown around about the landscape—then leisurely drove home.

Of our many friends in the prairie country the McCalls were perhaps most interesting. The two brothers were members of the school board, and Oliver, like Casper of Economy, had a deep respect for education and learning. But in his zeal for community and social improvement in our district, he was quite aggressive, brushing aside all opposition from the "small fry" with whom he was anything but popular. Those obstructing his path at first called him "Hog" McCall, but gradually their hatred became less bitter, and the nickname climbed to "King" McCall.

During our first winter on the prairies, the "old-fashioned" social events common to frontier communities took place; they proved a help in acquainting ourselves with the neighbors. The first major event was a community spelling bee at the schoolhouse—an event I have always treasured; for finally—through the maze of *daguerreotype, phthistic, queue, ptomaine*—King Oliver and I alone faced each other. It was a battle royal, and we kept on and on. At last on a comparatively simple word, *hydraulic,* King Oliver was dethroned.

I think it was during Miss Kate's first term at the school that, with the McCalls, we organized a Literary Society. At first Oliver and I had to do most of the debating, but by and by others threw their hats into the ring. Naturally Oliver and I were generally put down as leaders of opposing sides. In the course of time the Friday night performance at the Hummel Schoolhouse became a famous institution in our section. Following in our footsteps, the Walnut Creek School District, six miles away, organized a similar society. After awhile, some one suggested that the two Societies devote an evening to a literary contest. No sooner said than done. People looked forward to this event with great expectations. Recitations, orations, and the concluding debate were fervently prepared. It was a great night. From every direction came the crowds. Some even came from Kansas, across the border. King McCall and I led the affirmative, while a young and brilliant hermit, by name of Sanford led the opposition. . . . Considering that the audience was seated on rough, uncomfortable benches, had listened to the efforts of ten debators, and that it was two o'clock in the morning when I finally made the closing speech, one can imagine my pride when this same audience, after my last oratorical effort, gave me a tremendous ovation, even clamoring for *"more speech."*

Our literary society debates spread my fame through the nearby countryside, and soon I came to be hailed as speaker here and there. Deeply conscious of the actions of the Chicago beef combine and similar institutions in the financial web of our country, I fervently assailed them on any occasion that presented itself. Trusts and corporations to the western farmer in those days brought much grief, hence lambasting these capitalistic organizations proved a popular pastime. After the close of one Fourth of July address, an elderly gentleman stepped up to me, and shaking my hand said, "Young man, that speech was clever but it sounded far too anarchistic. Take my advice and talk in milder terms." However, such protests as I had made might have been heard throughout the western country, and doubtlessly helped in bringing about the creation of the Interstate Commerce Commission,

Talk of such anti-capitalistic nature naturally led me into political channels, so that when the Republican primaries drew nigh, my friends proposed my name for County Superintendent of Public Instruction. Having the support of the party leaders, this was tantamount to election. At this juncture an estimable, capable lady announced herself a candidate, and, knowing the full value of having a woman represented on the ticket, I hastened to withdraw my name in favor of Miss Eva King.

After such a gesture the party leaders assured me of their wholehearted support in case I should at any time become a candidate for any public office. Friends of mine began to talk of grooming me for Congress . . . when, as lightning out of a clear sky, came a new call.

A letter from my mother informed me that Henrici had called to see her about the matter of a competent teacher at the Economy schools. Henrici wanted me, and sent his appeal through my mother. This flattered me not a little, for Henrici had heretofore steadfastly refrained from asking any former "Economite" to return to Economy.

However since my financial outlook at the ranch was rosy; the livestock was doing well; I was in the political arena; and the future prosperity of the prairie country seemed assured; we could not bring ourselves to take a stand. Finally, we left the matter to Fate—if for two days good conditions should continue, I would not accept Henrici's proffered offer. But if something untoward should happen, we would return to the village on the Ohio. . . . On the following morning, coming from the stable to my breakfast, I said to Mrs. Duss: "We're going back to Economy—there's a dead colt in the stable. . . ."

9

Economy Again, and the Old Order Passeth (1888-1890)

EARLY ONE PERFECT SUMMER MORNING—July 28, 1888—we arrived at Economy. The dew, I remember, hung heavily on greensward, vine and shrubbery, and the myriad drops sparkled like diamonds in the sun. The rolling fields of Economy were lush, and charged with the fragrance of the gardens, the very atmosphere breathed an auspicious welcome.

Though I had lived most of my life on these same smiling acres, it seemed that everything had changed. Accustomed as I was to the vast reaches of the half-settled prairies, the landscape that I looked upon on the morning of our return seemed to have shrunk. The hills and woods had moved right up against the town, the steeple of the church no longer bored into the sky, and the great Ohio River seemed only half its former width.

Henrici came to greet us, bidding us a hearty welcome. Members of the Society and other friends, thronged about us happily, asking many questions and exchanging pleasantries. But the words of Henrici, aside from his simple welcome, outweighed the words of all the others. "Well, now you are here, and everything is all right." . . .

Words of welcome at Economy in import were not those of the world at large. Through the establishment of three settlements and the building of three towns, these people had been forcibly impressed with the value of manpower and individual worth to the general welfare of the commune. Their welcome and appraisal were determined according to one's worth, at least in part. Henrici apparently recognized in me not only a satisfactory solution to the school problem, but also a valuable acquisition in the realm of music, not to mention the orchards, farms and livestock. In other words he knew me as an all around handy man; one who in view of the decline of the Society, was most welcome. . . . But there was also an intangible something in Henrici's welcome that somewhat puzzled me. Later I learned that he, like Father Rapp, had earnestly prayed for the required help to be sent. And just as the coming of Henrici years ago was regarded by Rapp as the answer to his supplication, Henrici now regarded my coming as the answer to his prayer. . . .

The brick dwelling opposite the schoolhouse, which we were to occupy, was still in course of preparation, hence temporary quarters were assigned—the identical house which my mother and I had occupied in 1869.

When we arrived I noted that the Harmonists seemed in fine fettle. The Society had just been victorious in a law suit—one of those periodical assaults on the Society's treasury. This time the heirs of Elias Speidel, (a member who had withdrawn from the Society in 1831 to get married) laid claim to $30,000! The case had finally gone to the Supreme Court of the United States, where Attorney George Shiras, Jr., of Pittsburgh, represented the Society successfully against Ohio's ex-Governor George Hoadley, who represented the heirs.

Our return to Economy, however, was not a pleasure unalloyed—so many of our old friends were missing. Friend Casper Henning was no longer there to shake my hand. Yet he was only one of many absentees. Indeed, the membership of the Society had become so depleted that, in spite of recent acquisitions such as Lauppe and my mother, the Society could boast no more than thirty members, the majority of whom were women. The male membership was inadequate to supply even the number of foremen required; thus some of the departments had passed entirely into the hands of hirelings.

New names appeared among the roll-call of the foremen—some of my childhood acquaintances had taken the places of those who had passed; some who had joined the Society during my absence filled other vacancies; while some "outsiders" had become advanced to foremen. However here and there, a patriarch of the past still lingered at his post. Good-natured, rolypoly John Wirth still had charge of the flour and grist mill. The rough and ready John Scheid managed the butcher shop; he was also saddler and foreman of the teamsters. Placid Joseph Schwarz presided over the sawmill, lumber yard and carpenters. Among the newer members, the saturnine, aristocratic Michael Staib was boss of the shoeshop, while smug little Mortitz Friedrichs had ascended the tailor's throne once occupied by dear, dapper Little David Hauffler. Ernst Woelfel, one of the "big boys" of my childhood days (who when of age left Economy to take unto himself a wife, and after her death had returned to join the Society) now was boss of the wine and cider cellars. George Kirschbaum, another friend of my childhood days, after some years of experience in California, had returned to the peace of Economy. After functioning for a time as foreman of the farm laborers, he was now taking a commercial course at Duff's College in Pittsburgh. Meanwhile, the mantle of farm foremanship had descended—save the mark!—on the shoulders of easy going Lauppe, who shortly after his return from the West had joined the Society.

The remaining shops and industries were now under

the supervision of those who were not members of the Society—Gustav Schumacher at the cooper shop; George Grieshaber at the blacksmith shop; Theodore Liebermann at the tinsmith shop; Julius Aufferman at the bakery; William Straube at the dairy; Christian Kuemmerle at the steam laundry; Henry Breitenstein at the cabinet shop. Breitenstein with the assistance of his wife also managed the hotel, while his sister, Mrs. Elizabeth Ott, and his wide-awake, capable son, William H., kept the community store.

In this communal organization it was now my duty to take charge of the Economy school—a department which for several years had proven a thorn in the side of the administration. In the curriculum of the school the German language had at all times stood preeminent. During my childhood days the common branches of learning were all taught in the German language—English being taught merely as a branch. (All through the history of early Pennsylvania, German had been almost as important as English; the minutes of the Constitutional Convention were published in both languages, and until 1850 the proceedings of the Commonwealth's Legislature were likewise issued in both languages.) Along in the 1870's there were times when Economy's school was taught alternately three days in English and the remaining three in German. In the reorganization of the school, however, this fifty-fifty method of teaching was discarded and the position of the two languages of the earlier regime were reversed so that the common branches were now taught in English, while German became a separate study.

In 1885 the Society had built a new two-story frame schoolhouse containing four large rooms. Each of the two lower rooms contained some thirty desks, conformably

dividing the upper and lower grades; all that I needed
now was an assistant. For this post Henrici chose Herman
Fischern, a man of education and culture. Fischern had
wandered into Economy and applied for food and lodging like other pilgrims of the road. (Henrici was always
averse to calling them tramps; he preferred to call them
"pilgrims" or "unfortunates," and sincerely believed that
some of them were divinely sent to Economy as a help).
Fischern had asked for work, and was given the job of
whitewashing the stables. It was soon learned that, as a
nephew of a former professor at the University of Heidelberg, he had acquired education worth while. Quite properly, therefore, Henrici installed him at the school.

Besides the changes in the curriculum aforementioned
I made other innovations that somewhat startled the
people of Economy. It being my belief that in the training
of the youth, discipline and coördinated action are prime
requisites, I devoted fifteen minutes each fair day to
military drill as it pertained to formations and evolutions
in marching. This was a violent jolt to peaceful Economy,
and the town soon buzzed with excitement regarding this
"manifestation of militarism." Henrici soon heard of it,
and one evening after singing school came to me.

"I hear you are making soldiers of the children," he
said. "What's the idea?"

"You have evidently been misinformed," I replied. "The
matter is one of discipline pure and simple, and the children are not trained with an enemy in mind. The result
is that the children learn how to stand and walk correctly;
in other words to achieve that 'upright carriage' which
Father Rapp liked and exemplified. Moreover, as to
mental discipline, the value of concerted action and in-
stantaneous obedience can hardly be overestimated."
These things were all calculated to appeal to Henrici—the

reference to Father Rapp, to physical and mental discipline, to the importance of concerted action. Then Fischern, who had been skeptical of such training at the beginning, added his testimony and approval.

After a few seconds of working his jaw, a habit of Henrici's when giving serious consideration, he observed, "It's all right, John, but I suggest you do not start too many out-of-the-ordinary things. At any rate, hereafter tell me about it before you start anything."

"Very well," I said. "We are now installing on the playground a turning pole and springboard for the boys, and a simple merry-go-round for the girls. You will also hear that we teachers are taking part in the children's play—which will undoubtedly stir up criticism." To these matters he offered no objection. In any case further innovations in methods of instruction did not cause any disturbance and the school work continued harmoniously.

However, when Elder Joseph Schwarz departed this life on June 25, 1889, a new boss was needed for the lumber business. For this post, Trustees Henrici and Lenz selected my admirable assistant, Herman Fischern. The vacancy occasioned in the school was in turn filled by my wife. Mrs. Duss, by the way, had taught school in Wisconsin and was every whit as good a teacher as her sister Kate. For a year we continued this splendid working relationship; then other duties called me.

In the autumn of 1889 Jonathan Lenz, my one-time guardian, came to me to talk over the very serious problems confronting the Society. His greatest worry was the rapidly dwindling membership. Death had taken away so many of the Society's members that at this time there remained only twenty-five—ten men and fifteen women. Further reduction of male members would preclude the proper filling of vacancies in the Board of Elders, thus leaving the Society without its lawful body for the management of its affairs.

Throughout the village word went around that a number of men and women were to be admitted to the Society at the next "Harmoniefest" in February. Among these were the Feucht brothers, Benjamin and Henry, and their wives; Julius Stickel, his wife and stepdaughter, Bertha Geratsch; Jacob Niklaus, and perhaps others.

The matter of the Feuchts joining had already caused Trustee Jonathan Lenz much worry. Both Elder Kirschbaum, leading light of the Board and generally regarded as successor to Henrici, and Elder Ernst Woelfel, next in importance, strenuously objected to admitting the Feuchts. On the other hand, Henrici favored their admission. Lenz saw nothing ahead but serious controversy. As to the Stickels, Lenz thought they were of doubtful worth, and certainly not to be considered as prospective members of the Board of Elders. Jacob Niklaus, he thought, would do if he were placed between two men of character and ability. Trustee Jonathan therefore suggested that Herman Fischern, Niklaus and I should arrange to join the Society to help maintain its integral structure. Later came Henrici. He spoke in a similar vein, as did Gertrude Rapp to Mrs. Duss, and thus it came to pass that we decided to accept this invitation to membership.

The extensive list of prospective new members was a real source of joy to the old members, but to the hirelings it was a case of sour grapes and ill omen. Because the Harmony Society was reputed to be immensely wealthy, a supposition which the newspapers always headlined as a certainty, outsiders were all too willing to suppose that those who joined did so from absolutely mercenary motives. Some of us were dubbed as "carpetbaggers." The judgment of the public often goes astray, but in regard to certain of the novitiates it proved only too true, as later will appear.

In the light of events happening several months after Lenz's talk with me, his prescience was amazing. On December 27, 1889, Gertrude Rapp, who for almost three quarters of a century had been the Society's "First Lady," closed her eyes in death. As a true "mother in Israel" she had presided over the executive mansion of the Trustees with such perfect tact and geniality that her passing left a void that could not well be filled . . . Soon after the funeral, realizing that Gertrude's position had to be filled immediately, the Trustees asked my mother to assume the difficult post. Though a request from Henrici was in effect a command, my mother, because of difficulties in general and the jealousies she knew would be kindled, at first refused. But soon Henrici returned, and with authoritative charm induced her to accept the post.

But during the latter days of Gertrude's illness Rebecca Feucht, wife of Benjamin, had tried to insinuate herself in Gertrude's place. Thus the appointment of my mother caused the first breach in the friendship of the families of Duss and Feucht—a breach that was to grow as time went on.

Six days after Gertrude's demise, George Kirschbaum, who was being groomed as Henrici's successor, on January 2, 1890, lost his life in an explosion of natural gas. Scarcely had his funeral taken place when John Wirth, another member of the Board of Elders, was stricken with an illness that carried him away on January 12.

Ten days later, Jonathan Lenz, for many years our beloved junior trustee and kind, simple, human friend to all, came to the end of his earth-life. The very air seemed charged with sorrow and death's darkness. . . . Within

225

three weeks there came to be three vacancies in the Board of Elders, leaving only six members of the governing body—the exact number required for a quorum.

It thus transpired that on January 24, 1890, in order to fill these vacancies, Herman Fischern, Jacob Niklaus and I became members of the Harmony Society, and were simultaneously elected to membership in the Board of Elders. Other new members, Mrs. Duss and fifteen more, were admitted to the Society on the following festal, day when such admission usually took place—the day of the Harmoniefest—the fifteenth of February.

To provide a more complete picture of the Society's personnel at this time, so that the troublesome events of the Society's decline in the following years may be better understood, the Trustees, the members of the Board, and the lay members, both old and new are herewith listed.

The members of the Board of Elders were Jacob Henrici, Ernst Woelfel, Moritz Friedrichs, Gottfried Lauppe, John Scheid, Joseph Schwarz, Michael Staib, John S. Duss, Herman Fischern, and Jacob Niklaus. The Board chose Ernst Woelfel to succeed Jonathan Lenz as Junior Trustee.

Of the other members still living at this time who had joined the Society in previous years, Franz Gillman, Gottlieb Reithmueller and Jacob Schellhaas were the only men. Women who had previously joined and still participated in Society affairs were Anna Bauer, Barbara Boesch, Maria Diehm, Caroline Duss, Elizabeth Geiger, Sybilla Hinger, Dorothy Hoehr, Simira Hoehr, Regina Lautenschlager, Frederica Muntz, Barbara Nix, Magdalena Purucker, Christina Schoenemann Rall, Elizabeth Beck Stahl, Barbara Vogt, Lena Rall Wolfangel and Phillipina Wolfangel.

To the nine elders and the twenty other members, fifteen new members were added to the roll at the Harmoniefest of 1890: Susie C. Duss, Benjamin Feucht and his wife Rebecca, Henry Feucht and his wife Margaret, Lena Fritsch, Bertha Geratsch, Christine Haerer, Conrad Hermansdoerfer and his wife Johanna, Edward Kellerman, Hugo Mueller, Blasius Platz, Julius Stickel and his wife Pauline, and Sigmund Stiefvater. Altogether, therefore, as of February 15, 1890 the Society totalled a membership of forty-four—twenty men and twenty-four women.

The Society, through the recent infusion of new blood, almost doubled its numerical strength and more than doubled its vitality. We seemed on the threshold of a new era. The outlook augured well for peace, prosperity and permanence.

However, a lack of real unity among the membership led to a number of internal dissensions. The hirelings were a continuous worry, and sometimes, because they far outnumbered the Society, caused the members to separate into various camps. Also it must be remembered that there was wide divergency in religious belief—a circumstance that led to subtle disturbances among the members, and sometimes affected the actual government of the community.

A humorous example of the petty frictions within the Society was what might be called the style insurrection. To the newly elected members, the men's hats and trousers for many years made at Economy on one general pattern, brought no end of argument and friction; and to the hired help it provided endless merriment. The winter headgear of the men had always been a beaver or felt hat—ill shapen, unduly heavy, and exceedingly uncomfortable. But the hat question soon terminated to our satisfaction—instead of being manufactured at Economy, they were furnished by a Pittsburgh hatter who was easily influenced to make them neater and lighter. But the men's trousers, instead of having the modern fly in front, were ornamented with a "flap," which hinged at the groins and buttoned at the waist. Now the flaps turned out by the tailors of yore, were works of art—something that was beyond the ken of the new tailors. The argument as to whether the old should continue, however irksome to the men and delectable to gossips, through the adoption of the new style, soon died a natural death. The unwritten custom of not permitting moustaches, also caused annoyance.

The matter of hats and trousers being a dead issue, the moustaches of the new members were assailed with double vigor. With one exception all the new male members had moustaches—mine being the biggest and blackest of them all. Caroline Molt, a comparatively new member and pious "Stundengaengerin," originated the attack. She was always cantankerous, and soon stirred up Henrici.

Meeting me one day, Henrici playfully seized me by the moustaches. "John, don't you think these ought to come away?" he inquired.

"For what reason?" I asked.

"Because the members of the Society have always been without moustaches." When I asked him why they discarded them, he said, "That I do not know."

"Then there is no valid reason?"

"The fact that our members have always done so, John, should be reason enough," replied Henrici, "and I ask you to follow their example."

"Nevertheless," I argued, "there is no real reason, and I will not contribute to Sister Caroline's cackling joy. I think I will leave the moustache where it is until the warm spring or summer days come, then for the sake of pleasing you I will discard it." Thus came victory to the moustache camp, until the warm spring Sunday when I appeared minus the moustache, and from Sunday to Sunday moustaches decreased in number until their final disappearance—a regular theatrical event and source of merriment during Henrici's elaboration of The Word.

Religious differences often caused minor disturbances within the little group. Aside from a few of the aged members and the redoubtable Henrici, Father Rapp's mysticism and glowing piety by this time was of little consequence. Henrici, while he continued in the pulpit and as spiritual leader, was the most faithful disciple of Father Rapp's theology. Although in the golden days of the Rapps, the mystery of the biune nature of Adam and the Elect, or in the imagery of Revelations the 144,000 Virgins, might have been taken for granted as postulates by some, Henrici allowed no such liberty. Sunday after Sunday we were regaled with long sermons in the purest High German, as Henrici, with his compelling mastery of the language, drifted into his favorite themes. These were, first, the biune nature of Adam, the division of this image of God into two beings, and their eventual expulsion from Paradise; secondly, the immaculate conception, followed with high tribute to the Virgin Mary; and, finally, the Elect—the 144,000 Virgins. In addition to these three cardinal points, Henrici expounded other favorite Rapp topics, such as the Second Advent of Christ, generally referred to as the End of the World, and the exhaltation of chastity and the celibate life. Henrici's discourses, like those of the elder Rapp, were permeated with the mysticism of Jacob Boehme.

Sometime in the 1880's Henrici, slipping on an iron cellar door, had fallen and broken several ribs. Jonathan Lenz was thereby elevated to the pulpit; but great was the surprise of all when Henrici, after his recovery, insisted that Jonathan continue in the role of speaker. Though Jonathan's educational equipment was somewhat scant, and his delivery in the debased Swabian patois had little in common with Henrici's pure High German, his commonsense homilies gave general satisfaction.

Though in former times members here and there disagreed with the theology of Rapp, of Baker, or of Henrici, it may be stated that with the exception of the days of the Count Leon imbroglio the great majority had at all times proved loyal. The disgruntled elements even seemingly in agreement, there existed a harmony to which some of the new members did violence. In religion they ranged from superpietist to infidel. Aside from Henrici who signed the Society's articles in 1827, the Society in the 1890's, for the purpose of religious analysis, falls into three groups.

Those who signed the Articles of 1827—John Scheid and fourteen women (to which were later added the names of Jacob Schellhaas, Michael Staib and Phillipina Wolfangel)—tolerated rather than agreed with Henrici's theology. Nevertheless, through the crucible of time, these members had become fused into a unified group that still possessed much of the spirit of the early days. Some of these had known the high faith of Father Rapp, and they had not wholly outlived it.

The second group was composed of those who signed the Articles in 1887, just a year before my return to Economy and sixty years after most of the first group had joined the Society . . . On my table is the "Book of Life" (which contains the Society's various Articles of Association and the signatures of the members). I look at that group of 1887; my eye focuses on the name of my mother, the center of this group. Consider the divergence of religious faith among them. Old Brother Franz Gilman, a

Lutheran, uncommonly devout and a fine example of Christian humility. The same is true of Magdalena Purucker. Caroline, my mother, was in early life a Lutheran, but soon found that church not sufficient to her spiritual needs. She thus in time became a Superpietist. To her even the Stundengaenger lacked the necessary piety, as apparently did the Harmony Society, for how many pilgrimages had she made in search of spiritual peace! Her cousin Gottlieb Reithmueller once said of her, *"Ach was,* the Wuerttembergers were always thus, groping and groping after something better"*. Then there was Brother Lauppe, in youthful days a Lutheran, who now as Stundengaenger and Separatist was still in search of Truth. Lauppe, with the aid of Caroline Molt and Katherina Nagel, who had run the same gamut of faith, had tried to organize a Stundengang within the Society, only to have it stopped by Henrici. Still, the heart hunger of these extreme pietists again and again came to the surface to trouble us . . . Nor can we forget dapper, little Moritz Friedrichs, neat as a pin and proud as Lucifer, never missing an opportunity to vaunt himself as a Herrnhuter (a religious settlement of Moravians on the estate of Count Zinzendorf in Saxony). At heart a Pharisee, he nevertheless lacked the courage to proclaim, "O Lord, I thank thee that I am not as other men!" With unctous tongue and sardonic smile he blotted out the Rapp theology and all the other faiths but his.

The third group, namely those who joined in 1890, illustrate so many shades of faith that they cannot by any means be defined as a group. Consider, for example, Julius Stickel, who prided himself on being a Baptist— that is, if Baptists were only what he would have them be. In his plebeian way he had endeavored to reform the Baptist faith, but at last, discouraged with his utterly unavailing efforts, he joined the Harmony Society. Knowingly or unknowingly, back of it all there was a desire to transform the Society into the Baptist Church of his ideal. One might call the roll of faith—or the lack of it—in the rest of this group; but so great is the diversity and so complex the relationships that to the reader it would only be a case of "confusion worse confounded." What about my faith? From my second year to my ninth I listened to the homilies of Romeli Baker; whereupon followed three years of Rapp theology as dispensed by Henrici; and another three years of sermons by the Presbyterian Divine, Rev. W. G. Taylor at Phillipsburg. At 16 years of age I was confirmed into the Lutheran faith in the very church that the seceding Harmonists had built in Phillipsburg in the 1830's. Being of Württembergian extraction it may be taken for granted that of "groping" I did my full share. However as to later Harmony Society days when it became my duty to preach to a congregation, the members of which had various faiths and some no faith whatever, I adopted the theory of the Apostle Paul and by "Becoming all things to all men" I managed to keep our religious barque on an even keel.

One summer day—July 26, 1890, to be exact—I was busy with transit, chain and field notes making a survey of Economy lands at the request of Trustee Woelfel, who desired a complete map of the Society's Economy property pasture lands, woodlands, and village. Suddenly, like a bolt from the blue came word that Woelfel, good Brother Ernst, was stricken with a cerebral hemorrhage. This same day he closed his eyes in death . . . Two days later the Board of Elders elected Conrad Hermansdoerfer to the Board, and thereupon elevated me to the junior trusteeship.

Aside from the air of general expectancy that pervaded

the community, my elevation to the trusteeship was on the surface passably serene. But beneath that surface I could sense the currents of antagonism. Somehow I had to overcome this mischievious undertow. I think my first move was designed to please at least the numerically important womenfolk. Mrs. Duss and other Society women had complained of the physical exertion necessary on wash days. Now, though Economy had one of the first steam laundries in the world which in its day was regarded with just pride, there had never taken place any addition or improvement to the machinery originally installed. Having converted the Board of Elders, I installed throughout our laundry the most modern and improved machinery; also an elevator which carried both women and washing to the drying room upstairs. The effect of this alteration was almost magical—until the newness wore away, loud were the praises uttered in my behalf.

In the management of the Society, and especially in my job of supervising the farms and property, I continuously had to cope with the influence of the hirelings. The individual members during the decades of 1870 and 1880 had become greatly outnumbered by the hired help; and, not unified among themselves, now were surrounded with these groups of satellites—each with self-appointed confidants and advisors largely composed of favorites, gossips and mercenaries. Thus discord, petty jealousies, and the corruption of the cooperative spirit played havoc with the Harmony of former days.

Indeed, those golden days were now no more. When I returned to Economy in July, 1888, I naturally joined the workers in the harvest field. Here I received a rude awakening. Though in the old days at Economy we had not rushed our daily work to the extent that I had practiced in the West, we nevertheless worked with an earnestness and a purpose. Now a far different spirit prevailed. Arriving in the harvest-field I dived into the work of gathering the sheaves with the zest and speed of Nebraska days, quite unaware of the sensation I was causing. The whole force stood petrified watching me. Soon conscious of their staring, I tried to explain that my way of working was the ordinary way out West. All explanations were in vain—the whole working force seemingly taking umbrage at my innocent exhibition at harvesting.

"If I would work in such a crazy way," said one, "then for the other eight or ten there would be nothing left to do!"

There was nothing left for me but to subside, and in their dawdling way, work leisurely along with them. But the experience was to haunt me many, many days.

If one recalls the great exertions of the Society through the years, one is all the more shocked by the decadent spirit of its workers in this later period. During the Society's first great era, when the great migrations from the Old World took place, when three villages were built and three smiling settlements were hewn out of the American wilderness, everyone worked for the common welfare with every ounce of strength. Even in those earliest days of privation, the productive efforts of the Commune are nothing short of astounding.

Then came, in 1832, the insurrection under Count de Leon, clearing the Society of all discordant elements. Though greatly decreased in productive manpower the Society soon recovered from the storm and from 1832 to 1860 enjoyed a period of sane industry, efficiency, loyalty and comfortable mode of living. It was a time of placidity and communal happiness, of spiritual and moral uplift and of physical well-being.

But with the decline of membership and the influx of

hirelings and discordant voices, the vices of indolence, shiftlessness, waste and disloyalty to the Society gradually infiltrated. By 1880 a period of spiritual disintegration pressaged an impending financial doom.

Early in my trusteeship it was my duty to inspect and manage the outlying farms and the internal operations of the community in general. One day when driving over the Economy lands on a tour of inspection, I came upon a group of our men seemingly petrified. Some had climbed above an old stone quarry; others were in the branches of nearby trees.

"What seems to be the matter up there?" I called to them.

"He will not let us work," one of them answered, pointing to an angry Jersey bull.

"How long have you been up there?" I questioned.

"Ever since we came out this morning."

I looked at my watch—two hours! "How long do you propose to stay up there?"

"Until he goes away." This time there was no hesitation.

"If someone doesn't do something soon, he is liable to keep you there all day. This is no way to do," I continued. "You are spoiling the bull as well as yourselves. Here I jumped from the sulky, tied my horse, gathered some stones and climbed the fence, the bull meanwhile working himself into a fury. This was old stuff to me; I had learned how to handle such critters in Nebraska. On the instant, I charged the bull, and when within convenient distance, let fly one of the missiles. It caught the surprised bull above the eye. An additional bombardment sent his lordship wheeling about, and bellowing in disappointed rage, he disappeared through the hollow . . . This episode engendered a wholesome respect among the laborers.

The more I scrutinized the operations of the Economy farms and shops, the more foreboding the situation loomed. Most of the hired laborers, and many of the new members, were simply time-servers. The Harmonist days of order, diligence, thrift and efficiency were no more. While I am writing these words a hundred examples of incredible waste and indolence pass through my mind. Once, when inspecting one of the fields in plowing time, I came to Gerber's Meadow, where the entire force of teams had been plowing. In the center of the field there remained a core about two feet wide and possibly ten rods long. Two teams making one round could have finished the task. Any right-minded worker with the slightest respect for his employer would have completed the task before doing anything else. But the dinner bell had rung! Eight plowmen had unhitched their teams, had ridden a mile and a half south to their meals in the village—only to retrace this same distance, re-hitch their horses to finish a five minute job of plowing. And at the end of this five minute job, to retraverse the same mile and a half, not to go to the barn, but to a field situated another mile still further south.

The situation was just as disappointing in the village shops, and even in the households. Each family, it will be recalled, was entitled to a small flock of chickens—one rooster, four mature hens per person plus a reasonable number of spring chicks that were periodically disposed of. Requisite chicken feed was rationed out to the respective families at the grist mill, thus automatically regulating the size of each flock. Judge of my consternation when I discovered one household, composed of only husband and wife, feeding a hundred and fifty laying hens, yet the cost of feeding them was almost nothing! They practically fed this flock of chickens with bread from the bakery—

bread being one necessity of life that the Society did not ration.

Elder Fischern, in charge of the sawmill, longing for something more modern than the old muley saw which had been in use for half a century, convinced Henrici and the other Elders that a fine new mill with modern equipment should be built. The location of same was to be at a short distance north of the village, namely at French Point where the first pioneers had landed in 1824. But of what value is a splendid new mill when the workers are inefficient? Suppose we take a look at Mr. Helms, the expert millwright who has charge of the new construction. On this morning he is sitting astride a heavy, squared piece of timber, endeavoring to insert the tenon into the mortise of an upright. Behind him are twenty ablebodied men, who at his given signal, are to propel the beam along. Now the tenon is about to enter the mortise; Helms' eye is fastened on it as he sings out. "Ready now, Heave ho! Heave ho!" At each "Heave ho!" he lifts and tugs with his might—somehow the beam no longer moves. Perplexed, he turns about to find the cause, and—"Donnerwetter!" he yells, almost expiring with rage at the sight of the entire force gathered around the ciderkeg a hundred feet away! At the stroke of 9 o'clock, A.M., the twenty men had let go all holds.

In days gone by, Oekonomie (the German word which the Society used in the sense of Economics) was an ideal to which all unselfishly dedicated their lives. It was a noble experiment in Christian living—an aspiration of several hundred people working and singing together in harmony . . . But the passing of the good old stock also meant the passing of the pioneer spirit of devotion and industry.

237

During two decades—1870 to 1890—occupation of responsible positions by outsiders; the lack of unity among the members of the Society, both as to spiritual and material ideals; not to mention the prevailing out-and-out indolence, extravagance and waste, resulted in a condition which unmistakably manifested that twilight had descended on the noble Harmonist Experiment.

Let it not be understood that all the employees were indolent, careless or disloyal—as shining examples of faithful loyal workers there flash through my mind names such as Knoedler, Stoffel, Breitenstein, Wagner, Kroll, Stauffer, Rye, Ott, Thumm, Kuemmerle, Kropp, Loeffler, Liebermann, Wendel, Heberling and others.

10

Whistling on the Crater of a Volcano
(1890-1892)

To THE WORLD AT LARGE, even to many of our own little
aging band of celibate communists, Economy was
growing old gracefully and prosperously. It was commonly
thought that The Harmony Society's wealth could not be
counted at less than forty-five or fifty millions of dollars—
some imaginative folks drove the figure up to a hundred
million or more. Mary Temple Bayard, otherwise known
as "Meg," feature-story writer for the *Philadelphia Times*
and other papers, headlined her article of August 2, 1891
thus—

One Million to Each

To her, as to many another traveling journalist, "Economy was all peace, harmony, and quiet good living backed
by fabulous wealth."

At any rate this was the surface aspect of Economy.
The immediate region round about was not as yet industrialized. Pittsburgh's steel mills and blast furnaces extended only a short distance down the "Beautiful River,"
and the towns farther down had not yet greatly expanded.
The factories long since closed, Economy seemed all the
more wrapped up in silence . . . . "A Rip Van Winkle
lethargy has fallen upon the place," startled only by the
more frequently recurring rumble and whistle of the
locomotive puffing its way below the bluff, as though it
were a threat of days to come.

Walking down Economy streets, there hardly seemed to be time or movement in this little world. Occasionally one met a grey-haired, wrinkled old man in light blue jacket who would tip his broad-brimmed hat with a courteous "Guten Tag," or perhaps some buxom dame in Norman cap and gown. The hauntingly beautiful hamlet, with its tidy streets and gracefully simple espaliered brick or frame houses high on the bluff overlooking the Ohio, had its own intrinsic movement. Even the big church tower clock told not the time of the world at large, but still ticked off its own sun-time, eighteen minutes slower than Eastern Standard time and forty-two minutes faster than Central Standard time. Yet it was a strange anomaly in a region that was soon to become one of the most highly industrialized areas in the country.

I recollect a Sunday morning service in the 1870's, when supposedly the Society was still enormously prosperous, Henrici varied his usual theologic discourse by reading a German story about the Harmony Society. A thing that struck all of the congregation as ridiculous was the writer's low estimate of the Society's wealth—three million dollars. But what startled us even more was Henrici's own comment—"Of course, this is a gross exaggeration!" The whole world—Economy included—for years had had the Economy multimillions dinned into its eyes and ears, yet here was Henrici's own revaluation, and Henrici was truthful.

But the days went on without any change in affairs, except that imperceptible waste and inefficiency continued to multiply our losses and undermine our economic structure.

For many years the Trustees had not kept any system of accounts worthy of the name. Exact knowledge of where we stood financially was out of the question. After I was elevated to the junior trusteeship, I became more and more suspicious of the reports of our fabulous wealth. Merely observing the manner of work in the fields and workshops, as I had to do in my supervisory capacity, would have made anyone suspicious. Indeed most of the members knew that the Society was running at a loss, but no one bothered to make any fuss about it. It was simply taken for granted. Everyone was having a livelihood, and that, apparently, was all that mattered.

I soon realized that my position as a responsible trustee necessitated knowing the hard facts of the matter. And, since there were no authoritative records to which I could resort, I was truly in a quandary. After all, Henrici having tended the temporal matters of the Society since his elevation to office long years ago, even Jonathan Lenz, as co-trustee, paid no attention to the Society's external affairs. I, at that time but thirty years of age, and he a patriarch, of eighty-seven, it would seem presumptuous for me to question the venerable Henrici. However it was imperative that I learn the true condition of the Society's affairs. To this end, one day, I wended my way to W. H. Breitenstein, the manager of the community store—he being in a position that entitled him to hazard a guess.

"It seems to me," I said, taking him aside, "that the village and the farms are operating at a loss which annually must run into thousands. In order to direct the work to the best interests of the Society, I need first of all a fairly correct estimate of these losses. I am not asking for exact figures, but what is your approximate guess?"

Wary, and blushing as though he were partly responsible, he replied, "Well, there is no doubt about there being a considerable annual loss. But, suppose you first give me your estimate."

"Oh well," I conjectured, "I suppose we are losing something like $25,000 a year."

"I am afraid you will have to revise those figures," he replied, "at least doubling your estimate."

Although I had come prepared to hear the worst, the thought that we were losing annually about $50,000 somewhat upset my equilibrium. It took a little time to frame my next question.

"And how long has this sort of thing prevailed?"

"Ten years at least," said Breitenstein. "In recent years there has not been much change. You know how it is . . . no system of accounts to hold the hired workers in check. And everybody says, 'Oh well, the Society's rich, so what does it matter?' "

"Ten years!" I exclaimed. "Why that means Half a Million Dollars!"

"It is generally supposed," he added, "that these losses have been bridged over with revenue derived from other sources. But in that direction, I very much fear that you will meet with some surprises also."

The information as to the extraordinary loss at the Society's home left me bewildered and bereft. Yet this was but the first surprise. Penetrating into other phases of the Society's finances, discovery after discovery startled me, so that in time I came to be shock-proof. Inquiry into the external operations and investments of the Society disclosed that beginning with the later years of the Baker and Henrici trusteeship most of these investments had been unfortunate. During the 1850's the trustees in conjunction with other capitalists were operating coal mines at Cannelton in Beaver County. The coal was shipped over their own railroad, the Darlington and Cannelton, which connected with the Pittsburgh, Ft. Wayne and Chicago Railroad at New Galilee. Though for awhile in great demand, the so-called cannelcoal proved in the end a most expensive luxury, and the railroad itself a great headache. Hand in hand with these operations they experimented with the manufacture of oil from shale, the refinery being located at Cannelton. Now just when the demand for the cannelcoal was assuming profitable proportions it was discovered that the coal formation was in small pockets which were soon exhausted, rendering all the expensive equipment of railroad, switches, tipples and other heavy machinery utterly useless. Also, just at the time when the coal-oil was beginning to be commercially marketable, the great underground pools of oil in northern Pennsylvania were discovered . . . The whole property—including railroad, mines, machinery and sawmill—was finally sold at a staggering loss. A former associate in this venture told me that the Society must have sustained a loss of about Half a Million Dollars!

Another thing that startled me as time went on was the appearance, now and then via U. S. Mail, of notices addressed to "Henrici and Duss Trustees," that a note of, let us say, $20,000 was due at such and such a bank. Henrici of course took care as to extension of the loans. One must remember that each of the trustees had full power either in his own name or in that of both trustees to draw checks, borrow money, etc. Early in 1890 I began to tabulate these notices. This evidence that Henrici was borrowing large sums aroused my suspicion as to the whole financial status of the Society. Since the Society, represented by its trustees, owned eighty per cent of the Economy Savings Institution at Beaver Falls, why should we borrow large sums from other banks? Here is my tabulation of Henrici's borrowings from Pittsburgh banks, with the dates due in 1891:

Farmers Deposit National Bank, on demand $10,000
Farmers Deposit National Bank, April 1 10,000
Bank of Pittsburgh, April 5 60,000
Bank of Pittsburgh, April 7 60,000

Bank of Pittsburgh, April 17	50,000
Iron and Glass Dollar Savings Bank, April 26	10,000
Iron and Glass Dollar Savings Bank, May 12	26,900
Iron and Glass Dollar Savings Bank, June 4	32,058
Bank of Pittsburgh, June 26	10,000
Bank of Pittsburgh, June 30	10,000
Iron and Glass Dollar Savings Bank, July 3	10,000
Iron and Glass Dollar Savings Bank, July 4	12,000
Farmers Deposit National Bank, July 21	28,600
Farmers Deposit National Bank, July 27	12,000
	$341,558

Astounding as these figures undoubtedly are, they were but a small part of the picture. Gradually other items came to my notice, were jotted down in my little black book, and generally brought me to a new pitch of excitement. Soon I discovered that for H. W. Hartman, an enterprising promoter and founder of Ellwood City, Henrici had endorsed notes at the Bank of Pittsburgh to the extent of $130,000. And through the Economy Savings Institution we were surety for some sixty or seventy thousand dollars to a bank in New York. These items, which I kept adding together, spelled something like another Half a Million.

"Half a Million Dollars" was beginning to sound like a chorus chiming in from every side. I felt that we were standing on the crust of a rumbling volcano—it was decidedly time to put our house in order.

But there seemed to be innumerable obstacles to any plan of action that I could conjure up. First of all, in spite of Father Henrici's eighty-seven years, he was still remarkably vigorous, and no doubt, as a patriarch following in the footsteps of his beloved Father Rapp, in course of time he had naturally come to feel that the large interests of the Society were his own personal affairs. He had been trustee since 1847, and even prior to that date had acted as Father Rapp's financial agent. After the death of Trustee Baker, he had become clothed with power absolute. At this juncture the reader's attention should be called to the fact that neither George Rapp, nor Jacob Henrici, nor Jonathan Lenz, as Trustees, ever regarded themselves as accountable to any one. Their attitude is best described by trustee Baker on the witness stand in the Nachtrieb Case in 1849.

Question (regarding the sequestration of the $510,000 fund by Geo. Rapp): "What was the object in leaving it out of the general statement of the year 1845?" Answer: I don't know . . . except that the sum should be considered as a reserve, or church fund, spoken of in the Old Testament, where it is stated "that the Children of Israel for the purpose of rebuilding the Temple at Jerusalem contributions should be gathered . . . and placed in the hands of trustees, *and no account to be kept of them.*" (See 2 Kings, 12:15 and 22:7.)

That the Society as a whole fell into this same attitude is borne out by the fact that up to the time of the Leon imbroglio, the members never demanded that their Trustees submit an account.

The story was told how Frederick Rapp, having sent a considerable sum of money to George, later wanted to know how it was applied. George's reply was that he bought some lumber, some cattle, and miscellaneous things. The answer not being at all satisfactory to Frederick, George added, "Why be so particular, *it is ours isn't it?*"

The George Rapp dictum expresses precisely the quality of the Henrici and Lenz trusteeship. It is ours . . . we are honest . . . why waste time in keeping a complete system of accounts!

Having an alert mind, Henrici kept his accounts in his memory, or as the common saying had it "under his hat." But during the time in which Henrici became clothed with power absolute, the Society had entered into its decline. Through death, the custom of celibacy, and the aversion to admission of new members, the Society was forced to the recourse of hired help. Nevertheless the introduction of this element proved a necessary evil, undermining as it did, the morale of the whole community, and ushering in an era of waste and extravagance unparalleled. The change being gradual probably accounts for the fact that the Trustees gave it little attention—the same reason perhaps accounts for their lack of proper heed to the complexity developing in the Society's external investments and operations. Aside from this, it must be borne in mind that Henrici's main object, officially and personally, was simply *to do good.* Thus in the number of men employed at Economy and in the enterprises which he controlled in other parts of the region, he was not concerned with profit. Always unwilling to discharge employees, though convinced that the Society was losing money, he insisted on keeping them in service.

"In other words, Henrici was not given to what modern America would call "sharp practice". Being as much a mystic as was Father Rapp his imagination did not take root in material things. As spiritual leaders of men, the two were much alike. But now Henrici was filling the shoes of Frederick Rapp whose feet had always been on solid ground. Brother Jacob's absorbtion in matters spiritual were of a nature to cause Frederick's "little empire" to languish—perhaps to pass away.

Few understood the nobility of Henrici—this man, whose character, pure as purest crystal, made him seem like one from another sphere. If ever there was a man who lived and walked with God, he was that man.

Now there was no such thing as caste at Economy. But in spite of social equality, an aura surrounded brother

246

Jacob—the aura of prophet, priest and patriarch. There was something almost unapproachable about this aged, venerable man. I remember numerous occasions when I tried to tie him down to immediate demands which had to be met. He would look at me, somewhat troubled for a moment, then blandly smile and say, "Don't worry, John, the Lord will take care of it."

And when Henrici consigned matters to the Lord they were consigned. The only thing left me was the phrase from Kipling, "And the sons of Mary cast their burdens on the Lord who in turn puts them on the shoulders of the sons of Martha."

Sometimes the good man was exasperating. Being a born teacher, he had little patience with those who spoke or wrote incorrectly. He would have made a wonderful editor, for I often heard him mumbling contemptuously, something on the order of *"Ei was!* this should be a semi-colon, not a comma!" Even when he was playing the organ in church, it was not unusual for him to stop, take out his pencil, and declare to the congregation, "Such harmony! The altos should sing a C sharp, not an E. Printers are getting worse and worse!"

Through the long years, in Western Pennsylvania, Henrici came to be regarded as a personality passing strange. As the Head of the supposedly rich and religious Harmony Society, he was looked up to on the one hand as a prophet and on the other as a fabulous financier. In other words the world at large—especially the business world—knew the Society only through Henrici. The prestige therefore, that was his, both within the Society and without, was a vital element in my effort to save the Society from perdition. Hence I early made up my mind that come what may, the upholding of the Henrici prestige was of first consideration,

247

It was plain to me that with the name of Henrici as a talisman, there existed a possibility of saving the Society from utter ruin—it was a certainty that without such talisman, there was not a faintest ray of hope.

In my position as Junior Trustee in charge of internal operations of the Commune, it fell to me to remedy the obvious waste, which in part was caused by a superfluity of lethargic workers. Becoming thoroughly alarmed at the general financial condition of the Society, it seemed more and more ridiculous to keep so many workers employed; but in the real necessity to rid ourselves of useless hirelings and hangers-on, strongest opposition lay in wait for me. The foremen of the shops all vigorously opposed the reduction of workers. When I approached Scheid, Lauppe, and Hermansdoerfer—all Elders and foremen— about cutting expenses, the usual answer was: "Suits us, but please begin at some other place of the town."

To please Fischern a new model sawmill was being built at French Point on a level with the railroad switch. French Point jutted out into the current of the Ohio, and served as a splendid gathering place for the huge lumber rafts which floated down the Allegheny and Ohio Rivers from the Society's Warren County forest lands. In earlier days it was a splendid sight to watch the huge rafts tie into place at the Point . . . But now the husky raftsmen seldom sounded their "Land Ho!"

While the building of the mill required large sums of money, my friend Fischern was branching out more and more in the lumber business. This at the very time when we should have been retrenching. In order to curb his expenditures it became necessary to enlighten Fischern. So without mentioning the most glaring irregularities of our financial status, I told him about our precarious condition. This under the stricture of absolute secrecy.

Soon after—one hot day in August, 1891—a threatening resolution was left at the store for Henrici. It requested him within thirty days to render an accurate statement of all property of the Society. Moreover, the petition urged that the statutes of the Society be changed in such a way that the Board of Elders could conduct all external as well as internal business affairs of the Society. The document bore the signatures of Johannes Scheid, Herman Fischern, Hugo Mueller, Gottfried Lauppe, Jacob Niklaus, Moritz Friedrichs, and Conrad Hermansdoerfer (all the Board of Elders except Henrici and me).

The resolution, in terms polite and sauve, reveals the clever hand of Brother Hugo, an intellectual and learned man and close ally of Fischern. Both were outstanding members of the declining Society. Both had been reared in the cultivated atmosphere of old Germany. Mueller, it was stated, had once been high in the councils of Berlin. Fischern himself, according to a confession letter written to Henrici in 1888, was the illegitimate offspring of a high and influential nobleman and the daughter of an English ambassador, born in a castle of Thuringia, and at an early age was placed in the hands of a well established German scholar. Later he attended the University of Heidelberg, then in its full glory, thereupon traveled in Italy, Greece and the Orient, and settled down as a director in a large chemical factory. Unaware of his parentage he had fallen in love with a young English lady whom he decided to marry. The shock of learning that she whom he loved was his half-sister drove him to the verge of insanity. When he recovered, he left Germany to represent five large chemical firms at the 1876 Centennial in Philadelphia, where he first learned of Economy. Seeking spiritual peace from the troubles of his past life, he had wandered into Economy sometime in the year 1887.

One cannot wholly blame men such as Fischern and Mueller for becoming unduly excited about the financial status of the Commune. But unfortunately none of the signers fully understood the ramifications of Henrici's trusteeship, nor the importance of secrecy concerning our state of finances.

On my return from an arduous day abroad Henrici handed me the resolution of our seven Associate Elders. Anxiously he watched me read it.

"What do you think of that?" he asked nervously.

'Not much!" I replied.

With this simple reply he brightened up. Hammering the floor vigorously with his inseparable umbrella, he added, "Neither do I!"

Nothing was done about it immediately. But on the following Sunday morning I thought I detected a righteous gleam in the eye of the Patriarch. He had chosen for his text the episode of Ananias and Sapphira, recorded in the Book of Acts. With his choicest eloquence—and Henrici's power of speech was justly famous—he denounced the culprits in the text and led onward to a sensational climax: I can still hear his words ring out . . .

"We also have amongst us certain Ananiases, lusting to put their hands on money which is none of their concern . . . Their desires in no way shall be gratified . . . Let them take warning from the fate of Ananias and Sapphira."

This is the only reply the seven Elders ever received. Surprised, chagrined and bewildered, they realized that they had reckoned "without their host."

For a time the conspiracy was quieted. Having ignored me in their resolution, they could not very well use my trusteeship to pry at Henrici. But soon the conspirators rallied. A friend had told me that the discontented elders were planning a petition for the whole community to sign. Dr. Benjamin Feucht's aid was requested, but he would do nothing without my signature. This brought on a secret meeting at the home of Brother Lauppe.

Having through certain channels received knowledge of this meeting, the matter had worried me continuously during a very busy day in Pittsburgh. On the evening when the meeting was to be held I was scheduled to take a train for the West to purchase livestock for the Society. But the feeling that something at Economy needed most urgently my attention was so strong that I asked A. B. Starr, superintendent of the Pittsburgh, Fort Wayne and Chicago Railroad, to stop a late afternoon express for me at Economy, thus giving me an hour or so before my departure westward.

At Economy I headed straight for John Scheid, who next to Henrici was the oldest member of the Board. Lauppe was with him. Half in earnest and half in jest, my first words caught them off guard.

"Well," I said without introductions, "now I suppose you think you are on top of the roost."

Suddenly they knew I was aware of their contemplated meeting. They stammered and jabbered: "What else can we do . . . He is too old . . . Things are going from bad to worse . . . You can't do a thing with him . . . He ignores us!"

Apparently their plans had gone farther out of bounds than I had expected; they were going to depose Henrici from the Trusteeship!

Taking my cue from this, I ventured, "Now that you have decided to depose Henrici, you may as well accept my resignation!"

Loud was the protest. "No, no, you can't do that. We need you."

251

I paused a little. "Do you know what I think of you people?" I said. "You remind me of the man who not only locks his stable after the horse is stolen, but hires a brass band and leads a parade to the empty stall. If you would only subside awhile, I may be able, with Henrici's name as a talisman—(the world still regarding him a great financier) to save the Society from bankruptcy. But without his name we are absolutely lost . . . Besides, whom are you going to put in his place?"

Seemingly they had not considered that vital question. Turning to Scheid, I said, "I suppose it will be you, John?"

"Oh no, no, I am too old," he admitted, "besides I have not enough education."

"Well then," I said, turning to Lauppe, "then it will have to be you."

"No not me," he answered. "If it were in regard to matters spiritual, I might listen, but I have no ability in material affairs."

I suggested the name of Niklaus, but the verdict was thumbs down. I went through the roll of the others— Moritz Friedrichs, Hermansdoerfer, Fischern, Mueller. All were unsatisfactory in one or more particulars.

I shifted my approach. "Anyway whose proposition was this to oust Henrici?" I asked. "Why, this all came from the sawmill," they answered, referring to Fischern and Mueller. Whereupon Scheid remarked, "It begins to look as if those fellows were making fools of us. I guess we'd better nullify our proceedings." To which opinion Lauppe added an Amen.

To interview Jacob Niklaus, I rushed to the dairy. Here the same proceeding took place, with the same results . . . Satisfied that I had spiked the guns of the conspirators, I rested easily that night, assured that for the time being the trusteeship of Henrici and Duss was not in danger . . .

It was some months after the conspiracy had run its course, that Henrici's requests that I relieve him from his pulpit responsibilities became more insistent. Though still vigorous and mentally alert, the responsibilities of his position, coupled as it was with the regular Sunday preaching services, rested heavily on his shoulders. Specifically, the acoustics of the church called for a voice of power, hence the aged Patriarch more and more firmly tried to pass the speakership to me. But here is where I balked. Knowing that the spiritual leadership of such a motley group of diverse believers was an uncharted sea made treacherous by hidden rocks, I knew that whoever essayed to fill Henrici's place at the pulpit table would assume a task seemingly impossible. Also I was in the midst of such harrowing daily experiences in alleviating the financial distress of the Society that I was in anything but a preaching mood.

Came a Sunday morning ushering in Rike Kroll, my cousin, fairly beaming with suppressed merriment.

"Uncle John," she announced, "you have to preach this morning."

"Oh, I think not," I replied complacently. "I guess Henrici, as usual, can be talked into the notion."

"No use this time," she said. "He is ill in bed, and says that you *must* occupy the pulpit in his stead."

So, while blacking my shoes and putting on my collar and cravat, I selected for my text, St. Paul's undying tribute to love—Chapter thirteen in his first letter to the Corinthians. To which there flashed across my mind a hymn in perfect consonance: Frederick Rapp's *"Freut euch ihr Kinder der Freundschaft und Liebe."* . . . "Children of friendship and love be rejoiced."

That twenty minute sermon, (wherein I spoke of the true meaning of the Greek word signifying "love" or "charity" as best expressed in the Harmonist concept of "brotherly love") though at the time it irked me, turned out to be a blessing in disguise. My discourse seemed acceptable to all and elevated me to the rank of priesthood. Even the cultured and learned Hugo Mueller expressed both surprise at and approval of my discourse. All this came at a time when I greatly needed the moral support and faith of the community. Some time after this—in March 1892—Henrici permanently transferred the offices of the pulpit to me.

Meanwhile dark clouds were descending upon us.

Even before I assumed the Junior Trusteeship I had heard of certain difficulties arising from the Society's ownership of some 4000 acres of land in Warren and Forest Counties in Northwestern Pennsylvania. Gradually the history of that tract was unraveled for me. Sometime in the 1850's it seems that one Davidson had been interested with the Society in a glass factory in the Beaver Valley. With the failure of the factory, said Davidson had become insolvent, though he still possessed ownership of the 4000 acres in Warren and Forest Counties already mentioned. Though the lands were generally regarded "not worth the taxes," the then trustees, Baker and Henrici, for the purpose of helping Davidson, at highest bid had purchased this land at a sheriff's sale. From the purchase Davidson had realized more than he had paid for the whole tract seven or eight years previously.

Sometime after this transaction, some of this property turned out to be oil territory, and its value rose accordingly. As might have been expected, certain parties raked up an old tax title and entered suits against a portion of the property. In 1861 arbitrators voted against the trus-

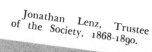

George Rapp. Spiritual leader and head of the commune, 1805-1847.

Jacob Henrici, Trustee of the Harmony Society, 1847-1892.

Jonathan Lenz, Trustee of the Society, 1868-1890.

tees, who thereupon appealed to the court and in the following summer, easily won the case.

With the enhancement in value of this property, the trustees remembered the case of Davidson, their former friend and business associate, and employed him and his sons as managers of the Society's oil wells. The family thus received various sums of money which in the aggregate totalled over $100,000. But the Davidsons, seeing the black gold derived from their former holdings, were by no means satisfied with this generous treatment. Accordingly the elder Davidson published a vitriolic pamphlet about his connection with the Society. When the trustees published a reply, Davidson threatened to publish another unless more money were given to him. To establish peace and harmony between the parties, the trustees thereupon made him a donation of $10,000 as a Christmas present, which led him and his wife to execute a formal release as to any possible claim.

This was in 1867. Some years later the property, under the supervision of the all too benevolent Trustee Johnathan Lenz, was used for various experiments. Jonathan's generosity was something that bordered on the incredible—exceeding perhaps the generosity of Henrici. For instance in the early 1880's there arrived at Economy a colony of twenty families of Russian Mennonites. In Dakota, whence they had come, their crops had failed, and, learning of the benevolence of the Harmony Society, they came bag and baggage. When the Trustees saw that they did not fit into the Economy scheme of things, Lenz led them to Warren County, placed at their disposal nearly a thousand acres, built them large dormitories and kitchens. But the colony failed to make things go, and so . . . the Society paid the whole bill of transporting them back to the Dakotas.

A little later four Swiss families from Ohio were placed on the tract. Every requisite for farming was provided, including additional help and money. Nevertheless, the project failed. Still later a band of Italians was placed on the tract and employed at burning charcoal. The market for charcoal varied so that Lenz built a large shed for storage. But instead of building this shed alongside of a switch at the railroad, he chose a high mountain on the far side of the river. Thereupon the charcoal was hauled from the three mile distant camp to the foot of the mountain, where it was shoveled into specially built crates, which the workers carried on their backs to the top of the hill and emptied into the shed. Upon receipt of an order for charcoal the same process took place in reverse. The object of it all was to give the men employment (an excellent example of what has taken place all over our blessed country during the recent depression).

About twenty years after the Christmas gift episode, Samuel, one of the elder Davidson's sons, and now the leading spirit of the family, proceeded to revive the question of the injustice that had been meted out by the Society to the Davidsons. Asserting that his parents had not been given the $10,000 gift, he stirred the interest of Trustee Lenz to the extent of searching for the quit claim receipt. Not finding it at Economy, at Tidioute, or at Warren, Lenz entered into an oral agreement with Samuel to the effect that 2200 of the best acres of the tract were to be deeded to the Davidsons, who in turn were to execute a quit claim deed as to the remaining acreage.

The deed was actually in course of preparation when death called Trustee Lenz. Lenz' successor, Ernst Woelfel, during his short term of office, had not taken any steps in the matter and Henrici paid no attention to it. But soon after I came to be trustee, a letter arrived from our agent, William Merkle, charging that Samuel Davidson with a crew of men had entered the property and that he was boring for oil, cutting timber and marketing it.

A crisis had come—the first in my stewardship—and I bounced into action. Instituting a thorough search in the vault, chests and bureau drawers of the Great House, every scrap of paper was carefully examined and, wonder of wonders, Mrs. Duss discovered the $10,000 receipt. Shortly Henrici and I, with our attorney Henry Hice (ex-Judge) journeyed to Warren County where we visited the Davidson camp. But to my chagrin, neither Henrici nor the Judge made any remonstrance in regard to the depredations that were taking place. However, I soon succeeded in the instituting of legal proceedings against the Davidson pillage.

Inasmuch as the case involved some 380 acres of Forrest County land, the first trial was held in the Forrest County court at Tionesta. Here the righteousness of our cause and the cleverness of its presentation claimed the admiration of both judge and jury. Frequently I had been called on the witness stand, and, indignant at the ingratitude of the Davidsons as well as at the bias in their favor on the part of the public, I wasted no words in leniency. The verdict was handed down in our favor, with the result that public opinion, as might be expected, swung in our favor.

When taken up in the Warren County court at the town of Warren the case, like all litigation involving the Harmony Society, had gained more than local publicity. Moreover, Davidson, smarting under his Tionesta defeat for which, by the way, he put the blame on me, publicly bragged that he was out for my scalp and to this end he would engage a lawyer "who had never been defeated".

257

This lawyer turned out to be George A. Jenks, one of Pennsylvania's distinguished attorneys—he was later nominated by the Democratic Party for Governor. W. H. S. Thompson, an eminent Beaver attorney, also was added to the Davidson staff.

When I was brought to the witness stand, Davidson's other lawyers retired while the estimable Mr. Jenks, with a let-me-at-him glint in his eye, began my examination with an air that clearly indicated an attempt at browbeating or bulldozing. Here is where he made a mistake— the more noisy and rampant he became, the more cool and calm were my replies—this to the amusement of his colleagues. At the close of a long hearing the jury decided the case in our favor, awarding us $2990. Hereupon, Davidson appealed the case to the Supreme Court of Pennsylvania, where our attorney, "Judge" Brown of Warren, easily won the approval of the findings of the lower court. To the $2990, at a later date I added $45,000 via a sale of 1700 of the 2200 acres in question, and in course of time the total sales of this land amounted to more than $70,000—a well worth while reward for all of my trouble in combatting an unjust claim and a welcome addition to sorely needed finances.

Of all the difficulties existent in the external economy of the Society, the most complex centered in the growing little city of Beaver Falls. To understand this economic entanglement, some history is necessary.

In 1859, the Society had acquired a tract of 500 acres at what is now the city of Beaver Falls; soon after, an additional 200 acres were obtained. By 1865 the trustees, Baker and Henrici, had plotted a considerable portion of this land into lots and streets, and placed them on the market.

Thus began the first forced-growth or "boom town" in

all this section of the country. Factory after factory, through one inducement and another, was built here and put into operation—cutlery works, file works, steel works, axe works, shovel works, pottery works, saw works, car works, a glass plant. The Trustees also founded a bank—the Economy Savings Institution.

An element of mischief, inherent in the policy of such forced development, is the over-anxiety of the promoters to secure the necessary industries. Successful plants are loathe to break up their establishments and move into a new environment, whereas such older industries as do move likely have not been successful. New industries located under such circumstances cannot be regarded as anything but experiments. This latter happened to be exactly the case at Beaver Falls. One after another of the industries became weak-kneed and clamored for support. Their cries were not in vain. They reached the heart of Henrici—also his purse. Inasmuch as the employees of these industries had purchased lots from the promoters and founded homes thereon, it seemed to Henrici that the sponsors were in a very real sense obligated to these home-builders. Wherefore the bank, primarily in the hands of the trustees (which meant Henrici himself), oftentimes came to the rescue by way of loans to the floundering enterprises, or Henrici himself saved the situation by purchasing an interest for the Society in these tottering ventures . . . Once started in this direction, the ball kept merrily rolling on. In numerous cases the entire responsibility came, in the end, to rest upon Henrici's shoulders.

From the beginning of the Beaver Falls development, one John Reeves had been the senior agent for the Society's Trustees, and sometime in the 1860's the young attorney, Henry Hice—"Judge" Hice—who assisted us in

the Warren County litigation—as legal advisor, became
the third member of a triumvirate that, so others thought,
ruled the roost—Henrici, Reeves and Hice—a combined
His Royal Highness.

An unpleasant sentiment lurked among the working
classes at Beaver Falls and the hirelings at Economy that
Reeves and Hice were "sitting pretty"—that, being in
touch with the supposedly fabulous Economy millions,
they could at will annex portions of these resources for
personal ends. Although not inclined to be suspicious,
and always scornful of such gossip, the constant recur-
rence of such whispers had brought matters to such a
pass that I was willing to be shown any such irregularities.
To me, however, both Hice and Reeves, like Henrici,
were august personages and entitled to my entire respect.

The suspicions which were dinned into my ears grew
most loud at the time that I began to feel the absolute
necessity for Henrici's complete confidence in financial
matters affecting the Society. Fond as he was of me, he
had not shown the least inclination of being communi-
cative. In a manner, he seemed to resent inquiry—and
no wonder. Mischiefmakers were at work, whispering,
whispering: "Keep hold of the reigns . . . don't give up
a thing . . . Duss is trying to push you aside . . ."

Casting about for some sort of opening, Providence
unexpectedly came to my aid. A delegation of business
men from Beaver Falls called on me to present a grievance against the H. R. H. combination. The city wished
to purchase the fire-engine house property, but Henrici,
Reeves and Hice were asking a relatively higher price
for this parcel of real estate than they were asking for a
similar property for a U. S. Post Office site, negotiations
for which were pending with the Federal government.
Now this providential set of circumstances not only gave

me an opening into the financial secrets of the revered Henrici, but with Reeves and Hice, as well as the whole Beaver Falls situation. Sympathetic with the delegation's claims, I resolutely refused to attach my signature to the deed for the postoffice site when Henrici placed it before me.

Henrici at first bristled mightily at this new stand, then tried to win me over.

"John, I don't understand. I assure you everything is proper. I've gone over the whole matter with Hice and Reeves—"

"That's just the point," said I. "But don't forget that no matter how wise and honorable you three may be, you cannot take from my shoulders the responsibility attached to my signature. And in the future you need not expect me to sign any document unless I have been consulted about its contents."

. . . Later I called on Hice and Reeves, both of whom were open and above-board about everything. And both freely admitted my rights in the matter. Thereupon I insisted that the price of the fire-house be somewhat reduced. From that time forth the Beaver Falls triumvirate was to function as a quaternity.

My conversation with Mr. Reeves must have impressed him, for when I next called at the Economy Savings Institution, of which Reeves was cashier and owner of ten per cent of the stock, the old gentleman took me into his inner sanctum for a heart to heart talk. I saw that he was leading up to something more or less momentous.

Finally he got to the point: Judge Hice had overdrawn his account some nineteen thousand dollars!

"What kind of banking is this?" I exploded.

Reeves lowered his voice. "You see," he said, "Henrici owes the Judge for years and years of service. Thus everytime I ask the Judge to take care of his overdraft, he promises to do so whenever Henrici pays him his due. Now the bank being in reality a Henrici institution, I have always felt that this overdraft was Henrici's concern, not mine. But obviously they ought to arrive at a settlement and take care of this unwarranted deficit."

I promised him I'd do what I could to expedite the matter.

"Good!" said Reeves, "but I have more to tell you."

"Henrici, unfortunately," continued Reeves, "has also overdrawn the Society's account—nearly thirty thousand dollars."

When I recovered from this jolt, I began working myself into a fine frenzy. Reeves listened patiently to my eloquence about "the sacredness of trusteeships," "responsibilities and duties of bankers," and "business integrity" in general.

"All very well," he said, deftly taking the wind out of my sails, "there is only one explanation—Henrici."

According to the Reeves recital, Henrici had dominated the situation from the beginning. No matter how great the loss at any of the works, they must be kept going so that the men—home-owners in Beaver Falls—would have work. Henrici, through the bank, always footed the bill. This sort of thing practised in the old days when the Society had plenty of money did not matter, but having become a fixed habit it now threatened disaster. Most of this overdraft in question, for instance, was the result of withdrawing money from the bank to meet the payrolls at the Leetsdale brickyard and at Economy.

"When the old gentleman comes in here to ask for money, what can I do but give it to him?" Reeves queried. "But now our cash is very low—sometimes no more than the daily balance of a few thousand dollars brought in by the local merchants. If one of our large depositors should happen to withdraw his account, it would clean us out—or what is worse, we might not have sufficient funds to pay him."

"Is there any likelihood of such occurrence?" I asked. "Just what are the amounts of the largest depositors?"

"There are depositors who have with us as much as thirty thousand dollars, and there are always the very large deposits of the State Treasurer, which amount to $162,000."

"Well," said I, after recovering my self possession, "there is one thing you can do at once. Stop all further overdrafts. Those on the books now must be taken care of as speedily as possible. This bank should be run like a true bank, and everybody must toe the mark."

"I am afraid," said Reeves, handing me a bank statement, "that there are some real difficulties to surmount before we can put the bank on such a basis."

After I looked over the bank statement, Reeves explained that we were much worse off than appeared by those figures.

"Now look here, Mr. Reeves," I remonstrated. "There is the overdraft of Judge Hice, that of Henrici himself; there is a large deposit due the State of Pennsylvania. And now you tell me there is more to come! Let me have the exact figures and be done with this agony."

Reeves handed me the following table:

OVERDRAWN ACCOUNTS—June 30, 1891

Beaver Falls Cutlery Company	$467,385.57
Beaver Falls Western File Company	351,038.89
Henrici and Duss	29,241.41
Henry Hice	19,486.54
Rowan and B.	3,460.78
J. C. Whitla	158.39
	$870,771.58
Ledger Balance	78,371.92
	$949,143.50

And so, to the nigh-unto half-million dollar debt to Pittsburgh and New York banks, nearly a million dollars was here added to our indebtedness.

But a million dollars in the 1890's was a far more stupendous sum than it appears today. Without the batting of an eye, our Congress at the present day appropriates billion after billion. Now, a billion is a thousand millions—of small consequence therefore is the million. Nevertheless an accurate significance of a million dollars is beyond the power of the human imagination.

But my problem was nigh unto a million and a half. Confounded and dumbfounded, I could hardly say a sensible goodbye to Mr. Reeves.

My mind became a merry-go-round of figures . . . O yes, there was another item of consequence—the indebtedness called for the payment of interest accruing at the rate of 6% per annum. On the loans from the banks this interest had to be paid in advance—that due to depositors in the Economy Savings Institution was simply credited to their accounts; but soon or late, it would have to be met.

Somehow I managed to walk to the depot, to take the train and to climb the hill at Economy. I recall that I was in a daze. And I vividly recall how between supper and bedtime—like a caged animal—a thousand times I circled around the eggshell coal stove in the center of my room; cogitating whether or not to walk away and leave the situation to Providence. However, a "wee sma" voice insistently demanded that I undertake this seemingly impossible task. "In all the world," it said, "there is no one aside from yourself who can possibly accomplish anything worth while in this situation. Being the only person in whom the members of the Society have full confidence, the only member who thoroughly under-

264

stands the Society as a whole and the only member who is capable of coping with the world outside—you have before you a duty which you dare not shirk." Wherefore, after some days of being thus weighed down, I proceeded to whistle as merrily as ever—not because I had become callous, but because of its beneficial psychical effect and the further reason that it acted as a "blind" to those whose prying eyes might discover something which would work havoc with my attempt at saving the Society from utter bankruptcy.

This sword above our heads soon led me to the conviction that, in order to liquidate our tremendous indebtedness, we would have to close out as speedily as possible many of our external holdings. At the same time it was imperative that we sell our stocks, bonds and other investments as near to par value as possible. After all, the good people of the Society had spent, collectively, about 85 years in honest, fruitful labor to build up this "little empire." They deserved par value, every bit of it. Brother Henrici growing more and more feeble, the responsibility all-round rested squarely on my shoulders. Upon investigation I found, much to my dismay, that most of the external investments of the Society had not been fortunate. Few of the stocks and bonds were immediately redeemable at anything like a fair price. Some were of dubious value, others only locally known and almost impossible to market, still others practically worthless, some even lost or mislaid! To find or to make a fair market for such a conglomerate group of assets seemed nothing short of superhuman.

Before recording my achievements in marketing our holdings, it is necessary to describe the vast extent of the Society's (for the most part unfortunate) external operations.

Aside from the craft and farming operations at Economy, the Society's greatest financial and industrial investments were in Beaver Falls. In the sale of lots, resulting from the laying out of the 700 acres purchased in 1859-60, the Society between 1865 and 1896 realized something over a million dollars. The Economy Savings Institution, eighty per cent of the stock being in the name of the Society and the remainder in the name of Reeves and Hice but in reality owned by the Society—was always a service institution designed to further the prosperity of the town rather than to make money. It constituted, in the hectic days to follow, the chiefest of my worries.

As already described, the Society had undergone the painful process of gradually assuming the financial burdens of most of the industries of the town. The greatest error of this process was in regard to the Beaver Falls Cutlery Works, incorporated in 1868, with a capital stock of $400,000, and the Western File Works. Due to the financial vagaries of the cutlery works, the Society, having originally a large amount of the stock, became sole owners in 1872, reorganized the company and reduced the capital stock to $250,000, seven-tenths (and later eight-tenths) of which was owned by the Society, while ten per cent each on Henrici's insistence was given to John Reeves, Henry Hice and H. T. Reeves. During all of its operations the works operated at great loss. Even under such circumstances and in spite of the protests of Reeves and Hice, Henrici insisted on continuing operations. The company reorganized in 1872; having no working capital, Henrici had the Economy Savings Institution advance large sums. The overdrafts continued, until in 1890 they amounted, in this one case alone, to more than Half a Million Dollars! Yet besides this the works was indebted $300,000 more on its note held by the E. S. I.

And though the full operation of the Cutlery Company was closed down in 1887, both note and overdraft were carried along by the bank from year to year. Thus the total debt as of February 4, 1896, was $736,590.87 . . .

Turn now to the other venture, or misadventure—the Western File Company. About 1875 a limited partnership had been formed, Henrici taking an interest of $40,000. About nine years later, though the company was losing money at a great rate, Henrici bought out the remaining interest at $37,000, then continued the management through his agents. The heavy losses continued until I shut it down in 1892. Its amazing indebtedness to the E. S. I. has already been quoted in the table of overdrafts—the debt amounting to $402,376.43 or five times the amount of the whole investment!

The C. C. Modes and Company, a glass manufacturing concern of Beaver Falls, had been sold to the Society at a sheriff's sale after the Economy bank had advanced it large sums of money. The concern was, to say the least, not successful—just another drag on the Society's financial resources. Another such venture was the Valley Glass Works, in which the Society held a large amount of stock. But the concern was operated at large losses until the time of its burning down in 1892.

Neither the Beaver Falls Steel Company nor the H. M. Meyers Company, a shovel manufacturing concern, were examples of financial gain. The former had been bought after the same old process of advancing large sums of money and was carried on without distinguished success until 1893. The Meyers Company underwent a similar process, except that the Society disposed of its share therein in 1889.

A car works had also been organized at Beaver Falls in 1879 with a capital of $50,000, $47,000 of which was held by Henrici for the Society. It seems to have been one successful but short-lived investment—the plant burned down in 1886 and for some unfathomable reason was not rebuilt. Henrici had bought outright an axe works from a man by name of Graff, to whom large sums of money had been advanced. The purchase was made to save the investment. After the manufacture of axes was carried on for a while, the works were sold. What the outcome was in this case I do not know. In a similar way the Society became owners of a pottery works, also in Beaver Falls.

The Society also had large interests in the Beaver Falls Gas Company and the Beaver Falls Bridge Company both of which were sold by me in 1892. The Union Drawn Steel Company and the Eclipse Bicycle Company interests, which I acquired, I also sold within two years at a profit of $25,000.

Looking at the other "assets" of the Society does not in any way enhance the picture. Remember that the Society had sustained a loss of roughly half a million dollars on the various Cannelton enterprises, and that the expenses of litigation took away some of the glory in my sales of the Warren County lands. After we were rid of the worries of these properties we still had the headache of 5000 acres of land in Michigan, fronting on Wild Fowl Bay, Lake Huron, and mostly of little value—on the books at $17,736, but by no means immediately redeemable in cold cash. The story is as follows: A number of well-meaning Pittsburghers, feeling that the disreputable tenements of that city were not conducive to health, morals or good citizenship, conceived the benevolent notion that deserving tenement residents should be given the opportunity to earn an honest livelihood under the clear canopy of heaven. To launch the enterprise, twenty thousand dollars were borrowed from the Harmony Society. The tenement people were moved to the tract on Wild Fowl Bay. But far from enjoying "the clear canopy of heaven," these tenement people, like the Children of Israel after their deliverance from bondage, harkened back to their former way of life. Thus the experiment in social uplift proved a dismal failure.

The Society had, through the years, become owner of other properties here and there in Western Pennsylvania, and these were roughly valued at $417,000; but the sale of them could be made neither immediately nor at a fair price.

Shares, some of them sizable, were held respectively in the Rochester National Bank, the Bank of Pittsburgh, the Allegheny Bank, and the Merchants and Manufacturers National Bank. Though these shares commanded a reasonably fair price, they had to be handled with kid gloves. The Society, being heavily indebted to various Pittsburgh banks, bankers here and there upon hearing of sales of these shares, would be inclined to look more closely into the financial resources of the Society and such scrutiny might bring about disaster.

It seems that the Trustees of the Harmony Society also dabbled somewhat in railroad stocks and bonds. Clutching about like a drowning man for a straw, I discovered our interests in the Pittsburgh, Chartiers and Youghiogheny Railroad. This short line, running from Chartiers to Beechmont, was organized in October 1881 with a capital stock of $593,600, of which the Society owned eighty per cent. The balance was purchased by a small number of men, not as an investment but for the purpose of obtaining such favors as switches. The cost of construction and equipment was slightly more than a million dollars, with a funded debt of over six hundred thousand. Largely due to the fact that it was at the mercy of two trunk lines with which it made connections, the road was never successful. The annual losses mounted, until two large mortgages were placed on it. As our share of the venture's costs, Henrici told me that he had sunk Half a Million Dollars (again that fatal amount). . . . Trying to get the two trunk lines, the Pittsburgh and Lake Erie R. R. and the Pennsylvania lines, to bid against each other at purchasing our holdings, they turned the tables on me by putting their heads together. However, I finally succeeded in wheedling out of them a reasonably fair price—$94,000 in cash and 276 bonds at a par value of $1000 each. But this sale gave us a year's lease on life; without it we soon would have floundered in irretrievable ruin.

Another railroad venture was that of the Little Sawmill Railroad, organized in 1857. In this the Society held stock of the par value of $105,025 and most of the bonds with a par value of $110,500. However, for our immediate purposes the stock was worthless and the bonds of doubtful value. Over a period of several years, entailing the most difficult maneuvers and careful reconnoitering, I managed to sell the greater share of this investment— believe it or not—at par.

At some time also the Trustees had been stockholders in the Pittsburgh Southern Railroad, and at the time of which I write still had 27 shares of Pittsburgh, Ft. Wayne and Chicago Railroad Company stock. But these stocks, due to the lack of any filing system, had disappeared from view, and only at a later day by accident came to light.

An excellent investment was Henrici's aid in the construction of the Pittsburgh & Lake Erie Railroad. Beginning in 1877, he is supposed to have fed into this

Susanna C. Duss, the author's wife. Last Trustee of the Society, 1903-1905.

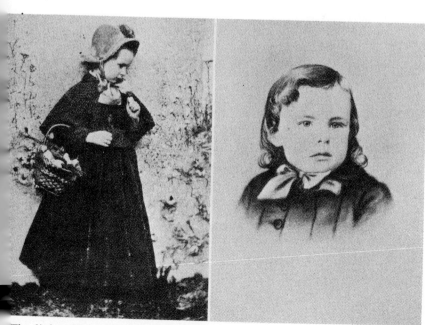

The littlest Harmonists." Vera C. Duss and John S. Duss, Jr., as children of the commune in the 1890's.

project the sum of $650,000. He was President of the Road from January 12, 1881 to January 14, 1884, at which time he sold the Society's interest, supposedly for $1,150,000. Too bad that he did not use this money to pay the Society's indebtedness, as of that time, instead of investing in projects that proved unfortunate.

Among other industrial holdings of the Society, were 2271 shares of Chartiers Block Coal Company, at a par value of $113,500, but really of little value. Sometime before the Society had also purchased stock in the Bridgewater Glass Company and later owned it, but as this was another losing venture, the Trustees sold out as soon as they could. (Would they had followed a similar procedure in other holdings!) Another losing venture and a favorite of Henrici's was the Leetsdale Brick Works, constantly losing money and kept alive only by repeated injections of borrowed funds.

The Trustees also invested in the building of bridges. Our stock in the Tidioute Bridge Company was the only stock of this sort which, given a little time, would be easily marketable. Our Point Bridge stock was not redeemable at this time because of litigation, and that of the Tenth Street Bridge Company was only locally known and difficult to market. Then too, the certificates were either mislaid or lost.

Out of this welter of investments and external operations, with the exception of the luckily discovered Pittsburgh, Chartiers and Youghiogheny holdings, only one was not pledged as collateral on Henrici's notes held by various banks—1610 shares of Monongahela Water Company stock had somehow been overlooked by Henrici. I discovered these in the vault in the Great House, and with this little weapon (par value $40,000) proceeded to attack the ever-growing giant of financial debt.

. . . These then were our "assets." Many of these holdings were being operated at a loss, requiring, according
to Henrici's method, frequent additions of money borrowed either from the Economy bank or one of the Pittsburgh banks. Interest kept on accruing with a lusty
growth. Most of the stocks were not regarded as marketable; others had been placed in banks as collateral on
notes . . . For too long a time we had been borrowing
from Peter to pay Paul. Judgment Day seemed just
around the corner. (See Appendix).

A tabulation of the sale of our stocks and bonds between April 1892 and July 1895 cannot possibly record
the drama of those years, the tremendous worries, the
sharp thrusts of fate, the miraculous twists of circumstance, the endless hours of scheming, fretting, work,
work, work. I confess that whenever I hark back to the
accomplishments of those hectic years feelings of awe
and wonderment overcome me. I marketed more than
$766,000 worth of stocks and bonds, exclusive of the
$175,000 gained from the sale of the Beaver Falls Steel
Company and the Union Drawn Steel Company. And,
miracle of miracles, the total amount of my sales approximated, within $500, the total combined *par* value of all
our complex stock and bond holdings! All this occurred
during years of litigation, when much of my time was
spent in the courts, or in securing witnesses, or in the
secret chambers of our lawyers, trying to ward off the
shocks that destiny seemed to hold in store for us. And
moreover these were "depression years" for the country
at large. But I am anticipating, so let us turn back to the
year 1891.

Not finding any consistent records of our financial affairs, I soon began to feel the necessity of employing an
expert accountant to remedy this state of affairs. What

I needed therefore was some sort of basis, verified by Henrici, on which to put the accountant to work. Hence I commissioned Judge Hice to labor with Henrici on a reasonable tabulation of assets and liabilities as of October 1, 1891, having already in hand the statements prepared at my request by various banks which held our notes. Time and again they missed the deadline date that I had in view.

Finally the Henrici-Hice statement as of April 1, 1892, was prepared. It was a lengthy document, describing the history of the Society, the family of George Rapp, the aims and purposes of the Commune. Though there was not much in the Henrici statement of assets which I had not known previously, it served my purposes, namely the provision of a framework for an expert accountant, and its coming to him directly from the hands of Trustee Henrici.

However, each delay in the completion of the statement entailed on my part another pilgrimage to each bank with requests for new statements. Such an unusual proceeding gave these bankers food for thought—all the more so because the newspapers at this time (of all wrong moments!), were flooded with sensational accounts about the subversion of the so-called Economy millions. Soon the cashier of the Bank of Pittsburgh evinced dissatisfaction and asked for a reduction of our indebtedness. For awhile I managed to hold him off, but as soon as I sold our holdings in the Pittsburgh, Chartiers and Youghiogheny R. R., I paid off some of our notes at the bank as they came due. Naturally I expected a return of the corresponding collateral security, and was I jolted when told that the bank did not permit this until the whole indebtedness was taken care of! Furthermore, this rule of the bank upset my plan of selling said collateral in order to take care of some other indebtedness. After raving at everybody from the cashier to the Board of Directors, and convincing them that it would enhance my efforts at lifting our notes, I finally succeeded in getting the return of collateral.

Thereupon I proceeded to the Farmers Deposit National Bank of Pittsburgh, to the office of T. H. Given, cashier—a banker who had sent me word that he wanted to see me. Given was hard as nails, but was looked upon as eminently capable.

"I sent for you, Mr. Duss," he began, "because Mr. Henrici was here the other day, and led me to do something for him that I would not do for my own mother. He said he needed $1500 for the payroll at the brickyards, and not having any collateral, he asked the loan as a personal favor. I let him have it, but"—and here Given grew almost purple with emphasis—"this sort of thing has got to stop! . . ."

"Now wait a bit," I interrupted, "it should have been stopped before this. Why is it you should do such childish banking?"

As justification, Given recited an event in the dark days of the Civil War, when there was a run on this bank. For a day or so the institution managed to meet the demands of the depositors. Then came Henrici, and the bank officers though their battle was lost, but instead of claiming the Society's deposits, Henrici brought in his carpet bag a deposit of $140,000 in cash. It saved the bank from utter collapse. "And now perhaps you will understand why Henrici got the $1500," said Given.

I admitted that there was real human beauty in Henrici's earlier action, as there was in his (Given's) of the present, but that from a legal standpoint, one was as unlawful as the other.

This interview led to further exchanges of confidence about Economy, though I carefully avoided any topics of danger. But Given, as a banker, soon started probing at our weakest· spot—the Economy Savings Institution. It seemed strange to him, said he, that the Society having its own bank, Henrici for years should have come to him for loans. And what about the reputed immense wealth of the Society? Given further reported that Henrici, Hice and Reeves had approached him about a loan for the benefit of the Economy Savings Institution, but when he asked for a complete statement of the E. S. I., nothing further came of the matter. It seemed that there "must be something rotten in Denmark."

Somehow, through this recital, I managed to assume an aspect of bold assurance, also I told Given that I was going to engage an expert accountant to put all the Society's affairs into ship shape so that we could know at any time exactly how we stood. For the post of expert accountant Mr. Given at once suggested James Dickson. Accepting Given's judgment, I interviewed Mr. Dickson; found him a man of considerable business experience and of wide knowledge in the field of accounting. He valued his services at $500 per month—which was agreeable to me, providing that I could secure Henrici's consent.

To my surprise (and that of everybody) Henrici was quite willing; whereupon I engaged Mr. Dickson as of April 1, 1892. It may interest the reader to know that from the moment that Henrici saw that I was bent on putting our house in order, he was with me heart and soul. He even confided in Mrs. Duss that the Lord had sent me to do the very things in which I was engaged and in general "to take over."

As to the affiliation with Mr. Dickson—fearing that he

might report the glaring irregularities of our financial status to such an one as Given, I first put him at the job of devising a system of accounts for the various internal operations at Economy. When this was successfully accomplished, he was led into the investigation of the enterprises in Warren and Forest Counties, the brick works at Leetsdale, the lands in Michigan and the works at Beaver Falls.

It was probably in late September, that, having found him faithful in these lesser matters, I put him to work on the Economy Saving Institution. After going about for some days with "the weight of the world upon his shoulders", he summoned up courage enough to enlighten me as to the status of the bank. Handing me the latest statement, he asked me to examine it. Nonchalantly I perused it.

"Do you understand it?" he inquired.

"Certainly", I replied.

"Why, Man-alive! Those items—cutlery works, file works, etc., are not assets, they are over-drafts!"

"That is only too true," I admitted.

"How long have you known of this condition?" he went on.

"Just about a year," I said.

"And you have been going in and out of this office whistling! Don't you know that you are standing on a volcano?"

"Yes, but the whistling is a help; and don't you forget that I have been standing on this volcano for a year!"

Thereupon Mr. Dickson opined: "This thing will prove to be the greatest disaster in the history of Western Pennsylvania when it becomes known!"

"Then," I replied, "we must see to it that it doesn't become known."

Earlier in 1892 our volcano almost erupted. Judge Hice, ordinarily a most placid gentleman, came to Economy one day in the greatest excitement, looking as though his whole world was about to disintegrate. Small wonder.

It seems that James Morrison, then State Treasurer, had somehow been informed of the doubtful standing of the Economy Savings Institution. Whereupon he was making an immediate demand for payment of the $162,000 which a former State Treasurer had deposited in the E. S. I. Judge Hice did not know that I was fully aware of the bank's condition, and made every effort to explain in a "reasonable" way the cause of the very low funds.

"But Judge," I answered, "you and Mr. Reeves as officers of this bank, as well as Henrici, must have known that you have been guilty not only of transgressing the rules of business integrity but even the banking laws of Pennsylvania."—Having for some time borne this burden myself, I could not resist having a bit of satisfaction at Hice's expense. Yet it was not all in fun, this roasting of the judge.

To his wail of lament; "What shall we do? What can we do?" I suggested: Suppose that we ask Morrison to wait until Reeves returns from his visit to the Pacific Coast. "No use," said Hice, "I made that request and Morrison flatly refused it. He wants his money and he wants it now, so I agreed that we would meet him tomorrow morning at ten o'clock at the office of his Pittsburgh attorneys—Lyon, Sanderson and McKee."

All at once I propounded what seemed at the moment to be a ridiculous question. "Do you want me to get you out of this fix?"

The question took the judge's breath away. He asked what I could do. "I am going to pacify Morrison," I replied, "all I ask is that you let me do the talking."

Promptly the next morning Hice and I appeared at the law offices and were joined by Messrs. Lyon, McKee and Morrison.

"What I wish to say," I began after the preliminaries, "will not take long. Frankly, the immediate payment of the $162,000 is utterly impossible. However, I am happy to state that, believe it or not, the bank is in a better condition than it was a year ago, when I first discovered its unsavory condition. Dead assets have been turned into live ones, live assets into cash." Here I explained the favorable litigation in Warren County, the sale of our share in the Pittsburgh, Chartiers and Youghiogheny Railroad, of which the $276,000 in bonds—due to the tardiness of the printer—had not yet been turned over to us by the Pennsylvania Lines and the Pittsburgh and Lake Erie Railroad.

"I propose, therefore, to place these bonds—as soon as they are printed—to the par value of $200,000 in the hands of Lyon, Sanderson and McKee, with the understanding that I be permitted to redeem them at par, depositing the cash to the par value of bonds withdrawn until the full $162,000 is paid. But not knowing just when the bonds will be available, I have brought along other stocks and bonds to the par value of $190,000 to leave as security (never mind the real value) . . . You have in your power to do one of two things—you can destroy the good work I have begun, force the Economy Savings Institution into bankruptcy, cause thousands of depositors to lose their money, force the Harmony Society into bankruptcy and its good old people into the poorhouse, or you can save all from disaster by the adoption of my plan." After a thoughtful pause, Mr. Lyon emphatically endorsed my plan and Mr. Morrison readily acquiesced.

A week later I proudly carried the promised two hundred $1000 bonds to Lyon, Sanderson and McKee. Thereupon, by selling the bonds in groups of various amounts, it was not long until I saw the entire $162,000 State deposit paid and the unsold bonds turned back to me.

So far, so good. What next?

In the Harmonist drama at Economy we had evidently arrived at a stage which foreshadowed the impending denoument as anything but placid and agreeable. I could sense it—the complex social relations and unrest within— the frenzied monetary affairs without—the growing sensationalism of newspaper reports—and, towering above all, and forecasting a shadow over our Great Experiment, the menace of serious litigation. In no direction was there any least ray of hope for peace. Had I been without faith in Divine Justice I could not have carried on.

11

The Dark Years That Held No Peace (1892-1894)

T HE STRAIN OF FINANCIAL MANIPULATIONS through the past several years might have been too much to bear had it not been for the constant, quiet encouragement of my wife. She, too, had a heavy burden to carry. When my mother, who had succeeded Gertrude Rapp as mistress of the Great House in 1889, had closed her eyes in death in April 1891, my wife Susanna was chosen by Henrici and the Board to fill this important post. With diligence, beneficence and dignity, she became the mother of the whole Commune, making our aged members as comfortable as possible, dispatching home duties (though such circumstances required that our children should be cared for by Mrs. Duss' mother, "Grandma Creese," much of the time), and, like a true wife of a diplomat, tactfully warding off newspaper reporters, cranks and fakirs.

The words of Mary Temple Bayard, newspaper columnist, who frequently had been our guest at the Great House, describe as well as mere words can do, my sincere regard and affection for my wife:

"It is the privilege of the writer to visit a good many families in the course of a year, and in all truth I am forced to say I was never in one where greater refinement prevailed, or where culture had reached higher tide. Never have I seen man and wife who were such good friends

as are John Duss and his wife. There seems to be
perfect understanding between them on all subjects and just appreciation of each other's love
and talents. Their tastes are in common, their
ideas in accord. Mr. Duss is of that variety of
man who is willing his wife should know as
much as he does; who believes in her mentality;
who values her counsel, her judgment, her intuition. . . .

A pretty woman is Mrs. Duss, red-cheeked,
clear complexioned, with plump figure, tiny
hands and feet, and speaking eyes that can flame
every emotion experienced by woman. In conversation she has a laughing face that looks but
half her thirty-five years; but, in repose, her face
would give a stranger the impression she had
seen great trouble. . . . But Queen of the Village she certainly is; a good wife, a good mother,
a good friend. What more could be said of any
woman?"

During these years of towering debts and financial
losses; of the creeping shadows of disintegration of the
Community; of slanderous headlines about the Society
and myself; of so many law suits that before the adjudi-
cation of one, another would be "on the tapis"—during
these dark years Mrs. Duss served also as a confidential
secretary.

For the good old folks of Economy she provided even
their recreation. Perhaps she would take the spryest of
her old friends, ranging from seventy to eighty-five years
of age, for an afternoon drive behind our milk-white
Welsh ponies. One time both of us accompanied them to
a circus, where the old women clapped their hands in

delight. Everything pleased them, especially the bareback riding! Even the "tights" of the performers caused no murmurs—and were accepted in the sense of "to the pure all things are pure."

All too seldom, however, were the times when I could emerge from the smoke and fury of those days into the pleasant, homey atmosphere of a quiet Economy evening; when the children, who were growing up now, and Susanna and I would talk, perhaps about new books, about favorite music, or about the quaint little things of our daily life. Sometimes I had recourse to my cornet; even the old pianofortes, that are still in the Great House parlor, were requisitioned which reminds me:

After my return to Economy in 1888, I served in various musical capacities—as cornetist, writer, composer and, after the death of Gertrude Rapp, as church organist. In 1893 I began in earnest to improve the personnel of the band. To the local group I added select professional talent from Pittsburgh, Beaver Falls and other sections.

The local members under my baton rehearsed three evenings weekly. At rehearsals of special music or music for special occasions, the entire group had to be on hand. As the band grew in efficiency so did its repertoire in size and in importance. Sunday afternoon concerts became a regular feature, and their fame spread far and wide. During the summer the wonderful Great House garden, blooming in amazing luxuriance, was the scene of these festivities. Around the graceful fountain, on benches and verdant lawn, sat or reclined folk old and young, who from Pittsburgh, and other towns and villages, came to listen to the music. For these concerts, by the way, I designed and had built a pavilion, which, from the standpoint of accoustics, was superior to any similar structure.

At times I not only conducted the band but appeared

as cornet soloist. The newspapers gradually sounded more and more the excellence of the band as well as that of my interpolated explanatory remarks in reference to important numbers on the program. They praised my conducting and vaunted my ability as cornetist even in times when they viciously attacked my trusteeship. Digging into my past, it seems that one reporter found that Jules Levy, in his day the world's greatest cornetist, hearing me play (when I was but eighteen years of age) and not seeing me, mistook my playing for that of Matthew Arbuckle—Arbuckle, one of the greatest cornet virtuosi of all time—whose beauty of cornet tone had never been equalled.

There also came to me the honor of being guest conductor at the Pittsburgh Exposition of large concert bands such as that of Fred Innis and John Philip Sousa. All in all I came to be regarded as a sort of musician-in-chief of a most musical Western Pennsylvania community.

Now and then important persons or famous musicians appeared at our concerts. The astonishment of these people at our work, as well as their intelligent criticism, gave assurance that we could get respectful recognition not only throughout America but in the European capitals. Among such was Madame Marie Luksch, prima donna of former days. She had studied at the Vienna Conservatory, and because of the beauty of her voice, had later became court singer in that faraway musical capital. She was the proud possessor of a beautiful gold bracelet which had been presented to her by Emperor Franz Joseph of Austria. Later she had appeared in various European courts, but her family being adverse to her public appearances, she settled down to teaching—attaining international fame. But . . . However at old Economy, far from the royal courts of Europe, Madame Luksch again made a public appearance—this time, as piano accompanist for my several cornet solos at the following Sunday concert. Needless to state that the concert was a success.

A most delightsome custom was that of the Reveille Concerts from the church-tower balcony on festal days. At early morn, the band played two numbers on each of the four corners of the balcony. It was the unanimous opinion that no music ever heard excelled in beauty that which thus awakened the sleeper. To the musicians on high came recompense by way of view . . . the prim, neat houses catching the shafts of the rising sun, the silver mists rising from the river, the dewy meadows stretching to the distant hills in cherry or apple-blossom time, constituted a scene that bordered on the Paradisiac.

Alas, Economy was no longer the active town of yore. Because of the difficulties in obtaining cash to meet payrolls; because of the general inefficiency and waste in the fields and workshops due to the employment of hired help; because in sheer numbers the Society had rapidly declined and the old members were unable to carry their former share of labor for the common good; and, finally because times were hard and a depression had set in over the country—it was imperative that we make still further retrenchments in our various internal operations.

Among the industries of the town which had ceased were the silk factory, as far back as 1850; the cotton factory in 1857; the woolen factory in the same year; the distillery in 1862; the brewery somewhat later; the shoe shop, tailor shop, weavers shop, tannery and harness making in the latter seventies, and the manufacture of wine in 1890. I think it was in 1893 that we decided to close down the sawmill, the planing mill and the barge yard.

In 1895, the Society still carried on the flour mill, cooper shop, machine shop, plumbing shop, carpenter shop, cabinet shop, butcher shop, laundry, bakery, dairy, orchard, farming and raising of livestock—employing seventy-nine men, among which were one clerk, two teachers and one policeman. Thirty-three took care of the farms and the livestock while three attended to the orchards. In 1889 the Society had employed 120 men in farming the same quantity of land.

It was in the fall of 1892 that I succeeded in getting the approval of the Board of Elders to place the hirelings on an entirely different basis from that of the Society members. Henceforth, instead of furnishing board, fuel, washing, housing and so on, plus an additional wage, to the hired help, the wages were now so increased that each worker could pay for these necessities. The result was a great saving to the Society. Of course, the Pittsburgh (and other) newspapers immediately proceeded to garble this event with sensational reports to the effect that the workers might threaten a strike, that there were growing rumors against my policy, and finally that I was abandoning the principles upon which the Society was founded. All of which, of course, was pure nonsense. Still, this change did heap some fuel on those low smoldering fires of disaffection apparent in the community.

Though inexperienced in the realm of frenzied finance, I readily grasped the significance of our huge debt and its accretion of interest. A problem of such proportions could not be solved merely by cutting expenses, making retrenchments, and trying to sell our stocks and bonds even if I could get them released from the banks where they were pledged as collateral. The whole problem could be solved only by handling it in a *big* way.

What the situation called for was the acquisition, from some private and sympathetic source, of sufficient funds for the liquidation of all our indebtedness. The finding of such a source required the utmost diplomacy. If, for example, the least authentic word or whisper of our true financial status should reach the ears of our bankers and other creditors untold disaster would follow. But where in all the world could I safely apply for wheedling such an enormous loan? Months of cogitation led to the consideration of two sources. Firstly, through Dr. Cyrus Teed, the Chicago "Messiah" who was trying to bring about a confederation of various communistic societies, my attention was directed to Elder Benjamin Gates, then head of the Shaker Society at Mt. Lebanon, N. Y. Since he occupied an office like mine in a similar community, and since the Shakers were likewise reputedly very wealthy, it occurred to me that Elder Gates might help me. If not, at least he would retain inviolate my secret.

Pursuant to correspondence, we met in New York City. But after a long and pleasant introductory talk, he completely dashed my hopes with the revelation that his community was having "a hard struggle to make ends meet." Indeed, he was on an errand similar to mine . . . trying to secure a large loan.

Secondly, in my journeys back and forth by train between Pittsburgh and Economy, I had become acquainted with J. T. Brooks, General Counsel of the Pennsylvania Lines. His home was at Salem, Ohio, where he spent weekends; the rest of his time he established headquarters in the Economy Hotel. Soon we became close friends, and he sometimes called my attention to defects in the village which attracted his attention. As the months passed, in order to prepare him for what I had in mind, I gradually placed before him, more and more of the details of the vast problems that beset me. One evening in October of 1892, we arrived at the juncture toward which during preceding months I had "groomed" Mr. Brooks.

"Have you any approximate idea of your assets and liabilities?" he asked, after I related some of our troubles to him. I told him about Dickson's satisfactory work in arranging our accounts. Thereupon Mr. Brooks asked me to confide the Society's status to him. This, of course, was exactly the thing for which I had been angling—so I told him my story, even the $900,000 overdrafts at the Economy Savings Institution. The news jolted him just as it had jolted Dickinson and myself. He actually grew pale and the cigar he was smoking fell from his mouth.

"For a number of years," said I, after he had recovered, "you have been enjoying the pastoral serenity of Economy; you have admired the industry, simplicity and singleness of purpose that typifies the life of our good old people; you know too of Henrici's purity and integrity. I know you don't want to see the property sold by the sheriff, but the only way to avert it is to borrow, by way of a mortgage on the home property, from some reliable and sympathetic source enough money to take care of these bank loans and the depositors of the Economy Savings Institution. When I first considered this plan I realized the impossibility of borrowing a million and a half, so I have been working out a plan by which, with utmost care, I believe that I can handle the situation perhaps with a loan on the Economy real estate of $800,000—"

"But John," Brooks interrupted, "that's simply out of the question; no one will let you have that amount on such security."

"That may be so," I answered, "looking at it from the standpoint of pure real estate value. But we need a sympathetic lender, one who fully appreciates what is back of it all. You are the one person in all the world who can help me . . . so you see I am absolutely in your hands. You are in touch with bankers, railroad magnates and other men of capital. If you cannot unearth a saving creditor, we might as well pull down our house before someone else proceeds to wreck it."

One may imagine how Mr. Brooks must have felt at having the responsibility of raising eight hundred thousand dollars thus thrust upon him. However, he promised to give the matter his most earnest thought. The next evening he came to me, suggesting that the best we might expect on a mortgage was $300,000, and argued for attempting liquidation of our debts with such a sum.

"No use," I said. "That would fall far short of assuring any success whatever, and I won't start the ball rolling without at least a fighting chance toward success."

"Well, John," said he, "next week I am going on an inspection tour with the officials of the Pennsylvania Railroad and will be in contact with men of large financial interests. I'll sound them out."

A week later I met Mr. Brooks at the old hotel. "Just what I thought," he said, "the highest estimate I could get was $300,000. Besides, I practically ruined the inspection tour, being so continually reticent and morose that one of the men even took me aside in confidence and talked to me about my mental condition!"

So hope was gone.

"But now wait a minute, John—" The voice seemed far away. Was there another answer? "You didn't let me finish my story," continued Brooks. "You know that I am one of the trustees under the will of the late former president of the Pennsylvania Railroad, J. N. McCullough. My associates in this are Harry Darlington and John Davidson, and I think that perhaps I can talk them into letting you have $400,000."

"No good," said I. "I appreciate your kind efforts, but—"

"Just wait till I finish," said Mr. Brooks. "It happens that I alone have charge of the affairs of the widow, Mrs. McCullough, and she will do whatever I advise. Now I propose to have her lend you $200,000, so that you can lift the entire indebtedness at the Farmers Deposit National Bank, thus you will be rid of the inquisitive Mr. Given and at the same time get back your collateral which we will proceed to sell. In this way you will practically get your $800,000." "Hurrah," said I "this will give us a fighting chance." Several evenings later Mr. Brooks came with the news that his associates had agreed to the $400,000 loan, providing Attorney David T. Watson would approve the title to the real estate.

Mr. Watson of Pittsburgh was one of the most brilliant lawyers in the country; he later gained an international reputation by obtaining a verdict in a London court advantageous to our country in the Alaska boundary dispute. Hieing myself to the office of the great advocate I told him our immediate problem, and asked him to consider himself retained in any and all litigation in which the Society hereafter might become involved.

"I appreciate your confidence in me," said Mr. Watson, "but first I will have to get rid of that fellow Stevens who has retained me in an escheat proceeding against the Society. I'll see what I can do."

I had known of certain escheat proceedings under way but not that Mr. Watson had been retained. I called at his office again after a few days, and was gratified to learn that he had severed his connection with Stevenson. Forthwith he undertook to examine the validity of our title to the Economy property. Five lawyers, John Freeman and Harry F. Stambaugh of the Watson firm and Judge Hice and his two sons, Richard and Agnew, went at the heroic task "hammer and tongs". Those were days when the pendulum swung from hope to fear and back again. At the same time Cashier Given of the Farmers Deposit National Bank in Pittsburgh was "putting on the heat" so severely for payment of our loans that I was planning to mortgage the brickyards at Leetsdale.

Just at the right moment the ever-kind J. T. Brooks stepped in, persuaded his associate trustees to let me have $35,000 to quiet Given, and furthermore made negotiations whereby we acquired $102,000 from Mrs. McCullough for the purpose of redeeming collateral in Little Sawmill Run Railroad bonds at the Farmers Deposit National Bank.

These were nerve-wracking days. A look at my diary entry of Friday, December 9, 1892, proves illuminative:

> I received the money from Mr. Davidson.
>
> Executed bond of Davidson and myself with Roseberg of Bank of Pittsburgh.
>
> Gave 500 shares Little Sawmill Run Railroad stock, together with six $1000 Little Sawmill bonds as additional collateral on a $102,000 note to Mrs. McCullough in Allegheny.
>
> Took up Sawmill bonds at Bank of Pittsburgh, gave check $4000.
>
> Sold 45 P. C. & Y. bonds to Robinson Bros. at 88½—$39,825.
>
> Paid some money to Bank of Pittsburgh.
>
> Deposited $35,585 in the F. D. N. bank.
>
> Checked out $15,000 for the E. S. I. at Beaver Falls.

The foregoing meant a feverish rushing about on foot, hither and yon, traversing many miles. The diary entries of this day are the last . . . At bedtime, in the days that followed, I was evidently too weary to bother with diary entries.

The legal lights found only 36 defects in the title to the Economy real estate. Most of these were of minor importance and were readily "cured." But there was one defect which at first blush seemed insurmountable—the title to the property was still in the name of Frederick Rapp Trustee! Were we happy soon to discover that providentially a recent Legislature had passed an act which enabled the County Judge to transfer the title to the present day trustees. The Society's title having thus been established as valid, Mr. Watson, to make assurance doubly sure, had prepared new Articles of Agreement, specifying the powers granted to the present trustees in great detail and he wanted these Articles signed and acknowledged by every member of the Socity.

"That cannot possibly be done," I told him.

"How many do you suppose will refuse to sign?" he asked.

"Probably ten or twelve, the four Feuchts and six or eight other malcontents."

"Oh, now look here, Duss," said Watson, "that won't do at all."

"Well," said I—in parlance of President Grover Cleveland—"this is a condition, not a theory."

However, Mr. Watson finally agreed that if only a few members refused to sign, he would not disapprove of the loan.

Now, on the day before I received the new Articles from Mr. Watson there came to see me Brother Hugo Mueller, secretary of the Board of Elders and now in charge of the sawmill and lumber business—operations which, as always, were being conducted at heavy losses. For eight months he had tried in vain to cancel the monthly losses, but it was futile. Brother Hugo was a man of education and culture, sensitive, suave and gentle,

291

"one to the manner born." He wanted to know whether I had made any provision for my family. "None whatever" said I—"being too busy at saving the Society, such thought never entered my mind". Hugo was worried about the Society's financial status; he believed we were doomed to disruption, complained that with his cultural background and "High German" dialect he could not fit in with these simple people of plebian ways and a South German patois. He wanted to sever his connection with the Society, and requested a $5000 settlement.

I told him that at present I could not pay him a cent but had underway a loan of $400,000 to liquidate the Society's indebtedness; that to obtain this loan required the signatures of the members on new Articles of Agreement. I told him further that, if he would help to secure the necessary signatures, I would do what I could at a later day to treat him fairly.

Through Brother Hugo's aid one recalcitrant signatory was secured. All except the four Feuchts signed the new Articles of Agreement. The great loan was thereupon granted, and the liquidation of our indebtedness begun. On the evening of December 21, 1892, Henrici and I executed the mortgage. Four days later Henrici closed his eyes in death . . . About five months later an additional loan of $100,000 was secured from the Harry Darlington Estate on the basis of a second mortgage on the Economy property.

Now the success in getting these loans was due almost solely to the kind efforts of one man—J. T. Brooks. Without his aid the liquidation of our vast indebtedness would have been impossible. In those last dark days of 1892, when I knew not where to turn, his sympathy and help was the one thing that sustained me. Though the securing of the large loans was a wonderful thing, it in no

way assured the success of our liquidation. After the release of the bonds and stocks held as collateral by the
banks, tremendous effort had to be put forth in order to
sell said assets at fair prices. Claims and charges against us,
appearing in the newspapers, forecast the fact that years
of litigation lay in wait. Thus success and failure trembled
in the balance.

Although the chances for success seemed preponder-
antly against us, Mr. Brooks had risked his entire professional standing as attorney and as financier on this matter
of successful liquidation of our debts. On account of the
pressing claims elsewhere, it was impossible to divert the
cash necessary for paying him for his inestimable services.

Earnest endeavor and cogitation led us to agree that he
should have a one-fourth interest in whatever remained
after the liquidation.

However we wanted the approval of wise and disinter-
ested counsel, so hied ourselves to the office of attorney
Watson. The great lawyer's only comment was, "aside
from the fact that you're a fool, Brooks, to enter such a
contract, I see nothing objectionable in it—one thing is
sure; no one else, knowing the circumstances, would risk
his reputation thus."

Christmas Day 1892. Day of rejoicing and happiness
for all the world—for Economy, a day of sorrow and of
tears. At early morn Henrici closed his eyes in last long
sleep. For two days his remains lay in state in the Great
House parlor, where from near and far, came men
and women to pay their last respects. The mantle of
responsibility in all things pertaining to the Harmony
Society having thus fallen on my shoulders, I had no
time for tears; but among the many, many details to
which I had to give attention, there came to me now and
then a sense of profound gratitude for the wondrous

Providence which had prolonged the life of Henrici to his signing of the Articles which enabled me to make the $400,000 loan—the big step toward saving the Society (a heritage he left me) from irretrievable disaster.

On that December morn when Henrici at the age of eighty-nine, passed into the Beyond, the snow lay on a barren earth. Even the Great House had a somber aspect. In the parlor was the black coffin, homemade like most other things in Economy. In death Brother Jacob's face looked infinitely old, and seemed to have a kinship with our visions of the days of Abraham. . . . Some forty reporters called that day, seeking among other things some information on the question of the Society's wealth—a question the answer to which required the utmost tact.

At the funeral services in the old church, where Henrici had for many years held forth in quaint but glowing discourse, there gathered some five hundred mourners—composed of the thirty-two members of the Society, together with employees and friends from Beaver Falls, Sewickley, Pittsburgh and other towns and villages of the region. The choir sang, while I presided at the organ. My address to the little multitude about this outstandingly pure man, "who seemed to be from another sphere," was in German. At the request of Dr. G. Y. Boal, our doctor, I gave a resumé of the address in English. I know my heart was in my speech as never it was before . . . After the *Maennerchor* also sang, we took a look at the dear face that henceforth we no longer were to see.

Through the snow we trudged to the orchard, now devoid of all foliage, to the open plot where 474 brothers and sisters already lay in unmarked graves. There by the apple trees, which in another season were to bloom as luxuriantly as ever; there, where lay the earthly remains of Father Rapp, of the noble Frederick, of plain and homely Romeli Baker, and of good-natured Brother Jonathan, we added those of Patriarch Henrici. . . . And now a prayer, a hymn, the casting of flowers on the coffin.

After the maze of funerary days the return to ordinary activity seemed something of an impact. Also, newspaper notices came to my attention which, though flattering, were nevertheless not pleasant to me. Glaring headlines— "Duss in Sole Control," "The Remarkable Rise of John Duss," "Master of Money," "$30,000,000 in His Power," "Duss on the Top." Such sensationalism could only be provocative of stirrings within and without. This yellow journalism, of which Economy had already tasted more than enough, was on the increase. However, for the time being it served the useful purpose of keeping people from probing into the Society's financial status. . . .

The truth of the matter was that the Board of Elders, meeting on December 27, 1892, elected me to the senior trusteeship and the spiritual leadership of the Society. One Samuel Siber, friend in my childhood near Zoar, who had recently been admitted to Society membership, was elevated to the junior trusteeship.

While the newspapers of the country continued to vaunt the so-called Harmony Society millions this publicity had two direct effects: On the one hand it helped to quiet minds of our creditors; on the other it attracted to our doors the most motley crowd of tramps, beggars, reformers, fakirs, messiahs, busybodies, sensationalists and spirit mediums imaginable. From every part of the nation they came; and, in true democratic fashion, we admitted them, heard what they had to say, and dismissed them from our minds. For the purpose of maintaining our credit, common sense, not to mention diplomacy, dictated the wisdom of continuing this policy.

But in itself this was more than a patience-testing job.

Some were exceedingly persistent, others seemed to be a little shady, still others really deserved attention. At the same time we were undergoing a crucial series of financial transactions. As to myself, the delicacy of these external maneuvers called for every minute of my time, and I could have audience with these seekers only at mealtime or during a spasmodic lull.

Moreover, the Society had an amazing reputation for hospitality. Henrici had always been exceedingly generous in this respect, especially in regard to tramps. Those who considered themselves of better clay expected a proportionately generous treatment, and got it—gratis of course. These were furnished lodging at the Economy Hotel, except in those rare cases when visitors especially distinguished—writers, statesmen, governors, European nobility—were invited to stay at the Great House as special guests. This was all very proper in the halcyon days of the Society's prosperity, but now it constituted an iniquitous burden.

The fakir fraternity—those who looked upon the Society as easy pickings—were treated politely but otherwise accorded short shrift. Some of these, however, descended upon us with fine recommendations backed by scriptural reference and other credentials, and with pet projects which seemed to require serious consideration. Always the scriptural injunction about "entertaining angels unawares" arose to plague us.

Those who came to solicit aid for humanitarian institutions such as hospitals, churches and schools usually departed with such gifts as the trustees were inclined to bestow. Larger benefactions were made only after the most sincere consideration.

The most troublesome were the reformers, among whom were many whose systems and projects were based and bulwarked in religion. These tried our patience almost beyond endurance. Being self-deluded fanatics, many of them, feeling quite sure of their mission, became mightily persistent. Though the world at large dismissed such like, Economy could not easily do so, for public opinion and newspaper sensationalism had placed us in a similar category, so that between these zealots and ourselves there lurked a bond of sympathy.

Most numerous were the religious enthusiasts, fanatics, and schemers. Some of these were worthy and sincere; others were unbalanced by their own indwelling spiritual revolutions, and some there were whom we today would call "definitely wacky."

Most noteworthy of the religious enthusiasts was one Dr. Cyrus R. Teed, already mentioned in connection with Elder Gates of the Shakers. Dr. Teed was well acquainted with a number of the American communes, for he had set out in an endeavor to unite them into one cooperative organization. He himself was leader of one such group in Chicago, called the Koreshan Unity.

His life story is as strange as that of Joseph Smith of the Mormons. Born in 1839 in a small village in New York State, he was forced to leave school at the age of eleven to take a job as driver on the then active Erie Canal. Later he studied medicine with his uncle in Utica. After marrying and begetting a son, he moved to New York City in 1862, then to Brooklyn, where he served honorably as an army physician and surgeon. Later he practiced near Utica, and in his spare hours studied what he called electro-alchemy, and was illuminated by the entire principia of "universology" and by the discovery of the "law of transmutation."

These strange-sounding metaphysical speculations soon led public opinion in his region to count him insane. He became estranged from his family, and friend and foe joined in destroying his medical practice. What did it all mean? First of all, Dr. Teed in his researches became convinced that matter is destructible as matter, and spirit as spirit. Moreover, according to the law of transmutation, matter and spirit are interchangeable, and in combination compose what is form and function. Everything in the universe, therefore, has limitation and form. Hence both Creator and Universe are limited in form and are perfect, without beginning or ending. This perfection was illustrated in Jesus the Messiah, who was but a Microcosmic reflection of the perfect goodness and grandeur of the Creator, the perfect Seed and Archetype of the coming perfect race of men.

This reasoning led Doctor Teed to believe in the literal fulfillment of the Lord's Prayer—"Thy kingdom come *in earth* as it is in Heaven." Thus it is a law of God that we should seek to put into actual life practice the commandment to love our neighbor as ourself, to do good to them that hate us, to seek the happiness of others by self-denial. This, then, is the key to a new social order, in which all products and wealth are to be held in communal interest. The true societal structure shall have the same functional organization as the physical universe, which is an imperial kingdom wherein center and circumference are co-related, for Doctor Teed believed that the earth is a concave sphere, a gigantic electro-magnetic battery, a vast alchemic-organic cell in which we have our being.

What Doctor Teed called "Koreshanity" was to come as fulfillment of prophecy. Koresh, messenger of the Covenant —no less than Doctor Teed himself—is to establish this new rebinding of God to man.

Furthermore, fantastic as it may seem, Doctor Teed was

successful in enlisting scientific methods, amazingly complex, and the interest of certain scientists in his new cosmogony. They actually erected a true perpendicular in the Gulf of Mexico, from which they projected a true horizontal line at the height of six feet. The ends of the line entering the water proved the concavity of the earth's surface—ergo, we are on the inside.

Among Doctor Teed's first converts was another prominent physician, Doctor Andrews of Binghamton, New York. With the aid of such, Doctor Teed organized a society of communists at Moravia, New York, and here published a periodical called the *Herald of the New Covenant*.

Sometime in the 1870's Doctors Teed and Andrews struck up a correspondence with the then Trustees of the Harmony Society, and in 1878 Koresh (Dr. Teed) and his chief disciple visited Economy.

In 1886 Dr. Teed was called to Chicago by the Mental Science Convention and became its president. Here he decided to remain, published another magazine and delivered lectures. In 1888 he established the Koreshan Unity with a membership of fifty. The communal group gradually grew in size, and by the time that the Unity moved to Estero in Lee County, Florida, he had some two hundred converts enlisted. Dr. Teed died in 1908, but the unity still abides.

One of the most troublesome factors in the recent years of financial difficulties in which we discovered ourselves resulted from the sensational propaganda in the press of the country against Doctor Teed and his community, especially in relation to the Harmony Society. The first charge in the newspapers appeared, I believe, in San Francisco, where a Mr. Speer and wife, disaffected one-time members of the Unity, charged that Doctor Teed, representing himself as the latter day Messiah, was on his way to Economy to get his hands on "the hundred and fifty million dollars" of the Society. It was reported that he had two girls at Economy to spy for him.

Of course, a charge of such sensational proportions was bound to be pounced upon and greatly elaborated by the press in general. When reporters came to me, I told them the truth so far as I knew it—that I had no knowledge of Dr. Teed's plans to come to Economy, that I had known him as a qualified scientist and scholar, that I knew he had a vast fund of learning (which indeed was the truth), that I found his beliefs and interpretations interesting, but that I and the Society were not in any way committed to him. Moreover, I emphatically assured these news-hawks that it was definitely not worth while for Doctor Teed or any other man, if indeed he had anything of the sort in mind, to attempt to put hands on the Society's wealth.

Nevertheless, it was soon noised about the country that Doctor Teed had arrived, and was negotiating with Henrici and me for a vast loan of $150,000,000! Furthermore, the newspapers began to paint me as one of his ardent disciples, which story was soon elaborated by portraying me as his spy at Economy—a story that told how, as a Nebraska ranch owner, I had been converted, wiggled my way into the Harmony Society and its trusteeship with the sole objective of seducing our good old folks into a Teed faction so that the doctor could completely get his hands on the Society's wealth. All of which leads me to opine that some newspapermen have amazing imaginations, even more fantastic than that which they assigned to Dr. Teed.

In many of the newspaper reports from Pittsburgh, and other cities, there seemed to be only one statement that had a modicum of truth: "Trustee Duss is in a state of high satisfaction." Since just at the time when our true financial status had to be kept from the minds of our creditors, this imaginative propaganda kept the eyes of the public on our supposed wealth, a thing that undoubtedly had to do with my being able to make sales of our stocks and bonds at fair value.

After a time, Dr. Teed did appear on the scene, but his main object, as I remember, was to enlist our moral support in his endeavors with the Koreshan Unity, and simply, for his own benefit, to find out about our communal organization. He seemed to be an altogether sincere and friendly man, with endless courage and spirit. We treated him with utmost cordiality. He was even given a hearing by the Board of Elders; it was a pleasant, affable, but non-committal meeting.

So I sent out to the press over the country a full report of our relationship with Dr. Teed. Not one newspaper to my knowledge ever printed a word of that report! . . . But the malicious lies continued. Still more printers' ink was wasted on headlines—TEED WILL LEAD . . . ALLEGED PLOT TO GET MILLIONS . . . TEED'S TRIUMPH . . . KORESHANS AND ECONOMITES WILL TRAVEL TOGETHER . . . TRUSTEE DUSS IS TEED'S TOOL.

A local bard of the *Pittsburgh Leader's* staff, possibly remembering Lord Byron's whimsical praise of Father Rapp in the famous poem of *Don Juan*, tried his hand at setting this sensational matter in verse, of which the following two stanzas are a part.

Alas! Alas!   *O Brother Duss*
It comes to pass   *Give ear to us*
That o'er those simple folk   *And shun this fakir brash;*
A monster low'rs   *Reject his claims*
Whose evil powers   *And tricky games—*
Would sear a heart of oak.   *He's strictly out for cash.*
With ghoulish greed   *Don't aid the plans*
Messiah Teed   *Of charlatans*
Abhorrence now excites;   *Or stir up faction fights*
He'd fain assault   *And none can say*
The money vault   *You're in the way*
Among the Harmonites.   *Among the Harmonites.*

All of which is . . . Hm! . . . Well, . . . not exactly Byronic.

Occasionally came others, neither as agreeable nor as real as Doctor Teed, but nonetheless strange and fantastic. For instance every age seems to bring forth its supply of "Sun Women," who believe themselves to be the ones designated in Chapter XII of the Book of Revelations:

> And there appeared a great wonder in heaven; a woman clothed with the sun and the moon under her feet and upon her head a crown of twelve stars.
>
> And she brought forth a man child, who was to rule all nations with a rod of iron: and her child was caught up unto God and to his throne.

Some of these strange claimants were highly cultured and otherwise personable. But the credentials of such ladies who came to us were hardly sufficient to convince us of the validity of their claims, so we politely refused to accept them.

Doctor Teed, as we were comparing notes on these

phenomenal characters, told me a story well worth repeating. One cultured, handsomely dressed, eloquent, domineering woman, with unusual emphasis put forth her claim as "the woman clothed with the sun." At the close of her argument she demanded, "do you accept me?"

"I do," came his reply, on the instant and with vigor, "and I ought to know because I am the man child that you brought forth." Which answer proved altogether too much for the woman with the assumed astronomical adornment. Totally "eclipsed" she made a hasty exit.

Due to the romantic possibilities of the Economy locale, the newspapers reported that Madame Dis DeBar, then the most famous spirit medium and clairvoyant in America, had come to Economy. This gave us one good hearty laugh, for she was one crank who did not intrude upon us. However, this Odelia Dis DeBar, as she called herself, had fleeced suckers from Wall Street to the country towns of the Midwest, and had served time in both New York and Illinois penitentiaries. Some time after this Economy report, she wormed her way into the confidence of several members of Dr. Teed's Koreshan Unity in Chicago, and managed to dematerialize several hundred dollars worth of jewelry. After this she married Frank Jackson.

Some time previously, at cherry-picking time, when, according to custom, the whole community joined forces in this activity, Jackson had sought me out and requested permission to join the pickers. Also he wanted to talk to me about a system of reform. Jackson was well-spoken, modest, rather handsome and well-dressed. The request as to the cherry-picking was therefore freely granted. As to talking world reform he had to do as others, *i.e.*, sit beside me and converse at mealtime. It soon came to my attention that he was eating an immoderate amount of cherries. But as to that he soon enlightened me.

Jackson's entire system of reform—"the salvation of mankind and the ushering in of the millenium"—was based on the biblical tenet: "The life thereof is in the seed thereof."

"The vegetarians are quite correct as far as they go," he explained, "but they do not go far enough. Thus whensoever your diet includes the destruction of any life whatever—as in the eating of beans, peas, tomatoes, etc.—in the light of the sixth commandment you become a murderer. You see, cherry-picking is just the thing for me; I eat the flesh and do not injure the seed."

Having convinced Jackson that men toiling at fiery furnaces or at heavy labor could not subsist on a diet of cherries, and that to live according to his standard would require the abolition of present day industrialism and the return to first principles, he at once proceeded to put into practice this total reform. He went about in scantiest attire of muslin shirt and trousers, and made a dwelling of a hogshead which he placed amongst the willows on the river bank below Economy. This existence, *a la* Diogenes, lasted until frost time when Jackson, like the birds, migrated southward.

It was sometime after this caprice that he married Madame Dis DeBar, his senior by many years. After defrauding a number of trusting people of funds and inveigling young women into nefarious ways in Australia, whence they had fled, they were found guilty in a London court and sentenced to heavy prison terms. Evidently, diet and spiritual clairvoyance had no effect on the severity of British justice.

Altogether different from the notorious Madame Dis DeBar was the famous feminine personality Victoria Woodhull. But here again the newspapers garbled the facts of a visit to the Pittsburgh area. It was alleged that on her way from New York to Chicago, in a vision she was told to stop off in Pittsburgh. At her hotel, so the story goes, she was visited by a Mr. Silverfriend, who was reputed to be a member of our Society and a close friend of mine; and whom Victoria, after a long conference, engaged as her private secretary. Now in reality Silverfriend was not a member of the Society at all. . . . By the way, the reporter missed his main chance—the interview between Victoria Woodhull and myself.

Victoria Woodhull, though much debased by newspaper reports, was a lady whose education, culture and experience entitled her to an audience. She had recently been happily married in England, and had returned at this time, as she believed, to bring salvation to the country of her birth. To this end she declared herself a *candidate for the presidency of the United States!* She was a sincere and ardent advocate of woman suffrage and other advanced ideas, for which in more youthful days she had been hounded by sensationalists and persecuted by public opinion.

Still another claimant that comes to mind, in some ways even more strange and fantastic than the others, was one Joshua Christian. Among the letters salvaged from a flood of criticism, admonition and advice is one beautifully edged in gold and embossed with stars, and written in the hand of "Joshua Christian, a Servant of God and the Lord Jesus Christ; to the Superintendent of the Society of the Ten Virgins." The writer records that God had shown him a heavenly vision, ordaining him for the job of announcing the Second Coming of the Messiah and of warning people of their evil ways. It seems that Joshua, writing from faraway Santa Barbara, California, wished to correct us concerning our fallacious belief about the Second Advent, for that event, according to the pious claimant, had already taken place. Moreover, Joshua also felt that all our beliefs and actions were destined to the flames, come Judgment Day. After twelve pages, teeming with fantastic prophecies, records of Babylonian assemblages and divine mysteries, the epistle comes to a majestic close with a commentary of the Book of Revelations.

In the maelstrom of confusion that followed, early in the year 1893 came an even more grandiloquent epistle. The letterhead stated that it was from a Dr. William H. Von Swartwout, President of the New Olumbia United States of the World, of "New York, London, Paris, Rome, Egypt and Palestine." Swartwout had apparently found out that certain legal proceedings were taking place against the Harmony Society. He writes me thus:

> I see by the papers that you are in legal complications and that certain parties are trying to acquire the Economy property. By the enclosed Proclamation and Declaration of Independence, etc., you will see that I am the owner of Economy, with all the rest of the earth, and I write to ask you if you would be willing that I should raise the Olumbia Flag over the Community property, and if you will use your influence to secure the consent of the others to do it?

This man who laid claim to ownership of the whole earth, added the alluring postscript: "This will be 'Harmony' to you and all the World besides, and is the *only way out*."

Busy as I was, I penned a polite reply, and tactfully (I thought) refrained from arguing either the question of ownership of the earth or that of the proffered protection. Apparently this only added fuel to the Doctor's burning zeal for soon he came in person.

Swartwout was a man of elegant appearance, education

and refinement, and I accorded him the usual Harmonist hospitality—freedom of the Economy Hotel. Of the Doctor's sincerity there appeared to be no question; he was thoroughly convinced that he was the saviour of mankind. We entered upon swift discussions of the wonders of the world unseen, as well as of present-day sociological problems. Not accustomed to disillusioning such fanatics, I let him ramble on and on.

One day in the discussion of reincarnation, in which he was an unwavering believer, he suddenly fixed me with his eye. "Do you remember me?" he asked.

Of course, I suspected something unusual, so for politeness' sake I pondered the question. "What I refer to," the doctor continued, "is the dim and distant past, when you and I each functioned in a different embodiment. Do you remember anything about Jerusalem?"

"No-o-o-," was my hesitant rejoinder.

"Perhaps Solomon's Temple—does that refresh your memory?" No, I persisted, while still playing his game except that as a boy—in an upstairs-room of the Great House wing—I used to greatly admire a picture of Schott's restoration of Solomon's Temple.

The eyes of Dr. Swartwout fairly gleamed. "Aha!" he broke out, "no wonder you admired the picture—for know you that when I was King Solomon, you were Hiram of Tyre. You built my temple!"

In those February days I had to step most carefully in the eyes of men. The Feucht Bill in Equity had been filed in the Beaver County Court. Also there came the run on the Economy Savings Institution. Although inclined to humor our would-be saviour, I gently but firmly told him that we would have to forego his Olumbianic aid. So he departed and I never heard from him again.

It is with awe and wonder that I look back on those fast-moving days. Just as the pendulum had swung from economy to waste, so too in the realm of human relationships, the use of the term "Harmony" was sometimes worse than travesty. Cliques sprang up, aided and abetted by hirelings and outsiders. New elements crept into our community, and these aggravated the factions, or, worse yet, organized or tried to organize them.

Shortly after my ascendency to the trusteeship, the Board of Elders at my suggestion, for the purpose of supplying the community with fish, had built a pond and stocked it with black bass. For the office of caretaker someone suggested David Creese, eldest brother of my wife. He was a veteran of the Civil War, and a true disciple of Izaak Walton. Creese and his family were brought from Iowa, and he was installed as caretaker of the fishpond, the cheese factory and a few other buildings. David proved to be quiet and gentle in manner, minded his own business, and soon gained the respect of the community in general. In no way did he sympathize or participate in the minor factions then becoming evident. But his peace of mind, as well as mine, soon was to receive a sudden jolt.

Altogether unheralded, George E. Ward with his wife (a sister of my wife) and their two little boys came to David's quiet home. It was night when they arrived, so David did not turn them away.

Ward had studied law, but did not practice. He declared to me that law practice was a hog's and robber's profession. To him all employers were despots and tyrants—all workmen merely wage slaves. To borrow money was just as sinful as to lend it—he would have nothing to do with either. With the ideals of socialists and communists he had no patience, in fact he proudly boasted that he was an anarchist. I had learned in the West that he was thoroughly undependable. Twice he had placed himself in my employ as self-appointed hired man, and both times left me without notice. Now, he had come from Illinois where he had stirred up labor troubles among coal miners. Withal he was endowed with a sharp intellect and a remarkable memory. With surprising facility he could quote from Holy Writ, from Shakespeare, from Milton . . . and twine and intertwine words of beauty and of wisdom with ridicule and invective. As an opponent in debate he was anything but mediocre. What a man of such characteristics could do in a community such as ours can readily be seen. So to all the problems thrust upon me, here was the extraordinary one of an undesirable, pestiferous brother-in-law and his family. Before I knew it he had interviewed the easy-going Elder Lauppe for employment. Representing himself as a relative of mine, it was natural for Lauppe at once to put Ward on the force. The reader should place himself in my position in order to experience the impossible situation. The people of Economy whether members of the Society or hirelings took for granted that Ward would be the recipient of special favors—also he was quick to trade on the matter of his being a relative of mine. Among the working force he proved a nuisance—doing little work himself and interfering with the work of others through his incessant talk.

After some months he did exactly what I suspected he would do—namely, he made application for membership in the Society. Knowing my opposition, he applied through my co-trustee Samuel Siber. Having previously made public accusations against me, he, in his application, admitted that he had been wrong in said attacks. Needless is it to say that the Elders promptly refused Ward's petition.

Thereupon Ward became vindictive and his attacks

more and more odious. Inasmuch as these attacks stirred public opinion against the Society as well as against myself at a time when of all times a favorable public opinion was desirable, I lay in wait for some act on his part which would enable me to oust him from our environs. In May 1893, he wrote a letter to the Elders in which he called me a fraud and a swindler, whereupon I took the matter to Court—charging the culprit with criminal libel. The jury handed in a verdict of guilty and the Judge sentenced him to jail. On promise to stay away from Economy, the Judge soon gave Ward his freedom, whereupon he wended his way West—never again to trouble us. The reader will readily understand that the author would much prefer to write only of the good and the beautiful. However, careless, misinformed or antagonistic tongues are still clacking, so let the truth be known.

Through the libels of Ward, to which for months I had not time to pay any attention, the discontented element within the Society became bolder; so I was not surprised when other charges drifted to my ears. Those elements, taking it for granted that I was too busy to combat charges—public or private—made against me or my management, soon came out in the open. It was their mistake.

The chief "fly in the ointment" was Henry Feucht; but to understand the Economy situation at that time, a bit of history is needful. To this end it is well that we have the words of Jonathan Lenz, delivered from the church pulpit, at a regular service: "The Feucht brother's grandparents, on the mother's side, were members of the Society and were united in marriage by Father Rapp in 1806. Of this union was born Conrad Feucht, who in time became the Society's doctor. At Economy, in the 1820's, Father Rapp, in his laboratory, busy with

310

chemical experiments and the brewing of medicines, had as helper a young woman of the Society, Hildegard Mutschler—a likeable young thing but *maulfertig* (loose-mouthed). Although Rapp was well advanced in years, his manifest partiality toward Hildegard gave rise to talk and indignation. Came a day in 1829, when Hildegard expressed a desire to marry. To this Father Rapp replied that she should marry Doctor Feucht. It must have been Father Rapp's idea that the community could not forego the services of a doctor, thus the couple would be permitted to remain at a time when it had become customary for matrimonially inclined couples to leave the Society. In this hope disappointment lay in store—the community would have none of it, so Hildegard and the doctor had to depart.

"It soon developed that Rapp grieved for the absentees—so much so, that in his sermons he castigated his brethren as being hardhearted, unforgiving, miserable sinners. Upon one of these diatribes, one of the bolder elders shouted, 'Oh, send for them so that we may again have peace.' Rapp at once took advantage of this advice—Hildegard and her husband were brought back and reinstated in full membership. As issue of this marriage there were two daughters, Tirza and another who died as a baby, and two sons, Benjamin and Henry. The mother on her deathbed, in December 1845, appealed to Father Rapp to be a father to her children. Claiming to be too old, Rapp put his responsibility on the shoulders of Henrici, who, I must say, has been more than faithful in carrying out the trust reposed in him. The three Feucht children grew up in the Society, and on arriving at majority became members. In 1865 both brothers withdrew from the Society in order to marry. Early in the 1880's, due to failing health Benjamin had to give up his practice as physician in the city of Allegheny. Henrici thereupon brought him, his wife Rebecca and daughter Estella, back to Economy, where they were treated as members of the Society. In 1889, Henry, his wife and four children, also were returned. Henry was given employment at the brickyard near Leetsdale. His conduct at the brickyard proving reprehensible to elder Kirschbaum, Henry was removed from his position. It also developed that Henry had written an anonymous letter charging me (Lenz) with immoral conduct."

On the Sunday following Kirschbaum's death, Trustee Lenz recited the foregoing history, thereupon announced that the Feucht brothers and their wives were to be admitted to membership. Immediately following the announcement Lenz severely censured the brothers and before the whole congregation, as a condition of their readmission, demanded from them a promise of future good behavior. The brothers gave such promise and shook hands on it both with Lenz and with Henrici.

Humiliating as was the scene—severe as were the strictures of Lenz—these matters are of small moment when compared to the contents of a letter of protest by Frederick Rapp to George Rapp in which he excoriates the Hildegard imbroglio in no uncertain terms. He charges Hildegard with being a falsifier—carrying tales to George Rapp—keeping the community in an uproar— taking his (Frederick's) place in George's heart—'Several times I had the mad idea to fill her feet with shot but, thank God, I did not do it.' Not only the members are talking but outsiders are commenting.

After the scene in church, Henry was given another chance at the brickyard, but soon he was again removed— this time by Trustees Henrici and Woelfel. The latter it will be recalled had been elected to the trusteeship upon the death of trustee Lenz in January 1890. Upon the death of Woelfel in the following July, Henrici proposed to make Henry a member of the Board of Elders. Henrici's idea was that thus Henry would be more immediately under our control. Inasmuch as most of the Elders could not see the matter in this light, Henrici abandoned the idea.

It so happened that before there was any contemplation of my becoming affiliated with the Society, both of the brothers, as well as their families, were friendly toward me—especially so Dr. Benjamin. He it was who advised my mother to employ the attorney who secured the Civil War pensions due to my mother and me. Also, it was upon Benjamin's suggestion that Henrici brought me from the West to take charge of the Economy school. Furthermore the doctor and Rebecca lived in an adjacent house and proved to be the best of neighbors. The doctor even divulged certain hopes or possibilities of becoming the chief administrator of Economy affairs with brother Henry in second place. The reader may imagine the surprise of Benjamin and the chagrin and jealousy on the part of Henry that resulted from my elevation to the very office which they had coveted. Much of the abuse and vituperation directed against me by Henry was due absolutely to this jealousy. Equally true is it that my realization of this made me feel sympathetic toward Henry whenever he was called before the Board for reprimand. Moreover, for the same reason, I rarely took any active part in proceedings of the Board against Henry. (See minutes of the Board of Elders.)

During the last year of Henrici's life, due to Henry's intrigues and defamation of the Board of Elders in the public press, Henry was repeatedly called before the board and hauled over the coals—all to no purpose. At

313

one meeting—I well recall it—John Scheid made a motion to expel Henry from the Society. Some of the Elders threatening to resign if Henry were not expelled at once, the motion was carried eight to one, Henrici half-heartedly dissenting.

Scheid, Lauppe, Niklaus, Hermansdoerfer and Reithmueller were the Elders who planned Henry's expulsion; as a committee they had so notified me previous to the meeting and asked my coöperation. But because of the financial volcano on which I was standing, I did not want to risk Henry's expulsion at this time. I argued against it, but they would have none of my reasoning. Finally, to preserve a semblance of harmony, Friedrichs, Mueller and I voted with the majority.

Soon thereafter, just as I feared, Henry started spreading a lot of wild talk among the Pittsburgh newspapers, which avidly sensationalized the whole matter. Soon Judge Hice notified me that George Shiras III, well-known Pittsburgh attorney employed by Henry, was about to bring legal proceedings. Hice was worried. "This is no time for such a drastic move," said he, referring to our difficult financial status.

Realizing that the Judge was right, I tried my best to influence the Board of Elders to rescind the motion of expulsion and reinstate Henry Feucht. Not daring to divulge our financial status, my efforts in this direction proved futile, the Board remaining firm in its stand. Sometime in June, Shiras drew up a document protesting the expulsion of Henry and advocating his re-instatement. This document bore the signatures of Henry's wife, Benjamin Feucht and his wife, Tirza Feucht, and eleven other lay members of the Society, some of whom—Marie Diehm, Regina Lautenschlager and Fredericka Muntz—*signed at my suggestion.*

314

With this instrument to threaten the Board, I finally succeeded in having the order of expulsion rescinded and the contumatious Henry reinstated. Elder Niklaus was the only member who refused to join in the reinstatement. However, the board insisted on depriving Henry of his job as superintendent of the orchards and the apiary. Henry—obstinant, vengeful and cantankerous—refused to give up his keys, and declared the Board to be vagabonds (*hergelaufene Lumpen*) who were ripe for the penitentiary! A second request brought only additional insults. At this time Henrici himself was so incensed that he declared himself in favor of removing Henry and his whole family from the Society and the village, come what may. Henry even refused to appear before the board, and generally gave full vent to contumely.

The matter stood at this highly unsatisfactory condition until February 1893, when the five Feuchts and four other lay members (Regina Lautenschlager, Dorothea Hoehr, Christiana Rall and Edward Kellerman) filed a Bill in Equity against the twenty-seven remaining members. Among the charges in this bill, Feucht (presumably through the pen of Attorney Shiras) claims that the Society, as a religious organization, had ceased to exist; that equality and brotherhood as a means of spiritual discipline had been forgotten; that I had sought to discredit the memory and teachings of Father Rapp; that I was preaching the doctrines of Cyrus Teed, and had given him large sums of money; that most of the members of the Board were common drunkards; that Trustee Siber was illiterate and wholly incompetent; that the principle of community of goods was no longer recognized; that I had grossly mismanaged the Society's affairs; that I had hoodwinked and co-erced the old members into mortgaging the whole property; that I had sold the stock assets of the Society to cover up debts contracted by my own mismanagement; and that the Society was rapidly approaching insolvency. The petitioners pleaded further that a receiver be appointed, the Society be altogether dissolved, and the assets of the Society divided among those entitled thereto—the petitioners receiving their just share in severalty plus "further relief." This bill was sworn to by Henry Feucht alone, with the names of Millard Mecklem, John M. Buchanan and Shiras & Dickey appearing as counsel.

After the filing of the bill, I proceeded to call a meeting at the Economy church on February 13. Feeling sure that Moritz Friedrichs deliberately refrained from signing the bill so that he could remain a spy in camp, and suspecting that there might be others also disloyal to our cause, I planned to "smoke out" all those who were inclined to treason. The ringing of the church bells in the evening brought together the whole population of the township, and the church was packed. I opened the service with our favorite hymn—a joint product from the pens of George and Frederick Rapp—*Harmonie, du Bruderstadt* (Harmony Thou Brother State). The text I chose was from the Epistle of James, Chapter one:

> For he that wavereth is like a wave of the sea
> driven with the wind and tossed. For let not that
> man think that he shall receive anything of the
> Lord. A double minded man is unstable in all
> his ways . . .

After commenting on the double-minded and unstable who might be among our own brethren, I praised those who had the courage to express their opinions, even if they were publishing their views to the world by way of the bill in equity. From the pulpit I could see that the signers of the bill looked amazed and half-abashed, while the "double-minded" folk were fidgety.

Thereupon I presented a resolution in writing protesting against the false charges of the bill and resolving to oppose it wholeheartedly by empowering the Trustees to employ counsel to defeat the bill. I asked all those who desired, to sign, and sent for pen and ink. Though so far my plan of action, giving the enemy no opening for protest or hostility, worked smoothly, suddenly "the monkey wrench was thrown into the machinery" by my co-trustee, Samuel Siber, who excitedly bounced up:

"It's just terrible!" but immediately his voice was lost in an uproar—every interested individual having something to announce. However, I soon gained control of the meeting by the simple expedient of quieting my own supporters—a move which left the opponents floundering.

By putting the quietus on Siber, Mueller and others, who rose to my defense, and permitting my adversaries to talk at random, they soon made a consummate fizzle of their case. After sundry expressions of sentiments, Margaret, wife of Henry Feucht, called across the church to her spouse: "Henry, you sit down!" Rebecca likewise urged her husband: "Benjamin, you keep still."

At another point in the discussion Benjamin reminded me that it was he who brought me here. "Of that you should be proud," I instantly replied.

As the doctor failed to grasp my remark, Henry poked him in the ribs, "Did you hear what he said?" Henry hissed. "He said that you ought to be proud that you brought him here!"

Doctor Benjamin, at heart a good-natured soul, appreciating my repartee, with a hearty laugh, came back: "Oh well, we all now and then have to have a bit of fun." This so incensed some of the sisters across the aisle that they shook their fists at him in protest.

317

Meanwhile, one after another added their signatures. Soon Regina Lautenschlager, one of the Feucht plaintiffs, started from the rear, but Henry tried to intercept her. Regina—a stalwart, stocky woman—elbowed him so violently that he fell over the end of a bench. Benjamin grew very serious, and charged me with causing Regina to commit perjury. When he forbade her to sign, I turned to Regina: "Are you sure that you understand the nature of this Bill in Equity and of these resolutions?"

"Give me the pen," she commanded, "I know what I want."

Thus three of the members—Regina Lautenschlager, Dorothea Hoehr and Christiana Rall—who were parties to the Feucht bill, now joined with the rest of us in protest. Finally the resolution was signed by all but Henry and Benjamin Feucht and their wives, Tirza Feucht, Julius Stickel and his wife and daughter, and Edward Kellerman, who was too ill to sign.

In spite of my confidence in victory, my friends and attorneys, Brooks, Watson, Hice and Fetterman were much perturbed about the pending Feucht bill. We soon gathered for a conference, and my attorneys proposed that, in view of our precarious financial condition, a compromise should be sought. To this plan I strenuously objected. Pointing out that compromise would only lead to further trouble, I preferred to fight to the bitter end. During the conversation attorney Watson remarked that George Shiras II, an Associate Justice of the United States Supreme Court and father of George III (Henry Feucht's chief of counsel) was now in Pittsburgh on a visit.

Whereupon Mr. Brooks, to pacify me and at the same time attain the ends sought by our attorneys, proposed that he talk over the pending matters with the elder Shiras. "In that way," he said, "I can properly inform him of the condition of the Society's affairs, and he himself will see the practical necessities and advise his son accordingly." The Conference having taken place, Mr. Brooks reported that Justice Shiras at once declared "so far as the talk of escheat by that fellow Stevens is concerned you and I know there is nothing in that," thereupon continued "when I was attorney for the society I obtained enough insight into its affairs to convince me that it was headed for financial wreckage. I even went so far as to talk with certain men of capital here in Pittsburgh to be ready to take advantage of the contingency whenever it should occur. But we then did not realize that men like Duss and yourself would come to the rescue." The eminent Justice finally promised that he would advise a compromise.

Upon hearing this Shiras' confession about having talked "with certain men of capital," I flew into a towering rage. So here was the seed, the first germination of suspicion about the Society's financial standing! And the younger Shiras, at the time when charging me with the dissipation of the Society's mythical millions, must have known that those millions did not exist! (That is how it appeared to me then, but now I am frank to confess that the father may not have imparted to the son the discovery of the Society's precarious condition).

As to the proposed compromise of the case, Henry Feucht was converted to the idea. But nothing came of it, for, so I was told, the Feucht women-folks would not agree.

After the case was noisily proclaimed in the newspapers of the region, the so-called Feuchts' suit was argued before Judge Wickham of the Beaver County court, and on March 3 he handed down his compendious decision, completely vindicating my efforts to save the Society from bankruptcy and dissolution, finding no proof of the absurd charges of the Feucht faction, and severely rebuking them for their falsehoods. "Summing the matter up," he said, "I shall not appoint a receiver. I find that Mr. Duss as the savior of the Society is the best possible receiver the Society could have."

To the plaintiffs the decision was a shock. Julius Stickel could not even talk of the matter to reporters and vanished from the court scene as quickly as possible.

When Judge Wickham's emphatic decision swept away all hope of court procedure, our opponents themselves began to make overtures for a compromise. When Watson presented this matter to us, he declared: "We've got them licked and they know it! And because of the scurrilous character of their bill and their pernicious newspaper activity, they don't deserve a bit of consideration from us."

"But you must remember, Dave," interposed Brooks, "Henry Feucht will probably be more vindictive than ever. The whole faction can keep the community in a state of ferment, which could easily lead to chaos and dissolution. Mr. Duss already has a list of four who wish to sever their connection with the Society, simply because they fear that there will be no peace. Thus, to relieve the tension of the whole situation, I think we ought to consider seriously any offer they propose."

When the decision was put upon my shoulders I finally admitted the wisdom of Mr. Brooks' point of view. "But mark my word," I added, "any such compromise will not be the end of this matter." Negotiations back and forth finally resulted in our agreeing to pay the five Feuchts a sum of $28,000. Soon after this settlement came one Mr. Delaney, son-in-law of Doctor Feucht. Delaney had cultivated my friendship for some time so I was not surprised at his plea for "something more." Specifically he had in mind a piece of property, our seven acres in Stowe Township. I told him plainly that, under the circumstances of their antagonism and false charges of fraud, I did not feel justified in doing anything extra.

It was not long before Delaney returned with a full and legal retraction (written in the handwriting of Judge Mecklem and attested to by him) with the signatures of Henry, Margaret, Benjamin and Rebecca Feucht, which concludes accordingly:

> . . . With full and better understanding of the whole situation, we now believe that we were mistaken in the assertions and charges made in said bill.
>
> In justice, therefore, to said John S. Duss and his co-trustee, we desire to say that we now believe his course to have been in harmony with the principles and purposes of said Society . . . that the results of his management thus far indicate that it has been able and wise . . .

And thus it came to pass that the Stowe Township property was added to the settlement.

(In the case of Schwarz v. Duss, to be mentioned later, our opposing attorneys tried to show that this retraction was a "white-wash" paper which I had purchased—they seemed not to realize that thus they were placing the signatories among the most despicable of liars and crooks).

But the efforts of our attorneys to bring about a compromise were more than once almost frustrated by the pernicious activities of newspaper scribes. In these hard days we were headline news, and when such a notable conclusion to the whole Feucht affair was near an end, the newspapers seemed to redouble their strongest efforts.

It should not be difficult to understand that during the Feucht litigation, a whole landslide of suits, claims and financial worries broke loose and nearly submerged us. Most pressing of these latter was that eternal thorn in the flesh, the Economy Savings Institution. The whirlwind of public opinion caused by the Feucht case and other pending litigation kept the bank tottering on the verge of ruin.

Even before the filing of the Feucht bill, the depositors of the bank had started a run for their money, at first slyly and quietly but gathering such momentum that on February 10, 1893, the very day the bill was filed, some $117,000 were drawn out by the panicky depositors. For several days, fortunately, I was engaged in such furious activity that I did not have time to be frightened. As fast as I could, I hunted fair markets for some of our securities, recently released from the banks, and with the cash realized from sales, plus a temporary loan of $42,000 from the Farmers Deposit National in Pittsburgh and another loan of $72,000 obtained through our friend Brooks, I stemmed the tide. When I looked back upon the disaster that threatened us and our miraculous feat of averting the same, I knew not whether I should collapse or be consumed with joy . . .

The stark figures of the whole E. S. I. history since 1891 seemed to contain an impossible drama. In three years, from early in 1891 to the end of 1893, we fed into its ravenous maw no less than $1,002,731.62! Very shortly after the Feucht hearing I sold the Economy bank property for $31,000 to John Reeves, though for a short time the Society still retained a majority share of its stock. This, plus the sale of our Union Drawn Steel interests, for $75,000 (a profit of $25,000) about the same time, helped to ease the financial situation.

Throughout the early part of 1893 we seemed to be surrounded by a swarm of hornets. To the flame of legal and financial gossip, the newspapers, from coast to coast, abundantly added fuel.

Even in our own quiet little community, several cases were causing trouble. One Benedict Bosch, then foreman of our sawmill, filed claim against Siber and myself for back wages amounting to $2797 plus interest. However, I had previously made a final settlement with Bosch and had paid his wages regularly. Perhaps he thought that, according to the former method, our accounts were not in shape. Bosch was a comparatively easy mark; I soon defeated him. About the same time a Mrs. Gebhart, employed at Economy for about a year, severely injured her arm in the community laundry, and threatened suit for damages. This case was taken care of outside of court and settled very amicably.

But such cases were only incidental to the day's work. Illustrative of the petty complexities that accompanied the major attacks against us, some of the most fantastic claims confronted us. A certain "Prince John" Devinney, a pure adventurer, swooped down on Pittsburgh with the sensational news that he was on the search for the lost Rapp will (which existed only as a figment of his over-active imagination). Prince John also declared that Rapp was originally a Catholic priest, that he repented having strayed from the Faith, and on his death bed called in a Catholic priest, made a full confession, wrote a will and received absolution . . . A singular fairy tale.

B. C. Henning, an oil speculator of Forest County, laid claim, as one of the heirs to the founders, and through the ever-active efforts of George Shiras III prepared to sue us for his share of the "Economy millions." Though Henning apparently got cold feet, others were more insistent. For instance, a group of former members and their offspring, who had settled in Mahoning County, Ohio, began to make efforts to force us to settle with them, on the absurd grounds that they or their sires had given their savings to Father Rapp and the best years of their life to the Society only to be expelled on various trumped-up pretexts. They certainly had waited a long time to air their grievances. In fact, altogether too long to make them effective.

If all the claims that were brought to light during those tempestuous years really had any validity, the heirs of Father Rapp alone constituted a veritable host. For example, some hundreds who claimed this distinction in Germany alone, upon hearing of the fabulous wealth of the Society, banded together and, as kin, through the offices of Consul Meyer, German consul in Philadelphia, applied to the Beaver County court, that letters of administration on George Rapp's estate be issued to him. One of the attorneys who argued the case was Gustaf Remak of Philadelphia. The name Gustaf Remak recalls the delightful story told me by Max Schamberg, Austria-Hungarian Consul at Pittsburgh. It seems that Schamberg had caused to be published in certain newspapers in Germany, a warning to the prospective "Rapp Heirs" not to throw away their money in legal proceedings which were only for the benefit of unscrupulous lawyers. Remak, on a visit to Schamberg, berated the latter for thus interfering with the business in hand. He also charged that Schamberg and Henrici were in cahoots. Schamberg in addition to a denial of this accusation, suggested a visit to Henrici. Remak, falling in with the idea, they took a train for Economy. Upon arrival, Remak, a high and mighty sort of aristocrat, received his first jolt when told that "Henrici was busy at the wash-house cooking jelly." Not caring to go to the "cooking," Schamberg suggested sampling the wines at the nearby cellar. No sooner said than done. Coming out of the cellar, Schamberg, seeing Henrici coming down the street, announced: "There comes the old gentleman—now I shall introduce you."

"Introduce me," ejaculated Remak. "Nothing of the sort. I am the higher in office, I shall introduce myself." Remak, well over six feet tall, arrayed in shiny beaver hat, elegant attire throughout, drawing himself to full height, adjusted his cravat and buttoned his frock coat. Henrici, having approached, at once shook hands with Schamberg meanwhile expecting to be introduced to the imposing figure alongside. However the latter grandiloquently began to babble that he had the privilege of introducing himself as the Imperial Consul from Philadelphia, plenipotentiary thus and so. Here followed a recital of titles— Knight of this, that and the other, Grand Minister, Marshal and what not—at the close of which Henrici smilingly remarked to Schamberg, "It doesn't matter, Schamberg, does it, that there must also be that kind of people in the world?"

Schamberg told me Remak was so thoroughly demolished that on the return journey he refused to be drawn into any conversation whatever; also that this experience was the high spot in all of his own official career.

Reverting to the "letters of administration sought," Judge Wickham in delightfully picturesque language dismissed the appeal at the costs of the appellants with these words:

> They never had and never can have any interest in George Rapp's estate . . . They are now chasing a Will o' the Wisp. Their claim is a dream born of a dream . . . It would be as profitable for the claimants to take out letters of administration on the estate of Adam as on the estate of George Rapp.

Such pleasantly positive language seemingly did not discourage others from laying claims. A blustering German journalist, one Schmidt of Stuttgart, plus a hundred more Rapp relatives, spread fantastic reports in the American newspapers of how Rapp (and hence his heirs) had sole property rights now held by the Society. Though threatening to take the matter through the highest courts of this land, nothing further was heard from Schmidt of Stuttgart.

A more persistent chap was P. H. Stevens, a well-known Pittsburgh lawyer, who in the period of nine years filed three reports with Attorneys General of the Commonwealth, claiming that, according to an Act of 1855, the Society was liable to escheat proceedings. Obviously, the act was in no way meant to apply to an organization such as the Harmony Society; in any event none of the Attorneys General took action.

12

The Passing of a Noble Experiment (1894-1903)

THE MULTIPLICITY OF ACTIVITIES that had so absorbed my energies during the past two years for the most part had their origin outside of the little village on the Ohio. But it should be readily understood that financial upheavals and venomous lawsuits without, naturally produced a restlessness within, which made the foundations of the old Society quake. Following the Feucht litigation, which in turn assisted in giving birth to a multitude of other suits, as well as threats in this direction, a number of the newer members, upon reading the sensational accounts published against us, became fearful of the future. One by one, these members came to me to appeal for an honorable dismissal from the Society, together with full money settlement. And during this time, others, grown aged in our peaceful environs, passed into the beyond.

On January 4, of that fateful year of 1893, Elder G. Lauppe was laid to eternal rest. A peculiar circumstance, illustrative of the fantastic imaginations of a restless community, bears repetition.

On the evening after Lauppe's burial, Trustee Siber came to me. In high dudgeon he exclaimed: "What do you think they are saying now?"

"I haven't the slightest idea," was my reply.

"Well, the talk is going around that we buried Lauppe alive—that we did not wait the customary three days between death and burial, but on the second day when the corpse took on a life-like appearance, we hurriedly put the body six feet underground!"

Immediately, I ordered Siber to exhume the corpse. Siber left, but soon returned with the report that the gossip was due to the fact that Lauppe's faithful housekeeper, the day before the last rites, had tinted red his cheeks!

About six weeks later, Elder John Scheid departed this life. He was the last of the original stock—a genial, good-hearted patriarch, whose birth in 1814 antedated Henrici's arrival by twelve years. During the controversies of these latter years, old "Hans" had been a tower of strength—always reliable, always true. I felt infinitely sad that no longer would his kindly smile and word of encouragement buoy me up in the days of trouble and darkness which surely lay ahead of me. His going was like unto the taking of a keystone away from an arch—presaging the crumbling of the entire structure.

Several weeks after this last sad event, we admitted a new member. He was destined to be the last. His name was Leonhardt Haerer, and we soon elevated him to the Board of Elders to take the place of the departed Scheid.

The reader will recall Hugo Mueller's application of withdrawal, and my promise of a donation in case we succeeded in securing the necessary signatures to the new Articles. Cultured Brother Hugo remained until March, when, with his son and $5000 he went forth into the world at large.

Julius Stickel (who had combined forces with the Feuchts), and his wife and daughter, Bertha, were the next to abandon the Society. On the day set for the Feucht hearing, Julius had met me at the railroad station, greatly excited and obviously worried. If I would settle with him now, he proposed, he would withdraw his affidavit prepared to aid the Feucht bill.

I told him that there would be no settlements before the hearing. "And as to withdrawing your affidavit," I continued, "that is the last thing I want you to do, since it is of no consequence whatever. Let your sins be on your own head!"

About a month after the hearing, we agreed to the Stickels' withdrawal from membership and the payment to them of $3620. That was one departure which I did not regret. Brother Julius had for some time been a thorn in the flesh—perhaps the dismissal of such disgruntled elements would tend toward uniting more closely those remaining.

The next one to apply for a settlement was a friend from whom I least expected such rash action. Elder Jacob Niklaus came to me one day in May to unbosom himself.

"You know," he said, "from the very first I have always stuck by you and tried faithfully to protect your interests and those of the Society. But with this agitation carried on by the Feuchts and everything else at sixes and sevens, I figure that we are not going to have any peace at all. John, I hope you'll understand—I want to go somewhere, anywhere, so that I can live in peace."

Good Brother Jacob, bosom friend of many years! Long and earnest were my protests, arguments, and entreaties. "No use," he declared, "my mind is made up. I am going. All I ask is that you treat me as you did Brother Mueller." He even hinted litigation, if the latter request were not granted . . . The records of the Board show that on May 5, 1893, Jacob Niklaus withdrew, with a $5000 settlement.

A realization of the fact that, up to this time, I had taken for granted that the Society would continue, will enable the reader to understand how Jacob's withdrawal shocked me.

Next came Sigmund Stiefvater. His complaint was that the others were continually finding fault because he drank too much, or could not carry his portion of wine or cider so well as the others, such as Brother Blasius; and that because we had suspended him from the blacksmith shop, he could not bear life in Economy any longer. Again my entreaties failed, and Stiefvater seceded, with the usual settlement of $5000.

Little Moritz Friedrichs, under the pretext that the Society would never get through its labyrinth of financial difficulties, withdrew in June. This meant one more settlement of $5000. It also meant that there were not enough male members of the Society left to fill the Board of Elders.

Something had to be done, and quickly. On the seventh of June, 1893, I called a meeting of all the remaining members. Since it was obviously necessary to establish new regulations in order to maintain the legal status of the Board, I proposed two methods: the first was to reduce the number of members constituting the Board; the second was to fill the vacancies by the election of women as its members. All but Leonhardt Haerer, approved the latter method. Whereupon, by a common vote, Fredericka Muntz, Susie C. Duss, and Regina Lautenschlager were elected to the Board of Elders, thus filling the vacancies made by the withdrawal of Mueller, Niklaus, and Friedrichs.

However, the exodus continued. On June 9, Blasius Platz, who had replaced Lauppe on the Board, complained that he could not get along with the other members, and withdrew from the Society. He was granted his $5000.

Even in those latter days, and among those elderly people, factions and inner controversies caused us many headaches. We in authority, forced to stand in judgment on such matters, had to deal tactfully, but firmly, to avoid that dreaded catastrophe, the disintegration of our little band, which would mean the total collapse of the Society. Especially was this authoritative firmness needed in such cases as that of Christina Hoerer, who complained that her sister, Katharina Nagel, and another member, Caroline Molt, had tormented her and made her life so miserable, that she had decided to leave Economy and the Society for good; and she threatened litigation if the Society did not allow her to withdraw and give her a proper payment.

When the Board attempted a reconciliation, the meeting resulted only in a weary exchange of innumerable grievances. However, it was obvious, as Elder Riethmueller expressed it, that Christina was after money, for after her withdrawal, it would only be a matter of time until her son, Leonhardt, would make application for withdrawal and ask for a share. Furthermore, I had gradually become aware that Brother Jacob Niklaus, who had already left us in our hour of need, had designed a plan whereby he and Christina were to withdraw separately for the best possible sum, and settle down on a farm, to which the young Leonhardt, with added lucre, would come later. But I am of firm belief that Leonhardt was not party to this conspiracy. The whole matter was further complicated with Katharina Nagel's threat to sue Christina, her sister, for slander. After temporarily pacifying Katharina, we finally awarded a release to Christina and Leonhardt, with a joint grant of $5000. Maria Diehm, and Franz Gillman were thereupon elected to the Board.

My faithful co-trustee, whose wife had abandoned the Society and in Pittsburgh, lived with a former boarder, declared that he would have to resign from the trusteeship and withdraw from the Society, because of the unsavory talk about his wife. Poor Samuel was heartbroken —the humiliation was too great to bear. It was hard to lose Samuel Siber; he had always been faithful and fully coöperative. To appreciate Brother Samuel's gentle honesty and sincerity, consider his words to a Pittsburgh reporter:

> "If I leave, I will not claim the large amount of money which the other members obtained . . . I have been a member for only a year and a half, and although I have done my duty with the Society, I have no right to ask for more than a start in the world when I leave. Trustee Duss has done more for this community than any other member was capable of doing . . ."

On his request that we give him no more, we granted him $1000. It wrung my heart to watch him leave to go to Zoar in Ohio, where finally he and his wife were reunited.

In the meantime Caroline Molt was elected to the Board, and friendly Gottlieb Riethmueller to the trusteeship.

Verily, these were days of unrest—but not for Economy alone. All America was emerging from an era of expansion, spiritual as well as economic, into one less spiritual and more intensely industrial. The result was a tremendous concentration of wealth and power. The old frontier was gone, economic independence was restricted, and the farmer stepped down to a subordinate position. Cities burst their bounds, the chasm between the poor and the rich was widened and deepened, the peaceful craftsmen were crowded out by hordes of factory workers, among which were many alien to the American way of life. The whole aspect of the country was changing; everything was in abnormal flux.

In 1893, came hard times. The economic growth of the country thus coming to a temporary impasse, a spirit of restlessness entered into the heart of the nation. Young people flocked to the cities, there to be swept off their feet by new, untested ideologies. Strange movements of reform developed. An outstanding one of such, was "General" Coxey's fantastic errand—the march of the unemployed to Washington—early in 1894.

Jacob Sechler Coxey, a Massilon, Ohio, business man, believed it to be the duty of the Federal Government to put an end to soup houses, breadlines, and other evidences of our lack of economic adjustment, by the simple expedient of utilizing the army of unemployed in the construction of a system of national highways. Failing to receive recognition by Congress, Coxey organized his famous "Petition in Boots." The army was to start moving on Easter Sunday, March 25. So sensationally had the fourth estate of the country headlined this project, that the whole world seemed to be in a state of expectancy. Many thought that Coxey's Army was but a prelude to a national revolution.

But we members of the Harmony Society, who were accustomed to giving aid and succor to all wayfarers who entered our gates, felt that this was an opportunity to do more good to greater numbers; so I gave orders to the Board of Elders, to arrange to feed the Army on the outskirts of Economy, which was directly on their line of march. Two weeks before, I had paid a visit to Coxey at

333

his hotel in Pittsburgh, and found him to be a genial, tolerant, big-hearted man, altogether sincere and honest in all his beliefs. He was overjoyed at the prospect of at least one good meal for his army.

Two days before their arrival at Economy, I paid an inspection visit to the more than two hundred men encamped just west of the Pennsylvania border. I was particularly impressed by Coxey's mystery man, his first lieutenant, "The Great Unknown"—whose identity no one had been able to discover. He was a splendid figure of a man, a born leader. Soon after my chat with him, General Coxey and I took a train for Pittsburgh.

"Strictly *entre nous*, General," I asked, "do you actually believe your walking petition is going to have any effect upon Congress?"

The General beamed entire confidence! "I tell you it is going to do those slick, fat-bellied congressmen much good to rub against those hardy, crude but wholesome fellows."

"Perhaps so," I answered, "but my candid opinion is that you will not get even a hearing. Congress, if it has any sense, will adjourn before establishing any such precedent. But if your efforts end in failure, what are you going to do? Any general worth the name must have at least one plan of retreat."

"I haven't even thought of that," he admitted.

Some days later, Coxey sent me his answer: "Now I know what to do if we fail. I will march my Army south, then west, and criss-cross the country until I have the whole nation thoroughly aroused." This word was brought to me by Frank Jackson, the same who had come to us in cherrypicking time. He had joined the Army, and was now distributing his booklet *The Dogs and the Fleas*— a burlesque on the workers and the idle rich.

The Grotto, Symbolic of man. External homeliness matters not so he be beautiful within.

Frederick Rapp's handsome doorway of the Music Hall, portal to music and solemn rejoicing.

The author conducting the Ambridge Community Band in the Great House Garden at the Economy Old Timer's Reunion, June 9, 1940.

On the night before the arrival of the Army at our peaceful village, there came the worthy "Indian guide," who cooked his supper over our burning gas well.

The next day the Army came to rest under the two long rows of budding trees, known as Lovers' Lane. We supplied them with twenty bushels of our own incomparable home-baked bread, two large boxes of boiled eggs, a hundred pounds of boiled ham, large cheeses, and many gallons of milk. Having eaten to their content, they gave hearty cheers for the good people of Economy, and moved on to Sewickley, where they established themselves for the night, and in my honor called the place "Camp John S. Duss."

Numerous groups, totalling an estimated 20,000 men, converging from various points of the compass, were on the march to join General Coxey. One snappy contingent of several hundred men under the command of Captain Galvin, had come all the way from the Pacific Coast. At Homestead, they were joined by the incorrigible George E. Ward. By the time they reached Greensburg, twenty-five miles away, he had the Army in an uproar.

Ward's contention was that Galvin should not be both captain and treasurer; evidently he was angling for the latter post for himself. Calling a meeting and addressing his men, Galvin stated: "Under my guidance, you have come more than two thousand miles, in safety and in peace. Suddenly, due to this fellow, you have become dissatisfied—now he goes, or I go. The voting which followed was overwhelmingly in favor of Galvin's continuance. So, exit Brother Ward.

Alas for the best-laid plans of mice and men! On the first day of May, the Army entered Washington, three hundred and fifty strong. The placing of police caused Coxey to make a strategic detour in order to reach the

335

Capitol steps. But here, with his two chiefs of staff, he was arrested, fined five dollars, and given twenty days in jail. "Petition in Boots"—Avaunt!

In this same year there occurred the Pullman Strike, producing the most extensive and alarming paralysis of traffic ever experienced in the United States. Violence flared forth in Chicago, mobs resorted to incendiarism, terrorism stalked the streets. Only a year before, the equally destructive Homestead Strike, one of the most deplorable social disturbances in our history, had brought Unionists and Pinkerton detectives into a pitched battle at the Carnegie Homestead Steel Works. In 1894, the great bituminous coal strike broke out, involving our own Chartiers Block Coal Company. The strikers realized, however, that we dealt fairly and squarely with them; thus our tipples escaped the destruction meted out to those of other operators. Finally in 1897, 157,000 coal miners in five States struck against low wages and the ignominious store system, where the miners were forced to buy their necessities at whatever price the company dictated. In one battle alone, eighteen miners were killed and forty wounded.

While our little ship of Harmony was floundering, the rest of the world also seemed to be on a tempestuous sea.

Although by 1894, our greatest financial difficulties were fairly well settled, obligations were still pressing, and the complex problems involved kept me on the jump. The transforming of almost dead assets into actual cash, called for ingenuity and great application. The annual loss of $15,000, small as it seemed in comparison to former years, needed still further pruning. Litigation, or threats of litigation against the Society, constituted a serious interference with the sale of real estate. In order to get the title away from the Society, we finally and unanimously adopted a plan devised by our attorneys, Brooks and Hice—the establishment of a corporation called "The Union Company," in whose name the real estate of the Society was to be held. The Society, in turn, was to hold the stock of this corporation. On April 11, the Board of Elders and all the remaining eighteen members of the Harmony Society signed an agreement authorizing the Trustees to convey to the Union Company all of our real estate. In return, the Society received 7950 shares of the capital stock, valued at fifty dollars each. Also, as officers of the corporation, Gottlieb Riethmueller, Conrad Hermansdoerfer, and I, as well as Henry Hice and James Dickson, received ten shares each in severalty. The shares of these officials were held in trust for the Society. The real estate, subject of course to two Darlington mortgages, was thereupon conveyed in fee to the new corporation, of which I was president, and James Dickson secretary and treasurer.

Before this transaction, I had already paid off the interest and $10,000 of the principal, on the mortgages; and by June 13, 1895, the whole of the $100,000 second mortgage was paid in full. About six weeks later, we paid $50,000 on the $400,000 mortgage. Meanwhile, to facilitate the activities of the Union Company in liquidating the indebtedness of the Society, the Society loaned to the Union Company $119,740.43.

By these efforts I was so successful in my liquidating, that in February 1896, our entire indebtedness, including our liability as partner in the Economy Savings Institution was reduced to $350,000 still owing on our first mortgage, a $10,000 item, and a contingent liability of $11,000 to the depositors of the Economy Savings Institution who could not be found. At the same time we had some questionable assets at face value of $500,397, and the

337

2600 acres of cheap Michigan lands, and the property at Economy.

After the formation of the Union Company in April, 1894, there seemed to be hope of peaceful days to follow. We had successfully weathered the long years of litigation and financial turmoil, of unrest within and without, and were therefore entitled to a respite. Alas, the days of peace were all too short! In June occurred an event that caused me once again to sally forth to fight the dragon.

Through the Associated Press and other journalistic channels, we were noisily informed that Christian Schwartz, and other seekers after the Society's wealth, were now prepared, through the efforts of Attorneys Shiras and Dickey, to bring suit against me and the Harmony Society. The newspaper propaganda was adroitly manufactured by our adversaries. For a year or more there had been insinuations that were bound to poison the minds of newspaper readers. All of our former malcontents, including Henry Feucht who had previously withdrawn all charges against me, seemed to contribute to the Shiras charges. From the Atlantic to the Pacific, the press pointed their flaring headlines.

We, on the other hand, decided not to try our case in the newspapers. Thus, as to publicity, the enemy, for the time being, had the advantage.

Though the enterprising propagandists in the opposing camp were loud in their predictions that sensational matters were to be unearthed, the bill, as actually presented, was practically a rehash of the charges in the
. Feucht bill of the preceding year. However, the new bill did contain additional charges of drunkenness, adultery, and general laxity on the part of various members; my tyranny in the case of Sister Elizabeth Beck, whom I "incarcerated in a chicken-coop," and my alleged selling

of intoxicating liquors without a license; and there were also charges of conspiracy against Judge Hice, John Reeves and me.

Because the plaintiffs in the case were residents of different States, the suit was brought in the United States Circuit Court, Western District of Pennsylvania, at Pittsburgh. The plaintiffs included Christian Schwartz of West Virginia, Anthony Koterba, David Strahaker, and Allen Shale, of Ohio, and G. S. Shale, of South Dakota. These men, working with Henry Feucht, had spun the most daring web of falsehoods ever to entangle the Society. So outrageous were these charges that, when the bill was finally filed and made public, Attorney Shiras left for Michigan, allegedly to look for witnesses.

It was palpably plain that a settlement with the Feuchts had only whetted their appetites for further easy money. As to the charge regarding my morality, this was but a villainous lie, and I feel certain that neither of their attorneys believed a word of it. Honest, upright Judge Marcus W. Acheson, must have felt as I did, when, at the close of the findings he reprimanded them for having this charge in the bill.

To our attorneys and to me the bill showed every evidence of having been drawn for a compromise. The insinuations regarding my personal character were intended to frighten me into a hasty settlement. Stripped of all fancy verbiage, the case seemed one of extortion.

In a high passion I left a meeting with my attorneys to look for George Shiras. But the bird had flown. Attorney D. T. Watson, suspecting my state of mind, lured me away to Philadelphia, under the pretext of needing me in the preparation of our answer to the bill. There, after several days, my mental turbulency subsided and my feelings settled down to a disciplined but bitter and efficient scorn.

339

In times of trouble and distress, I used to turn to the Great Book for comfort. But in the rage that permeated my being, the injunction of the Master: "Love your enemies, bless them that curse you, do good to them that hate you"—I could truthfully apply this to Henry Feucht, who was enslaved by nature with an unruly tongue; but regarding the lawyers, whose gang of plaintiffs, for the sake of money, with deliberate malice aforethought, fabricated monstrous falsehoods, no mantle of Christian charity seemed to fit.

Albeit, the tongues of the gossips clacked away. People, even some of my friends, began to look askance at me. I felt them secretly probing my inner consciousness. One of the most trying of the situations was my occupancy of the pulpit in the old Economy church—even there I felt the eyes of the curious, the suspicious, and the mongers of scandal.

The old folks, however, remained true, and often met me with words of encouragement. I remember the words of Rike Muntz: "As far as the ugly accusations against your personal character are concerned, don't pay any attention to them. That's old stuff. None of us believe a word of it. The same things were said about Father Rapp and Romeli."

In August answers to the Schwartz bill were filed by Trustee Gottlieb Riethmueller and the members of the Society, one by myself, and a third by John Reeves, Henry Hice and the Union Company. After a thorough airing in the newspapers, the case came to a hearing on September 4, 1894. Meanwhile, Attorney Shiras, evidently realizing that his activities against me were beginning to look too conspicuous, tactfully pushed one Mr. Sol. Schoyer into the limelight as prosecutor in chief. As examiner in the case, Judge Marcus Acheson appointed H. B. Gamble to take the testimony. Time after time questions arose, seemingly beyond the examiner's horizon, which had to be referred to Judge Acheson. Under such circumstances progress was at a snail's pace, hence the attorneys requested Judge Acheson to appoint a Master. Accordingly, in February, 1895, W. W. Thompson was appointed Examiner and Master.

It became evident, as the case proceeded, that Shiras and Dickey had been unpardonably careless in the preparation of the Schwartz bill. In their anxiety to force me to make a settlement, they were so concerned with heaping abuse and contumely upon me, that many contradictory averments, puzzling to the Master, so confused their case that they made a consummate fiasco of it.

I recall the surprise of Attorney Watson at the stand taken by counsel of the plaintiffs on certain legal points involved in the case; and he deftly turned from amusement to invectives and biting sarcasm in his arguments before the Master and Judge Acheson. At times, the great advocate rose valiantly to the defense of the plaintiffs themselves in his denunciation of the position taken by Shiras and his aids. "They have cut the ground from under their clients, the plaintiffs," proclaimed Watson, "through their declaration that grants to the Trustees were void. Self-evidently, it is solely under said grants to the Trustees that anything could be claimed by anyone!"

Watson often winked at me during the hearings, and otherwise expressed his astonishment at the utter lack of wisdom displayed in the preparation of the bill. His usual comment was, "Oh well, this bill was never prepared for a fight in the courts."

And, by the way, Sol. Schoyer himself, said the same thing to me one day at the close of one of the hearings.

While speaking of Attorney Watson, I want to mention my appreciation for the friendship and encouragement of Philander C. Knox, United States Attorney General under President McKinley and President Theodore Roosevelt, and later, Secretary of State under President Taft. During those dark years, through Mr. Watson, Mr. Knox took a sympathetic interest in my case, and watched its progress through the courts; and for a quarter of a century or more, until his untimely death in 1921, "Little Phil" and I were the best of friends. On one occasion—in a letter to two United States Senators—he paid me one of the highest compliments ever received by anyone. The friendship and encouragement of men like Philander Knox serves as a kind of storage battery from which faith and hope can be drawn in darkest hours.

Unless one has passed through a similar ordeal, one cannot have any idea as to the amount of work involved in the preparation of our defense. Such a seemingly simple thing as the procuring of competent witnesses—a matter which devolved entirely upon me, led me on many a weary chase. Take for instance the charge that I, as Trustee, was engaged in the selling of liquor without a license, and that this constituted an abandonment of the Society's principles. Now the whole world knew that the Society had always manufactured intoxicants; in earlier days Economy whisky was known far and wide; our wines also had acquired a wide renown. Despite those facts, it was no easy matter to find competent witnesses to substantiate the truth, for, by this time, the distillation of whisky and the manufacture of wines and beer were no longer regarded as respectable occupations.

To my surprise and disgust, one after another of the multitude of persons who had purchased alcoholic beverages at Economy, refused to take the witness stand. However, after a long search, I luckily found a willing witness in Mr. Charles Fowler of Freedom; after his valiant testimony, others became willing to follow his lead.

When actual testimony had effectually disposed of the plaintiffs' claim that the Society was worth four million dollars before I became Trustee, and when it became evident to all that I had saved it from bankruptcy, the opposing attorneys trimmed their sails to the wind and took an entirely opposite course—attempting to prove that the Society was so hopelessly bankrupt that neither I nor anyone else could save it. This brought up the question of the second mortgage loan of $100,000. Our opponents argued that we were utterly powerless to meet this obligation. Questioned as to how I expected to accomplish this impossible feat, I flatly refused to answer, claiming that it might be fatal to my plans to do so.

Attorneys who find themselves on the wrong side of the fence, often frame their questions to please their clients, so that the resulting answers may be gradually constructed into a semblance of truth advantageous to their case. Even though counsel on the side of truth by cross-examination will destroy the structure bit by bit, the opposing counsel for a time at least, has the satisfaction of feeling a psychological uplift in the minds of his clients.

At a subsequent hearing, Attorney Schoyer, attempting to show the worthlessness of our stocks and bonds, called attention to our holding of stock in the Little Sawmill Run Railroad of a par value of $105,025. Schoyer proceeded to prove that this was of little or no value. Moreover, I showed outward evidence that the subject was a very painful one. Schoyer questioned me, therefore, regarding my own estimate of its worth. Seemingly worried, I conjectured for a time, then, to every one's sur-

343

prise, managed to gulp out that the stock was worth—about par! My answer was delivered in a fretful, doleful mien, which led the adversary to disbelieve every word of it.

Further questioning brought to light the fact that not a single share of this stock had changed hands in four years, and that the few shares sold at that time, had passed for twenty-five cents on the dollar. "And so you still contend," he sarcastically blustered, "that this stock is worth about par?"

However, after leaving the courtroom, I closed a transaction with A. A. Tustin, a broker, for the sale of our Little Sawmill Run Railroad stock at par, and after paying the broker's commission, although the $100,000 second mortgage note in the hands of Harry Darlington was not yet due, I lifted it forthwith.

At the next hearing, I was on the witness stand. Schoyer, who had read of the transaction as reported in the papers, came to the point immediately, asking what, since our last meeting, had become of the Little Sawmill Run Railroad stock. Cold-bloodedly but on the instant came my answer: "I sold that stock at par and paid off the Darlington $100,000 mortgage."

"That's not what I asked you!" shouted Schoyer . . . and the court reporters snickered.

Not until April 11, 1898, was the testimony and the Master's Report completed and filed. The complainants filed their exceptions to the report on the same day—exceptions totalling twice the number of paragraphs in the original bill.

But consider what the Master had to say. In the huge volume of his report, of the many charges brought by Shiras and his gang of plaintiffs, not a single one was proven or accepted.

344

A closer look at the Master's findings will shed a flood of light not only on the litigation, but on the life of the Harmonists as well.

In the first place, the Master established the fact that none of the plaintiffs had any claim whatsoever on the property of the Society through any of their ancestors, for the simple reason that none were ever members of the Society; and furthermore, all the property was held by the Trustees in trust for the Society in joint ownership, and therefore the plaintiffs could have no share in the property even in case of its dissolution.

It was also charged that the Society had already been dissolved by common consent, our opponents offering the ludicrous proposal that by deaths and withdrawals, the Society's membership was so depleted that it constituted a virtual dissolution of the whole organization! Naturally, the Master had pointed out that no minimum membership had ever been established, and the Society, through its Elders and Trustees, still continued, and—so far as anyone knows—intended to continue.

To the next charge that the Society was dissolved by the abandonment of the purposes for which it was founded, the Master held that to cause a dissolution of the Society by the abandonment of its purposes, would call for *such abandonment by all its members.*

In support of this abandonment charge the opposition claimed a conspiracy on my part to admit Dr. Cyrus Teed and the members of his Koreshan community to membership in the Harmony Society, with a view toward transferring all our property to the Teed group. It was further alleged that Henrici, being aged and weak, was under my complete power, that the Board of Elders under my domination became wholly demoralized, and that I had obtained membership in the Society fraud-

345

uently . . . The Master's report relates simply the true story of my ascendency (with which the reader is already familiar), and maintains that the above charges were not substantiated by any evidence or proof whatsoever—which indeed was the case.

The next charge is here quoted: "Upon the failure of the plot to turn the Society to the said Teed, the said Duss concluded to wreck and dismember the Harmony Society, and thereby attain for himself and his confederates what he had lost . . ."

It was also charged that I insisted that no new members be elected to the Society under any circumstances, and that my wife and I were the last members elected. These charges the Master found were entirely unsupported by evidence, and absolutely disproved by the fact that I was admitted to membership on January 24, 1890; Mrs. Duss and *fifteen others,* on February 15, 1890; Gottlieb Riethmueller, and Samuel and Elizabeth Siber, on February 15, 1892; and Leonhardt Hoerer in March, 1893.

The next averment of the bill charged me with entering into a conspiracy with Henry Hice and John Reeves, to use the money of the Society, without consent of the members, to pay off the enormous indebtedness of the Economy Savings Institution. The reader need not be informed of the detail of the Master's findings in this respect, since they parallel the true facts heretofore recorded, that the Economy Savings Institution was in reality the Society's own bank, and its financial difficulties were a result of poor management before I arrived on the scene.

The ridiculous charges of fraud in regard to the Darlington mortgages were likewise refuted by the Master's findings, as was the charge of my coercing members to withdraw.

346

Regarding the Board of Elders, the Master found that, in spite of all the charges, it was neither "packed nor incompetent, and that the mere election of women to the Board in no way constituted an abandonment of purposes, as alleged by the plaintiffs."

The more I consider the charges, the more amused am I regarding the utter ludicrousness of the plaintiffs' case. For example, they charged that I had transferred Economy and other properties to the Union Company, without the knowledge of the Society's members in a wholesale attempt to terminate the Society's long career. Naturally the Master found that the members had known of the transfer, had even authorized the proceedings; and that the whole transaction was an attempt to facilitate the liquidation of our indebtedness by the sale of properties, especially real estate which the Society no longer required; and, in view of prospective legal attacks affecting title to the property, to remove the title from the attention of prospective purchasers.

The charges against me as a tyrant, who continually threatened intimidation and oppression if members refused to follow my dictates, were based upon a cock-and-bull story, that I had incarcerated poor old Elizabeth Beck in a chicken-coop. The actual truth of this story is as follows: In 1894, Elizabeth was eighty-one years of age, and no longer able to take care of herself. Fredericka Muntz reported to me that Elizabeth was not properly cared for, and proposed at the Board meeting that a small frame house be put into condition especially for Elizabeth. The place was entirely renovated, cleaned and painted—for indeed at one time some "peepers" had been put therein to protect them from the rats. Elizabeth was then brought to her new quarters, and placed under the constant care of Frederika, Mrs. Louisa Scharf, and Mary

Nagel. Every care was provided, and Mary Nagel's wages were increased on account of her added duties. Dr. Boal, the Society's physician, who attended Elizabeth, testified that the little house was the best possible place for her in Economy. Elizabeth, herself, was quite contented, and doubtless was greatly perplexed by the story regarding her imprisonment.

Henry Feucht's own testimony finally proved that he was the author of the story.

The bill also averred that I was 'a man of bad moral character,' that my religious views were utterly at variance with those held by the Society, and that I had been guilty of the gravest duplicity with a girl eighteen years of age. The only evidence to support this charge was the testimony of John Weggel, a disgruntled and discontented worker at Economy, who previously brought suit against us unsuccessfully.

Some time after Weggel had so testified, he confessed in open court to perjury, and furthermore that he had never really known of any improper conduct on my part. Moreover, other testimony proved that the girl had not even been in Economy at the time in question!

The general charges of drunkenness and illegal sale of liquor were totally disproved. And, concerning the general abandonment of celibacy, as constituting an abandonment of the Society's purposes, the Master justly pointed out that even in the days of its greatest prevalence, celibacy was only a semi-custom.

The report finally dismissed the case at the cost of the plaintiffs.

Filed in April, 1898, the plaintiffs' attorneys vigorously attacked the report by filing a list of exceptions, fifty in all. Whereupon the exceptions were argued before Judge Acheson. The Judge, confronted by such an altogether one-sided affair, made it his business to read the entire testimony of several thousand pages. Thereupon, in February 1899, he filed his opinion, upholding the Master's report in every particular, as well as the decree. As a parting shot at the plaintiff's attorneys, Judge Acheson added: "The charges of immorality against John S. Duss were disproved and are not true." In August 1899, upon the petition of the plaintiffs, the case was entered in the United States Circuit Court of Appeals at Philadelphia. Mr. Watson brilliantly argued the case; but almost another year had passed by the time this Court filed its decree—upholding that of the lower court.

Pursuant to a conversation between attorneys Shiras and Watson, Shiras and I met "to talk things over." Mr. Shiras at once proceeded to excuse his attacks upon me as being simply in the line of professional duty—that "lawyers oft were misled by clients." What Shiras really wanted was some sort of a compromise—his clients "not being the paying kind, why carry the case to the United States Supreme Court?"

"But that is exactly what I want you to do," said I. "Having gone to all the trouble and expense that has befallen us, I want the questions at issue settled once for all, and if you put up a vigorous fight in the Highest Court, I shall be ready to continue our conversation."

Accordingly, in January, 1901, the plaintiffs petitioned the U. S. Supreme Court for a writ of certiorari. Chief Justice Melville W. Fuller granted the petition. Early in 1902, the case was vigorously argued before this high tribunal, and on October 27 (Justices Fuller and Brewer, dissenting) Associate Justice Joseph McKenna, delivered the majority opinion—fully sustaining the finding and decree of the lower courts.

It would be interesting to know how the minds of the

349

Justices reacted in case they read in the daily press, that on that very day, under my baton, the Duss Band, which had lately risen to the peak of fame in the musical world, was giving two concerts in the city of Boston. . . . But that is a story which in itself deserves a chapter.

However, the important decree of this Highest Court gave us such profound satisfaction that I found it easy to recall my implied promise to Mr. Shiras and forthwith employed him and his associate Schoyer as attorneys in another matter which brought them a commensurate return. Frederick Rapp, in his day, in the case of Eugene Miller, must have felt similarly jubilant—paying, as he did, the attorneys on both sides.

Harking back to the intervening "nineties," I must chronicle the deaths of Elizabeth Beck, Dorothea Hoehr and Christina Schoeneman in 1894; Lena Rall Wolfangel in 1895; Conrad Hermansdoerfer, Philippina Wolfangel and Regina Lautenschlager in 1896; Gottlieb Riethmueller and Edouard Kellerman in 1897; and of Friedericke Muntz in 1901.

Three outstanding events were the passing of Hermansdoerfer, Marie Diehm and Trustee Riethmueller. Dear, honest Brother Conrad had always been a staff of loyalty upon which to lean. When at times it seemed that all were on the point of forsaking me, Conrad firmly stood by me. No wonder that while officiating at his last sad rites, my emotions, refusing to be controlled, almost overcame me.

The funeral of Marie Diehm shook the Commune. This was due to the fact that she was not only a cousin to Gertrude Rapp but very much resembled Gertrude in character. For Marie Diehm, I unhesitatingly selected as funeral text, the first seven Beatitudes. In all the throng present at the service, there was not a dissenting voice re-

View of Economy from the East. Background, hill beyond the Ohio River. A, Sight f the Labyrinth; **B,** Silk Factory; **C,** Slaughter House; **D,** Soap Factory; **E,** Steam aundry; **F,** Piggery; **G,** Sheepfold; **H,** Cotton Factory.

Dwelling and one of Economy's numerous Street Hydrants. Economy Store and Post fice. Shoe and Tailor Shops in lower story. Millinery department in upper story. est Facade of the Music Hall.

garding the propriety of applying all the virtues inherent in the text to Marie Diehm.

The death of Trustee Riethmueller caused some consternation. To me he had been a source of encouragement at times, and now there was the question of a vacancy on the Board of Trustees. The Board decided to reduce the number to one—thereafter I was to be sole trustee. Seemingly I was to bear a double burden—factually it relieved me from useless consultation and explanations due to a co-trustee. In any case, the only added burden was that heaped upon me by my friends, who from every side, for a time bestowed upon me the title "Pooh Bah," the ludicrous character in Gilbert and Sullivan's *The Mikado*.

The eight year battle in the Schwartz case having come to an end in October, 1902, only a handful of members remaining, and most of them too old to engage actively in the great amount of work entailed by our extensive and complex holdings, the only feasible plan was to continue to dispose of considerable portions of our property.

Near the close of the year 1899, one Charles M. Jarvis, President of the Berlin Iron Bridge Company of East Berlin, Connecticut, called on J. T. Brooks in the latter's official capacity as second vice-president of the Pennsylvania Lines. Jarvis was on the search for a good manufacturing site for his company, and Brooks at once imparted this information to me. Thereupon, Mr. Charles A. Dickson (successor to the elder Dickson after the death of the latter) and I scheduled a conference with the treasurer of the Berlin Iron Bridge Company, which resulted in granting them an option by the Union Company on thirty-eight and a half acres of land in Harmony Township, at five hundred dollars per acre. The deal was closed on May 1, 1900.

In the meantime a vast combine of bridge companies

throughout the country was being widely heralded. This proposed gigantic merger, in the name of the American Bridge Company, was soon to increase its normal capital to $70,000,000, and to control ninety per cent of the bridge and structural trade of the country.

At about the same time, two officers of the A. & P. Roberts Company, which had acquired the Berlin Iron Bridge Company's 38-acre tract in Harmony Township, came to see us in an endeavor to get about 70 acres additional territory lying adjacent, for the purpose of building a mammoth bridge plant. Unfortunately there arose the question that this entire acreage was subject to inundation by the Ohio River when at flood tide. Thus our effort at locating the industrial mammoth came to naught.

However it was not very long until at one of our nightly meetings, Mr. Brooks surprised me with a plan so fantastic that it bordered upon the miraculous. He contemplated the enormous undertaking of raising the level of this manufacturing site to a height beyond the reach of the river floods—eight, or even ten feet. The great furnaces of Pittsburgh and environs would be more than willing to give us all the slag required, but the problem of transporting it to our site seemed insurmountable. As a high official of the Pennsylvania Lines, however, Brooks finally succeeded in getting the consent of his fellow officials to have the Pennsylvania Railroad transport these acres of slag to the proposed site at Economy.

Immediately, we reopened negotiations with the Roberts Company, and soon reached an agreement to the effect that, if the Pennsylvania Railroad Company would obligate itself to haul all the slag necessary for raising the ground level above flood tide, the bridge company would purchase the Economy site. The two companies reached this agreement. Upon what terms, I never knew

—having had the good sense not to inquire. But I do know that, since our good friend Brooks was at that time in a precarious state of health, his colleagues, in their anxiety, were willing to go the limit in doing him a favor. And so once again we were indebted to friend Brooks. Nowadays when I look upon the terrain of the great American Bridge Company, I think of those perfect words of St. John: "Greater love hath no man than this, that a man lay down his life for his friends." Good friend Brooks soon closed his eyes in death.

On the last day of the year 1900, the A. & P. Roberts Company paid us $10,000, in consideration of which the Union Company, holding title to Economy real estate, gave two options involving the purchase of two hundred acres at $1000 per acre. The options were of about equal acreage—one for a factory site, the other a residential site.

While the Roberts Company was merging into the American Bridge Company combine, the great United States Steel Corporation came into being. It seems that after Andrew Carnegie had amassed his tremendous wealth, his dealings with his fellowmen became more and more dictatorial. To fight the Pennsylvania Railroad, he began mapping out another railroad from Pittsburgh to the Atlantic. He ordered a whole little fleet of ore-carrying steamships to fight Rockefeller. He began to develop new mills to fight other companies, planning to spend ten million dollars to kill all other steel competition. These were by no means mere threats, for he was at the controls of the largest industrial empire in the world.

I could well sympathize with those who had felt Mr. Carnegie's iron fist, for after we granted options to the Roberts Company, which was really negotiating for the American Bridge Company, the "canny Scot" insisted that the new plant be located adjacent to the Carnegie

Steel Works at Homestead. Other prominent officials in these mergers were opposed to this, claiming that there was not enough room for expansion at the Homestead property. I suggested that Carnegie buy the whole Economy property. Alas, my suggestion came too late—Carnegie had already purchased several thousand acres at Conneaut, whither, if necessary, he would move his entire Homestead mill, and where there was abundant room for the American Bridge Company plant.

Meanwhile, other industrialists and business men saw the necessity of combatting the "Laird of Skibo," and to this end enlisted the services of J. P. Morgan, the most powerful banker in the country. Morgan saw that the only solution to the problem of combatting Carnegie lay in the amalgamation of segregated trusts on a larger scale than had ever been dreamed of. Offering Carnegie a price for his properties that proved acceptable, Morgan proceeded with formation of the United States Steel Corporation— the crowning achievement of his career.

Meanwhile, the options of the Roberts Company on our property had lapsed, and I was almost ready to bid goodbye to the hoped-for $200,000 which I had expected to develop out of the sale of this land.

But early in January, Charles A. Dickson and I accepted an invitation to dinner at the old Duquesne Hotel in Pittsburgh, as the guests of A. J. Major, president of the American Bridge Company. He had come to see what could be done as to a resurrection of the options. I readily agreed to extend the options to March 31, for a further payment of $2500. After another lapse of the options, I granted a further extension on April 11, 1902, for a payment of $20,000. Finally, on November 24, 1902, the Union Company sold to A. J. Major a little more than 105 acres, now occupied by the American Bridge Works, and on December ninth, 25 acres of land, now the site of the bridge company's office.

The Ambridge Land Company which had plotted its purchase into a town site, were making rapid sales of lots at prices that netted the owners a handsome profit. With this example I was able to impress upon James A. Houston, district manager of the American Bridge Company, the importance of the remainder of the Economy tract for industrial and residential development. After further talks of this nature, the Liberty Land Company, of which Mr. Huston was president, bought some 2523 acres of our land in Beaver County and 20 acres in Allegheny County, May 1, 1903. For this sale we were paid not in cash, but in bonds at a face value of $2,000,000— practically three times the then cash value of the property.

It was a handsome sale, perhaps, but it cost me many a pang to watch those pleasant acres lose their pastoral peace and beauty. Only a few acres remained to us—the three blocks containing the Great House, the Music Hall, the woolen factory and some dwellings; also, last of all, the little cemetery beneath the apple trees.

One day I called on Theodore Lieberman, in charge of the Society's tin shop. Theodore prided himself on being an anarchist and free-thinker, but in spite of his attitude, he was a most faithful and industrious servant of the Society. As a highly skilled mechanic and craftsman, Theodore fashioned and repaired tinware not only for the Commune but for people living miles distant, with such an energy and industry that it should have brought a blush of shame to some other employees. After disposing of our immediate business, Theodore proceeded to give me some fatherly advice, urging me to visit Sisters Caroline Molt and Katharina Nagel frequently and talk religion with them by the hour.

355

"These Stundengaengers require this sort of thing," he said, "and besides, there is a Rev. Bersch from Chicago after them, visiting around day and night."

But at this time I was so embroiled in Society business outside the boundaries of Economy that practically no time remained for such visitations. Moreover, my attitude was that expressed in the words of Rike Muntz, a member tried and true: "If they don't know the way by this time, neither preachers nor preachments will be of any use."

"Nevertheless," persisted Theodore, "if your own visits and instructions don't displace these parleys of the Rev. Mr. Bersch, he will succeed in forming a schism that might prove fatal to the Society."

Theodore's prophecy proved only too true. A religious circle had formed around Sisters Caroline and Katherina. In their jubilation, they thought of the Reverend Doctor Reiner, who in years gone by had ministered unto them in Germany. He was invited to come and share the beneficence of their new religion. Before doing so, however, he came to see me to find out what it was all about. All that I could tell him was that I understood that Sisters Caroline and Katharina were becoming interested in some new religion called the Apostolic-Catholic church.

Late in the evening of the same day, Doctor Reiner returned to my quarters, calmly reporting his adventure. "We met at the house of Lauppe," he said, "and after the usual greetings and a long silence, I broke the quietness to ask why we were there. Then Bersch (the preacher from Chicago) told me that he wished to argue some points of religious faith with me. Looking him through and through, I said: 'Oh, indeed! Now let me tell you something. My whole life has been spent in the bulwarking of my creed and faith. If you want to come to me in the proper spirit of humility to seek instruction, I may help you—but argue with you? Never!' And with that, I picked up my hat and bade them goodnight."

To appreciate fully this grand manifesto, one should understand Doctor Reiner's inborn aristocratic temperament, his leonine mien and cast of eye. But the rose he handed me was not without its thorns, for now Caroline and Katharina, thoroughly at outs with Reiner, became more and more enmeshed with the doctrine of Mr. Bersch.

The efforts of Bersch and the tempting expectations of huge profits from the impending sale of most of our property, brought matters to a climax early in 1903. Sisters Caroline and Katharina concluded that now was the time to strike for their share in the Society's property and to withdraw. "For wheresoever the carcass is," saith the Book of Matthew, "there shall the eagles be gathered together."

Knowing full well that I had opposed all withdrawals from the Society except those of the Feuchts and the Stickels, they enlisted our secretary, K. R. Wagner, to plead their cause. They knew also, that I had to have their full support and agreement to consummate our then impending sale to the Liberty Land Company. Taking full advantage of the situation, their claims for a donation reached the amazing figure of $75,000 each. Johanna Hermansdoerfer, also taking advantage, came to me in person. More modest than the others, she asked for only $70,000. Realizing that these settlements meant practically a dissolution of the Society, I told her that she should receive the same sum as the others.

Settlement with these three seceders thus totalled $225,000. What else could I do? Sufficient cash simply was not available, and to consummate the sale of our property to the Liberty Land Company, I needed their support. Therefore, I agreed to their demands, and in

357

April, 1903, concluded negotiations, paying each of the three $15,000 in cash, three interest-bearing promissory notes of $15,000, one note of $10,000, and one of $5000 —a total in each case, of $75,000. As collateral on the notes, we gave each of them four hundred shares of stock in the Union Company, to be replaced with seventy-five of the $1000 bonds of the Liberty Land Company upon consummation of the sale of the property. At a meeting of the whole Society, every member concurred.

Thereupon, Christine Rall petitioned, not that she wanted to withdraw, but that she wanted adequate provision made for her daughter, Mrs. Louise Schumacher, of whose ministrations Christine wished to be assured for the rest of her life. Her claim was just and fair, and in May, 1903, I placed seventy-five $1000 Liberty Land Company bonds for Christine and Mrs. Schumacher in the hands of her trustee, Henry Hice.

Knowing of our heavy obligations to J. T. Brooks, and to John Reeves and Henry Hice, the Board authorized me to make complete settlement with them. Inasmuch as Reeves at all times had made settlement with the Trustees of the Society for his services by simply retaining the amount due him out of the collections, this final one was one of quit claim. But the case of Henry Hice presented a different situation. For nearly a quarter of a century, he had represented the Society as attorney, receiving little if any compensation. Now he placed his service at a value of $100,000.

Of course I went to attorney Watson about this matter. Watson gravely shook his head. "Your troubles seem to come in bunches," he said. "I suppose there is only one thing to do—pay it." And so Henry Hice was paid $100,000 in Liberty Land Company bonds, which were to be redeemed with cash.

The reader will recall that, in our very darkest and most trying days, I had made an agreement with Mr. Brooks, that if he would assist me in saving the Society and act as our legal advisor, I, as Trustee, would assign him, after all of our debts were paid, one-fourth of the remaining possessions. Having arrived somewhere near thi juncture, I spoke about this matter to Mr. Watson.

Watson was greatly perturbed. "Look here, Duss," he said, "this won't do at all; you can't make any such settlement." I called his attention to the time when he called Brooks a fool for entering into such an agreement, at which time, nevertheless, he approved of the contract. "That is true," he replied, "but in those days no one realized what you would be able to accomplish." An ensuing conference between Watson, Brooks and me, resulted in the payment of $100,000 to Brooks—five thousand in cash and the rest in stock of the Union Company, later replaced by 95 Liberty Land Company bonds. After a time, the Brooks estate handed back forty-five of the thousand dollar bonds, to Trustee Susie C. Duss.

The weary years of tribulation and pitiless publicity had exacted their toll of me. By May, 1902, I was in a state bordering on nervous prostration. In that month, however, I began my first summer concert season in New York as director of the Duss band. Immersed in music and far from the "field of hostilities," I managed to forget my worries. In November when I returned to the Great House at Economy, my state of health was almost normal. But this return to old and new vexations, soon again affected me adversely.

At the same time, to continue my musical career where alone I could find peace and health, I entered into negotiations to carry on a summer concert season at Madison Square Garden in New York. Having made provision for

359

the payment of the Society's outstanding indebtedness as well as for the material welfare of the remaining members, it seemed that I was no longer indispensable. Sensing the continuation of the Society as impossible, I decided to devote myself heart and soul to music, all of which naturally led to my withdrawal from the Society. Thereupon on May 2, 1903, the Board of Elders elected my wife, Susanna, as sole Trustee. Pursuant to legal advice and a gentleman's agreement that if the remaining members, through litigation or for other cause, should come to want, I was to come to their aid, the Board presented me with five hundred Liberty Land Company bonds.

The two thousand Liberty Land Company bonds at a face value of $1000 each (but actually worth about one-third of that amount) were apportioned as follows: seventy-five each to Caroline Molt, Katharina Nagel, Johanna Hermansdoerfer, and Christine Rall; one hundred to Judge Hice; ninety-five to estate of J. T. Brooks; and five hundred to me; making a total of 995. The Harmony Society was thus left with 1005 bonds.

Well and good on the surface. But we had to redeem the bonds issued to Caroline, Katharina and Johanna, as well as the hundred held by Judge Hice, at face value, in spite of the fact that their true appraised value was not more than one-third of their face value. To satisfy these people, we had to borrow large sums of money, paying six per cent interest to the banks in advance. To clear up these obligations required no less than twenty-five years of ardent endeavor. It was a heroic struggle, and at one time I even sold my life insurance to keep our ship afloat.

The reader should comprehend that although I was no longer a member of the Society, said fact was ignored in ensuing litigation. Hence, for all practical purposes, I was "counted in" and had to "go along."

Redeeming the above bonds at face value thus released 325 more bonds to the Society, although the transactions were a great loss in cash. Forty bonds were also used in payment to Mrs. Louise Schumacher, this was counteracted by the return of forty-five by Mrs. Brooks; the Society was therefore left with a total of 1335 Liberty Land Company bonds.

In order to complete the affair of the Liberty Land Company bonds, let us look ahead of our story several years: The Society was formally dissolved in 1905. The heritage of the 1335 bonds descended to Mrs. Duss and Franz Gillman, but it turned out to be no handsome inheritance, for more than three-fourths of these bonds were consumed by way of land releases of Economy real estate (for development) from under the mortgage. The remaining bonds, together with 153 of my own, went a-glimmering via subsequent litigation and other expenses —not to mention settlements with attorneys who had rendered special services to us in the past. The number of bonds here and there, fluctuating in number, as they did, from time to time, according to how many were pledged as collateral on large loans, the number redeemed or used as attorney's fees—I am dealing in sum totals—not in exact figures. (See also Chapter XIV.)

My withdrawal from the Society in 1903, marked the end of my little world. The severance loosened the ties of friendship and of principle forged through the years of boyhood, youth, and manhood. Everywhere I looked, phantoms of youthful days rose up to haunt me and bring sorrow to my heart. Here I had helped to clear the fields of rocks, of mullein, and Canada thistle; there I had gathered the fruits of the orchard, the vineyard, and the berry patch. On other acres I had planted, trimmed, and grafted trees which I had grown to love; had planted and gathered corn and potatoes. Looking on the rolling fields beyond the village, I could see myself swinging the cradle in grain fields in the summers gone by and singing in the fields with the harvest hands at the close of the day—climbing nut trees in the tangy days of autumn. I thought of the lambs, which, born afield, I had carried to the fold. In the village some of the shingled roofs bore evidence of my handiwork, the old steeple clock had told its sun-time by my winding, and on various occasions I had rung the towerbells. Looking on the graceful church-tower balcony, I thought of days when in the sweetness of an Easter morn or that of a crisp Christmas, I had played the cornet or clarinet to rouse the village. Inside the church stood the same old organ which I had played, and, last of all, I saw the pulpit where for more than a decade, I had preached and prayed.

In the lowering twilight, the old village reminded me of those soft, proud, sad and perfect lines of Goldsmith, when he wrote of a village he had loved:

> *Sweet-smiling village, loveliest of the lawn!*
> *Thy sports are fled and all thy charms with-*
> *drawn.*

> *Yes! Let the rich deride, the proud disdain,*
> *These simple blessings of the lowly train,*
> *To me more dear, congenial to my heart,*
> *One native charm, than all the gloss of art.*

> *Proud swells the tide with load of freighted ore,*
> *And shouting Folly hails them from the shore;*
> *Hoards, e'en beyond the miser's wish abound,*
> *And rich men flock from all the world around.*
> *Yet count our gains; this wealth is but a name.*

All too soon, this quiet scene by the majestic Ohio, would fade, consumed in the hot fires of industry—to be recalled only in "the sessions of sweet, silent thought" . . .

13

An Interlude of Music
(1895-1905)

DURING THESE LAST SEVERAL YEARS we were making retrenchments of every kind and on every hand. Operations both in shop and field grew less and less in significance. The process, though painful, was as inevitable as fate.

One part of the organization alone grew both in size and in importance—the Economy Band. The terrific strain to which I was subjected by the requirements of—and attentions to—our legal and financial complications called for something in the way of recreation. What better could I do than to immerse myself in music—that magic tonic of creativeness! Hence I issued a decree that during my band rehearsals I was not to be disturbed by any caller, be he president or potentate.

Inasmuch as my whole life had been so closely interwoven with the latter day history of Economy, a just appreciation of the development of music in the Society as related to myself can be made only by surveying the spendid musical heritage which, from the days of the pietistic movement in eighteenth century Germany on down through the years, came to me as a precious part of my life at Economy.

Nearly all of the Harmonists were Germans—familiar with the high musical standards of eighteenth century Germany, and by nature endowed with a strong deep love of music. When these people came to battle with the wilderness of Western Pennsylvania and to encounter other great difficulties, they found sweet recompense in song. To them, moreover, music stood forth as the earthly yet divine embodiment of the *Harmonie ideal.*

To illustrate the deep love and understanding of music which pervaded the minds of most Harmonists, I call to mind an essay written by an anonymous Harmonist, evidently of the early days of the Society. I found the little essay pasted in the flute book belonging to Walrath Weingaertner, flutist in the Society's orchestra—the same Walrath who taught me freehand drawing and watercolor sketching. There is beautiful but almost untranslatable sentiment in these lines:

> Through the slowness or rapidity by which the sounds follow upon each other, through their heighth or depth, their strength or weakness, through their intimate confluence, and their wonderful change in variety—those sounds assume forms of sensations or passions which carry over and blend with the mind . . . How magnificent is music, as it holds the listeners apart from each other in timidity and purblindness, then again unites them all as one, yet at the end leaving them languishing, finally transporting them into a dream of rapture.

Among cultural activities the Harmonists from the very beginning of the Society placed music on the highest pedestal. Most of the leaders were musicians. The writing of hymns by both of the Rapps, George and Frederick, has already received notice. Though perhaps less powerful than George as a poet, Frederick was a much more capable musician and composer. For any stirring occasion

365

Frederick could write both words and music. For example, when the migration from Harmonie, Pennsylvania, to the Wabash took place—down the Ohio on flat boats, Frederick composed a gay, happy, hopeful song which the members sang to while away the hours. In the composition of solemn or serious music Frederick was equally capable. I need only point to his "Freut euch ihr Kinder" (Children in Friendship). He also collaborated with George Rapp in writing the Society's favorite hymn, "Harmonie, du Bruderstadt" (Harmonie, thou Brother-State).

Gertrude, Father Rapp's granddaughter, likewise was a splendid musician, an artist at playing the pianoforte and Harmonium, and familiar with the classics of her day. From her childhood her grandfather saw to it that Gertrude received the best training available. Among her studies was Karl Philippe Emmanuel Bach's method for the pianoforte. (See Duss Memorial collection at "Old Economy".) For many years distinguished visitors to Harmonie, Ind., and Economy praised the fine talents, the distinguished and discriminating taste, and the cultured bearing of Gertrude. I have at hand an old manuscript volume of Chorals, dated 1822, collected and copied for her use. Other manuscript volumes of those early days, of music arranged especially for the young girl, and betraying beautiful handiwork and painstaking craftsmanship, are still in the Duss Memorial exhibit.

Another outstanding musician of the early days was the estimable Doktor Christoph Mueller. It was probably he who organized the first orchestra in the community—at Harmonie in Butler County. During the sojourn on the Wabash, he was constantly active in developing the musical organizations of the Society. After the settlement at Economy was established, Dr. Mueller's activities began to bear real fruit. However, in 1832 Count Leon and his followers came to Economy, and Mueller became one of the Count's converts. When the disaffected members of the Society, together with the followers of Leon, moved to Phillipsburg, Mueller went along, but not without bitterly and justly complaining that the arbitration committee had deprived him of his beloved flute and violin.

The Leon disaffection naturally impaired Economy's workaday life; and especially true was this of the Society's musical activities. The departure of Mueller and other musicians marked for a time the end of both rehearsals and concerts. Yet the musical organizations of the Society soon again were prospering.

The deep sorrow experienced by the remaining members at the loss of their brethren is reflected in some original compositions. Yet these same works of music show a firm determination for a closer unity and a new happiness. The title of the 1833 oratorio, presented by the singers and instrumentalists of the Society, is significant: "Arise, Harmonie, Be of Good Cheer." One finds such noble lines as these:

Despair not, little flock,
Thy shepherd's arm is o'er thee . . .
Adorn thyself festively, for quickly cometh
*   thy King to claim thee as his bride . . .*
Solemn will be thy bridal day, festive for earth
*   and heaven—*
Clear and strong the sound of triumph in thy
*   victory . . .*

And doubtlessly they sang these words with full hearts and inspired souls.

Thus music within the Society continued to excel and to receive the acclaim of discriminating critics and men of culture who visited the Commune. The gradual advancement in music, after the building of Economy, was due very largely to the talented Jacob Henrici. He had studied composition and harmony in Germany; it was but natural that at Economy he should stimulate a greater interest in the musical classics of his native land.

At versification Henrici reminds me somewhat of Father Rapp—thus Henrici shone both as composer and as poet. Some of his compositions are among the very best in the collection—for example, his "Harmonie, Listless as to Place and Change of Time," written in 1839.

For many years Henrici presided at the piano in most of the rehearsals and at the concerts. Indeed much of his leisure time was faithfully devoted to writing words and music, as well as scoring and rearranging old hymns.

Among the names of leading musicians of the Society is that of Friedrich Eckensperger, Economy's first school teacher. Eckensperger, it will be recalled, was somewhat of a general factotum and active in all phases of Economy's cultural life. A man of good taste and common sense, his opinions were greatly respected by all. Among his musical compositions are difficult piano exercises and orchestral numbers . . . still another Society musician of note was my good friend Jonathan Lenz, who played both the French Horn and the String Bass.

It will interest the reader to know what kinds of music were presented throughout the history of the Society by the different musical organizations—chorus, band and orchestra. One might suppose that the sober Harmonists were interested only in music of a solemn or religious character. Not so—for the Harmonists knew that, as in the harmony of life so in the harmony of sound, a proper balance and variation was necessary between the deep and solemn and the light and festive.

Though the Harmonists had no time for the dance and at no time cultivated the terpsichorean art, the musical programs, printed by Dr. Mueller and recorded by later musicians, betray a marked weakness for waltzes, polkas, minuets, quadrilles and hornpipes. This applied to the repertoires of both piano and orchestra. True, some of these were compositions of Mozart, Haydn, Beethoven and other eighteenth century masters, but many pieces were of the ordinary popular type of the day. I recall an incident in the 1870's when one of the super-pious hired hands remonstrated with Henrici about permitting the band to render "this outrageous music of the street and the bawdy house."

Henrici, with a characteristic twinkle in his eye, replied, "You seem to know something which doesn't much interest me. In any event we are not going to let the devil monopolize what we regard as good music." To which we all said an emphatic "Amen."

Throughout the days of the Society, members not only hummed and whistled the light popular songs of the day, but some even essayed to write in a similar vein. I recall one ambitious effort to compose "light o' love" lyrics . . .

My heart was free; you caught it.
My friends looked on and thought it
  A feather in my cap to win your love.
Your love—so many sought it,
  A feather in my cap will prove.

Though we're no more together,
  Go, trifler, go,
  Your fickle love
  Was nothing but a feather.

Then go, some other victim find.
Forgetting, I'll forgive you,
Since vanity has changed your mind,
I'll change my own and leave you.

. . . Shades of the Elizabethan lyrists, the troubadours, the minnesingers! That such delightful doggerel should take its place beside the stately strains of Handel, Bach, Mozart, Beethoven, and the more somber words of the Harmonist composers, is something that can be readily understood only by the student of psychology.

As might be expected, the self-effacement practiced by the Harmonists resulted in the omission of the names of authors and composers from the printed and manuscript music of the Society. Not one of the hymns in the "Harmonie Gesangbuch" bears the name of author or composer. But pencil marks here and there, plus the clues offered by handwriting and style of composition, have enabled me to make surmises which are probably correct. In some cases, self-evidently, the product is the handiwork of several authors and composers working in collaboration. Also, in the manuscript books of music still extant, I find original compositions freely interleaved with standard classics.

Much of the original poetry of the Society relates to the spiritual ideal of Harmonie. Especially is this true of the earlier original cantatas rendered at regular intervals by chorus and orchestra. "Schön bist du Harmonie" is one of the most beautiful of these cantatas. Though a translation into English of the mystical splendor of the text is impossible, the following effort may give an inkling of its inherent beauty:

Fair art thou, Harmonie!
The glory of thy conscience is scattered o'er thy
    premises

AN INTERLUDE OF MUSIC (1895-1905)

Full of charm as thy blossoming Spring.
Lovely is thy companionable joy where thou
flowerest in God's garden . . .

Unhesitatingly, in the breath of fragrant air,
thou standest in full innocence,
Tender and gentle as a Spring-shoot,
Fairer than the rose on the green bush,
As passing fair as youth, fair as a festal day of
atmosphere serene,
And fully innocent as nature . . .

O thou, smiled upon by joyous hope,
In festive dawn of morn thou soarest in advance
of day,
As the cooling of pure breezes aereate thy cours-
ing blood.

More beautiful than the summernight art thou,
When dew, bright as a shining light, drops from
thy locks.

Thou sweet-scented balsam, spice of the flower
exhaled in the twilight;
Buds of roses blossom for thee, and with subtle
fragrance fold thee.
Sing thy songs of sweet enjoyment that the glad
hills may resound.
Crowns of victory await thee,
O fair Harmonie,
At the great feast shalt thou triumph
And thy Sabbath solemnize.

Such lines, teeming with the rhythms and imagery of the

Psalms and the Song of Solomon, lifted the spirit of the early Harmonists to a new Eden. True songs of praise were these, and endless Hallelujas. . . .

In Chapter V the story of the passing of the orchestra has already been told; likewise the organization of the band and its ups and downs, the advent of Professor Rohr, as well as my own training in the musical arts.

So in the declining years of Economy, after having saved the Society from utter ruin, I devoted more and more time to music, principally to the development of an outstanding concert band. To this organization, composed of young men in the employ of the Society, I added more and more expert talent from Pittsburgh and other nearby communities.

Thus the Economy Band grew steadily in importance and renown. We began to fill engagements throughout Southwestern Pennsylvania, and from these parts words of praise spread down the Ohio Valley and eastward. As early as 1895 our concert band participated in the G. A. R. national encampment at Louisville, where we caused a furore and were entertained by the great Henry Watterson, editor of the *Courier-Journal*. The next year we were at St. Paul, and the year following at Buffalo.

One must remember that in the 1890's, and even until the first World War, nearly every community had at least one band. Band music was as popular and competitive as dance music is today, and bandmasters of outstanding bands were nationally known and highly respected figures. Those were the days when public parks in summertime sponsored the best traveling musicians that the country could boast, and truly vast crowds assembled for band concerts.

Balmy days . . . Every barefoot boy whistled the newest band numbers from morn till eve, and young lovers sat dreamy-eyed under the influence of the organ-like music of the best bands. Gilmore was a name familiar to all, and justly so; John Philip Sousa was attaining the peak of popularity . . . Soon the name of Duss would also rise to fame.

By 1899 the Economy Band was accepted as the best organization of its kind in the region of Pittsburgh. In May of that year we performed the chief concert at the Dewey Celebration, commemorating the victory at Manila the year before. A Pittsburgh paper conceded our superiority: "It was the best effort made by any local musical organization in the parks, and Mr. Duss proved himself to be a great leader and a popular one, too."

On Memorial Day we were again the chief musical attraction at Schenley Park, and it was estimated that twenty-five thousand people listened to the concert. For this occasion I composed a band selection called "America Up to Date." The vast crowd put on a noisy demonstration so that it had to be repeated four times.

The return of the Tenth Regiment from the Philippines to Pittsburgh on August 28, 1899, was another occasion that called my band to the attention of thousands. Awaiting the return of the soldiers and their reception by President McKinley, we played almost incessantly from ten A.M. until late in the afternoon. Finally President McKinley arrived, but the Guenther Band, stationed at the point of his arrival, missed its cue, so impromptu we trumpeted forth our "Hail to the Chief".

Two days later a reception was tendered to Company B at the city of Beaver, where we again furnished the music. Ten thousand people listened to our concert, and again and again encored "America Up to Date" and "The Fighting Tenth" (a new composition of mine for this occasion). The listening scribe of the *Beaver Times* was no less than rhapsodic and went off the deep end in praise of us: "The concert was the finest ever given by any band in the country."

Early in the year 1900, after I had improved the personnel of the band by recruiting some of the best players of the region, we merged with the Great Western Band of Pittsburgh. Under this new banner our first important appearance was at a place where I had successfully weathered many a suit at law, namely the Court House at Beaver. In these congenial surroundings we were a brilliant spot throughout the four day Beaver County Centennial Celebration.

On the last day I met with a surprise. During an intermission, the Reverend Doctor J. S. Ramsey gave a flowery speech of appreciation of our band music, and concluded his remarks by presenting me a handsomely wrought gold medal—the first I received for my musical accomplishments. . . . I was really so taken off my guard that my acceptance speech sounded inadequate, so I set the band to work on the Beaver County Centennial March which I had composed for the occasion.

More and more our services were required, until we were able to fill only the most important engagements. Early in December 1901 came R. E. Johnston, prominent New York impressario and "discoverer" of such artists as Nordica, Sauer, Plançon, Ysaye. Apparently the word of our Band's excelling musicianship had reached New York, and Johnston made a special trip to Economy to hear us. I quickly arranged an impromptu concert. The New York *Musical Courier* of December 11, quoted Johnston's own enthusiastic first impression:

It was a sensational surprise; in fact, a revelation. I have heard all the prominent bands of Europe and America, but I never was so thrilled and de-

lighted as I was by this wonderful organization
and never have I sat under a more magnetic and
forceful conductor than Mr. Duss . . .

Those were not empty words, for Mr. Johnston immediately urged me to forsake my obligations as trustee of
the community and bring the band to New York. I kept
putting off the impresario, declaring that it was impossible to forsake my trust. Submitting the matter to the remaining members, they voted in the affirmative and thus
it came that I promised to appear in a limited number of
concert engagements during the coming summer, under
the name of the Duss Concert Band.

The *Musical Courier,* as early as January 22, 1902,
heralded our coming in glowing terms, with special reference to my versatile and varied background:

He has become one of those striking phe-
nomena—this business man, philanthropist,
financier, economist, interesting himself in literature, and at the same time, conducting and re-
hearsing a concert band; but so it is, and it becomes therefore the most versatile and unique
appearance that one can imagine.

The first Duss Band concert will take place in
New York at the Metropolitan Opera House on
Sunday evening, May 25.

I hardly expected Mr. Johnston to give us such a magnificent start—an initial concert at the "Met," but
throughout the remaining winter months I held rehearsals nearly every night—this for the purpose of enlarging
our repertoire. By the time we journeyed to New York,
my local boys were competent to hold their own among
the professional musicians gathered from the four winds.

375

The first rehearsal proved that I had under my baton an organization symphonic in character and the equal of any band of that day. Music by such a band together with my explanatory remarks between numbers would constitute an unusual—indeed, a really unique—combination. Nevertheless when concert time approached that evening at the Metropolitan, I realized the full import of the occasion. Backstage, word came that an illustrious audience had assembled, fairly filling the huge auditorium. The critics were there, of course, probably not a little scornful of our provincial background and notoriously rapid rise to fame.

As to the success of our undertaking I had not the least particle of doubt. Every number on the program was there for a purpose. From the opening strains of Wagner's "Rienzi Overture" to the final chords of the National Anthem, our music kept the audience on the *qui vive*. Even the speeches between numbers—an unprecedented procedure—caught on; though they gave rise to ensuing controversy as to their propriety, the controversies were of incalculable advertizing value.

The following morning every major newspaper carried a generous approval of our debut. The *Musical Courier's* next issue, among other comment, carried the following:

Duss is decidedly original in his methods . . .
everything taken into consideration. He opened
his New York engagement brilliantly; the enthusiasm of the audience was commensurate
with its size, every number on the program
being applauded vociferously.

The New York *Evening Post* commented that the audience "insisted on having an extra or two for every number on the program," and concluded its article thus:

". . . He combines the enthusiasm of the reformer with that of the music lover, which gives his performance commendable vitality."

Then followed the daily engagements at St. Nicholas Rink. On Monday night, flushed with the success of the night before, and confronted with an audience of a different type, my manner of conducting was in accordance. And this is the report of the facetiously inclined scribe of the *Concert Goer:*

> There is not another combination on this section of the earth's surface like Duss and his band— particularly there's nothing like Duss! Duss is a Pooh Bah . . . But Monday night . . . he let himself loose—soon he had the audience letting itself loose also.

Throughout the summer the critics were more than kind, and our audiences increased. The New York *Press* called us "a phenomenal success," and the adjective was not excessive for our house was crowded every evening. "One of the season's most popular hits, wrote the *Press* scribe, "is 'The Battle of Manila,' one of Duss' compositions." The *Times* complimented us for mixing classical with popular music in such a way that "even the rather popular Sunday night audience enjoyed it as much is if it had been made up of favorite airs." The New York *Herald* Oct. 5, 1902, carried a full page illustrated article, "Who's What and Why in America", in which the writer humorously advocates the merging of Damrosch, Sousa and Duss into a billiondollar combination for the purpose of giving America some much needed original music.

My first New York season of 128 consecutive nights came to a dramatic close with a mammoth affair for which

I engaged the Madison Square Garden. It was a brilliant windup, and in spite of the threatening weather, more than 5000 people came to bid us farewell. "Duss has created a furore in New York," wrote the reporter of the *Mail and Express.* "The popular expression of opinion is that he is the best band leader since the days of Gilmore."

Thereupon followed a widely heralded tour to various eastern cities. From Pittsburgh, where of course I felt very much at home, to that formidable citadel of conservative culture, Boston. Some of my artists were quite worried about what kind of a reception Boston would give us. Some of the other cities had critics and audiences who knew worth while music when they heard it, but Boston was different. Boston people knew that they knew.

In spite of all fears, however, we were well received, and throughout the series of three programs at Symphony Hall, the large and fashionable audiences were "frantically applausive," as the Boston *Journal* recorded. I knew what they wanted—Wagner, Tschaikowsky and other masters interspersed with lighter compositions but rendered with artistry and finesse.

The press was as enthusiastic as the audience, even exceeding my fondest hopes. The *Transcript,* after comparing me with Nikisch, Eduard Strauss and Sousa, all of whom had been recently heard in that city, wrote: "The salient qualities of all these conductors with an additional dash of easy nonchalance and a hearty cordial way of taking the audience into his confidence are combined in Duss." The *Post* was full of praise: "All in all, the band showed some of the best ensemble effects possible." The *Advertizer* went the limit: "Duss' Band is undoubtedly the best band before the public."

During the intermission of the first Boston concert, I

received a telegram stating that the United States Supreme Court in the Schartz Case had handed down a decision in our favor. To the surprise of my men neither the applause of the audience nor the decision of the court produced any excitations on my part. Why should they? I knew the psychology of the Boston audience and had made preparations accordingly. As to the Supreme Court, that august body had practically no choice in the premises, confronted as they were by the findings of the Master, the decision of Judge Acheson of the U. S. Circuit Court, and that of the U. S. Circuit Court of Appeals—all in our favor.

After the Boston engagement, I returned . . . half regretfully . . . to Economy. Of what awaited me there, I had not the slightest suspicion. It turned out to be a welcome like that accorded unto a conqueror. Pittsburgh newspapers heralded it with encomiums. At Economy in the evening oldfashioned candles stood in the windows of the houses. All of the members of the original Economy Band who could be found were gathered to play old-fashioned airs and to lead a torchlight parade through the town. Meanwhile I was in the Great House, once again united with my family; but soon a committee of residents came to take me to the Music Hall where nothing less than a popular ovation was tendered. I was so overcome that I heard only half of the good Doctor Baskerville's welcome address. After some other speeches, the assembled multitude presented me with a resolution, signed by a committee of townspeople, expressing their unanimous delight at my spectacular career as a musician and their loyalty to me as a faithful trustee and neighbor.

This indeed repaid me for all the difficulties I had undergone for the community, and in my response I found no difficulty in assuring those assembled that this

379

demonstration of affection at home naturally meant more to me than the applause of large audiences elsewhere or the critical approvals in metropolitan newspapers. Still a gratis announcement such as the following is not to be underestimated. The New York *Press*, April 2, 1903, featured a musical staff on the lines of which were suspended fourteen "Famous Musicians of America"—Frank and Walter Damrosch, Sousa and Duss leading the procession. . . .

The management of Madison Square Garden, highly gratified at the success of my farewell concert, soon made me an offer regarding the use of the Garden for the following summer concert series. The offer was so flattering that I could not afford to turn it down. However, one stipulation was that I conduct the Metropolitan Opera House Orchestra and that is what came to pass.

To make the amphitheatre of the Madison Square Garden properly serviceable for concert purposes required a transformation of the entire interior. One day at the Sportman's Show I noticed the unique island stage-set arrangement for an Indian scene, and then I knew I had the germ of an idea. With an island "stage" for the orchestra, and a huge Venetian backdrop, I proposed to encircle the island with a canal, span it with bridges and float a number of gondolas manned by real Venetian boatmen. The development of these ideas resulted in what was looked upon as the most noteworthy setting ever seen in the city. As late as 1920, Frederick Dean, writing in the New York *Times,* said, "The most elaborate setting for Summer music in New York was planned by Bandmaster John S. Duss in 1903, when Madison Square Garden, for the first and only time, was transformed. Exact figures are wanting, but, from those given at the time, Mr. Duss must have spent somewhere between $75,000 and $100,000 before he opened the doors."

Arthur Voegtlin painted the immense drop at the end of the Garden, said to be the largest curtain ever painted. Settings of the Doges Palace, Desdemona's House, and St. Mark's Cathedral were built, some true to original size. Spanning the canal was a facsimile of the Ponte De Rialto. Tiffany Studios for one line of advertising in our programs loaned us $40,000 worth of decorative marble, sculpture and fountains. A blue bunting sky with suspended electric stars and moving clouds, produced cinematographically, added still more to the atmospheric setting. I believe it was *Harper's Weekly* that proclaimed, "Mr. Duss has accomplished the seemingly impossible—he has given New York a novelty." At any rate that same magazine, instead of charging us $1500 for advertising, asked permission to print a full-page picture of the production.

A half-circle of curved glass at the back of the orchestra —my invention—served as a splendid soundingboard, a prime requisite in the huge auditorium. The setting was musically valuable as well as esthetically pleasing.

For the opening concert we had Madame Nordica, then one of America's favorite operatic stars, and Edouard de Reszke, the great Polish operatic basso, with a chorus of a thousand voices, augmenting the orchestra. When the night of the opening concert arrived, people flocked to this new showplace, so that the receipts of the first two nights practically covered the entire costs of the installation.

The attendance throughout the summer continued satisfactorily, but to keep it thus—the engagement being a long one—shrewd publicity was a necessary adjunct of the concerts. My manager, R. E. Johnston, was a forerunner of the modern high-pressure publicists of Hollywood. At least he showed almost alarming ingenuity in publicity schemes and gags that caught the public eye.

One lovely summer evening I was conducting the orchestra in Saint-Saëns' *Danse Macabre*. Under the influence of this deeply melancholy "Dance of Death," the audience sat very still. Suddenly I heard a commotion behind me, and the orchestra, almost to a man, stretched necks and gaped toward one point in the arena, neglecting to perform. Continuing to conduct and to sing until I brought the men back into line, we finished the selection; whereupon I turned to my illustrious concertmeister, Nahan Franko, with a questionmark in my eye, to which he replied: "Somebody fell into the canal, or tried to commit suicide."

The next day the press carried a romantic story, embellished with all sorts of trimmings, of a young and lonely Iowa girl—leaning too far over the side of the gondola, falling headlong into the canal; how a gallant gentleman arrayed in full dress plunged to her rescue (the water was only three feet deep). A clever publicity hoax, engineered for fifty dollars by our efficacious press agent. . . . But it worked.

The press agent is a necessary evil. To keep his artists in the public eye he oft resorts to the publishing of sensational stories. In the Spring of 1903 Johnston had scheduled a Spring tour for the orchestra under my direction, with the famous artists Lillian Nordica and Edouard de Reszke as guest stars. Upon Johnston's suggestion, a clever caricarturist prepared a sketch representing Johnston pushing a wheelbarrow in which De Reszke, Mme. Nordica and the author were seated, while a tiny Nahan Franko sat astride one of the handles. This daring poster, as advance publicity but unknown to the artists it portrayed, had been sent far and wide and had the whole country agog . . . Mme. Nordica threatened to cancel her contract, and De Reszke, ordinarily a big good-humored fellow, protested vociferously in his best broken English. Let the New York *Sun* (April 5, 1903) conclude the story:

The protests of these two artists might not have availed but for the objection that came from Economy, Pa., bearing the signature of the great Duss himself. It came, however, by telegraph. It was peremptory and it announced the speedy arrival of the sender in New York.

He did arrive soon in person and the result was the destruction of the 100,000 cards that had cost so much money in addition to the mental wear and tear that Mr. Johnston and the designer had undergone.

"I push my business" was the legend that stood at the bottom of the poster. Mr. Johnston says he is pushing it still, but not in a wheelbarrow.

However the laugh was really on us, for Johnston had attained his objective; and the case of the suppressed posters and those that had already been sent proved an advertisement extremely valuable.

The just fame of our artists and the sparks of our publicity combined to bring us tremendous crowds on that Spring tour. At Topeka, Kansas, for instance, where we were booked as the chief musical attraction for that city's May Festival, the newspaper told of "the scramble for the Duss-Nordica-De Reszke tickets." Sale of tickets was scheduled to open Monday morning at seven o'clock, but the first man arrived at the boxoffice at eight o'clock the night before. Fifty men held their places throughout the night. Early the following morning came police and handed numbered tickets to the men in line to enable them to go to breakfast and return to their respective places.

This visiting of the main cities of the eastern half of the states and Canada constituted a virtual march of triumph. The Topeka *Journal* pronounced our engagement there "the greatest musical event in the history of Kansas." The whirlwinds of applause often almost doubled the length of the program. As one journalist said, "At the Duss concerts the encore fiend is in his element."

From Topeka we headed eastward to cities like Des Moines, Toronto, Montreal and Hartford where the tour came to a close. Hereupon followed the engagement at Madison Square Garden.

After the summer concerts came a tour to the West, booked by impresario Loudon G. Charlton: Indianapolis, Omaha, Denver, Salt Lake City, Tacoma, Seattle, Portland, Sacramento and the Golden Gates of San Francisco.

Members of the orchestra, who with the Metropolitan Opera had been in San Francisco, warned me that this city was a law unto itself; far from being influenced in our favor by the glowing notices we had received elsewhere, the critics there would probably prove skeptical, perhaps even antagonistic.

Wherefore with utmost care, I prepared the five concert programs for which we were under contract. But lo and behold, the local impresario in charge of our engagement devastatingly rearranged my programs! Then too, at the matinee at Stanford University, Nahan Franko, gaping at an acquaintance in the audience during a critical moment in an involved Richard Strauss number, led the whole first violin section astray —whereas on the one hand it was a good joke on one of America's greatest concertmasters, on the other it meant some forceful singing on my part to bring order out of chaos. Nor was this all. At the first evening concert, scheduled for 8:15, when the orchestra was already seated on the stage, I began to hear the audience clamor for the rise of the curtain. Ten minutes passed . . . fifteen . . . No longer able to contain myself I rushed out from my dressing room only to find that our baggage (which had arrived at five o'clock) was just being transferred to the stage—by my own men at that. Labor union rules had caused the trouble. Half an hour late, I faced an angry, antagonistic audience. But after an hour of music I knew that the audience had been won, and next morning reports in the newspapers were favorable.

But still trouble did not cease. At our concert the next afternoon the rearranged program was a most incongruous concoction. We opened with Berlioz's "Roman Carnival Overture". After a few vigorous opening measures comes a grand dramatic pause—and in this moment of tension one of our trombonists, without rime or reason, gave forth a tremendous blast. This naturally upset the temperament of the others, and presto! the English Horn player missed his cue in the solo that follows. I sang frantically to bring the orchestra to a harmonious finish, and then the audience, to my utter disgust and amazement, broke forth in tumultous applause. . . . At intermission I discovered that the boys, elated by the compliments in the morning newspapers, had paid visits to the Poodle Dog Inn and other such rendezvous of liquid refreshment, with the result that at concert time the notes on their scores played little impish dances. In the midst of the concert one culprit had to be led off the stage. But the newspaper scribes proclaimed that this concert was even superior to that of the previous night!

. . . And so to Los Angeles, Dallas, Galveston, Little

Rock, Chicago in unbroken success to the closing concert at Washington, D. C.

Thereupon back to Economy to plan for the year 1904, when once more I was to direct the Metropolitan Opera House Orchestra in its summer season. As to that, our concerts at Madison Square Garden were hailed with as much enthusiasm as that accorded us during the previous summer.

. . . But dark clouds were on the horizon.

14

Final Tempest and Twilight Calm (1905-1941)

EXCEPTING FOR a touch of sadness in retrospect—memories of the erstwhile Harmony Society, its "ups and downs" and the lamentable passing of a noble experiment—my life as a successful bandmaster was supremely happy. Nothing can be more enrapturing than the swinging of a baton over a large body of artist-instrumentalists. Thus sweet music cast the worry and fret of a former day into oblivion.

During the winters of 1903 and 1904, Mrs. Duss for health's sake, spent some months in Florida. Finding the climate beneficial, she purchased a wild tract of scrub-oak and palmetto on the Atlantic beach opposite the near-by town of New Smyrna; where, in a modest home we lived for twenty years and thereupon moved into the town.

In the year 1905, Mrs. Duss and the other members decided to dissolve the Society and, as joint owners of its property, to distribute the same among themselves. The agreement of dissolution was entered into December 5, 1905. According to one of the provisions of this document, Mrs. Duss became the owner of property at Economy, the title of which was still in the name of the Society.

As to myself, my musical career continued unmolested for a time, then came a sudden jolt. On February 8, 1907, a bill of complaint against John S. Duss and Susie C.

Duss, was filed in the U. S. Circuit Court, by two citizens of New Jersey—Ada J. Everitt and Louisa R. Tryon. They claimed to be heirs of George Rapp.

In the main, their bill followed the footsteps of Schwartz *vs*. Duss, but it omitted all of the abuse and villification in reference to which former courts had dealt with in no uncertain terms. However one new and novel idea was advanced—"that the contributions of George Rapp were donations in a strict sense; not given for a valuable consideration, but as a voluntary disposition, to found the Society," and "that he used his own means to purchase a site for the Society before it had any existence". It was also averred that none of the several last members of the Society, among whom the last remnants of the property were divided, ever made any contribution in property or in goods. None of this was true, but the truth or falsity nevertheless had to be established—thus once again we were enmeshed in court proceedings.

One of the most pestiferous and trying incidents of the case was the rule served on us to produce the deposition of Dr. Smith, in the case of "Schreiber *vs*. Rapp". This simple demand gave us no end of trouble, vexation and expense. The root of it all was an innocent seven-word footnote appearing in the "History of the Harmony Society" written by John A. Bole in 1904. Mr. Bole had come to see me in 1902 to obtain permission to consult the documents of the Society. The permission was granted on the sole províso that the manuscript of the story which he was about to write was to be submitted to me for my approval before it went to press. Unfortunately, the manuscript did not reach me and the perplexing footnote—."Testimony of Dr. Smith, Schreiber *vs*. Rapp"—thus came to appear in print.

It seems that the opposing attorneys imagined that

through this footnote, which referred to a contribution by Peter Schreiber to the Society, they could find a clue advantageous to their case. Failing to find any trace of Dr. Smith's deposition, we filed a reply declaring that we had neither knowledge nor possession of the deposition—in fact, we did not believe that it existed. The court ordering a continuation of the search, other parties examined all the documents extant—all to no avail. After Mr. Bole testified that he had no idea where he got hold of the Smith deposition, and it also appeared that the testimony in the Schreiber-Rapp case was taken orally. After more than six months of worry and work on the Smith testimony Judge Lanning discharged the rule.

The taking of testimony had lasted until 1910—three years of fret and worry, not to mention the very considerable expense, and the further fact that the necessary attention to the legal proceedings brought to a sudden termination my meteoric career in the world of music.

And now, as if to add insult to injury, yet another bombshell burst in our midst. Even before the Everitt-Tryon case came up for argument, M. Hampton Todd, Attorney General of Pennsylvania, on behalf of said Commonwealth on May 4, 1910, entered proceedings in escheat against us.

Be it noted that this was not simply "another law-suit" but one which was diametrically opposed to the suit of Everitt-Tryon.

Self-evidently, so long as there are heirs to a property, it is not subject to escheat—and the Everitt-Tryon suit challenged us on the basis that the plaintiffs were rightful heirs. Equally evident is it that property subject to escheat cannot be subject to claim by heirs. Thus were we suddenly caught 'between the Scylla of escheat and the Charybdis of the heirs.'

Preparation or argument, or both, demanded utmost circumspection in both cases. Argument the least bit too far in one direction naturally would be seized upon with avidity by the Attorneys in the other case.

After the lapse of nearly two years, namely on January 30 and 31, 1912, the Everitt-Tryon case was argued in the U. S. Circuit Court before Judge Charles P. Orr. About six months later the Judge filed his opinion. It was altogether in our favor. Nevertheless, the plaintiffs carried the case to the U. S. Circuit Court of Appeals in Philadelphia, where in June of 1913—more than six years after the filing of the suit—this latter Court affirmed the decree of the lower court.

Though these six years of litigation were troublesome and expensive, our relations with the plaintiffs and their counsel were altogether fair and amiable—precisely opposite to the belicose attitude that had prevailed in the case of Schwartz *vs.* Duss.

Void of any personal animus, the hearings in the Everitt-Tryon case partook of the nature of family reunions. Also we faced the ludicrous situation of the Commonwealth's proceeding in the Beaver Court to escheat the very property to which in the U. S. Circuit Court, Everitt-Tryon—as heirs of George Rapp—laid claim.

The suggestion for Quo Warranto was entered in the Court of Common Pleas of Beaver County, Pa. as No. 275 of June Term, 1910.

The Commonwealth of Pennsylvania
Ex Relatione M. Hampton Todd
versus
The late Religious Society, known as the
HARMONY SOCIETY; SUSIE C. DUSS, last
elected Trustee of said Society; JOHN S. DUSS,

De Facto Trustee of said Society, and SUSIE C. DUSS and FRANZ GILLMAN, sole surviving members of said Society.

Why were the other members, still living, thus flagrantly omitted?

Viewing the Escheat Case as objectively as possible, first from the moral angle, I failed to find any justice in it. Inasmuch as the escheat of our property was on the ground that it was impressed with a "religious use," or that the Society had been a "Religious organization," the Commonwealth in all fairness, should return all the money, which as taxes, it had erroneously or unlawfully collected during the years 1824 to 1905. Selfevidently the Commonwealth could not or would not do any such thing.

The Harmony Society had always paid its taxes—local, county, state, federal—even though its property generally was assessed at a higher value than was other similar property. After the Civil War for several years the Society paid a federal tax on annual income. All its obligations to the county, State and Nation had been fulfilled. Also not only had the Society contributed to many State Institutions such as hospitals and schools, but in times of disaster such as the great Pittsburgh fire, the Civil War, and the Johnstown flood, had borne its full share in alleviating distress. In any case the existence of whatsoever property the Society possessed at the time of its dissolution or whatsoever we as defendants possessed, was due absolutely to my almost superhuman efforts; and no amount of wealth could possibly remunerate me for the gauntlet of harassment, villification and persecution through which I had had to pass in order to save the Society from total ruin.

Also be it noted that if attempt at escheat had been

391

made in the years 1886 to 1892, the depositors in the Economy Savings Institution would have lost all, or nearly all, of their savings while the good old folk of the Society would have ended their days in the County Poor House.

Regarding the legal aspect of the case, the proceedings were based solely upon an Act, passed in 1855, for the purpose of curbing the growth of Catholic institutions. The irony of it all was that against such institutions the Act had never been invoked and that more than half a century later, Attorney General Todd sanctioned proceedings against us—the disbanded remnants of a Society, not religious in a sectarian sense or purpose and not of a character such as the framers of the Act had in mind.

After two Attorneys General in the 1880's had turned a deaf ear to petitioners for the bringing of such escheat proceedings, Attorney General W. U. Hensel during his term in office (1891-1895) emphatically refused the petition of the Pittsburgh attorney Stevens. Thus, one Attorney General after another decided that the Act of 1855 was not applicable to the Harmony Society. Let us also recall that in the conference regarding the Feucht case, twixt Mr. Brooks and U. S. Supreme Court Associate Justice George Shiras, the latter said "so far as concerns this talk of escheat by that fellow Stevens, we know that there is nothing in that."

Nevertheless, since this question bobbed up now and then, we had given it careful study and were not by any means unprepared to meet it.

In December of 1892, before approving the title to the Society's property, Attorney Watson thoroughly scrutinized the question of escheat; but like the several Attorneys General, concluded that the Act of 1855 was not applicable to the Harmony Society.

Since the "Quo Warranto" was based on the assumption that the Society had been a "religious society" our answer had to be yea or nay. In accordance with the facts and the opinion of eminent theologians, who negatived the question and who were ready thus to testify, our answer was in the negative.

Throughout the history of the Society the Courts had steadfastly viewed the Society in accordance with the stamp the Society had placed on itself, namely that of an economic association—agricultural, industrial and commercial. Decisions, for or against, usually were not on the assumption that the property of the Society was impressed with a "religious use."

However the best evidence of the Society's character is in the Articles of Association, which on February 15, 1805 brought into being the Harmony Society. Let the intelligent reader judge for himself.

A duly organized religious society means "a formally organized body of believers, having a system of faith and form of worship". There is no such language in the Articles of 1805.

A careful study of the Articles reveals that in strikingly democratic spirit, the ordinary members retain supremacy as follows: The Agreement is "between us, subscribers of the one part and George Rapp and his Associates of the other part."

The subscribers on their part, and that of their heirs and descendants, deliver up . . . all their estate and property . . . to George Rapp and his Associates, as a free gift . . . for the benefit and use of the Community there (at Harmonie).

They promise to labor with their hands, to promote the good and interest of the Community and to hold their children and families to do the same . . . .

In consideration of which George Rapp and Associates adopted the subscribers as members and gave them the "privilege to be present at each religious meeting" . . . and that all "shall and will receive the same necessary instruction in church and school which are needful and requisite for their temporal good and welfare as well as eternal felicity."

Note that attendance at religious meetings is not obligatory and that palpably plain is the fact that the decision as to the needful instruction lay not in a specific doctrine, preached by a particular individual, but in the judgment of the individual members. Equally plain is it that, having forsaken their homes and, through stress and storm, come 3000 miles into a wilderness, the individual members were not inclined to place themselves in a position of having thrown off one religious yoke only to take up another one.

George Rapp and his closest friends likely would have preferred to begin the Articles with "Whereas a Religious Society is being founded by George Rapp." But in view of the various shades of belief, as well as of unbelief, on the part of the colonists, not to mention the caution necessary on the part of the attorney, who in drawing the Articles had to avoid stamping the Society as being of a type not capable of holding property, such preamble was out of the question.

Noteworthy is the fact that it took George Rapp twenty-two years to bring the Society to a unity which he deemed sufficient to warrant the attempt of drawing new articles and presenting them to the members for execution. The bitterness and opposition that ensued is shown in Chapter IV.

Reverting to the Quo Warranto proceedings:

The "informer," who under the Act was entitled to

one-third of the value of the property in question if the escheat proceedings were successful, was a Pittsburgh attorney, George C. Buell. As early as 1903 he had threatened us with legal proceedings on behalf of Mrs. Everitt and Mrs. Tryon, but in the preparation of their bill he made the discovery that he could accumulate more money by way of escheat proceedings. Attorney General Todd, undoubtedly misinformed by Buell as to the "millions" involved and not interested in the decision of two former Attorneys General who refused to undertake escheat proceedings against us, in a careless moment agreed to the Buell proposition. Anyway, Todd was about to step out of office—so why should he worry?— let his successors wrestle with the matter as they might. Meanwhile, Attorney Buell soon found that he needed a capable assistant, someone intimately acquainted with Economy and watchfully alert to developments "on the ground floor." Thus he took into partnership Charles F. Straube, then a resident of Economy.

In reference to this partnership the Pittsburgh *Chronicle Telegraph,* March 1, 1907, has the following "Buell and Straube, the informants, were seen this afternoon at the home of Mr. Buell at Allegheny. Mr. Buell said that he and Straube were actuated in the first place by personal motives, as the law of the State . . . provides that the informants should receive one-third of any escheated property." Mr. Straube at a later date put it that "they were engaged in the project in order to remove the cloud that was on the title of the real estate formerly of the Harmony Society." However, instead of removing any cloud, the proceeding actually constituted a cloud.

Nevertheless, during the years when the case was pending, no less than 391 transfers of this real estate were recorded. All of the attorneys, both of Beaver County and Allegheny County, to whom the question of title was submitted, approved the title. Also be it noted that among said attorneys was one of the staff representing the plaintiff. Attorneys evidently had no fear regarding the outcome of the proceedings. Now, at the time when actual proceedings were opened against us—in May 1910—Mrs. Duss and I were residents of Florida. Franz Gilman, who like Mrs. Duss was one of the three last members of the Society at the time of its dissolution, was living with us.

By order of Judge Holt of Beaver County Court, the County Sheriff came to Florida with subpoenas for the three of us. But since we were now citizens of another State this proceeding attracted attention far and wide. At that time, residents of other states were hailed into local courts by way of extradition only if they were criminals. In civil cases there was no such provision. When Sheriff Hartzell served the papers on us in Florida, he laughingly remarked that the Beaver lawyers had told him that he was going on a wild goose chase.

The whole affair had the populace guessing. Again the newspapers were headlining our case; attorneys pricked their ears when they read of the unusual Quo Warranto—while a thousand or more landholders both in the counties of Butler and Beaver became jittery. As to the legal procedure itself, the machinery proved so entangled that three years and five months elapsed before I filed my answer.

Two Attorneys General who succeeded Mr. Todd, seemingly took no interest in the case—thus it did not come up for trial until early in 1916. Having steadfastly stood on our constitutional right to be tried in our place of residence, we had avoided service in Pennsylvania. But now our attorneys, desiring my presence for consultation, requested me to come to Youngstown, Ohio, just beyond the Pennsylvania border, but sternly urged me to travel by lines beyond said border.

Ignoring the injunction, I journeyed to Washington where I boarded a Baltimore and Ohio train routed directly through Pittsburgh. Having notified accountant Mr. Dickson by code telegraph of my itinerary, I was not surprised to find his secretary awaiting me at the Pittsburgh depot.

He fairly rushed at me. "Good morning," he beamed, "we are all glad you came this way—you are very much wanted—I am to take you to Mr. Watson's office at once."

After a "good morning" at Watson's office, I asked, "What's this all about?"

"One day's real fight in court," said Watson, "seems to have been too much for them. I understand they are anxious to make a settlement; we are to have a meeting here this morning with them."

Closeted in one of the rooms, these chambers brought back many memories of twenty-four years of law suits and incidental tribulations. I wondered would I ever see the end of these troublesome suits at law.

Soon the conference of opposing attorneys took place in an adjoining room. Now and then one of our camp came to consult me about this or that. A friendly spirit seemed to prevail, and after fencing about for a time, the attorneys for the Commonwealth proposed a settlement amounting to payment on our part of $100,000 in cash and the transfer of three Economy blocks held by the Beaver County Land Company.

This proposition was quickly rejected as "altogether exhorbitant." The opposing Counsel having departed, we continued pro and con. Finally Mr. John Freeman,

397

Mr. Watson's enterprising young partner, proposed a "take-it-or-leave-it" ultimatum, offering $15,000 in cash and a deed to the Great House block and about three-fifths of the Music Hall block. The rest of us had no faith in the ultimatum, but Mr. Freeman succeeded in putting it over. After the Freeman proposition was accepted by the opposing attorneys, it was submitted to Attorney General Francis Shunk Brown. But on account of the wide and blatant publicity given the case, he refused to act except by sanction of the Legislature. To this end a meeting was held in Harrisburg.

The minutes of said meeting disclose the presence of Attorney General F. S. Brown, Auditor General A. W. Powell, State Treasurer R. K. Young, attorney John Freeman, accountant C. A. Dickson, Charles F. Straube and his attorney D. J. Mulvahill, also a joint committee from both houses of the General Assembly. The only jarring note at the meeting was Mr. Straube's demand of $300,000 in whatever settlement was to take place. His attorney being the only individual to hold such view, the others decided to submit the proposition to the Assembly.

On January 25, 1916, a formal stipulation was signed by plaintiff and defendant. After the Assembly passed a resolution of approval, Governor Martin G. Brumbaugh on January 27 approved the stipulation. However Attorney Watson insisted on a trial by jury. Thus a week later a jury in the Beaver Court recognized and accepted the compromise, also stating that none of the Harmony Society's property "ever was or is held for any religious or charitable uses and that the defendants, their heirs, grantees, successors and assigns have a good and indefeasible title thereto."

This additional finding by the jury was of course for

The Author at the age of 82 on February 22, 1942.

the purpose of forever quieting the question of title to a thousand or more parcels of land formerly in the name of the Harmony Society.

Reverting to the question of escheat. It may interest the reader to note that even if the Society had been primarily a Religious Society rather than an Economic Commune, and if its property had been subject to escheat under the meaning of the Act of 1855, there were other reasons why this property could not be escheated. The Act stipulates that at the time of such escheat the Society whose property is subject to escheat must have real and personal estate within the Commonwealth of a clear yearly value of $30,000. But the tables prepared by our accountant showed an annual loss of $30,000. Moreover, the Act was decidedly prospective—not retroactive—and the Society had held undisputed possession of its property and income for thirty years prior to 1855. Finally, previous suits at law had established the validity of transmission of titles as well as that the distribution in severalty of the Society's property, upon its dissolution was altogether according to law.

Aside from the legal obstacles inherent in the Act itself as applied to the Society, the suggestion was filled with numerous discrepancies and conflicting averments. For example it asked that the property of the Society, which no longer existed, should escheat as of the time of the Society's dissolution—for this no legal or other reason was offered. In one paragraph the Society is mentioned as composed of four members at the time of its dissolution —at another place is mention of six members; and, error of errors, it is declared that the Society ceased to exist January 1, 1903, and that the Society's property then consisted of stock in the Beaver County Land Company—a corporation not yet in existence.

399

Looking at the stupid and glaring discrepancies in the Suggestion, one might have serious doubts as to the sobriety of the attorney who prepared the document.

The reader may imagine the jubilation with which the settlement of this pestiferous case was greeted in Ambridge.

Though Mrs. Duss and I were still in Florida, we received many invitations to come back to our former home. So we finally journeyed to Ambridge, where preparations for a great celebration were being made by D. L. McNees, K. Rudolph Wagner and many others. Owners and prospective buyers of former Society property, and friends and acquaintances throughout the region were on hand at a banquet at which we were the guests of honor. A sudden attack of influenza prevented me from attending, but the guest band played some of my compositions and a galaxy of orators outdid each other in rejoicing and eulogy. They told me later that the good Rev. J. F. Martin of the local St. Veronica congregation, while speaking of the notable leaders of the Harmony Society, had proclaimed me "the greatest Roman of them all!"

And now the last tempest had spent its fury, and the throbbing sea subsided to a rhythmic calm.

Ten years before, my life had been in mid-career, flushed and enlivened with success—my name upon the lips of many—my talents and those of my associates at high tide. But tempestuous litigation having blotted out the course which I had charted, the world of music by 1916 but faintly remembered me—so fickle are both fame and fortune.

Now that the waves of legal proceedings which for a quarter of a century had engulfed us had spent themselves, one might suppose that we henceforth could sail upon a sea of calm. Not so. Soon we were again beleaguered with letters, more or less threatening, from persons claiming to be heirs of former members of the Society. A particularly annoying group was one in Germany. It consisted of several hundred collateral heirs of George Rapp. As late as 1932 they sent an emissary here to collect "the $200,000,000 estate" of George Rapp. Although we proved to him that no George Rapp estate whatsoever existed, the group sent him again the next year. One chap threatened to blackmail us in the press if we refused to come across. But I wrote to that gentleman that if he started anything of this sort he could expect to see me in person.

Certain parties also still labored under the impression that they were entitled to inherit monies sent to America about the middle of the nineteenth century by a wealthy banker of Honfleur, France—one Johannes Huber. The story of the Huber money has always been a mystery. We do know, however, that Huber sent certain sums to his American heirs, some of whom were members of the Harmony Society while others at one time or another seceded. Being of the opinion that the Society could not survive, Huber wanted to make some provision for those of his heirs who were members. When he sent drafts, he made specific provision that none of the funds should go into the Society's treasury. With this specification, he also wrote certain allusions to Father Rapp which incensed his heirs who were members of the Society. So incensed were they, indeed, that they instructed Frederick Rapp to return the money to Huber together with a letter expressing their indignation at Huber's words.

After Huber died and failed to leave a will, Jacob Wagner, one of the 1832 seceders, went to France to collect the shares due the various heirs. Returning with the money, Wagner refused to turn over to those heirs, who were members of the Society, their rightful shares. A quarrel ensued, resulting in certain litigation between R. L. Baker, then trustee of the Society, and Jacob Wagner. The case, however, was not concerned with the Huber money, but rather with certain slanderous utterances for which Wagner received a jail sentence.

Although I spent much time and effort at trying to find out just what became of that money, my efforts proved futile. To begin with, Henrici said that he did not know anything about it—that the matter had been altogether in the hands of Romeli Baker and that it did not concern the Society. Such documents as were among our papers did not shed any light on the subject. The only specific mention in reference thereto is in the Secession Agreement of March 6, 1832; it states that a sum of 60,000 francs is to be paid to Mrs. Jacob Wagner and a Mrs. Bentel. The money due the heirs who died in the Society seemingly was borrowed from Trustee Baker by one who forgot to make any report thereof after the death of Baker. Those funds, at interest, by this time, should amount to a very sizable sum . . . I heartily wish that somebody would find it, since for many years it has been a thorn in the flesh, some of my best friends off and on becoming estranged over the issue.

Though I realized that the years of litigation had quite broken my public musical career, I nevertheless continued in the art in a semi-private way—functioning now and then as guest-conductor and as a composer for special occasions. Worthy of mention perhaps is my "Mass in Honor of St. Veronica." The burden of planning several memorials and participation therein, also devolved upon me. But the most pressing activities during the years immediately following the last law-suits were the industrial and residential development of the town of

Ambridge, and placing on a firm footing the Harmony Society Memorial "Old Economy."

After the sale of 105 acres to the American Bridge Company and that of 100 acres to the Ambridge Land Company, I sold the remaining acreage to the Liberty Land Company for bonds at a face-value of $2,000,000—a figure that was three times the actual value of the property. The reason why I was able to secure this exorbitant price lay in the fact that the purchasers expected to bring to Ambridge the development which came to pass at Gary, Indiana. Had such development materialized at Ambridge, we all would have prospered; but when Judge Gary decided to take the great industrial enterprise to Indiana the Ambridge site was left "high and dry." Instead of being quickly developed, the land lay as just so much acreage along the Ohio River, between Pittsburgh and Beaver.

The interest on the bonds, outrunning the amount coming in from sales, the Liberty Land Company soon defaulted on its interest payments. Thereupon, to prevent a Sheriff's sale of the property, C. A. Dickson proposed the following plan: Inasmuch as the stock in the Liberty Land Company was worthless, he felt that probably he could acquire it, form his own company and proceed with the development of the Ambridge site, providing Mrs. Duss and I would contribute the necessary number of bonds for the release of land under the mortgage, so that it could be plotted. To this we agreed, and by 1910 Mr. Dickson succeeded in acquiring the Liberty Land Company stock.

Under this Dickson-Duss arrangement we located a number of factories, laid out residential plots, and, with the able assistance of the local firm of Wagner and Kerr, managed to realize a small income. But when it came to

403

releasing land from under the mortgage, our losses in bonds were stupendous.

The property thrown back into our laps as it were—beside the fact that the face of the bonds was three times its actual value—there came to pester us the question of releases. One of the terms in the mortgage required that plots to be released must join property formerly released or be along the boundary; and another very silly term required that the plots released must be exactly twenty-five acres in extent. Thus, for instance, in order to make a sale of forty-five acres to the Standard Seamless Tube Company, a sale amounting to $67,500, meant release of two 25-acre plots and the surrender of bonds amounting to fifty times $2500 or $125,000. On most of the acres sold in the $2500 Zone, we sacrificed $1500. The hillside zone was under the mortgage at $2000 per acre, hence in the development of that terrain we sacrificed only $1000 per acre.

Also we found ourselves confronted with a silly oversight in the mortgage—there was no provision for the exemption of streets. This cost us, in the first zone alone about 60 acres multiplied by $2500 per acre or $150,000.

A firm believer in "going while the going is good," shortly after we received the Liberty Land Company bonds, I set in motion negotiations toward turning them into cash. I asked 85 per cent of their face-value—the prospective purchaser talked of 75 per cent—when the deal came to naught through the opposition of Agnew Hice, attorney for the Society, who thought it "too great a sacrifice."

Had this sale taken place, Mrs. Duss and I would have been able to carry out a dream of years—namely the establishment of a worthy Memorial to the Harmony Society.

But holding on to the real estate and assisting in its development called not only for work and worry but for frightful depletion in our resources. Said depletions, by way of aforementioned releases, continued until 1927 when I prevailed upon Mr. Dickson to "sell out."

Remaining through the winter and working at the proposed sale, I found a purchaser. There being nothing left but my 347 Liberty Land Company bonds the transaction was quite simple. In the Spring of 1928 I sold said bonds and all the accumulated interest coupons at $173,500.

This amount I promptly divided equally between Mr. Dickson, Mrs. Duss and myself. Thus, with certain emoluments accruing by way of land formerly released, after twenty-five years of additional financial struggle and litigation, we received about the same share as was paid to some of the seceding members in 1903.

Due to the custom of celibacy, the extinction of the Society long since had been taken for granted. Concomitantly had arisen the query, "what is to become of the Economy millions," the answers, in later years, had coalesced into, "Oh presumably the lawyers will get it all."

I do not have any exact figures regarding the attorney's fees; we paid them partly in cash but in greater part with Liberty Land Company bonds. But I do know somewhat of what the lawyers did not get.

They did not get the more than a million dollars cash paid the depositors in the Economy Savings Institution, nor the $300,000 which I paid to three Pittsburgh banks, nor the $70,000 paid to a New York bank, nor the $162,000 paid to the State Treasurer, nor the $338,600 that I paid to twenty seceding members and Mrs. Schumacher, nor the $173,500 which I distributed between

Mr. Dickson, Mrs. Duss and myself—all of it amounting to more than $2,000,000.

May I be pardoned for mentioning an interesting sidelight, namely that with my Liberty Land Company bonds I saved the day for another bank. Lending said bonds to the Directors, they were able to borrow sufficient funds to carry on. No one the wiser, everything worked out to perfection and the unusual procedure has ever been a high spot in my memory as well as a source of delight.

Meanwhile, Economy and the Harmony Society had become history. Early in 1913 I received a letter from George C. Taylor of New Harmony, Indiana, informing me of the New Harmony Centennial Celebration and asking me to participate by delivering an address on the opening day, the first of eight days of "the biggest birthday party ever celebrated west of the Cordilleries." I was given a rousing welcome, the band played my compositions, and the newspapers were eulogistic. said one:

> Duss was one of the figures of the celebration. For it wasn't so much what Duss said, as Duss himself that centered the attention. Well known to the general public as a musician of distinction, he has a vivid and dramatic manner, an ideal of artistic perfection, a certain sardonic humor, a vast amount of unlabelled erudition, and a desire for an absolute exposition of the truth, which makes him a striking personality, to be ranked with the great misunderstood.

The truth is that steadily confronted, as I was, with the silly legends of the "Gabriel Stone" and "Rapp secret underground passage," my tongue grew eloquent in vitriolic and sky-rocketing anathema.

Some time after the Great House, Music Hall and Garden had been deeded to the Commonwealth, Mrs. Duss and I received a letter from Gilbert A. Hays of Sewickley, suggesting that the property thus acquired by the state should be set apart as a memorial to the Harmony Society. Now the Hays family, at the time of the death of Gilbert's father, General Alexander Hays, in the Civil War, lived on Big Sewickley Creek along the boundary of Economy, and thus for years were the very friendliest and best of neighbors. A daughter, Agnes Hays, later the Mrs. George A. Gormly, grew up in close friendship with some of our women members, and later collected her experiences at Economy into a charming and delightful booklet, which somewhat helped the outside world to a better understanding of the Society.

Gilbert, the brother of Agnes, was a boyhood friend of mine. He often played his merry pranks on us Economy boys, but throughout his life he had a special soft spot in his heart for Economy, never for a moment forgetting the many kindnesses and practical help which the Society had extended to his war-widowed mother and her children.

Gilbert's plan was to ask the General Assembly in Harrisburg to pass an Act setting apart as a perpetual memorial to the Harmony Society the property which in the escheat case we had deeded to the state. Also to organize an historical association to administer a museum in the Great House. To this end, he asked if we would lend the paintings, furniture and other paraphernalia formerly belonging to the Society. At once we assured him of our utmost cooperation; in fact having had a similar project in mind for years, Mrs. Duss had assiduously collected and preserved items of particular interest precisely for such purpose.

407

Thus it came that Gilbert A. Hays, John M. Tate, Jr., Robert T. M. McCready and Franklin T. Nevin of Sewickley; Charles A. Dickson and Thorson E. Bilquist of Pittsburgh; and Frederick Knoedler of Ambridge, petitioned the court at Beaver for a charter of incorporation under the name of The Harmony Society Historical Association. The corporation received its charter on June 4, 1917.

In 1919 an Act was passed by the General Assembly and approved by Governor Sproul, designating the Economy property a state memorial to be known as "Old Economy," and delegating the preservation, restoration and maintenance of the property to the Pennsylvania Historical Commission. The Commission, in turn, placed the management of the property in the hands of the Harmony Society Historical Association. My effort, covering a period of many months, and those of this organization resulted in partial restoration of the Garden and partial renovation of the Great House.

By way of a formal dedication of this memorial, a large audience of several thousand gathered on Sunday afternoon, June 26, 1921, to witness a long program in the Garden. For the occasion I assembled a band of thirty choice musicians as well as a chorus. The band and chorus united in the first rendition of my "March of Time" composed expressly for this occasion. Another number of the well-balanced program was the "Gloria" from my recently composed *Mass in Honor of St. Veronica.*

This memorial program gave the project a triumphal start, but serious disappointments soon ensued. The local association found but little support toward sharing the burdensome expenses of repairing the large buildings, hiring attendants, and operating the memorial in general.

Wealthy neighbors failed to come to the rescue—having the very good excuse that "since the state owned the property, the state should pay the expenses appertaining."

Soon after the establishment of the Memorial, Mr. J. M. Tate, Vice-President of the Harmony Society Historical Association, in the matter of restoration of the Great House Garden, succeeded in enlisting the interest of the Allegheny County Garden Club. Having known this garden intimately from my ninth year, and in 1903 taken out of it thirty-six disreputable fruit and evergreen trees; also turned the one-third of the block heretofore planted in vegetables, into lawn and floral display; I naturally felt that my advice would be of help—so offered it—alas, to little purpose. The committees sent by the Garden Club quite naturally were not interested in my experiments of recent years—what they wanted was the Garden of 'ye olden time'. A valiant effort and an expenditure of several thousand dollars soon resulted in bright spots of color and of beauty here and there, while borders of *viburnum nana* outlined the paths. However the committees from time to time appointed to attend to the Garden, reckoned without their host—said host being the coke-ovens and smoke-stacks of the Jones and Laughlin iron mills directly across the river. The soot and cinders belching forth from these mills took the life out of most of the foliage and considerable of heart out of the gardeners. In connection with this subject there should be mentioned the fact that at this very moment (Oct. 31, 1941) the Pennsylvania Historical Commission is having an expert landscape gardener busy at determining what plants to use in the restoration of the garden according to the plan that I have furnished him.

In 1922 I began to groom the town of Ambridge toward

the hoped-for Economy Centennial Celebration in 1924. Nothing developed until November 1923, when in spite of the local apathy, a few of us decided to forge ahead on the project. Still living were a number of old-timers whose lives had been closely identified with the old community. A sufficient number of these were yet in the vicinity to guarantee an organization for the support of the centennial and to this end Frederick Knoedler and I called a meeting of all those who had resided in Economy before 1901. Thirty-seven gathered and formed an organization appropriately called "The Old-Timers"; they responded immediately with subscriptions totalling six hundred dollars for a three-day celebration—June 6th, 7th, and 8th. Mr. Max Liebermann, appointed treasurer, soon raised an additional $3000.

As the centennial executive committee appointed me to prepare the program, I spent the winter of 1923-24 in Florida translating the diary of Heinrich Jung, (an account of the 1824 journey from New Harmony on the Wabash to Economy), writing an historical pageant, an address, and the words and music of the "Centennial Ode," and at selecting historical data. As my assistant I selected Mr. Andrew F. McKee of Ambridge who chose the singers and attended to other details. After my return to Ambridge I was kept busy with band rehearsals in Pittsburgh and chorus rehearsals at Economy, the spread of publicity in Pittsburgh newspapers, the presentation of two radio talks over KDKA, and local arrangements. After the last rehearsal on the Sunday preceding the celebration, everything was in readiness. I went peacefully to sleep. The next morning I found myself ill—pneumonia developed. On Thursday, the day before the opening of the centennial, I was taken to the hospital . . . .

However, Mr. McKee saw to it that the program was carried out. My son read the Jung diary and my keynote address, and P. C. Funaro, my great euphonium soloist of former days, conducted the band and chorus . . . The touching testimonial and resolution which the Association sent me for my efforts compensated for the loss I felt at missing the celebration. Due to the efforts of the committee in charge, the celebration was indeed an artistic success—except perhaps for the secret opening of twelve hundred-gallon casks of Economy wine (which turned out to be water) by certain adventuresome scamps.
. . . Ever since the establishment of the Harmony Society Memorial in 1919, I have consistently devoted much of my time toward the development of the Memorial. There being no one else so well qualified in the traditions and history of the Society as I am, the details of restoration are often referred to me. For this and the further reason that Mrs. Duss and I have donated the invaluable collection of furniture, paintings, tools, silks, books and manuscripts (formerly of the Harmony Society) to the Commonwealth, the Pennsylvania Historical Commission has invited us, for the remainder of our days, to make our home in the Great House.

After the first ten years of struggle, with the aid of W. H. Stevenson, of the Pennsylvania Historical Commission, we prevailed upon said Commission to set aside from its 1930 budget the sum of $3900 for the repair of buildings. This sum together with $900 raised by J. M. Tate, Jr., Vice-President of the Harmony Society Historical Association, constituted the first real step in this direction.

In 1935 we secured a $10,000 appropriation from the Legislature for repairing the Great House. This had taken a great amount of correspondence and journeys on my part as well as on the part of members of the Association. In 1937, the Pennsylvania Historical Commission began to take a serious interest in the memorial—OLD ECONOMY—so that in 1938 under the General State Authority, $38,000 were spent at repairing other buildings.

Later, with the assistance of a Works Progress Administration unit, many thousands of dollars were spent in renovation of buildings, preparation of relics for installation in museum, translation and cataloguing of letters and documents. In 1941 the Commission and the General State Authority pooled resources to the amount of $14,500 for a program of improvements now under way. (I am hoping that some day my pet project, the construction of ECONOMY in MINIATURE, will materialize).

The Commission has wisely districted the Commonwealth, and Commissioner Mr. Gregg L. Neel, in charge of Western Pennsylvania, is wideawake regarding Old Economy, its importance and its requirements.

From August 7 to 14, 1938, Harmony, Pa., celebrated the centennial of its creation as a borough. In 1929, at the removal of the steeple of the old Harmonist church, enterprising citizens had salvaged the old tower clock (likely brought to America by Frederick Rapp). Now, after having it carefully repaired, they installed it in the belfry of the schoolhouse. The committee in charge graciously invited me to take part in the festivity. So it came that via radio station KDKA, I had the privilege of dedicating to new use what is said to be "the oldest tower clock in the Western Hemisphere."

(A. J. Whitehill the expert who repaired the clock, places the date of its manufacture at about the year 1650).

My address closed with the wish: "May Heaven smile upon the clock and on the inhabitants for whom henceforth it is to mark the time. And may it proclaim the hours to a people industrious, frugal, peaceable and harmonious as were the people of the Harmony Society; who, in the early years of the last century SET UP THIS CLOCK IN THE STEEPLE OF THEIR HOUSE OF WORSHIP." The success of OLD ECONOMY as a famous historical shrine assured, the members of the Harmony Society Historical Association may take a just pride in having brought about the establishment of a monument, the like of which—if organized according to the plan that I outlined to Messrs. Melvin and Cadzow of the Commission, in 1937—will not be found elsewhere between our Atlantic and Pacific Coasts.

It goes without saying that the relics or contents of the buildings donated by Mrs. Duss and myself are the very soul of the Memorial, hence the contract of Oct. 1, 1937, twixt the Dusses and the Commonwealth very properly states that the collection of relics is to be known as "the Duss Memorial Exhibit."

As for myself, I feel fully requited for all of my work and worry and I know that it must be a source of satisfaction to Mrs. Duss to see that her toil of gathering and preserving the relics in question has not been a thing in vain but one that has led to something which will be a joy forever.

In March of 1939 the Indiana Legislature, created the New Harmony Memorial Commission. Said body, consisting of three ex-officio and seven appointive members, were to select a suitable, qualified person to serve as Director. The duty of said Director being the investigation of all information as to feasible restoring and furnishing of buildings and with the support of the Commission to plan projects to memorialize outstanding ideals and customs promulgated by the Harmony Society and

413

the Owenites at New Harmony. Said Commission promptly elected the unique Indiana historian Ross F. Lockridge,
Litt.D. to this important post. Although Director Lockridge and the members of the Memorial Commission are
men and women of outstanding ability, I can safely pre-
dict (according to my 23 years of experience in further-
ance of the OLD ECONOMY MEMORIAL) that they will find
ahead of them a wearysome, tortuous trail in the direction of whatsoever goal they may have in view. But
Cheerio, good friends—where there is a will there is a way.

On June 23, 1939, Director Lockridge and Judge
Herdis F. Clements of Mt. Vernon, as speakers; together
with the Kibler Band of Evansville and New Harmony's
leading vocalists under my baton, gave a creditable performance in honor of the One Hundred and Twenty-
fifth Anniversary of the founding of New Harmony.

I value highly my association with Director Lockridge.
Being the first historian to apperceive, evaluate and
properly appreciate the Spirit of the Harmony Society
and to assign to the hardy pioneers composing the same
that place in history to which they are justly entitled, he
is a man after my own heart. The two memorials—Old
Economy and New Harmony—to me are a wonderful
gratification in that they are proof of the fact that there
are still men and women possessed of noble aspirations
similar to those of the well-meaning pioneers of the early
part of the nineteenth century—else would there not have
come into being these two memorials.

Harking back to the New Harmony Centennial, June,
1914: Several days after said birthday party came the fearful news that Europe was inflamed by war. I watched the
fire spread as the leviathans of propaganda worked over-
time at inflaming the hearts of men on every side with the
sting of deadly hatred.

414

In 1917 the boys went. In 1918 they returned—some of them. Not many recognized it at the time, but they had changed—in fact everybody and everything had changed. Normal sanity and discipline of life went off at a tangent, became more loose, irresponsible and un-balanced. Old foundations giving 'way, there came "pro-hibition" and the delirium of bootlegging, the speakeasy, the racketeer, the kidnapper, ruthless gangster warfare, modernistic art, jazz, sophistication . . . Whatever of it all fell short of being criminal was nevertheless in de-plorably bad taste.

The winter months which I spend with my family at New Smyrna, Florida, are supposed to mark a vacation—in reality they mean a change in activity. There is always a voluminous correspondence to be attended to—much of it from persons related to former members of the Harmony Society. (I do wish that such writers would en-close stamps for reply.)

A considerable portion of this story was written in Florida, as was my "Mass in Honor of St. Veronica" and other compositions. For some years I was director of the New Smyrna Choral Society, and at all times I have coached one or another of the Church Choirs. The yearly absences from Old Economy probably have been a help to me in keeping the proper perspective in regard to the Economy Memorial.

The panorama of my life, passing before my mind's eye—in spite of the wars of nations, antagonisms of classes and ideals—nevertheless unfolds a germ of life that links the past with the present; an explanation, as it were, of the past and a questioning of the present . . . In child-hood days—I knew the solid substance and abundance of a socio-economic harmony, built on simplicity, equality and brotherhood. As a young man I experienced the

415

energy and marvellous expansiveness of the West and of its people—hardy, buoyant, flexible. Upon my return eastward to the scenes of my childhood, I became aware of the passing of certain sterling qualities, the growing irresponsibility of men, and the coming of colossal industries, which by their very size and organization presaged an era of difficult adjustment materially and spiritually, and in which the old qualities, inherent in the very foundations of our New World, seemingly, were to be forced to recede into the twilight of history.

In the present conflict—World War II—from various quarters comes talk of "a new order." Whether the talkers really have sufficient knowledge to usher in the dispensations they have in mind, remains to be seen. However, in all humility I offer the taking of a leaf out of the history of the Harmony Society. The experience of the Society demonstrates:

That the proper place to begin is at the beginning.

That the climb on the "ladder of success," begins not at the top but at the foot.

That money is not a commodity but a medium of exchange; wherefore it should play a part in an economic system only after exchange of commodities calls for a medium. As to the Society's inner workings, money was utterly useless.

That a substantial economic structure is like unto a pyramid, resting on a broad base of land, material and production with finance, mayhap, as the apex. The turning over of the pyramid so that the apex becomes the base—as some new and false prophets prefer to have it—calls for the application and continuous addition of props on every hand in order to keep the tottering structure in position—entailing an amazing waste of time and effort.

Finally, and most important, the necessity for the cultivation of a spirit of integrity, unselfishness, devotion and religion, beautifully summed up in "the Golden Rule."

And now let me close my story with six choice stanzas from the Harmony Society's favorite hymn—the joint work of the two Rapps, George and Frederick.

Harmonie thou Brother—State,
Peace unto thee ever.
God be with thee soon and late,
Foes affright thee never.
For it doth enow appear,
Thou art steadfast, holy;
God unto his flock is near
And He will extol thee.

Harmonie, denotes the space,
Where henceforth and ever,
Brethren in this dwelling-place,
Crowned are for endeavor;
Where all hate, strife, jealousy,
Cease their wicked stressing.
Harmonie means Symphony—
Sphere of golden blessings.

Thou dost favor but the ONE—
TWO has no subsistence;
Who would save himself alone,
Wrecks but his existence.
Blest is he who here finds thee
And submits to training

From thee, who find'st speedily,
All self-love remaining.

Brethren, rise, and falter not,
Here to dwell as burghers.
Many tasks as yet unwrought,
Wait on skillful workers.
Only in Harmonious soil,
Finds the spirit essence—
All else is but toil and moil
Without convalescence.

Harmonie—Love's holy band,
Of God, highly rated;
Grasp us firmly hand in hand,
So that unabated
Sweet impulses multiply—
Through love's might extended.
And all sin and perfidy,
In us may be ended.

God we pray thee: With Thine eye,
Watch o'er and protect us.
Thou, alone, canst satisfy,
Guide us and protect us.
Thine, with heart and soul, are we,
Let us grow in measure;
That, Immanuel, in Thee,
We may find our pleasure.

Appendix

Be it hereby known to all who need to know it, that the following Agreement has this day been made and concluded, between us Subscribers of the one part, and George Rapp and his Associates of the other part.

1st. We the Subscribers on our Part and on the Part of our heirs and Descendants deliver up, renounce & remit all our estate & property, consisting of cash, lands, chattles or whatever it may be to Geo. Rapp and his Association in Harmony, Butler County, Pennsylvania, as a free gift or Donation for the Benefit & use of the Community there; and bind ourselves on our own part as well as on the Part of our heirs & descendants to make full renunciation thereof, and to leave the same at the disposal of the Superintendents of the Community as if we never had nor possessed it.

2nd. Do we pledge ourselves jointly and severally to submit to the Laws and Regulations of the Community and to show due & ready obedience toward those, who are appointed and chosen by the Community as Superintendents in such a manner that not only we ourselves endeavour by the Labor of our hands to promote the good & interest of the Community, but also to hold our children and families to do the same.

3dly. If, contrary to our expectation, the case should happen, that we jointly or severally could not stand it in the community, and would within a few or more years break our promise and withdraw from the community for whatever cause it may be, never to demand any Reward, either for ourselves, or children, or those belonging to us, for any of our Labors or Service rendered, but whatever we jointly & severally shall or may do, we will have all done as a voluntary Service for our Brethren.

In consideration whereof George Rapp and his Associates adopt the Subscribers jointly and severally as members of the community, whereby each of them obtains the privilege to be present at every Religious meeting and not only they themselves, but also their children and families shall and will receive the same necessary Instruction in church and School which is needful and requisite for their temporal Good and wellfare as well as eternal Felicity.

4th George Rapp and his Associates promise to supply the Subscribers jointly and severally with all the necessaries of Life, as Lodging, meat, Drink, Clothings &c; and not only during their healthfull days, but also when one or more of them become sick or otherwise unfit for Labor, they shall have and enjoy the same support and maintenance as before, and if, after a short or long Period the father or mother of a family should die or be otherwise separated from the community and leave a family behind, they shall not be left widows or orphans, but partake of the same Right and Maintenance as long as they live or remain in the community as well in sick or healthfull days, the same as before, or as circumstances or Necessity may require. 5th And if the case should happen as stated above that one or more of the Subscribers after a short or long Period should break their promise and could or would not submit to the Laws and Regulations of the church or community and for that or any other cause would leave Harmony. Then George Rapp and his Associates promise to refund him or them the Value of his or their Property brought in, without Interest in one, two or three anual Installments, as the Sum may be large or small and if one or more of them were poor and brought nothing into the Community, they shall, provided they depart openly and orderly, receive a Donation in Money, according as his or their conduct while a member, or as his or their circumstances and necessities may require, which George Rapp and his Associates shall determine at his or their Departure.

In confirmation whereof both Parties have signed their Names; Done in Harmony, February 15th, 1805.

Compared, and corrected Some word to produce the Same meaning as written the German Language which was Shown to me as the original September 10th 1835.

CHRISTIAN BUHL.

N.B.

The translation is by Jacob Henrici. Both he and Buhl make the same mistake in reference to the name of the place. That should be HARMONIE as it is in the German.

J. S. DUSS.

TABLES PREPARED BY ATTORNEY D. T. WATSON FROM TABLES PREPARED BY PUBLIC ACCOUNTANT JAMES DICKSON IN SCHWARTZ VS. DUSS

Statement of Assets of the Harmony Society as of April 1st, 1892.

	Stock in Economy Savings Institution	$360,000.00
I.	Other stocks	545,700.00
	Bonds	402,500.00
		$1,308,200.00
II.	Industrial factors, etc.	$320,503.00
		$1,628,703.00
III.	Economy Items	$18,873.24
		$1,647,576.00

IV.	Union Drawn Steel Co. Loan	$18,750.00
	P. C. & Y. R. R. ....special	18,466.89
		$1,684,793.65

Also

	Beeler Real Estate Contract	$3,000.00
V.	Beaver Falls Contracts, Mortgages and Judgments	127,805.17
	Meyer Mortgage	28,922.25
	Deposit in Farmers Deposit National Bank	2,623.46
		$1,847,144.53

Also

	Economy Savings Institution, Special	$28,895.33
VI.	Beaver Falls Car Works, Special	26,431.70
	Economy Savings Institution Deposit Balance	62,117.93
		$1,964,589.49

And Their Debts Were

Bank of Pittsburgh, four notes	$142,000.00
Farmers Deposit National Bank, four notes	60,600.00
Iron and Glass Dollar Savings Bank, five notes ..	88,958.00
Hartman Notes	13,600.00
L. Power Notes	1,874.75
Valley Glass Co. Notes	4,000.00
Economy Account	2,685.90
Five Mortgages	35,350.55
Economy Savings Institution Special	39,383.36
Little Saw Mill Run R. R.	50.00
Monongahela National Bank	5,000.00
	$393,502.56

The foregoing Tables show assets in excess of liabilities
to the amount of $1,571,086.00
But when we subtract the worthless stock
of the Economy Savings Institution $360,000.00
And the indebtedness of said bank for
which we were responsible 1,080,436.02
The assets shrink to $130,630.91
Item six of assets, a mixture not immedi-
ately available $117,443.96
Assets in excess of liabilities seemingly resolve themselves
into $13,185.95

TABLE II		
	Nominal Value	Worthless or Unavailable	Available
Beaver Falls Steel Works ..	$263,098.14	$263,098.14	
Harmony Brick Works	16,554.82	16,554.82	
Economy Lumber Company	13,942.10	13,942.10	

Economy Planing Mill Co.	8,737.26	8,737.26	
Economy Oil Company	4,500.00	4,500.00	
Economy Oil Co. Cash Account	13,671.00	13,671.20	
Economy Sundries	18,873.24	18,873.24	
P. C. & Y. R. R. Special ..	18,466.89	18,466.89	
Union Drawn Steel Co. Loan	18,750.00	18,750.00	
Beeler Contract	3,000.00	3,000.00	
Beaver Falls Mortgages, etc.	127,805.17	127,805.17	
Meyers Mortgage	28,922.25	28,922.25	
Deposit in Bank	2,623.46	....	$2,623.46
Economy Savings Inst. Special	28,895.33	28,895.33	
Beaver Falls Car Works ..	26,431.70	26,431.70	
Economy Sav's. Inst'n. Deposit	62,117.93	62,117.93	
	$656,389.49	$653,766.03	
Stock in Economy Svg's. Inst.	360,000.00	360,000.00	
	$1,016,389.49	$1,013,766.03	$2,623.46

TABLE III

Securities more or less marketable but not available because they were held by banks as collateral for loans.
Held by Bank of Pittsburgh

	Par	Loans
150 Bonds P. C. & Y. R. R.	$75,000	
406 Shares Stock Beaver Falls Gas Company....$100	40,600	
200 Shares Stock Beaver Falls Bridge Company....$100	20,000	........$142,000.00
Bonds of Little Saw Mill Run R. R.	12,000	
Bonds of Little Saw Mill Run R. R.	12,000	
193 Shares Bank of Pittsburgh Stock	9,650	

Held by Iron and Glass
Dollar Savings Bank

3650 Shares Monongahela Water Co. Stock	89,000	..........88,958.00

Held by Farmers Deposit National Bank

178 Shares M. & M. National Bank ..	8,900	
78 Shares Allegheny National Bank	3,500	
Bonds Little Saw Mill Run R. R. Co.	12,500	...........60,600.00
Bonds P. C. & Y. R. R. Company	32,500	
Second Point Bridge	13,000	
	$332,650.00	........$291,558.00

Held by Bank of America
New York

Little Saw Mill Run R. R. Bonds .. 82,000.00 ....75,000.00

$414,650.00   ....$366,558.00

TABLE IV.

A complete list (by Master Thompson in the case of Schwartz vs. Duss) of Stocks and Bonds, more or less available and more or less marketable.

" 600 shares stock of Point Bridge Co. ....par value $ 15,000
  386 shares Tidioute Bridge Company .... "   "   19,000
2271 shares Chartiers Block Coal Co. .... "   "   113,000
2100 shares stock Little Saw Mill Run R. R. ...... "   "   105,025
  500 shares stock Union Drawn Steel Co. .... "   "   50,000
   11 shares stock Beaver Falls Gas Co. .... "   "   1,100
   30 shares stock Beaver Falls Bridge Co. .... "   "   3,000
   27 shares stock P. Ft. W. & C. R. R. .... "   "   2,700
   50 shares stock Rochester Nat'l Bank .... "   "   5,000
1610 shares stock Monongahela Water Co. .... "   "   40,250
Bonds of the Chartiers Block Coal Co. .... "   "   3,000
  483 shares of Tenth Street Bridge Co. stock ...... "   "   12,075

$369,450"

According to the above table I should have been in possession of stocks worth $369,450.00 for the purpose of beginning my work of liquidation. But the Point Bridge Co. Stock could not be sold on account of litigation between the Company and the West End Passenger Railway. The Stocks of the Chartiers Block Coal Co. and of the Little Saw Mill Run R. R. Co. had no market value whatever.

With the exception of the stocks of The Monongahela Water Co.; the P. Ft. W. & C. Ry. Co.; and that of the Tenth St. Bridge Co.; the other stocks were not known in Pittsburgh and were difficult to sell; their value, if any, lay in the future.

It will thus be seen that instead of the $369,175 there remained only $55,025.

        P. Ft. W. & C. Ry. Co. .... $ 2,700
        Monongahela Water Co. 40,250
        Tenth St. Bridge Co. 12,075

                             $55,025

But of these three stocks the Railway and Bridge stocks were lost or mislaid, which brings us to the naked fact that I had exactly 1610 shares of Monongahela Water Stock of the par value of $40,250. with which to attack the indebtedness amounting practically to $1,500,000.00. Interest on this sum at 6% per annum approximated $90,000.

    N.B. Any apparent discrepancy in the Tables must be ascribed to the time element. We moved so fast at times that Mr. Dickson complained that he had difficulty in keeping pace with my transactions.

———

Schedule of Real Estate, also from Schwartz vs. Duss.

Item		Estimated Value	Actual Sales	Date of Sales
1	Cannelton, Pa.		$ 3,124.20	1893
2	McKees Rocks, Pa.		1,640.00	1893
3	Stowe Township Allegheny County	$ 20,000		1893
4	32d Ward, Pittsburgh		55,000.00	1893
5	23d Ward, Pittsburgh		4,000.00	1893
6	Rochester, Pa.	3,000		
7	New Brighton, Pa.	2,500		
8	Collier Township Allegheny County		250.00	1894
9	Economy Home, 2600 acres problematical			
10	Leet Township Allegheny County	100,000		
	Sold part of this at various dates		3,700.00	
11	Beaver Falls houses, lots, etc.	97,000		
	Sold parts of this at various dates		50,291.00	
12	Beaver Falls Water Power			
13	Michigan Lands at various dates		10,736.04	
14	Waren County Lands at various dates		71,089.76	
15	Philadelphia real estate at various dates		9,750.00	

N. B.

The real estate items above enumerated, for the time being were useless assets. To convert real estate into cash takes time and effort.

The $20,000 item (No. 3) was swept away completely by the settlement with the Feuchts; and it took me from one to four years to market items 1, 2, 3, 4, 5, 6, 13 and 13; and of parts of 10 and 11.

Item 14 (Warren County Lands) meant careful salesmanship after a battle royal in the Courts of Forest and Warren Counties, as well as of the Supreme Court of the Commonwealth.

The Home tract itself, even for the purpose of security as the reader will recall, had first to undergo a thorough renovation as to title.

Trustee R. L. Baker's tabulation of the Society's holdings in the year 1866.

Mortgages $183,030; Bonds $836,000; Stocks $132,265; Real estate $650,000; Cash $17,550; a total of $1,818,845.

Value of Buildings comprising Economy Village.

1	Brick Store House	$ 2,500.00
1	Family warehouse	200.00
1	Brick B'l'g. (tailor, shoemaker, miliner)	3,000.00
1	Large Brick B'l'g. for Museum	4,500.00
1	Tavern, Frame and Brick	3,500.00
1	Church.... (brick)	3,500.00
2	Bells and Clock	2,500.00
1	New Granery	1,500.00
1	Brewery	1,000.00
1	Distillery	800.00
1	Soap boiling shop	400.00
3	Steam Wash houses	225.00
	Barn, threshing Machine & Steam Engine	1,800.00
	Stables	1,800.00
1	House with wine press	250.00
	Rapp House and Stables	4,000.00
1	Tannery	1,500.00
1	Hat Shop	400.00
1	Blacksmith Shop, 5 furnaces	400.00
1	Wagon maker's Shop	100.00
1	Saddler's Shop	100.00
1	Turner's or Cabinet Maker's Shop	150.00
1	Linen Weaver's Shop	350.00
1	Tinsmith's Shop	100.00
1	Carpenter's Shop	150.00
1	Potters Shop	150.00
1	Doctors Shop	100.00
1	House for Silk Worms	500.00
1	Cooper's Shop	100.00
1	Oil & Saw Mill	1,000.00
1	Schoolhouse.... (frame)	600.00
1	Old Granery	400.00
43	Family Brick Houses at $600	25,800.00
6	Double frame Houses at $600	3,600.00
47	Single Frame Houses at $500	23,500.00
8	Small Frame Houses at $350	2,800.00
9	One-story Frame Houses at $200	1,800.00
1	Cotton Factory & machinery	20,503.00
1	Woolen Factory & machinery	25,036.00
1	Grist Mill & Machinery	9,000.00

$149,614.00

The above list is as of an earlier date. With the exception of the bells, clock and last three items (amounting to $57,039) the village valuations could be enhanced 50%.

To the foregoing, to the best of my judgment, should be added Farm and Shop equipment $2500; Furniture, bedding etc. $3000. Horses' and other livestock $6000.